YOSEMITE
WILDFLOWERS

Help Us Keep This Guide Up to Date

Every effort has been made by the authors and editors to make this guide as accurate and useful as possible. However, many things can change after a guide is published.

We would appreciate hearing from you concerning your experiences with this guide and how you feel it could be improved and kept up to date. While we may not be able to respond to all comments and suggestions, we'll take them to heart, and we'll also make certain to share them with the authors. Please send your comments and suggestions to the following address:

FalconGuides
Reader Response/Editorial Department
246 Goose Lane
Guilford, CT 06437

Thanks for your input!

YOSEMITE
WILDFLOWERS

A Field Guide to the Wildflowers of Yosemite National Park

Judy and Barry Breckling

GUILFORD, CONNECTICUT

FALCONGUIDES®

An imprint of The Rowman & Littlefield Publishing Group, Inc.
Falcon, FalconGuides, and Outfit Your Mind are registered trademarks of The Rowman & Littlefield Publishing Group, Inc.

Distributed by NATIONAL BOOK NETWORK

Copyright © 2020 Judy and Barry Breckling

Map © The Rowman & Littlefield Publishing Group, Inc.

Photographs by Barry Breckling unless otherwise credited

Cover photo: Half Dome from Olmsted Point by Olof Carmel, www.carmelgallery.com

British Library Cataloguing-in-Publication Information Available

Library of Congress Control Number: 2019953897

ISBN 978-1-4930-4066-7 (paperback)
ISBN 978-1-4930-4067-4 (e-book)

∞™ The paper used in this publication meets the minimum requirements of American National Standard for Information Sciences—Permanence of Paper for Printed Library Materials, ANSI/NISO Z39.48-1992.

This book is dedicated to the memory of our
mothers, who encouraged us to
go out and play
and not to pick the wildflowers.

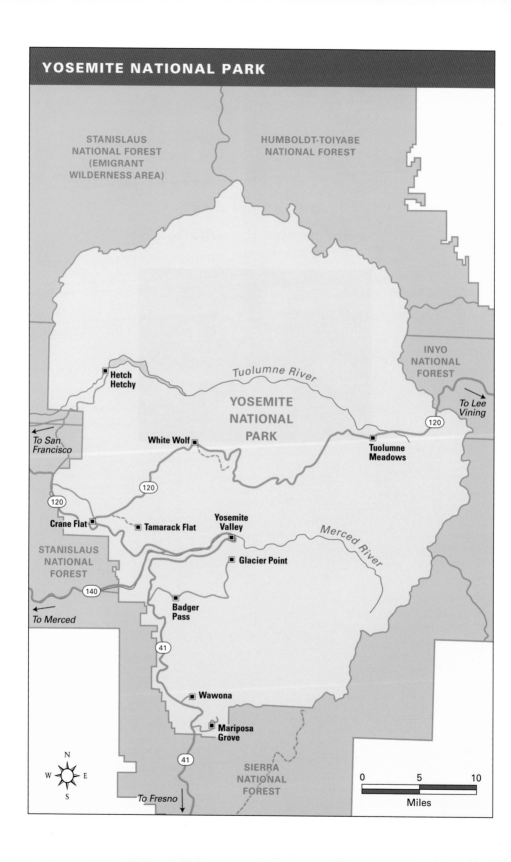

CONTENTS

As long as I live, I'll hear waterfalls and birds and winds sing.
I'll interpret the rocks, learn the language of flood, storm, and the avalanche.
I'll acquaint myself with the glaciers and wild gardens,
and get as near the heart of the world as I can.

—John Muir

ACKNOWLEDGMENTS

Our botany buddy Doug Krajnovich edited and proofread all the text at least three times and suggested quite a few valuable improvements. He also let us use several of his photographs. Lynn Robertson, another botany buddy, and Dave Jigour, our esteemed neighbor, also provided photographs for the book.

Alison Colwell, Peggy Moore, and Garrett Dickman, former and present Yosemite botanists, have given us all sorts of useful information and have provided encouragement as well. Jennie Haas, botanist for the Stanislaus National Forest, provided plant location information and lots of encouragement.

Steve Schoenig (known fondly by many as Mr. Monkeyflower) helped us sort out the latest monkeyflower changes and provided a photo for the book.

Several photographers allowed us to use photos that we selected from their collections on the CalPhotos website. Those generous photographers, listed in alphabetical order, are Michael Charters, Debra Cook, John Doyen, John Game, George W. Hartwell, Neal Kramer, Steve Matson, Keir Morse, Anuja Parikh and Nathan Gale, Jean Pawek, Steven Perry, Aaron Schusteff, Mike Spellenberg, and Dean Wm. Taylor. Their photographs are listed in the photographer credits section on page 322.

We constantly make use of *Jepson eFlora* (ucjeps.berkeley.edu/eflora) in conjunction with *The Jepson Manual: Vascular Plants of California*, second edition, 2012. We used the online manual, which is frequently updated, as the authority for the family classifications, scientific names, and plant information in this book.

The Calflora website (calflora.org) is another resource that we find incredibly useful and that we highly recommend. You can use the website to find out what plants grow where, and you can use their location information to locate plants in the field. You can also designate an area on a map and retrieve an illustrated list of the plants that grow in the area.

The plant section of the CalPhotos website (calphotos.berkeley.edu/flora) is one of our most indispensable resources. The CalPhotos site was established in 1995, when the Internet was just getting going, and it was one of the first online image databases specializing in natural history subjects. At this writing, the site had more than 370,000 plant photos, a number that grows every day.

We also frequently refer to *An Illustrated Flora of Yosemite National Park*, 2001, by Stephen J. Botti. When we're not out in the field with the book, it usually sits open on our desk. Unfortunately, the book is out of print, but copies are still available online.

ACKNOWLEDGMENTS

We highly recommend Michael Charter's California Plant Names website. His botanical name derivations pages (calflora.net/botanicalnames/index2.html) explain the meanings of botanical names. He also provides detailed information about the people for whom plants have been named. If you want help deciding how to pronounce botanical names, you'll probably want to bookmark his pronunciation guide (calflora.net/bloomingplants/pronunciationguide.html).

We also recommend *A Field Guide to Pacific State Wildflowers*, 1976, by Theodore F. Niehaus and Charles L. Ripper. Although the book is somewhat old, it's still quite useful, and even experienced botanists carry it in the field.

INTRODUCTION

Yosemite's towering cliffs, majestic domes, and magnificent waterfalls make it one of the country's most popular destinations. Its serene mountain lakes, lush meadows, sparkling creeks, and Giant Sequoias add to the scenic grandeur. The wide variety and abundance of wildflowers in the park are the icing on the cake, and they are, of course, the worthy subject of this book.

The book was designed to make it possible for park visitors to identify most of Yosemite's wildflowers. It covers the native and non-native flowering plants that are known to grow in the park, with the exception of the graminoids (grasses, sedges, and rushes), mistletoes, non-showy aquatic plants, and a few plants that have been reported in the park only in the highlands north of Hetch Hetchy Reservoir. Shrubs and trees that have conspicuous flowers are included in the book.

Three groups of plants in the park (plants in the *Cryptantha*, *Plagiobothrys*, and *Cuscuta* genera) often require dissection and high-power magnification to identify the species and can be extremely difficult even under those circumstances. We mentioned those genera in the book, pointed out the difficulties, and described a single plant in each genus that is readily identifiable.

Over 1,000 plants are covered in the book. Many of them have a photo unit of their own, and the rest are covered in the similar plants text of the plant they most closely resemble. Ideally, every plant would have its own photo unit. If that were the case, however, the book would be far too big to fit in a book bag.

Vegetation zones

This book uses five vegetation zones to classify the plant communities in the park. Other resources have similar classifications but sometimes use different nomenclature. For example, what we call the mixed conifer zone is also called the yellow pine belt and the lower montane forest. The zones intermingle and often overlap considerably, and they're primarily influenced by elevation, moisture, temperature, and slope aspect. The elevation ranges specified for the zones apply to the Yosemite region rather than to the entire Sierra Nevada.

The **chaparral/oak-woodland zone** ranges up to about 4,000 feet and occurs mainly in the Tuolumne and Merced river canyons in the lower elevations around the park's western border. It's the dominant plant community in the El Portal and Hetch Hetchy areas, but the zone also extends up into western Yosemite Valley and is represented by isolated pockets around Wawona. The principal plants in the zone are grasses, annual wildflowers, low-elevation chaparral shrubs, oaks, and Gray Pine.

The **mixed conifer zone**, also known as the Great Green Wall, ranges roughly from 3,000 to 6,500 feet. Big Meadow, the Giant Sequoia groves, most of the Wawona area, and most of Yosemite Valley are in the mixed conifer zone. Ponderosa Pine, Sugar Pine, Incense Cedar, White Fir, and Douglas Fir are predominant conifers in the zone. Black Oak, Big-leaf Maple, Mountain Dogwood, Western Azalea, and Mountain Misery are common in the zone.

The **montane zone** runs between about 6,000 and 8,000 feet and includes most of the area traversed by Glacier Point Road and the land along Tioga Road up to about Olmstead Point. Lodgepole Pine, Jeffrey Pine, Western White Pine, and Red Fir are predominant conifers in the zone. Aspen, Western Juniper, Huckleberry Oak, Bush Chinquapin, and several *Ceanothus* species also grow in the zone. There is a rough rule of thumb to tell if you're in the mixed conifer zone or the montane zone. If most of the fir trees you see are White Fir, you're in the mixed conifer zone. If most of them are Red Fir, you're in the montane zone. A trick to differentiate the two firs is to find a needle on the ground and try to twirl it between your thumb and finger. If it twirls somewhat easily, it's a Red Fir needle. White Fir needles are flat and can't be twirled.

The range of the **subalpine zone** is about 8,000 to 10,500 feet, basically up to the tree line on the mountain peaks. Lodgepole Pine, Whitebark Pine, Western White Pine, and Mountain Hemlock are predominant conifers in the zone. Tuolumne Meadows, Dana Meadows, and much of the northern part of the park reside in the zone.

The **alpine zone** in Yosemite is restricted to areas above the tree line, which makes it the most clearly delineated zone in the park. The zone ranges from about 9,500 feet to exactly 13,114 feet, which is the top of Mount Lyell, the highest point in Yosemite. Most of the zone is made up of rocky, gravelly areas with sparse vegetative cover.

The park's lower elevations have fine spring wildflowers displays that typically begin in April and peak in May and early June. During those spring days, Yosemite Valley, the Hetch Hetchy area, and the Wawona area are good destinations for plant hunts. By the end of May and into June, plants start to bloom in the upper mixed conifer zone and the lower montane zones. The Ackerson Meadow area, Crane Flat meadows, and the Giant Sequoia groves are good destinations for wildflower treks on those early summer days. By late June and early July, it's time to travel up Tioga Road and Glacier Point Road into the upper montane and subalpine zones. And finally, in late July and early August, it's time to visit the subalpine meadows and climb the mountains in search of alpine wildflowers. Even in middle and late summer, it's a good idea to return to the lower elevations to look for later blooming plants.

Suggested reading

The following books provide a wealth of information about Sierra Nevada natural history.

An Island Called California: An Ecological Introduction to Its Natural Communities, second edition, by Elna Bakker. Published in 1984 by the University of California Press. One reviewer's comment: "As a naturalist often bored by nature writing, I am stunned by *An Island Called California*. I first read it two decades ago, and I've just rediscovered it. Bakker's survey of the ecosystems of this massive and diverse state is lyrical, lively, and full of ecological anecdotes."

California's Changing Landscapes: Diversity and Conservation of California Vegetation, by Michael Barbour, Bruce Pavlik, Frank Drysdale, and Susan Lindstrom. Published in 1993 by the California Native Plant Society. A reviewer's comment: "If you want to know more than just the names of California plants, but also their connection to the many different habitats of the state, you can't do much better than to read this book."

Geology Underfoot in Yosemite National Park, by Allen F. Glazner and Greg M. Stock. Published in 2010 by Mountain Press Publishing Company. One reviewer's comment: "An excellent introduction to the geology of the Sierra Nevada and the Yosemite area. The photos and illustrations are stunning and clearly illustrate the concepts covered in the text. Best of all, none of the areas described are far from the main roads, so even the less adventurous among us can explore the fascinating geological history of this national park."

Suggested reference books

At least *one* of these two books, preferably both, should travel with you whenever you're on Sierra Nevada outings.

The Laws Field Guide to the Sierra Nevada, by John Muir Laws. Published by the California Academy of Sciences in 2007. Review comment by *Sierra Magazine*: "If you have room for only one Sierra Nevada guidebook in your pack, make it this little gem."

Sierra Nevada Natural History, An Illustrated Handbook, by Tracy I. Storer, Robert L. Usinger, and David Lucas. Published by the University of California Press in 2004.

HOW TO USE THIS GUIDE

Organization

The plants in this book are organized in six color sections based on the most prominent color of the flower or the inflorescence. In some cases, closely related plants were put in the same color section if most of them have flowers that clearly belong in that color section and others are not quite as clear cut. For example, many monkeyflowers have flowers that are pink to purplish, but since most of them are more pink than purple, and it's useful to compare them as a group, all the monkeyflowers with pink to purplish flowers are in the section for pink, rose, and magenta flowers. Flower colors are highly variable and the colors can change at different stages of development. For that reason, if you can't find a plant in one color section, we encourage you to look for it in similar color sections.

Many plants have bicolored flowers. When a plant's corolla has a vivid color and a paler color, it's usually included in the section for the more vivid color. For example, if a plant has flowers with petals that are white at the base and have purple tips, chances are good that you'll find the plant in the section for blue, purple, and lavender flowers. If you don't find it there, look in the white section.

In each color section, the plants are sorted alphabetically by scientific family names. Plants in the same family are then sorted alphabetically by their scientific names.

Common names

The common names in the book are those that are most often used by online botanical resources and regional field guides.

Common names are easy to pronounce, fairly easy to remember, and sometimes nicely descriptive. But one plant can have more than one common name, and the same common name is sometimes used for more than one plant. Common names can also be misleading. For example, Blue-eyed Grass is not a grass, Owl's-clover isn't a clover, and Toad Lily looks nothing like a toad and isn't a lily. Despite their shortcomings, common names are a stepping-stone to establishing familiarity with plants, and once you know a plant's common name, the natural next step is to get to know its scientific name.

Scientific names

The scientific family and plant names in the book are those used by the online *Jepson eFlora* as of the publication date of this book.

Each plant and animal species has a binomial (two-part) scientific name. The genus is the first word in the name and the second word is the specific name, which is usually referred to as the specific epithet. The scientific name is formatted in italics, the first letter of the genus name is capitalized, and the specific epithet is all lowercase. For people not familiar with the concept, let's say the Smith family has three siblings. They all have the last name (genus) Smith in common, and their specific epithets are Sally, Tim, and Lee. So they would be formatted *Smith sally*, *Smith tim*, and *Smith lee*.

Scientific names are usually derived from Latin or Greek words. The names are often difficult to pronounce and challenging to remember, but they're the same worldwide (more or less), and are necessary for acquiring in-depth knowledge of plants and for communicating with other plant enthusiasts.

Scientific names change for a variety of reasons, most recently because DNA research sheds new light, but also when a researcher unearths an old, dusty specimen that, by international code, takes precedence over a more recently named specimen. The names that are no longer valid are called **synonyms**. Many plants in this book have scientific names that have changed somewhat recently, and the names that are no longer valid are included as synonyms. It's important to include synonyms so that people who are using older plant references can make a connection between the plant names. The plant unit headers in the book have synonyms in parentheses after the currently accepted name, and synonyms are also included in the similar plants text. For a summary of some of the most significant recent changes, see page xxiii.

Native status

For plants that are not native to our area, the term "non-native" is included under the plant's common name in the header. Non-native status is also indicated for plants of that status in the similar plants text. Plants that don't have the term non-native associated with them are native to our area.

There are probably more appropriate terms to use for plants that are not native to a particular area, such as "introduced" and "naturalized," since every plant is a native somewhere, but non-native is a familiar term and probably more readily understood.

Plant descriptions

The plant descriptions provide somewhat detailed information about plant characteristics. In all cases, priority was given to the characteristics that help differentiate a plant from similar plants. A description of a plant's fruit and information about its reproductive parts (number of stamens and pollen color, for example) were included where space allowed.

When plants in the book are described as common, uncommon, rare, and so forth, the reference is to the plant's abundance in Yosemite, rather than to how common the plant is throughout its range.

Botanical terms

Botanical terminology can be challenging, and this book uses simple descriptive words whenever possible. More technical terms are used only when they serve to significantly reduce wordiness. For example, to avoid the word *oblanceolate* (a common leaf shape), a description would have to say something like "lance-shaped with the widest end away from the point of attachment."

All botanical terms used in the book are defined in the glossary. You should have a fairly easy time understanding the plant descriptions if you become familiar with the terms in the illustrations on pages xx through xxii and with the following terms: appressed, axil, ciliate, clasping, claw, graduated, hypanthium, involucre, node, perianth, petiole, receptacle, reflexed, sessile, stellate (in reference to hairs), and tepal.

Flowering time, habitat, and range

The flowering period, habitat, and elevation range specified for each plant are specific to the Yosemite region. Keep in mind that the specifications are not strict limits. They simply represent the data currently available based on herbarium specimens and reported sightings.

Location information

This book was designed to help people identify flowering plants that they find in the park. Although plant location information is included where space was available, such information was omitted when the available space was required for plant identification information. If you want to search for specific plants and would like information about where you might find them, we suggest that you use the Calflora website (calflora.org). You can specify a plant name and generate lists that tell you when and where the plant has been collected or reported in specific counties.

Similar plants

The similar plants text includes plants that are not covered elsewhere in the book, as well as plants that have a separate photo unit of their own. The names of plants that have their own photo unit in the book are highlighted with green text.

Tips for identifying plants

First, the tools. If you don't already have one, we highly recommend that you get a 10x hand lens and carry it with you whenever you're out in the field. Even when you don't need magnification to identify a plant, you might want to use the lens to get a closer look at some of its details. You should also carry a six-inch ruler with you, one that has 16th-inch increments and preferably one that's flexible. A ruler is provided on the back cover of this book, but you can't always position the book in such a way as to get an accurate measurement of plant parts.

Whenever you've got the time and inclination, thumb through the plant photos in this book. The more often you do, the more familiar you'll get with the look of the plants and the layout of the book. If you thumb through the photographs often enough, when you see a particular flower in the field that looks familiar, you might remember seeing it in the book and may even be able to flip right to it.

The easiest way to learn plants is to go on field trips with people who are botanically knowledgeable. During the spring and summer, Yosemite offers guided wildflower walks. To access the schedule, search the Internet for "Yosemite calendar." The Sierra Foothills chapter of the California Native Plant Society also offers field trips. If you live in the area, you might want to consider joining the chapter to meet new botanically inclined people. To access their field trip schedule, search the Internet for "CNPS Sierra Foothills."

How your camera can help. When you find a plant in the field and you can't find an exact match for it in the book, find the photo that comes closest to a match and check the similar plants information. The information may get you to a positive or tentative identification of your plant. Either way, first take photos of the plant, focusing on the parts used to differentiate the plants in the similar plants text. Then take a photo of the page in the book. Later, when you've got the photos in front of you and you have access to the Internet, bring up CalPhotos plants (calphotos.berkeley.edu/flora). Access photos of the plant (or plants) in the similar plant text until you find a good match.

If you carry a smartphone in the field, you definitely should consider downloading the Seek app, which was developed by the iNaturalist team at the California Academy of Sciences. You can point your phone's camera at a plant and the app will provide identification information for the plant at the top of the screen. The more specific the image is, the closer the app will come to narrowing down an identification. In areas with no Internet connection, you can take photos of plants with the app. Later on, when you have a connection, you can instruct the app to identify the plants in your photos.

Cautionary notes

Plant edibility. Many of the plants described in this book are edible, but many others are highly toxic. To complicate matters, many edible plants have one or more look-alikes that are inedible or downright poisonous. Plant edibility information is included in this book because people often find such information of interest. But, please refrain from consuming any part of any plant you find in the park, not only for your own protection, but also because harming plants is prohibited in the park.

Mountain weather. Anyone who's spent time in the mountains knows that weather at high elevations can change almost instantly. Summer storms develop quickly and can occur with little warning, bringing strong wind, lightning, and heavy rain, hail, or snow. Hunkering down in such circumstances can be an unforgettable experience, but probably not one that you'd want to repeat. Your best bet is to get going early in the morning, keep your eyes on the sky, and leave plenty of time to beat a retreat.

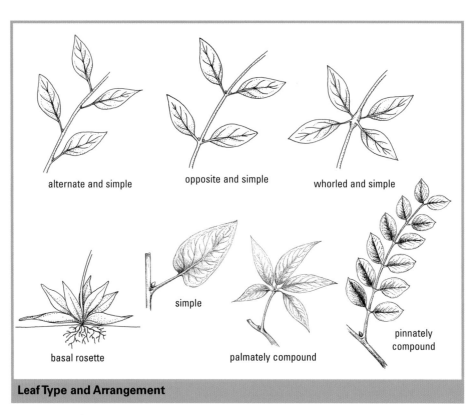

alternate and simple

opposite and simple

whorled and simple

basal rosette

simple

palmately compound

pinnately compound

Leaf Type and Arrangement

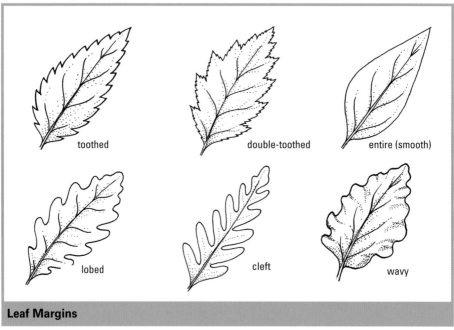

toothed

double-toothed

entire (smooth)

lobed

cleft

wavy

Leaf Margins

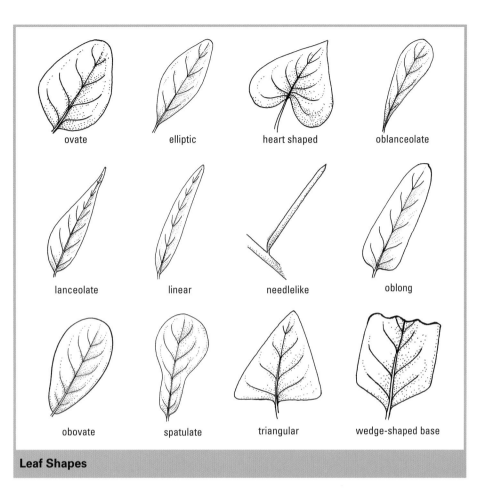

Leaf Shapes

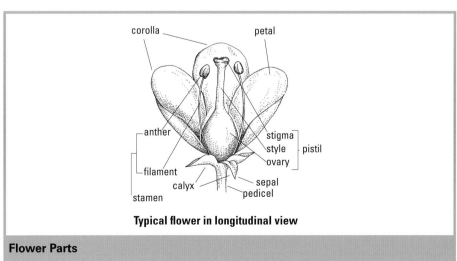

Typical flower in longitudinal view

Flower Parts

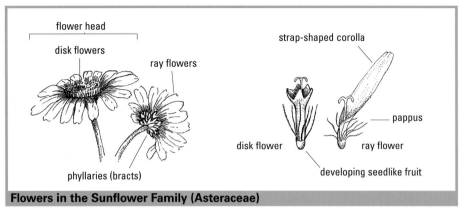

Flowers in the Sunflower Family (Asteraceae)

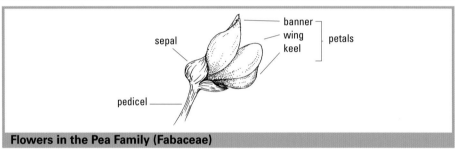

Flowers in the Pea Family (Fabaceae)

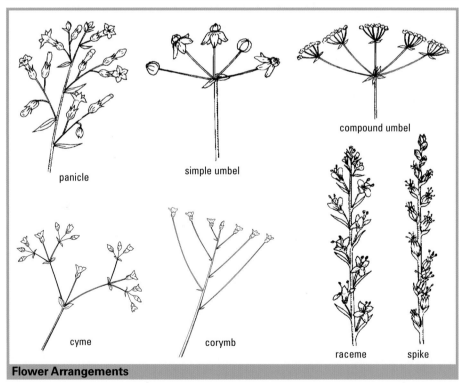

Flower Arrangements

BOTANICAL CHANGES

Quite a few botanical name changes have taken place in *Jepson eFlora* somewhat recently.

Family changes

Some of the more significant family changes are described below.

Several years back, the borage family (Boraginaceae) was expanded to include all members of the waterleaf family (Hydrophyllaceae) family.

More recently, several genera in the snapdragon family (Scrophulariaceae) were moved to other families. The *Castilleja*, *Cordylanthus*, *Orthocarpus*, and *Pedicularis* genera (plural of genus) were moved to the broomrape family (Orobanchaceae). The *Antirrhinum*, *Collinsia*, *Digitalis*, *Gratiola*, *Keckiella*, *Lindernia*, *Penstemon*, and *Veronica* genera were moved to the plantain family (Plantaginaceae). The California native monkeyflowers, previously in the *Mimulus* genus, were assigned to the *Diplacus*, *Erythranthe*, and *Mimetanthe* genera and were moved to the lopseed family (Phrymaceae). The *Scrophularia* and *Verbascum* genera remain in the snapdragon family.

A number of genera in the lily family (Liliaceae) have been assigned to different families. The *Allium* genus was moved to the onion family (Alliaceae). The *Brodiaea*, *Dichelostemma*, and *Triteleia* genera were moved to the brodiaea family (Themidaceae). The *Camassia* and *Chlorogalum* genera were moved to the century plant family (Agavaceae). The *Narthecium* genus was moved to the bog asphodel family (Nartheciaceae) family. The *Tofieldia* genus was renamed *Triantha* and was moved to the false-asphodel family (Tofieldiaceae). The *Smilacina* genus was renamed *Maianthemum* and was moved to the butcher's-broom family (Ruscaceae). The *Zigadenus* genus was renamed *Toxicoscordion* and was moved, along with the *Trillium* and *Veratrum* genera, into the false-hellebore family (Melanthiaceae). The *Calochortus*, *Clintonia*, *Erythronium*, *Fritillaria*, *Lilium*, and *Prosartes* (previously *Disporum*) genera remain in the lily family.

Yosemite native plants that were in the purslane family (Portulacaceae) have been moved to the miner's lettuce family (Montiaceae).

Plants that were in the milkweed family (Asclepiadaceae) have been moved to the dogbane family (Apocynaceae).

Plants in the *Sambucus* genus have been moved from the honeysuckle family (Caprifoliaceae) to the muskroot family (Adoxaceae).

Genus changes

Some of the more significant genus changes are listed below.

Sunflower family (Asteraceae). Yosemite plants in the *Aster* genus have been moved to the *Eucephalus, Eurybia, Oreostemma, Sericocarpus,* and *Symphyotrichum* genera. Several plants in the *Senecio* genus were moved to the *Packera* genus.

Mustard family (Brassicaceae). Most Yosemite plants that were in the *Arabis* genus were moved to the *Boechera* genus.

Pink family (Caryophyllaceae). All Yosemite plants that were in the *Arenaria* genus are now in the *Eremogone* genus.

Pea family (Fabaceae). California native plants that were in the *Lotus* genus have been moved to the *Acmispon* and *Hosackia* genera.

Phlox family (Polemoniaceae). Several plants that were in the *Gilia* genus are now in the *Navarretia* genus. Most of the Yosemite plants that were in the *Linanthus* genus have been moved to the *Leptosiphon* genus.

Primrose family (Primulaceae). Plants that were in the *Dodecatheon* genus have been moved to the *Primula* genus.

Rose family (Rosaceae). Some plants that were in the *Potentilla* genus are now in the *Dasiphora* and *Drymocallis* genera.

Saxifrage family (Saxifragaceae). Some plants that were in the *Saxifraga* genus were moved to the *Micranthes* genus.

The previous names are indicated in the plant description and similar plant sections and are included in both the family and general indexes.

Western Azalea (*Rhododendron occidentale*)

The plants in this section have flowers with predominantly white to cream corollas. The section includes plants with flowers that are white at maturity and become red with age.

If you've gone through this section and haven't found a plant you're looking for, check the sections that include pink and blue flowers. Many plants that have white flowers can also have pink, blue, or lavender flowers, especially plants in the sunflower and evening primrose families.

Many plants have bicolored flowers. A plant with a corolla that's partially white or cream and also has a more vivid color is usually included in the section for the more vivid color. For example, if a plant has flowers with petals that are white at the base and have purple tips, chances are good that you'll find the plant in the section for blue, purple, and lavender flowers.

Note: The similar plants sections include plants that are not covered elsewhere in the book, as well as plants that have a separate photo unit of their own. The names of plants that have their own photo unit in the book are highlighted with green text.

BLUE ELDERBERRY
Sambucus nigra ssp. *caerulea* (*S. mexicana*)
Muskroot family (Adoxaceae)

Description: Blue Elderberry is a large, many-branched shrub, 6–25' tall, with deciduous leaves that can be over 1' long. The leaves are pinnately divided into 3–9 oval to lanceolate leaflets that taper to a pointed tip and have small, sharp teeth along the edges. The showy, flat-topped flower clusters, up to 13" wide, have many tiny, white to cream-colored flowers with 5 rounded petals. The flowers mature into black berries with a white, powdery coating that makes them look blue.

Flowering time: June–September

Habitat/range: Forest openings; chaparral/oak-woodland and mixed conifer zones; up to 7,000'.

Comments: Elderberry herbage and the berries of some species are toxic to humans. Cooking the berries makes them safe to consume, and people often use the fruit to make pies, jellies, and wine.

Similar plants: Red Elderberry (*S. racemosa* var. *racemosa*, previously *S. racemosa* var. *microbotrys*) and Black Elderberry (*S. racemosa* var. *melanocarpa*, previously *S. melanocarpa*), have smaller, dome-shaped flower clusters. Red Elderberry **[inset]** has leaves with mostly 7 leaflets, and its flower clusters are up to 4" wide. Black Elderberry, which is rare in the park, has leaves with mostly 5 leaflets, and its flower clusters are no more than 2¾" wide.

WAVY-LEAF SOAP PLANT
Chlorogalum pomeridianum var. *pomeridianum*
Century Plant family (Agavaceae)

Description: This slender perennial arises from a bulb that has many coarse, brown fibers from old bulb coats. The stem is 1½–8' tall and has a waxy, powdery coating. The linear basal leaves are ½–2¼' long and have parallel veins and conspicuously wavy margins. The stem leaves are much reduced and become scale-like toward the top of the plant. The inflorescence is an expansive, usually much-branched panicle. Each flower has 6 curved tepals, ½–1" long, that are white with a dark midvein. The 6 white stamens have yellow anthers, and the green ovary has a single white style. The tube-like flower buds have conspicuous green or purple lines.

Flowering time: May–August

Habitat/range: Openings in grasslands, woodlands, and chaparral; chaparral/oak-woodland and mixed conifer zones; up to 4,300'.

Comments: The flowers open in late afternoon or evening and close for good several hours later, each flower having only one chance to become pollinated. Native Americans used the copious fibers from the old bulb coats to make stiff brushes. They crushed the bulbs and mixed the bulb material with water to create a soapy lather, which they used for cleaning clothes and baskets.

GLASSY ONION
Allium hyalinum
Onion family (Alliaceae)

Description: This attractive, bulbed perennial has an erect stem, up to 1½' tall, and it often grows in scattered patches. Like all plants in the *Allium* genus, its herbage has an onion odor. Each plant has 2 or 3 narrow basal leaves. The flower clusters have 5–25 flowers with 6 white or pink tepals, up to ⅜" long, that become transparent as they age. The flowers have 6 white stamens and an ovary with no crests at the top.

Flowering time: March–May

Habitat/range: Moist, shady canyonsides; chaparral/oak-woodland zone; around 2,000'.

Comments: Glassy Onion grows along the north-facing slopes of the Merced River Canyon in the vicinity of El Portal. If you enter the park on Highway 140 and the plants are in bloom, you're likely to notice them. *Allium* is the Latin name for garlic. The genus includes several ornamentals and many plants that are cultivated for food.

Similar plants: Somewhat similar Narrow-leaved Onion (*Allium amplectens*) **[inset]** grows in the Hetch Hetchy area and has been reported elsewhere in the park. It has denser flower clusters, and the flowers have an ovary with 6 crests at the top. White Brodiaea (*Triteleia hyacinthina*) looks similar, but its anthers are conspicuously broad at the base and its herbage has no onion odor.

SUBALPINE ONION
Allium obtusum var. *obtusum*
Onion family (Alliaceae)

Description: This bulbed perennial's small, dense flower clusters are less than 1" wide and appear to be emerging at ground level because most of the plant's stem is usually buried in gravel. Each plant has 2 or 3 basal leaves, less than ¼" wide, that are green when the flowers are in bloom. The flowers have 6 obtuse-tipped tepals, up to ½" long, that are white with a pale purple midvein. The tepals are slightly longer than the 6 stamens.

Flowering time: May–August

Habitat/range: Open, sandy and gravelly areas; upper mixed conifer, montane, subalpine, and alpine zones; 6,000–10,800'.

Comments: This plant blends into its surroundings, making it easy to overlook. When a flower cluster dries up, it detaches from the stem and drifts over the ground, dispersing its seeds.

Similar plants: Less common Red Sierra Onion (*A. obtusum* var. *conspicuum*) never has more than a single leaf, and the leaf can be broader, up to ½" wide. Its tepals, which are also slightly longer than the stamens, are acute at the tip and have a slight to pronounced pink tint. Yosemite Onion (*A. yosemitense*) **[inset]** is rare in the park. It has similar white to pink, somewhat low-growing flower clusters, but its flowers have stamens that are noticeably longer than the tepals.

POISON OAK

Toxicodendron diversilobum
Sumac family (Anacardiaceae)

Description: Poison Oak is extremely variable in growth habit and leaf appearance, and it can cause people to develop a mild to severe blistery rash when they come into contact with it. It can grow as a dense shrub, as a vine that can climb up trees to incredible heights, or as a tree with a trunk that's 3–8" wide. The leaves, which range from paper thin to thick and leathery, are divided into 3 leaflets that are 1–4" long, are often glossy, and have toothed, scalloped, or lobed margins. The leaves are usually bronze colored at first, turn bright green in the spring, turn yellow-green to reddish in the summer, and become bright red or pink in the fall. The tiny flowers, which grow in loose clusters from leaf axils, have 5 greenish-white petals. When temperatures drop sharply in late fall, the leaves are discarded, but the cream-colored or greenish-white berry clusters often remain long into the winter.

Flowering time: April–May

Habitat/range: Canyons, thickets, and wooded slopes; chaparral/oak-woodland zone; up to 4,600'.

Similar plants: Fragrant Sumac (*Rhus aromatica*) has similar leaves with 3 leaflets, but the middle leaflet is usually much larger than the lateral leaflets, and the leaflets have a wedge-shaped base. Poison Oak's middle leaflet is about the same size as the lateral leaflets or only slightly larger, and the leaflets don't have a wedge-shaped base.

BREWER'S ANGELICA

Angelica breweri
Carrot family (Apiaceae)

Description: Brewer's Angelica is a perennial, 3–6½' tall, with somewhat hairy herbage. It has plentiful leaves clustered at the base of the stem and several alternate stem leaves. The base of each leaf widens to a balloon-like sheath that clasps the stem. The leaves are 6–14" long and are triangular shaped in outline, and each leaf is divided 2 or 3 times into smaller segments, ending up as lanceolate, toothed leaflets, up to 4" long. The umbrella-shaped compound umbels have 25–60 spreading rays that end in a round-topped cluster of tiny flowers with 5 white petals.

Flowering time: June–September

Habitat/range: Streamsides and other moist places in coniferous forests; mixed conifer and montane zones; 3,400–8,800'.

Similar plants: Brewer's Angelica is one of four Yosemite carrot family plants that have lanceolate, toothed leaflets. Western Cowbane (*Oxypolis occidentalis*) is the only one in the group with leaves that are divided only once. Ranger Buttons (*Angelica capitellata*) is the only one that has distinctly ball-shaped umbellets. Highly poisonous, non-native Water Hemlock (*Cicuta douglasii*) is similar to Brewer's Angelica in many respects, but its herbage is hairless and it tends to grow in rather than near water. Water Hemlock has been reported in meadows near Gin Flat and north of Hetch Hetchy.

RANGER BUTTONS

Angelica capitellata (*Sphenosciadium capitellatum*)
Carrot family (Apiaceae)

Description: The stout stem of this robust perennial can get up to 6' tall and is sometimes branched. The basal leaves are 8"–2½' long and are 1 or 2 times pinnately divided into lanceolate, pointed leaflets that are sometimes irregularly toothed. The base of each leaf is greatly expanded into a sheath that clasps the stem. The plant is hairless, except for the inflorescence. The compound umbel has 4–18 stout, densely soft-hairy stalks that end in a tight, ball-shaped cluster of tiny flowers with 5 white petals. The clusters are often pink when they're immature.

Flowering time: July–August

Habitat/range: Wet places and open, rocky slopes and flats; mixed conifer, montane, subalpine, and alpine zones; 4,000–10,500'.

Comments: This plant would fare well in any wildflower popularity contest. It's instantly appealing to almost anyone who encounters it for the first time. However, like many plants in the carrot family, all parts of Ranger Buttons are highly toxic. Cattle and other livestock have died from eating the plant.

Similar plants: Other carrot family plants that look somewhat like Ranger Buttons have looser, more hemispheric umbellets (the secondary flower clusters), and they don't have densely soft-hairy umbel stalks.

POISON ANGELICA

Angelica lineariloba
Carrot family (Apiaceae)

Description: Poison Angelica is a large perennial, 2–5' tall, with leaves that are clustered at the base and are alternate along the stem. The base of each leaf widens to a pale, thin, balloon-like sheath that clasps the stem. The leaves are 4–14" long and are divided 2 or 3 times into smaller, linear to linear-oblong segments with smooth margins. The attractive, umbrella-shaped compound umbels have 20–40 spreading rays that end with a round-topped umbellet of tiny flowers with 5 white petals. The umbels and umbellets have no bracts at their base.

Flowering time: June–August

Habitat/range: Open rocky slopes and flats; montane and subalpine zones; 6,000–10,600'.

Comments: The carrot family contains many cultivated culinary plants, such as celery, parsley, dill, and cilantro, but the family also contains quite a few poisonous plants, and Poison Angelica is one of them. Another poisonous plant in the family is notorious Poison Hemlock, which was used to execute Socrates. The non-native has become a common weed throughout North America and has been reported to grow in the Wawona area.

Similar plants: Bolander's Yampah (*Perideridia bolanderi*) looks similar, but its umbels and its umbellets have bracts at their base.

AMERICAN WILD CARROT
Daucus pusillus
Carrot family (Apiaceae)

Description: This annual is 11–30" tall and has bristly leaves, 2½–10" long, that are dissected into narrow, pointed, parsley-like leaflets. The flowers have 5 tiny, white petals and are tightly clustered in a flat-topped or concave umbel that looks as if it's nesting in a ring of leaves. As the flowers age, their stalks bend inward and eventually form a roundish cluster of bristly, oval fruit. The taproot of the plant is a small, edible carrot.

Flowering time: April–June

Habitat/range: Dry slopes in sandy or rocky areas; chaparral/oak-woodland and mixed conifer zones; up to 5,000'.

Similar plants: Closely related Queen Anne's Lace (*Daucus carota*) is a showy, non-native biennial that can get up to 4' tall. The European native grows sporadically throughout much of California along roadsides and in other disturbed areas and has been reported to grow in El Portal. Its leaves have long, thread-like segments, and they don't resemble parsley. Its flower clusters, unlike those of American Wild Carrot, often have a single purple flower in the center. Our culinary carrots were developed from a subspecies of Queen Anne's Lace.

COW PARSNIP
Heracleum maximum (*H. lanatum*)
Carrot family (Apiaceae)

Description: This robust, strong-scented perennial has stout stems that are 3–10' long, are finely hairy, and have longitudinal grooves. The impressively large leaves are rounded in outline, are 8–20" wide, and are divided into 3 coarsely toothed, irregularly lobed leaflets. The large compound umbels, which are up to 1' wide, have 15–30 rays that end with a cluster of numerous tiny flowers. The flowers, which have no sepals, have 5 white petals that are usually notched at the tip. The flattened, obovate fruit often have prominent dark lines.

Flowering time: May–July

Habitat/range: Moist, wooded or open areas; mixed conifer and montane zones; 3,500–9,000'.

Comments: This conspicuous plant is somewhat common in the park, and the larvae of the Anise Swallowtail Butterfly feed on it. Native American groups peeled young Cow Parsnip shoots and ate them raw or cooked, and they dried the hollow stems and used them as straws and flutes and as blowguns for shooting berries or pebbles. They chopped and dried the mature lower stems and used the material as a salt substitute in cooked food. *Heracleum* is for Hercules, who was said to have used this plant medicinally.

GRAY'S LOVAGE
Ligusticum grayi
Carrot family (Apiaceae)

Description: This common, widespread perennial grows up to 2½' tall from a taproot and has hairless herbage. Its pinnately divided leaves are up to 22" long, grow mostly toward the base of the plant, and look very much like the leaves of Italian Flat-leaf Parsley. The compound umbels, which are slightly rounded at the top, have 5–18 rays, each ending in an umbellet of small flowers with 5 white or sometimes pinkish petals. The small, oblong fruit have narrow-winged ribs.

Flowering time: June–September

Habitat/range: Meadows and other moist areas; montane, subalpine, and alpine zones; 6,100–11,000'.

Comments: The plant was named for Asa Gray, a Harvard professor who was an eminent American botanist in the 19th century. He started the Harvard Herbarium, now called the Gray Herbarium, and he collected many plants in the American West.

Similar plants: Though Gray's Lovage resembles other carrot family plants in the park, it's the only one with leaves that look almost exactly like Italian Flat-leaf Parsley. The leaves of non-native Poison Hemlock (*Conium maculatum*) are somewhat similar but are more lace-like, and its stems have distinctive purple blotches. The highly poisonous plant has been reported in the Wawona area.

MOUNTAIN SWEET-CICELY
Osmorhiza berteroi (*O. chilensis*)
Carrot family (Apiaceae)

Description: The foliage of this slender perennial has a sweet, anise-like fragrance. The 1–3 erect stems, 1–4' tall, can be smooth, hairy, or bristly and are branched and leafy near the top. The leaf blades are 2–6" long and are divided into parts of 3. The thin, somewhat hairy leaflets are narrowly ovate to somewhat round, are less than 2½" long, and are coarsely toothed, cut, or lobed. The plant has several long-petioled basal leaves, and its short-petioled stem leaves are single, paired, or in a whorl of three. The loose compound umbels have 3–8 rays that end in small flowers with 5 greenish-white petals. The flowers mature into a narrow, densely bristly fruit that tapers toward the base.

Flowering time: April–July

Habitat/range: Shaded forest; mixed conifer and montane zones; 3,400–7,500'.

Similar plants: Yosemite has three similar plants in the *Osmorhiza* genus. California Sweet-cicely (*O. brachypoda*) is the only one that has bractlets at the base of its umbellets (the secondary flower clusters). Both Mountain Sweet-cicely and California Sweet-cicely have greenish-white flowers and bristly fruit. The other species, Western Sweet-cicely (*O. occidentalis*), has yellowish flowers and smooth fruit, and it's less common and more shrubby looking than the other two.

7

WESTERN COWBANE
Oxypolis occidentalis
Carrot family (Apiaceae)

Description: This hairless, water-loving perennial is 2–5' tall and has a simple or few-branched stem. The basal leaf blades **[inset]** are oblong in outline, up to 1' long, and pinnately divided into 5–13 narrow to ovate leaflets. The leaflets are 1½–2½" long and have rounded to saw-like teeth. The few stem leaves have smaller leaflets and have an expanded sheath that clasps the stem. The compound umbels are flat topped to umbrella shaped, often have bracts at the base, and have 12–24 rays that end in umbrella-shaped clusters of many tiny flowers with 5 white petals. The small, oval fruit are flattened and have conspicuous ribs and wings.

Flowering time: July–August

Habitat/range: Lakes, streams, bogs, and meadows; mixed conifer, montane, and subalpine zones; 4,000–10,000'.

Similar plants: Western Cowbane's leaves are divided only once into leaflets and it grows in boggy places. Howell's Yampah (*Perideridia howellii*) is uncommon in the park. It also grows in boggy places and its upper leaves are sometimes divided only once, but its lowest leaves are always divided twice. Brewer's Angelica (*Angelica breweri*) and Gray's Lovage (*Ligusticum grayi*) have leaves that are usually divided twice into leaflets, but they don't grow in boggy areas, though they often grow along streambanks.

BOLANDER'S YAMPAH
Perideridia bolanderi ssp. *bolanderi*
Carrot family (Apiaceae)

Description: Bolander's Yampah is a slender, hairless perennial that's 6-36" tall. Its basal leaves are 5–14" long and are pinnately divided 3 times into linear to thread-like ultimate divisions **[inset]**. The flower clusters are dense, round-topped compound umbels with 10–20 rays that terminate in delicate clusters of small flowers with 5 white petals. Both the umbels and umbellets have small, persistent bracts at the base. The small, oblong fruit have thread-like ribs.

Flowering time: June–August

Habitat/range: Mostly dry meadows, sometimes in seeps and along damp rock fissures; mixed conifer, montane, and subalpine zones; 2,800–8,500'.

Comments: Yampah roots, with their sweet, nutty flavor, were an important food source for many Native American groups. Some groups used the seeds (similar to caraway seeds) as a seasoning. Blackfoot Indian kids dug up the roots and ate them as snacks when they got hungry during playtime.

Similar plants: Poison Angelica (*Angelica lineariloba*) has similar leaves, but its flower clusters have no bracts at the base.

PARISH'S YAMPAH

Perideridia parishii ssp. *latifolia*
Carrot family (Apiaceae)

Description: Parish's Yampah is a slender, hairless perennial that's 6–35" tall. Its basal leaves **[inset]** are 5–12" long and are usually divided into 3 linear to narrowly lanceolate leaflets that are 1–6" long. The inflorescence is a compound umbel with 5–20 rays of almost equal length. Each ray ends in a cluster of tiny flowers with 5 white petals. The small fruit are round to ovate and have thread-like ribs.

Flowering time: July–September

Habitat/range: Meadows and open conifer forests; mixed conifer, montane, subalpine, and alpine zones; 5,000–10,000'.

Comments: Native Americans ate the sweet-tasting tuberous roots raw or cooked them in a fire pit. They also dried the roots and pounded them into a flour, which they used to make bread or soup.

Similar plants: Parish's Yampah is extremely difficult to distinguish from Lemmon's Yampah (*Perideridia lemmonii*), and they often grow together. To tell them apart with any certainty, you'd need to examine a cross section of a fruit under magnification. Parish's Yampah has 3 or 4 oil tubes between each rib. Lemmon's Yampah has 1 oil tube between each rib. The oil tubes can be difficult to discern even under 10x magnification.

TALL SOCK-DESTROYER, FIELD HEDGE PARSLEY

(non-native)
Torilis arvensis
Carrot family (Apiaceae)

Description: This slender European annual, up to 3' tall, has a spreading or erect, branched stem with alternate leaves. The lower leaves, up to 8" long (including the petiole), are pinnately dissected 2 or 3 times and have coarsely toothed segments. The inflorescence is an open compound umbel of small flower clusters on long, slender rays. Each flower has 5 white, unequal petals. The small, oblong fruit are uniformly covered with tiny, straight, barb-tipped prickles that are about as long as the fruit is wide.

Flowering time: April–July

Habitat/range: Disturbed places; chaparral/oak-woodland and mixed conifer zones; up to 5,000'.

Similar plants: Four similar carrot family plants grow in the park. Non-native Bur-chervil (*Anthriscus caucalis*) is the only one with fruit that have curved prickles. Native California Hedge Parsley (*Yabea microcarpa*) has straight prickles on its fruit, and it's the only one of the four that has small, pinnately divided, leafy-looking bracts in its flower clusters. The other straight-prickled species, non-native Knotted Hedge Parsley (*Torilis nodosa*), sometimes called Short Sock-destroyer, has fruit with prickles only on the outer-facing surface.

INDIAN HEMP

Apocynum cannabinum
Dogbane family (Apocynaceae)

Description: Indian Hemp is a hairless perennial, 1–4' tall, with stout, leafy stems that are branched above. The opposite, lanceolate to ovate leaves, 2–3" long, are sessile or have short petioles. Clusters of flowers grow at the stem end and from the upper leaf axils. The small, white, cylindric to urn-shaped flowers, less than ¼" long, have erect lobes. The fruit is a pendant pair of long, cylindric, often red-tinged pods that contain numerous seeds, each with a tuft of silky hairs that catch the wind.

Flowering time: June–August

Habitat/range: Damp to wet areas; chaparral/oak-woodland and mixed conifer zones; up to 6,600'.

Comments: Indians used the long, tough fibers of the stems to make twine, thread, fishing line, bowstrings, nets, blankets, and baskets. In the Great Basin, Indians made large nets from Indian Hemp (and other fibers) to catch rabbits. The nets were 2–3' tall and could be over 300' long (some sources say as much as a mile long). The hunt was a communal effort, with neighboring groups working together, and included men, women, and children. One or more nets were set up near an area where rabbits lived; people formed a line and moved through the area, driving rabbits into the nets. Indian Hemp is poisonous; the genus name is Greek for "away from dog," for a similar European plant's ancient use as a dog poison.

COMMON YARROW

Achillea millefolium
Sunflower family (Asteraceae)

Description: This highly aromatic perennial, 8–40" tall, has 1 or more stems that are branched near the top and are covered with soft-woolly hairs. The alternate, fern-like leaves are pinnately divided 2 or 3 times into narrow segments. The numerous small flower heads, in flat- to round-topped clusters, have 3–8 round, white ray flowers and several greenish to cream-colored disk flowers with bright yellow anthers.

Flowering time: June–August

Habitat/range: Many habitats; chaparral/oak-woodland, mixed conifer, montane, subalpine, and alpine zones; up to 12,200'.

Comments: Achilles, the mythological Greek hero for whom the genus was named, was said to have saved the lives of many of his soldiers during the Trojan War by staunching their wounds with Common Yarrow. The legend has validity; lab experiments have verified that the plant contains an alkaloid that reduces the clotting time of blood.

Similar plants: With its finely divided leaves and umbel-like flower heads, Common Yarrow could be mistaken for a member of the carrot family, from a certain distance. A closer look confirms that the small flower heads are made up of ray and disk flowers.

TRAIL PLANT
Adenocaulon bicolor
Sunflower family (Asteraceae)

Description: This common perennial has slender, widely branched stems that are 1–3' long and are white-woolly below and glandular above. Most of the leaves grow on long, flexible stalks at the base of the plant. The triangular leaf blades are usually heart shaped at the base. They have wavy margins and are smooth and green on top and silver-woolly below. The flower heads, which grow at the tips of long branches in an open arrangement, have tightly packed, tiny, white disk flowers. The fruit (achenes) are club shaped, have stalked glands, and are up to ½" inch long.

Flowering time: June–August

Habitat/range: Moist, shaded woods and forests; chaparral/oak-woodland and mixed conifer zones, up to 6,000'.

Comments: Trail Plant got its name from its bicolored leaves. When animals (including people) walk through patches of the plant, their feet can flip a leaf over and trample it upside down, revealing the silver underside. A silver leaf shows that someone has walked there, and its arrowhead shape indicates the direction of travel.

PEARLY EVERLASTING
Anaphalis margaritacea
Sunflower family (Asteraceae)

Description: This aromatic perennial, up to 3½' tall, typically grows in large, crowded patches from rhizomes. The unbranched, usually solitary stem is densely covered with white-woolly, nonglandular hairs. The linear to lanceolate, sessile or clasping leaves are alternate along the length of the stem. The leaves have a conspicuous midvein and woolly hair, mostly on the underside, but sometimes on both surfaces. At the end of the stem is a dense, more or less dome-shaped cluster of small, round flower heads. Each flower head has many layers of pearl-white, papery phyllaries surrounding yellow disk flowers that turn brown with age.

Flowering time: July–October

Habitat/range: Open forest, meadow borders, roadsides, and disturbed places; mixed conifer, montane, and subalpine zones; 3,500–8,500'.

Comments: Although the plants don't actually last forever, the flowers keep a fresh look long after they're dead, and they're often used in floral arrangements. The plants have a delectable fragrance that's been described as smelling like maple syrup, vanilla, butterscotch, and caramel.

Similar plants: California Everlasting (*Pseudognaphalium californicum*) is quite similar, but it doesn't grow in large, crowded patches and its stems have sticky glands.

ROSY PUSSY-TOES

Antennaria rosea ssp. *rosea*
Sunflower family (Asteraceae)

Description: This mat-forming perennial has erect stems, 3–16" tall, and a network of stolons by which it spreads. The basal leaves, ¾–1½" long, are spoon shaped and woolly on both surfaces. Several small flower heads grow in a dense cluster at the stem end. The tips of the phyllaries can be pink, red, white, yellowish, or brownish, and they have no spots. Male and female flowers grow on separate plants, though most individuals are female.

Flowering time: June–August

Habitat/range: Woodland, meadow edges, and rocky areas; mixed conifer, montane, subalpine, and alpine zones; 4,000–11,500'.

Similar plants: The leaves of almost identical *Antennaria rosea* ssp. *confinis* are no more than ¾" long. Flat-top Pussy-toes (*A. corymbosa*), possibly the most common *Antennaria* in the park, has white-tipped phyllaries with a dark spot toward the middle. Alpine Pussy-toes (*A. media*) has blackish-green phyllaries, and its longest leaves are more than ½" long; Beautiful Pussy-toes (*A. pulchella*) also has blackish-green phyllaries, but its leaves are less than ½" long. Brown Pussy-toes (*A. umbrinella*) is the only *Antennaria* in the park with a somewhat woody base. Silvery Pussy-toes (*A. argentea*) is the only *Antennaria* in the park that has no stolons and doesn't form mats, and it's the only one that grows only in the mixed conifer zone.

SOFT ROSINWEED

Calycadenia mollis
Sunflower family (Asteraceae)

Description: Soft Rosinweed is a sticky annual with 1–6 wand-like, sometimes reddish stems, 11–35" long, that are soft-hairy at the base and glandular-hairy above. Its narrow, grayish-green leaves are up to 2¾" long and are covered with soft, appressed hairs. The flower heads are about ½" long. They have 2–10 disk flowers and 1–4 white, rose **[inset]**, or yellow ray flowers. The tips of the rays have 3 lobes that are about the same size. The bracts beneath the flower heads have long, ciliate hairs and interesting little saucer-shaped tack glands.

Flowering time: May–September

Habitat/range: Dry, open meadows; chaparral/oak-woodland and mixed conifer zones; up to 5,000'.

Comments: The Soft Rosinweed populations in the Yosemite area seem to have mostly white-flowered plants with a scattering of rose-flowered plants mixed in.

Similar plants: Sticky Rosinweed (*Calycadenia multiglandulosa*), which looks a lot like Soft Rosinweed, is rarely encountered in the park. Its ray flowers also have 3 lobes at the tip, but the middle lobe is noticeably smaller than the outer 2 lobes. Like Soft Rosinweed, its ray flowers can be white, yellow, or rose.

SIERRA PINCUSHION
Chaenactis alpigena
Sunflower family (Asteraceae)

Description: This low-growing, matted perennial is less than 3" tall and is easily overlooked. The gray-green to mint-green leaves are densely white-woolly, somewhat fan shaped in outline, and variously lobed. The woolly flower stalks, which rise slightly above the leaves or lie along the ground, end in a single flower head, about ½" long. Each flower head has narrow, pointed, woolly phyllaries and cream-colored disk flowers. When the flowers are mature, they have extended magenta anthers that are fused around a 2-branched style. The anthers and style are the "pins" in the pincushion.

Flowering time: July–August

Habitat/range: Open, sandy or gravelly slopes and flats; subalpine and alpine zones; 9,000–11,800'.

Comments: People who hike the gravelly granite slopes and flats in the Yosemite high country are likely to walk by patches of Sierra Pincushion without noticing them, even if they're searching for plants. The woolly-gray foliage makes the plants blend in perfectly with granitic gravel. They're much easier to spot in less granitic habitats (like in the photo above). Good places to look for the plants are in gravelly areas on Mount Watkins and along the upper part of the Mount Hoffmann trail.

DUSTY-MAIDENS
Chaenactis douglasii var. *douglasii*
Sunflower family (Asteraceae)

Description: This biennial or perennial has erect to spreading stems, up to 1¼' long, that are densely gray-woolly initially and become less so with age. The stem is usually branched above, and each branch ends with a flower head. The alternate, fern-like, glandular stem leaves are 2 or 3 times pinnately divided into thick, narrow, curled segments. The leaves are woolly when they're young, become smoother with age, and get smaller upward. The basal leaves are usually much larger than the stem leaves and are sometimes withered when the flowers are in bloom. The flat-topped flower heads are about ⅝" long and have a glandular cup of unequal phyllaries. The numerous white to pinkish disk flowers often have extended anthers fused around a style with 2 linear branches.

Flowering time: May–August

Habitat/range: Open, sandy, gravelly, or rocky areas; mixed conifer, montane, and subalpine zones; 3,000–9,900'.

Comments: The woolly, cobwebby hairs on the stems and leaves give the plant its dusty look. The plant was valued medicinally by several North American Indian tribes, who used it to alleviate a variety of conditions, but especially to treat skin problems.

DINNERPLATE THISTLE, MEADOW THISTLE

Cirsium scariosum var. *americanum*
Sunflower family (Asteraceae)

Description: This stemless, taprooted perennial or biennial native thistle has a dense basal rosette of oblong, spiny, sometimes deeply divided leaves that are up to 1¼' long and are often persistently cobwebby-woolly toward the base. One to many flower heads, with white to cream-colored disk flowers, are nestled in the center of the rosette of leaves. The flower heads are about 1" wide, and there is often only a single flower head in full bloom, alongside others that are fading or just beginning to develop.

Flowering time: July–August

Habitat/range: Moist places in the open, usually on slopes and at meadow edges; montane, subalpine, and alpine zones; 7,500–11,000'.

Comments: This species is extremely variable. Our variety has no stem, but others have a stem that's up to 3' tall, and some have bright, colorful flowers. According to *Jepson eFlora* (2020), "Past taxonomic treatments have variably recognized members of this complex as multiple species, some as subspecies and/or varieties or have merged all or most variants into a single polymorphic sp. with extraordinary variability." Botany, like most things in life, is a work in progress; "needs more study" is a common phrase in botanical literature.

HORSEWEED

Erigeron canadensis (*Conyza canadensis*)
Sunflower family (Asteraceae)

Description: Horseweed is an invasive annual that's native throughout most of North and Central America and is becoming naturalized in Europe, Asia, and Australia. The erect, sparsely hairy stem is up to 5' tall and is much branched throughout the upper half. The alternate, slender, sessile leaves, up to 4" long and less than ½" wide, are rough-hairy, are sometimes minutely toothed, and grow in a distinctive spiral up the stem, often looking as though they're whorled. The lower leaves tend to wither as the plant matures. The many small flower heads, which grow in panicle-like clusters, have 7–13 yellow disk flowers and 20–45 white or pale pink ray flowers that are often inconspicuous.

Flowering time: all year

Habitat/range: Disturbed places; chaparral/oak-woodland and mixed conifer zones; up to 7,500'.

Comments: Horseweed is commonly considered a weed since it infests fields, meadows, gardens, and roadsides throughout its native range. A vigorous fire follower, it rapidly invades areas cleared of vegetation by fire. *Erigeron* in Greek means "early old man," in reference to the fact that some early blooming species in the genus already have white, whiskery seed heads in early spring.

CUT-LEAVED DAISY
Erigeron compositus
Sunflower family (Asteraceae)

Description: This tufted perennial, 1–6" tall, has unbranched stems and herbage that's densely glandular and sometimes sparsely covered with bristly hairs. The leaves are mostly basal and are up to 2½" long, including the long petiole. The leaf blades are divided several times in a fan-like manner into multiple segments. The alternate stem leaves, if any, are small and are usually undivided. The flower heads, up to ¾" wide, grow solitary at the stem ends. They can have yellow disk flowers only **[inset]** or yellow disk flowers and 30–60 white (sometimes pale pink) ray flowers. The rough-hairy, minutely glandular, bell-shaped involucre has more or less equal phyllaries with purple tips.

Flowering time: July–August

Habitat/range: Open, rocky areas and fellfields; subalpine and alpine zones; 9,500–12,500'.

Comments: Cut-leaved Daisy is common in alpine fellfields throughout the park, and plants that have ray flowers are just about as common as those that don't.

Similar plants: When it has ray flowers, Cut-leaved Daisy looks a lot like Rambling Daisy (*Erigeron vagus*), but Rambling Daisy's leaves have 3 lobes at the tip rather than multiple fan-like segments.

COULTER'S DAISY
Erigeron coulteri
Sunflower family (Asteraceae)

Description: Coulter's Daisy is a showy perennial, 8–26" tall, with a leafy stem that's hairless at the bottom and sparsely hairy toward the top. The lanceolate to oblong, petioled basal leaves, 2–5" long, are hairy and sometimes have 2–6 pairs of shallow teeth. The alternate, clasping stem leaves are a bit smaller. The unbranched or few-branched stem has 1–4 flower heads that are about 2" wide. Each flower head has many yellow disk flowers and 45–140 white ray flowers. The bell-shaped involucre **[inset]** has somewhat equal, minutely glandular phyllaries with spreading hairs that have distinctive black markings at the base.

Flowering time: July–August

Habitat/range: Streambanks and wet meadows; montane, subalpine, and alpine zones; 7,000–11,000'.

Similar plants: Non-native Ox-eye Daisy (*Leucanthemum vulgare*) has similar flower heads, but its lower leaves have deeply scalloped margins and it grows in disturbed areas. Wandering Daisy (*Erigeron glacialis*) grows in the same habitat and vegetation zones. It sometimes has flower heads with white ray flowers, which could cause it to be confused with Coulter's Daisy, but Wandering Daisy's phyllaries are densely glandular and they have no hairs with black markings.

SHORT-RAYED DAISY
Erigeron lonchophyllus (*Trimorpha lonchophylla*)
Sunflower family (Asteraceae)

Description: This dainty composite grows in moist meadows, where it's often hidden among taller grasses. Its stems, 1½–8" tall, are covered with stiff, spreading, white hairs that give them a bristly appearance. The basal leaves, about 1" long or less, are narrowly oblanceolate, have smooth margins, and taper to long petioles. The alternate, linear stem leaves are sometimes longer than the basal leaves. Each stem usually has several flower heads, less than ⅜" wide, with numerous yellow disk flowers and 70–130 tiny, white to pale pink ray flowers. The nonglandular, hairy phyllaries are overlapping and purple tipped, and the flower heads don't always seem to open fully.

Flowering time: July–August

Habitat/range: Damp meadows and other moist places; subalpine zone; 8,200–10,500'.

Comments: This diminutive plant often grows on alkaline ground, such as the grassy borders of the paths around the Soda Springs area in Tuolumne Meadows.

Similar plants: Somewhat similar English Daisy (*Bellis perennis*) is a non-native annual that grows in lawns around developments at lower elevations; it has fully open flower heads, more than ½" wide, and oval leaf blades with shallowly toothed margins.

RAMBLING DAISY
Erigeron vagus
Sunflower family (Asteraceae)

Description: Rambling Daisy is a charming, compact perennial that's only 1–2" tall. It has hairy, unbranched, sometimes glandular stems. The spoon-shaped leaves, which are crowded toward the base of the plant, are densely soft-white-hairy, are minutely glandular, and have 3 rounded lobes at the tip. The alternate stem leaves, if any, are much smaller. The flower heads, which grow solitary at the stem ends, have many yellow disk flowers and 25–35 white to pale pink ray flowers with rays that are up to ¼" long. The bell-shaped involucre has hairy, minutely glandular phyllaries that are green on the lower half and purplish on the upper half.

Flowering time: July–August

Habitat/range: Talus, scree slopes, and fellfields; alpine zone; 11,000–13,000'.

Comments: Rambling Daisy has been reported from only a few locations in the park, such as the ridge above Gaylor Lakes, on Mount Gibbs, and along the northwest side of Mount Dana.

Similar plants: When Cut-leaved Daisy (*Erigeron compositus*) has ray flowers, it looks a lot like Rambling Daisy, but the leaves of Cut-leaved Daisy are divided several times in a fan-like manner into multiple segments.

16

WHITE-FLOWERED HAWKWEED
Hieracium albiflorum
Sunflower family (Asteraceae)

Description: White-flowered Hawkweed is a perennial with a slender stem that's up to 2½' tall. The stem is unbranched and long-hairy toward the base and is loosely branched and mostly hairless toward the top. The coarsely long-hairy, alternate leaves are 3–5½" long. Most of the leaves are crowded at the base of the stem and sometimes look like a loose rosette. The leaves are oblong or oblanceolate, are occasionally purplish, and sometimes have a few teeth. Several to many small flower heads, a little less than ½" wide, grow in loose clusters at the branch tips. Each flower head has 15–30 white ray flowers. The squared-off tips of the rays have 5 tiny, pointed lobes.

Flowering time: June–August

Habitat/range: Dry, open or shaded forest; chaparral/oak-woodland, mixed conifer, montane, and subalpine zones; up to 9,000'.

Comments: White-flowered Hawkweed is a leggy, weedy-looking native plant that's widespread and common throughout the western United States, Canada, and Alaska. The small, white ray flowers have a tidy appearance with their squared-off, 5-lobed tips. Hawkweeds have a milky sap that Native Americans used to make chewing gum.

OX-EYE DAISY
(non-native)
Leucanthemum vulgare
Sunflower family (Asteraceae)

Description: Ox-eye Daisy, a Eurasian native perennial, is considered by some to be the quintessential daisy. Its stem is up to 3' tall and is sometimes branched above. The alternate, long-petioled lower leaves are up to 5" long, are broader at the tip, and are deeply scalloped or toothed along the margins. The smaller, clasping stem leaves are sometimes toothed. The solitary flower head is up to 3" wide and has many yellow disk flowers and 15–30 white ray flowers. The leathery, lanceolate, overlapping phyllaries have reddish margins.

Flowering time: June–August

Habitat/range: Meadows and grassy disturbed areas near present or historic habitation sites; mixed conifer zone; 3,700–4,600'.

Similar plants: Non-native Mayweed (*Anthemis cotula*), has similar large flower heads, but its leaves are finely divided and fern-like. Non-native Prairie Fleabane (*Erigeron strigosus*) **[inset]** is much branched toward the top, has smaller flower heads, and has 60–119 ray flowers. Like Ox-eye Daisy, Mayweed and Prairie Fleabane do not grow above the mixed conifer zone. The leaves of native Coulter's Daisy (*Erigeron coulteri*) have smooth margins or a few scattered teeth, and it grows from the montane zone up into the alpine zone.

17

WOOLLY DESERT-DANDELION

Malacothrix floccifera
Sunflower family (Asteraceae)

Description: This appealing annual has 1–8 erect or ascending, simple or branched stems, up to 16" long, and herbage that's often reddish. The fleshy lower leaves are up to 3" long, are oblong to oblanceolate, are pinnately toothed or lobed, and form somewhat of a rosette. The alternate stem leaves are smaller and are sometimes toothed or lobed. The leaf lobes often have tufts of white hair on the upper surface. The flower heads, which grow in loose clusters, have 20–60 ray flowers that are up to ⅝" long. The rays are solid white, white with yellow bases, or occasionally all yellow, and they often have a broad purplish strip on the lower surface. The phyllaries are in 2 or 3 series, and the outer phyllaries are about half as long as the inner phyllaries. The fruit is a ribbed achene with deciduous bristles.

Flowering time: April–August

Habitat/range: Open areas in loose soil of burns, slides, and road cuts; chaparral/oak-woodland and mixed conifer zones; up to 6,500'.

Comments: This plant is uncommon in the park. It has been reported along Wawona Road, Snow Creek Trail, and Yosemite Falls Trail, but it's much more common in the barren, often serpentine soil of road cuts along Highway 49 in the foothills west of the park.

CALIFORNIA EVERLASTING

Pseudognaphalium californicum
(*Gnaphalium californicum*)
Sunflower family (Asteraceae)

Description: The green stem of this annual to perennial is 1–3' tall, branched above, and strongly aromatic. The lower leaves are up to 6" long and are oblong-lanceolate. The stem leaves become smaller toward the top and have a sessile base that extends down along the stem. The glandular leaves are sometimes whitish when young but are green at maturity. The small flower heads, in clusters at the branch tips, have pearl-white phyllaries that become straw colored and shiny with age. The yellowish disk flowers are often inconspicuous.

Flowering time: April–July

Habitat/range: Dry areas; chaparral/oak woodland and mixed conifer zones; up to 4,000'.

Similar plants: Three related plants in the park differ in that they have white-woolly herbage throughout their lives. Lowland Everlasting (*Gnaphalium palustre*) is the smallest (under 1' tall), and the only one with woolly flower heads nestled in leafy bracts that extend beyond the heads. Small-flowered Everlasting (*P. stramineum*, previously *G. stramineum*) has clasping stem leaves and flower heads in a tight spherical cluster at the top of each stem. The stem leaves of White Everlasting (*P. thermale*, previously *G. canescens* ssp. *thermale*) are sessile, but not clasping, and its flower heads grow in clusters at the branch tips.

OREGON ASTER

Sericocarpus oregonensis ssp. *californicus*
(*Aster oregonensis* ssp. *californicus*)
Sunflower family (Asteraceae)

Description: Oregon Aster is a leggy perennial with hairy stems, up to 3½' tall, that are branched toward the top. The basal and lowest stem leaves wither early. The rest of the stem leaves, up to 3" long and less than ½" wide, are oblanceolate to oblong and are rough to the touch above and rough and somewhat glandular below. The flower heads, which grow in tight clusters at the branch ends, have 9–20 white disk flowers with purplish anthers and 2–6 white ray flowers with rays that are up to ¼" long. The distinctive shingled phyllaries are in 3 or 4 series and are white to cream colored with green tips.

Flowering time: July–September

Habitat/range: Dry to moist, sandy soils in open areas; chaparral/oak-woodland and mixed conifer zones; up to 5,000'.

Comments: This is one of many composite plants that used to be in the *Aster* genus. A 1994 study of plants assigned to the *Aster* genus revealed that Eurasian members of the group are substantially different from North American members. By rules of scientific nomenclature, the Eurasian plants, which were named long before the North American plants, kept the *Aster* genus name, and about 180 North American plants were assigned to other genera.

GRAY CHICKENSAGE

Sphaeromeria cana
Sunflower family (Asteraceae)

Description: This subshrub has many erect stems that are up to 2' tall and are branched throughout. Its gray-green, gland-dotted herbage has a sage-like odor. Its alternate leaves are up to 1½" long and are covered with fine, gray, silky or woolly hairs. The upper leaves are linear-oblong, and most of the lower leaves are divided into 3 or 4 linear lobes. The flower heads grow at the branch ends in small, crowded clusters. Each head has 10–12 pale, woolly-hairy phyllaries in 2 or 3 series and 30–60 cream-colored disk flowers that have soft-hairy corolla lobes. The flower heads turn brown as they age.

Flowering time: July–August

Habitat/range: Dry, rocky ledges and crevices in cliffs; subalpine and alpine zones; 9,000–12,000'.

Comments: If you climb Mount Dana, Mount Gibbs, or the Dana Plateau, you might encounter this attractive plant. Or you can simply drive to the east side of Tioga Pass and find it growing on rocky ledges below most of the scenic view parking areas.

SIERRA CAT'S-EYE
Cryptantha nubigena
Borage or Waterleaf family (Boraginaceae)

Description: Sierra Cat's-eye is a hardy perennial with several erect to ascending stems, up to 1' long, and herbage that's densely covered with long, bristly hairs. The plant has alternate stem leaves and usually has several leaf rosettes at the base. The basal leaves are narrowly oblanceolate to spoon shaped. The small flowers are clustered in a somewhat ball-shaped head and have a corolla with 5 white lobes and a yellow center. The fruit is a set of 4 small nutlets.

Flowering time: July–August

Habitat/range: Moraines, fellfields, and scree slopes; subalpine and alpine zones; 9,800–12,500'.

Similar plants: There are about ten species of *Cryptantha* in Yosemite, and they're very difficult to tell apart. It's also difficult to distinguish plants in the *Cryptantha* genus from plants in the closely related *Plagiobothrys* genus. For many of the plants, identification requires microscopic examination of features on the tiny nutlets when they're dry. Most plants in the two genera are under a foot tall, are bristly-hairy, and have coiled inflorescences. Sierra Cat's-eye is the only biennial/perennial *Cryptantha* or *Plagiobothrys* species that grows in the park, *and* it's the only one that's easy to identify, with its ball-shaped flower clusters and high-elevation habitat. The annual species grow in various habitats below the alpine zone.

DWARF HESPEROCHIRON
Hesperochiron pumilus
Borage or Waterleaf family (Boraginaceae)

Description: This low-growing, stemless perennial has a rosette of 2–10 basal leaves that are up to 3" long. The oblong to oblanceolate leaf blades have ciliate margins and taper to a petiole. The leaves can be sparsely hairy above but are hairless below. The plant has 1–8 flowers, each on its own slender stalk that's up to 2½" long. The flowers have 5 (or 6) usually unequal stamens and a white, wheel-shaped to shallowly bowl-shaped corolla, about ½" wide, with 5 (or 6) rounded lobes and netted purple veins. The corolla is partially fused at the base and has a yellow throat with long, soft hairs.

Flowering time: June–July

Habitat/range: Wet meadows and moist slopes and flats; mixed conifer and montane zones; 5,000–8,700'.

Comments: The *Hesperochiron* genus contains only two species. The first part of the genus name was derived from the Greek word *hesperos*, which means western or evening, in reference to the fact that both species grow only in western states.

Similar plants: California Hesperochiron (*Hesperochiron californicus*) has been reported in the park and looks much like Dwarf Hesperochiron. However, its flowers have funnel- to bell-shaped corollas, and its leaves are usually hairy on both surfaces.

VARIABLE-LEAVED NEMOPHILA
Nemophila heterophylla
Borage or Waterleaf family (Boraginaceae)

Description: This common annual has slender, hairy, sometimes branched stems that are up to 1¾" long. Its opposite lower leaves are pinnately divided into 5–7 well-separated divisions. The uppermost leaves have 0–5 lobes and are alternate, though some plants lack alternate upper leaves. The long-stalked flowers grow from the leaf axils. The soft-hairy calyx has 5 lance-ovate lobes and small, reflexed appendages between the lobes. The 5 white, partially fused petals form a bell-shaped corolla that's less than ½" wide.

Flowering time: March–July

Habitat/range: Partly shady slopes; chaparral/oak-woodland and mixed conifer zones; up to 5,000'.

Comments: *Nemophila* comes from Greek words that mean grove and love, for the shady habitat of many species in the genus; *heterophylla* refers to the variability of the plant's leaves.

Similar plants: Sierra Nemophila (*N. spatulata*) and Meadow Nemophila (*N. pedunculata*) have flowers that look much like those of Variable-leaved Nemophila, but both plants grow in mostly flat, moist to muddy places and have opposite leaves only. If you find a white-flowered nemophila growing on a somewhat dry slope and the plant's leaves are all opposite, it's probably a Variable-leaved Nemophila without alternate upper leaves.

MEADOW NEMOPHILA
Nemophila pedunculata
Borage or Waterleaf family (Boraginaceae)

Description: Meadow Nemophila is a low-growing annual with fleshy stems that often trail along the ground. Its herbage is nearly hairless to sparsely bristly-hairy. The leaves, all of which are opposite, are oblong to ovate in outline and are deeply divided into 5–9 lobes. The long-stalked flowers grow from the leaf axils. The 5-lobed calyx has distinctive reflexed appendages between the lobes. The 5-lobed, bell-shaped, white corolla is less than ½" wide, has noticeable purplish veins, and usually has dark purple dots or lavender spots.

Flowering time: April–August

Habitat/range: Damp, mostly flat, somewhat shaded areas; chaparral/oak-woodland and mixed conifer zones; up to 4,300'.

Similar plants: Sierra Nemophila (*N. spatulata*) **[inset]** also has opposite leaves only, and it grows in flat, moist to muddy places, but its leaves are spoon shaped or spatula shaped and have only 3–5 somewhat shallowly divided lobes, most of which are triangular shaped. Variable-leaved Nemophila (*N. heterophylla*) has alternate upper leaves, but the upper leaves are sometimes missing. Its habitat sets it apart from Meadow and Sierra Nemophila; it grows in drier places, usually on somewhat shady slopes.

LITTLE COMBSEED
Pectocarya pusilla
Borage or Waterleaf family (Boraginaceae)

Description: Little Combseed is an inconspicuous, slender annual with an ascending to erect stem, 7–16" long, that has stiff, appressed hairs and is sometimes branched toward the base. Its linear to narrowly oblong leaves are up to 1½" long and have stiff, more or less appressed hairs on both surfaces. The lower leaves are opposite and fused at the base, and the upper leaves are alternate. The tiny flowers, which grow solitary from leaf axils, have a short, curved stalk and 5 narrow, spreading sepals with hook-tipped hairs. The white corolla has 5 rounded lobes and a shallow tube. The fruit **[inset]** is a set of 4 radially arranged, spreading nutlets that are diamond or kite shaped and are covered with hooked hairs.

Flowering time: March–June

Habitat/range: Dry, sparsely vegetated places in grasslands and chaparral; chaparral/oak-woodland and mixed conifer zones; up to 6,000'.

Similar plants: This plant is similar to cat's-eye (*Cryptantha*) and popcornflower (*Plagiobothrys*) species. However, cat's-eye and popcornflower nutlets are compact and are mostly concealed, unlike the readily visible, spreading nutlets of combseed plants. Northern Combseed (*Pectocarya penicillata*) may grow in the park, though it hasn't been reported yet. Its nutlets are elongated and are arranged in 2 distinct pairs.

KAWEAH RIVER PHACELIA
Phacelia egena
Borage or Waterleaf family (Boraginaceae)

Description: This common perennial has mostly basal leaves, has several branched stems, up to 2' long, and has short hairs throughout. The basal leaves are 2–10" long and are pinnately divided or dissected into 5–11 leaflets or segments that are themselves undivided and unlobed. Numerous flowers grow in one-sided, coiling inflorescences at the branch ends. The 5 calyx lobes are linear to oblanceolate and don't overlap each other when the fruit has developed. The cream to white, bell-shaped, 5-lobed corolla is up to ⅜" long.

Flowering time: April–August

Habitat/range: Dry, open areas; chaparral/oak-woodland and mixed conifer zones; up to 6,000'.

Similar plants: Imbricate Phacelia (*P. imbricata* var. *imbricata*) and Variable-leaved Phacelia (*P. heterophylla*) are the only other phacelias in the park with basal leaves that have numerous leaflets or segments that are undivided and unlobed. Variable-leaved Phacelia is distinct in that its coiling flower clusters encircle the entire upper stem. Imbricate Phacelia's inflorescences are similar to those of Kaweah River Phacelia, but its calyx lobes are broader (broadly lanceolate to ovate), and they overlap each other when the fruit has developed. Imbricate Phacelia grows around El Portal and has been reported in Yosemite Valley and in the Wawona area, but it's mostly a foothill species.

TIMBERLINE PHACELIA, COMPACT PHACELIA

Phacelia hastata var. *compacta*
Borage or Waterleaf family (Boraginaceae)

Description: Timberline Phacelia is a perennial with several reclining to ascending stems, 2–10" long, that are sometimes glandular. Its gray-green herbage is covered with fine, silvery, bristly hairs. Most of the leaves grow in tufts at the base of the plant, and they're rarely lobed or compound, though they can have 1 or 2 pairs of lobes or 2 leaflets toward the base of the blade. The leaves have prominent veins and a lanceolate to widely elliptic blade that tapers to a narrow petiole. Numerous flowers grow in 1-sided, coiled inflorescences toward the stem ends. The linear to lanceolate calyx lobes are often purplish, are usually glandular, and have long, stiff, white hairs. The urn- to bell-shaped corolla is up to ¼" long and has 5 fused, white or pale lavender petals that become dirty white with age. The stamens and style extend well beyond the corolla lobes.

Flowering time: July–September

Habitat/range: Dry, rocky places; montane, subalpine, and alpine zones; 7,000–13,000'.

Similar plants: Changeable Phacelia (*Phacelia mutabilis*) is the only other perennial/biennial phacelia in the park with leaves that are unlobed or few lobed toward the base of the blade. Unlike Timberline Phacelia, many of its basal leaves are withered when the plant is in bloom, leaving mostly stem leaves, and its stems are up to 24" long.

VARIABLE-LEAVED PHACELIA

Phacelia heterophylla var. *virgata*
Borage or Waterleaf family (Boraginaceae)

Description: This distinctive biennial or perennial has mostly basal leaves and usually has a single central stem that's 8"–4' tall, though it occasionally has several shorter lateral stems. Its herbage is densely covered with short, soft or bristly hairs. The basal leaves, which often form a rosette, are up to 6" long and are lanceolate to ovate in outline. The leaves are pinnately dissected into 5–7 leaflets, and the terminal leaflet is larger than the lateral leaflets. The upper leaves are much reduced and can have a few lobes. The distinctive elongated inflorescence has many dense, coiling flower clusters that encircle the stalk. The linear to linear-oblong calyx lobes are covered with yellowish-green hairs. The white to pale lavender, bell-shaped corolla is up to ¼" long, and the stamens and style extend well beyond the corolla lobes.

Flowering time: May–July

Habitat/range: Dry, open slopes and flats; chaparral/oak-woodland and mixed conifer zones; up to 5,000'.

Comments: Phacelia flower buds grow along one side of a coiled stalk. The flowers begin to open when the inflorescence is tightly coiled, and the flowers at the base of the stalk open first. As the coil unwinds, the next buds in line open at the "new" top of the coil, where pollinators can more easily find them.

BRANCHING PHACELIA
Phacelia ramosissima
Borage or Waterleaf family (Boraginaceae)

Description: Branching Phacelia is uncommon in the park. It's a woody-based perennial with several sprawling to ascending, profusely branched stems that are 1½–3½' long. Its herbage is finely grayish-hairy to bristly throughout and sometimes glandular. The leaves are up to 6" long, are oblong to broadly ovate in outline, and are pinnately compound, with several toothed or lobed leaflets. The flowers are nearly sessile in dense, short, coiled clusters at the branch ends. The densely glandular-bristly calyx has 5 spatula-shaped lobes, and the dirty-white or bluish corolla is about ⅜" wide. The 5 rounded lobes of the corolla spread outward, making the face of the corolla look like a flat disk. The stamens protrude well beyond the corolla.

Flowering time: May–August

Habitat/range: Open, somewhat moist, often rocky areas; mixed conifer zone; 4,900–6,800'.

Similar plants: Caterpillar Phacelia (*Phacelia cicutaria* var. *cicutaria*) also has bristly foliage, pinnately divided leaves, and dirty-white flowers, but its stems are erect (or lean against rocky banks), they aren't profusely branched, and they're not woody at the base. Caterpillar Phacelia has been reported to grow in the Merced River Canyon nearly up into Yosemite Valley, but it grows mostly west of the park and is widespread and common in the Sierra Nevada foothills.

RUSTY POPCORNFLOWER
Plagiobothrys nothofulvus
Borage or Waterleaf family (Boraginaceae)

Description: Rusty Popcornflower is an annual with branching, mostly erect stems that are 8–26" long and have sharp, spreading hairs that make them rough to the touch. Its oblanceolate, sparsely hairy basal leaves are 1–4" long, grow in a rosette, and are pointed at the tip. The alternate stem leaves are linear or lanceolate. The flowers grow in a coiled cluster and open from the bottom upward as the coil unwinds. The 5 calyx lobes have dense, tawny hairs, and the small, 5-lobed corolla is white with a ring of pale to bright yellow appendages at the center.

Flowering time: March–May

Habitat/range: Grasslands and open woodlands; chaparral/oak-woodland and mixed conifer zones; up to 5,000'.

Similar plants: With its leaf rosette and the tawny hairs on its calyx, Rusty Popcornflower is fairly easy to recognize. The rest of the plants in the *Plagiobothrys* genus (the popcornflowers) and most of the plants in the closely related *Cryptantha* genus (the cat's-eyes) can be identified to species only by a careful magnified or microscopic examination of features on their tiny nutlets when they're fully developed.

MOUSE-EAR CRESS
(non-native)
Arabidopsis thaliana
Mustard family (Brassicaceae)

Description: This annual has 1 or more erect stems and is 2–16" tall. Its oblanceolate, hairy basal leaves are up to 1½" long, form a rosette, and are sometimes minutely toothed. The alternate stem leaves are smaller. The flowers, which grow on slender stalks near the top of the plant, have 4 sepals and 4 white, unnotched petals that are less than ¼" long. The cylindric fruit are about ½" long.

Flowering time: April–July

Habitat/range: Open, grassy, disturbed areas; mixed conifer zone; 4,000–5,300'.

Comments: Mouse-ear Cress is native to Eurasia and Africa and has become naturalized throughout the world. It has also become the most widely used model organism in plant biology, due (in part) to its small size, fast growth cycle, and small genome size. In the year 2000, it became the first plant to have its genome fully sequenced.

Similar plants: Spring Whitlow-grass (*Draba verna*) **[inset]**, a common, early blooming non-native, has a basal leaf rosette and is similar in several other respects, but its 4 white petals are deeply notched and its tiny, somewhat flattened fruit are football shaped. Rockcresses (*Boechera* species) look similar, but their fruit are somewhat flattened rather than cylindric.

YOSEMITE ROCKCRESS
Boechera repanda (*Arabis repanda*)
Mustard family (Brassicaceae)

Description: Yosemite Rockcress is a biennial with stout stems that are 16–28" long and are covered with star-shaped hairs. The obovate to spatula-shaped basal leaves are up to 3" long, have rounded teeth and wavy margins, and are mostly in a rosette. The lower stem leaves usually have a winged petiole. The inflorescence has 7–25 flowers with 4 sepals and 4 white petals that are up to ¼" long. The fruit (siliques) **[inset]** are up to 5¼" long, are ⅛–³⁄₁₆" wide, and are spreading and ascending and almost always curved.

Flowering time: June–August

Habitat/range: Dry forests in partial shade; mixed conifer, montane, and subalpine zones; 3,900–10,200'.

Similar plants: Yosemite Rockcress is one of four rockcress species in the park with ascending but not completely erect fruit. Davidson's Rockcress (*B. davidsonii*, previously *Arabis davidsonii*) and Spreading Rockcress (*B. divaricarpa*, previously *A.* x *divaricarpa*) can have spreading *or* ascending fruit, but their mature fruit are narrower, less than ⅛" wide. Pioneer Rockcress (*B. platysperma*, previously *A. platysperma*) has mature fruit that can grow up to ¼" wide; its fruit have wavy margins and are straight or only slightly curved.

25

REFLEXED ROCKCRESS

Boechera retrofracta
(*Arabis holboellii* var. *retrofracta*)
Mustard family (Brassicaceae)

Description: This biennial or perennial has a single stem that grows from the center of each basal leaf rosette. Its basal leaves, up to 2" long, are densely hairy and are sometimes shallowly toothed. The stem leaves have 2 lobes at the base. The inflorescence **[inset]** has 15–140 flowers with 4 sepals and 4 white to pale lavender petals, about ¼" long. The fruit stalk is mostly straight and points downward, and the fruit are usually straight and tend to grow toward one side of the stem.

Flowering time: May–August

Habitat/range: Rock outcrops, open hillsides, and sandy banks; mixed conifer, montane, subalpine, and alpine zones; 3,000–10,500'.

Similar plants: This is one of four rockcresses in the park with fruit that hang downward. Dropseed Rockcress (*B. pendulocarpa*, previously *Arabis holboellii* var. *pendulocarpa*) is the only one in the group that has stem leaves with no lobes at the base. Bristly-leaved Rockcress (*B. rectissima*, previously *A. rectissima*) is the only one in the group with a stem that's mostly hairless from top to bottom. The last of the group, Woodland Rockcress (*B. pinetorum*, previously *A. holboellii* var. *pinetorum*) is much like Reflexed Rockcress, but the stalk of its fruit is arched rather than straight and its fruit are often curved rather than straight.

DRUMMOND'S ROCKCRESS

Boechera stricta (*Arabis drummondii*)
Mustard family (Brassicaceae)

Description: This biennial or short-lived perennial has 1 to several stems, 12–35" long. Its oblanceolate lower leaves, up to 3½" long, are slightly hairy. The sessile stem leaves are oblanceolate, have 2 lobes at the base, and are usually hairless toward the top of the stem. The stem leaves overlap and conceal the lower stem. The inflorescence **[inset]** has numerous flowers with 4 sepals and 4 milky-white petals that are about ⅜" long. The slightly lumpy, narrow fruit (siliques) are 1½–4" long, are distinctly erect, and more or less hug the stem.

Flowering time: June–July

Habitat/range: Gravelly slopes; subalpine and alpine zones; 8,700–11,500'.

Similar plants: This is one of four rockcresses in the park that have completely erect fruit. Howell's Rockcress (*B. howellii*, previously *Arabis platysperma* var. *howellii*) is the only one in the group with mature fruit that can be more than ¼" wide, and its fruit have wavy margins. Lyall's Rockcress (*B. lyallii*, previously *A. lyallii* var. *lyallii*) and Small-flowered Rockcress (*B. paupercula*, previously *A. lyallii* var. *nubigena*) have lavender to purplish flowers, and their lower stem leaves don't conceal the stem. The basal leaves of Lyall's Rockcress are hairless except sometimes along the margins. The basal leaves of Small-flowered Rockcress are densely hairy on both surfaces.

SHEPHERD'S PURSE

(non-native)
Capsella bursa-pastoris
Mustard family (Brassicaceae)

Description: Shepherd's Purse is an annual or biennial with an erect to ascending, sometimes branched stem that's 5–20" long. Its hairy basal leaves are 1–3" long, are unlobed to deeply lobed, and form a rosette. The sessile or clasping stem leaves are shaped like narrow arrowheads and have 2 lobes at the base. The inflorescence, which becomes elongated with age, has many flowers with 4 sepals and 4 white petals that are less than ¼" long. The flattened, hairless fruit (silicles) are heart shaped.

Flowering time: February–October

Habitat/range: Disturbed areas; chaparral/oak-woodland and mixed conifer zones; up to 7,000'.

Comments: The seedpods of this European native are shaped like leather purses that shepherds used to carry. The plant has become a common roadside weed throughout much of North America. It grows in Yosemite Valley, near Wawona, and around El Portal. Its tiny black seeds, when moistened, secrete a thick, sticky substance that attracts and engulfs tiny creatures in the soil and leaf litter. Some scientists believe that the seeds might be able to extract nutrients from the creatures, which would enable Shepherd's Purse to grow in nutrient-poor soils where not much else can grow.

CALIFORNIA MILKMAIDS

Cardamine californica
Mustard family (Brassicaceae)

Description: This plant is a mostly hairless perennial with 1 or 2 erect, unbranched stems, 8–25" tall. The basal leaves, which arise from the rhizome, are simple or divided into 3 or 5 broad leaflets, the terminal leaflet larger than the lateral leaflets. The alternate stem leaves are simple or divided into 3 or 5 leaflets. The leaf margins are smooth, toothed, or shallowly wavy. The flowers, which grow in a raceme, have 4 sepals and 4 white to pale rose, obovate petals that are ⅝–1" long. The fruit are slender, erect siliques, up to 2½" long.

Flowering time: January–May

Habitat/range: Shady areas in woodlands and canyons; chaparral/oak-woodland and mixed conifer zones; up to 4,600'.

Comments: The white, saucer-shaped flowers, which act as a beacon to pollinators, expose pollen to the elements of late winter and early spring, but each flower bows downward when it's rainy, forming an umbrella that protects the pollen. In their drooping state, the flowers look a little like the caps once worn by Dutch milkmaids.

Similar plants: Brewer's Bittercress (*Cardamine breweri*) has similar leaves, but its petals are less than ¼" long and it grows in standing water in wet meadows, marshes, and streams, such as the meandering streams in the Happy Isles fen.

27

FEW-SEEDED BITTERCRESS
Cardamine oligosperma
Mustard family (Brassicaceae)

Description: Few-seeded Bittercress is a common, but often overlooked annual or biennial with 1 or more ascending to erect stems that are 3–12" long and are sometimes branched. The basal leaves, which form a rosette, are pinnately compound and usually have 5–9 leaflets. The terminal leaflet is larger than the lateral leaflets and often has shallow lobes. The alternate stem leaves are similar to the basal leaves but smaller. The inflorescence is a terminal raceme. The flowers have 4 green sepals and 4 white, spatula-shaped petals, about ⅛" long. The 6 stamens are unequal, 4 of them longer than the other 2. The slender fruit (siliques) are up to 1" long and are ascending to erect.

Flowering time: March–July

Habitat/range: Shady, usually moist or wet places; chaparral/oak-woodland and mixed conifer zones; up to 4,000'.

Comments: Some people consider this charming little native to be a garden weed. The pods open somewhat explosively, propelling the seeds a foot or more away in all directions. Native Americans ate the plants raw or cooked, and they used the plant medicinally as a digestive aid.

BREWER'S DRABA
Draba breweri
Mustard family (Brassicaceae)

Description: This alpine perennial is ¾–4½" tall and has a few to many stems. The stems and both leaf surfaces are covered with gray, star-shaped hairs. The densely clustered basal leaves, up to ¾" long, are oblanceolate to obovate, and the alternate stem leaves are smaller. The somewhat dense inflorescence **[upper inset]** is a raceme with 7–20 flowers that have 4 sepals and 4 white petals, about ⅛" long. The fruit **[lower inset]** are twisted, linear-oblong, hairy siliques.

Flowering time: July–August

Habitat/range: Open, rocky areas; alpine zone; 10,800–13,100'.

Comments: William H. Brewer was a member of the famous Whitney geological survey party in California in the 1860s. Among his other duties, Brewer was in charge of the team's botanical collections. Mount Brewer in King's Canyon National Park was named in his honor, and many plants have been named after him too. The classic book *Up and Down California, 1860-1864* is Brewer's journal of his California travels.

Similar plants: Slender White Draba (*Draba praealta*) also grows only in the alpine zone, and it too has flowers with 4 tiny, white petals. Its fruit are similar, but they aren't twisted, and it grows in wet or moist habitats rather than dry, rocky areas.

VIRGINIA PEPPERWEED
Lepidium virginicum ssp. *virginicum*
Mustard family (Brassicaceae)

Description: Virginia Pepperweed is an annual with alternate leaves and a branched stem that's 6–22" long. The early withering basal and lower stem leaves are up to 5" long and are pinnately lobed or toothed. The upper stem leaves are often lobed or toothed. The flowers grow in an elongated inflorescence and have 4 sepals and 4 white petals, ⅟₁₆–¼" long, that are at least as long as the sepals. The round, flattened fruit **[inset]**, less than ¼" wide, have a stalk that's cylindric throughout.

Flowering time: March–September

Habitat/range: Disturbed or grassy areas; chaparral/oak-woodland and mixed conifer zones; up to 7,000'.

Similar plants: The fruit stalk of Menzies' Pepperweed (*L. virginicum* ssp. *menziesii*) is flattened, at least where it meets the fruit. The fruit of Branched Pepperweed (*L. ramosissimum*) are elliptic (broader in the middle and narrower at both equal ends). The fruit of Miner's Pepperweed (*L. densiflorum*) are obovate (narrower at the base and broader at the tip). Branched and Miner's Pepperweed either have no petals or petals that are less than ⅟₁₆" long and are hard to see without magnification. Non-native Pennycress (*Thlaspi arvense*) has much larger fruit (¼–¾" wide) than the fruit of the park's *Lepidium* species, which are less than ¼" wide.

WATERCRESS
Nasturtium officinale
(*Rorippa nasturtium-aquaticum*)
Mustard family (Brassicaceae)

Description: Watercress is a rapidly growing, aquatic perennial with hollow stems that root freely at the nodes. The plant's stems can grow up to 4' long, and its herbage is mostly hairless. The leaves are 1–6" long and are pinnately divided into 3–11 round to ovate, oblong, or lanceolate, sometimes toothed leaflets, with a terminal leaflet that's larger than the lateral leaflets. The flowers, which grow in a dense, terminal raceme, have 4 small sepals and 4 bright white petals that are less then ¼" long. The ascending, curved fruit (siliques) are up to 1¼" long and are constricted between the seeds.

Flowering time: April–October

Habitat/range: Slow water in streams, springs, marshes, and ponds; chaparral/oak-woodland, mixed conifer, and montane zones; up to 8,000'.

Comments: Watercress is one of the oldest known leaf vegetables consumed by humans, and it's still commonly used as a salad and sandwich ingredient. The nutritious plant is particularly rich in vitamin K and also contains significant amounts of vitamins A, C, and B6. Watercress is treated as a native by the *Jepson eFlora* (2020), but *Flora of North America* treats it as an introduced plant.

MOUNTAIN JEWELFLOWER, SHIELDPLANT

Streptanthus tortuosus
Mustard family (Brassicaceae)

Description: This common biennial or perennial has a simple to many-branched stem, 8–40" long, that often reclines toward the ground as the plant matures. Its rosetted basal leaves wither early. The oblanceolate lower stem leaves are 1–3" long, taper to a winged petiole, and are often toothed. The oblong to round middle stem leaves clasp the stem, and the shiny, round to oblong-ovate upper leaves deeply clasp the stem, essentially surrounding it. The leaves fade to yellow or bronze with age. The urn-shaped sepals vary impressively in color and can be white, cream colored, green, purple, rusty red, or magenta **[inset]**. The 4 narrow, wavy-margined petals are up to about ½" long and are sometimes purplish but are usually white or cream colored with purple veins. The spreading fruit (siliques) are 2–6" long and are curved and flattened.

Flowering time: May–August

Habitat/range: Dry, open slopes and flats; chaparral/oak-woodland, mixed conifer, montane, subalpine, and alpine zones; up to 11,500'.

Similar plants: Variable-leaved Jewelflower (*Streptanthus diversifolius*), which is common in the Hetch Hetchy area, has similar flowers and shield-like upper leaves, but its lower and middle stem leaves are pinnately divided into linear or thread-like segments.

LACEPOD, FRINGEPOD

Thysanocarpus curvipes
Mustard family (Brassicaceae)

Description: Lacepod is a common, early bloom-ing annual with erect stems, 4"–2' tall, that are branched above. Its rosetted basal leaves are ½–3" long, are oblanceolate to obovate, have smooth or wavy-toothed margins, and sometimes have coarse, stiff hairs. The alternate, lanceolate stem leaves have a 2-lobed base that clasps the stem. The tiny flowers, which grow in an elongated raceme, have 4 sepals and 4 white petals. The small, round, flattened fruit (silicles) are about ¼" wide and are winged along the margin. The wing is often perforated and shallowly scalloped.

Flowering time: February–June

Habitat/range: Grassy places; chaparral/oak-woodland and mixed conifer zones; up to 5,000'.

Comments: Native Americans roasted and ground Lacepod seeds, along with seeds from other plants, to make a valuable flour mixture called pinole. They made a tea from the whole plant and sometimes used the tea to relieve stomach aches.

Similar plants: Common Sandweed (*Athysanus pusillus*) grows in the same zones and is also an early bloomer. It has long, slender stems with many dangling fruit **[inset]**, but its fruit are only slightly flattened, are densely hairy, and are less than ⅛" wide. The fruit tend to grow along one side of the stem, and they don't have winged margins.

TOWER MUSTARD

Turritis glabra (*Arabis glabra*)
Mustard family (Brassicaceae)

Description: Aptly named Tower Mustard is a biennial or short-lived perennial, 1¼–4' tall, with a stem that's sometimes branched toward the top. The stem is usually hairy below and hairless above. The hairy basal leaves are 2–5" long, are oblanceolate to oblong, and have large teeth along the margin. The alternate, narrowly arrowhead-shaped, hairless stem leaves are smaller and clasp the tower-like stem. The flowers, which grow in an elongated raceme, have 4 yellowish sepals and 4 yellowish-white (rarely purple) petals that are up to ⅜" long. The linear, erect fruit (siliques) are 1½–4" long, are cylindric or somewhat 4-angled, and press close to the stem.

Flowering time: April–July

Habitat/range: Meadows, roadsides, and other open areas; chaparral/oak-woodland, mixed conifer, and montane zones; up to 8,000'.

Comments: This plant, like many others that grow in dry, sunbaked habitats, has a waxy coating that prevents excess water evaporation and gives it a gray-green or blue-green look.

Similar plants: Tower Mustard is similar to some rockcresses (*Boechera* species), but the rockcresses have flattened fruit, and Tower Mustard's fruit are not flattened, though they can be 4-angled.

SIERRA THREADSTEM

Nemacladus interior
Bellflower family (Campanulaceae)

Description: This wispy annual has somewhat stiff, wiry stems, 2½–10" long, that are diffusely branched. The small, hairless, oblanceolate to elliptic leaves, up to ¾" long, are mostly in a loose basal rosette and have shallow, irregular teeth. The flowers grow in strongly zigzagging racemes, with a tiny bract at each junction. The thread-like, ascending flower stalks, ¼–½" long, are straight at the base and curve upward at the tip. The flowers have a white, conspicuously 2-lipped corolla **[inset]** and 5 tiny, triangular sepals above a partially inferior ovary. The lower lip of the corolla has 2 spreading lobes without markings. The upper lip has 3 deeply divided, erect lobes, ⅛–³⁄₁₆" long. The lower part of each lobe has a purple or red, jagged band with a greenish-yellow spot below it.

Flowering time: May–July

Habitat/range: Dry, gravelly slopes and recently burned areas; chaparral/oak-woodland and mixed conifer zones; up to 5,500'.

Similar plants: Common Threadstem (*Nemacladus capillaris*) has been reported from the Hetch Hetchy area. It has similar leaves and zigzagging racemes. Its corolla has a similar shape but has even tinier lobes (less than ¹⁄₁₆" long). The corolla lobes lack prominent markings, and the flower stalks are completely straight from the base to the tip (rather than curved at the tip).

31

BLUE FLY HONEYSUCKLE
Lonicera cauriana
Honeysuckle family (Caprifoliaceae)

Description: Blue Fly Honeysuckle is an erect, sparsely branched shrub, 1–3' tall, with shredding bark and soft-hairy herbage and flowers. Its thin, opposite, oblong-ovate leaves are up to 2" long and taper to a short petiole. The leaves are ciliate along the margins, hairy below, and mostly smooth above. Below the paired flowers are 1–3 pairs of green bracts; the inner pair of bracts is fused and tightly encloses the partially fused pair of ovaries. The white, cream-colored, or pale yellow, funnel-shaped corolla is up to ½" long and has a narrow tube and 5 spreading lobes. The stamens have a white filament and a yellow anther, and they extend beyond the corolla lobes. The 2 blue berries are so completely fused that they look like a single berry.

Flowering time: May–July

Habitat/range: Bogs, streambanks, and wet meadows; montane and subalpine zones; 7,000–10,500'.

Comments: The fruit's resemblance to a bluebottle fly may be how the plant got its common name. *Lonicera* was named for Adam Lonitzer (1528–1586), a German botanist who taught university level mathematics and later became a medical doctor. His primary interest was botany, and he wrote extensively about herbs.

FIELD MOUSE-EAR CHICKWEED
Cerastium arvense ssp. *strictum*
Pink family (Caryophyllaceae)

Description: This attractive perennial has non-flowering stems that form mats and flowering stems that are ascending to erect and are 2–10" long. Its opposite leaves are up to 1" long, are linear or lanceolate, and are sometimes hairy. Small leaf clusters grow in the axils of the lower stem leaves. Groups of flower stalks that are often branched arise from a common, 2-bracted point on the stem. The flowers **[inset]** are up to ¾" wide and have 5 sticky-hairy sepals and 5 white, broad-lobed petals that are about twice as long as the sepals.

Flowering time: May–August

Habitat/range: Damp, shaded, rocky cliffs and slopes near seeps or waterfalls; mixed conifer and montane zones; 3,900–8,200'.

Similar plants: If you find a plant with smaller, but otherwise almost identical flowers along the Sierra Crest, it's Alpine Mouse-ear Chickweed (*C. beeringianum*), a native alpine plant that's rare in the park. Two similar, non-native *Cerastium* species have petals that are *not* twice as long as their sepals. The sepals of Sticky Mouse-ear Chickweed (*C. glomeratum*) have glandular hairs mixed with longer white hairs, and its sepals are often dark tipped. The sepals of Common Mouse-ear Chickweed (*C. fontanum* ssp. *vulgare*) have shorter, non-glandular hairs. Both plants grow mostly in disturbed areas up into the mixed conifer zone.

KING'S SANDWORT

Eremogone kingii var. *glabrescens*
(*Arenaria kingii* var. *glabrescens*)
Pink family (Caryophyllaceae)

Description: King's Sandwort is a common perennial with erect stems, up to 8" long. The mostly basal, awl-shaped leaves are tufted or grow in dense mats, and the stem leaves are in opposite pairs. The flowers grow at the branch tips of open inflorescences. The 5 free sepals are narrowly ovate, have membranous margins, and are often glandular-hairy. The 5 white petals, up to ¼" long, are longer than the sepals and are sometimes slightly notched. The anthers on the 10 stamens are red before they open to release their pollen.

Flowering time: June–August

Habitat/range: Dry, gravelly or rocky slopes and flats; mixed conifer, montane, subalpine, and alpine zones; 6,000–12,000'.

Similar plants: The park's perennial sandworts have crowded, linear leaves and 5 white petals that are not conspicuously lobed (or no petals). Four of them, including King's Sandwort, have petals that are longer than the sepals. Ball-headed Sandwort (*E. congesta*, previously *Arenaria congesta*) is the only one that has head-like flower clusters. Prickly Sandwort (*E. aculeata*, previously *A. aculeata*) is the only one with leaves that have a waxy coating, often giving them a grayish look. Alpine Sandwort (*Minuartia obtusiloba*) is the only one with vividly bright green leaves that often have ciliate margins.

DOUGLAS' SANDWORT

Minuartia douglasii
Pink family (Caryophyllaceae)

Description: This wispy annual has a slender, much branched, green or purple stem, 2–11½" long, that's glandular-hairy above. The opposite, linear leaves are ¼–1¼" long. The small flowers grow in open clusters on slender, glandular-hairy stalks. The 5 dark-tipped, glandular-hairy sepals have inconspicuous narrow, translucent margins. The flowers have 5 white, ovate petals that are noticeably longer than the sepals, 10 stamens with yellow anthers, and a pistil with 3 styles.

Flowering time: April–June

Habitat/range: Dry, open areas; chaparral/oak-woodland and mixed conifer zones; up to 6,000'.

Similar plants: Very similar California Sandwort (*M. californica*) also has petals that are noticeably longer than its sepals, but its sepals have no hairs or glands. Annual Sandwort (*M. pusilla*) has similar leaves, but its calyx is hairless and its petals are shorter than the sepals. Non-native Four-leaved Allseed (*Polycarpon tetraphyllum*) **[upper inset]** has somewhat similar flowers, but it has broad, crowded leaves and its sepals have conspicuous translucent margins and are much wider than the petals. Highly invasive, non-native Corn Spurry (*Spergula arvensis*) has been reported in the park and has similar flowers. Its leaves, which appear to be whorls of many leaves, are pairs of opposite leaves that are deeply divided into linear lobes **[lower inset]**.

33

NUTTALL'S SANDWORT
Minuartia nuttallii var. *gracilis*
Pink family (Caryophyllaceae)

Description: Nuttall's Sandwort is a densely glandular-hairy perennial that has ascending to erect flowering stems, along with trailing, non-flowering stems that form loose mats, up to 8" wide. The dried remains of stems from the previous year usually persist at the base of the plant. Its dense, needle-like to awl-shaped leaves are less than ½" long. The small flowers grow in open, terminal clusters. The flowers have 10 stamens, 5 lanceolate sepals with narrow membranous margins, and 5 white petals that are about the same length as the sepals or slightly shorter.

Flowering time: July–August

Habitat/range: Sandy, gravelly, and rocky areas; subalpine and alpine zones; 10,000–12,100'.

Similar plants: All the perennial sandworts in the park have crowded, linear leaves and 5 white petals that are not conspicuously lobed (or no petals). Three of them, including Nuttall's Sandwort, have petals (if present) that are at least sometimes shorter than the sepals. Nuttall's Sandwort is the only one of the three with leafy stems that form dense mats. Bog Sandwort (*M. stricta*), has leaves that form clusters, but not mats, and it's the only one of the three that is completely hairless and that often has no petals. Reddish Sandwort (*M. rubella*) also has leaves that are clustered, but not matted, and it has glandular-hairy herbage.

STICKY STARWORT
Pseudostellaria jamesiana
Pink family (Caryophyllaceae)

Description: This common perennial has an ascending to erect, square stem, 4–17" long, that's often branched and has stalked glands in the inflorescence. Its sessile, opposite leaves are ½–5" long and are linear, lanceolate, or elliptic. The flowers, which grow at the stem end or from the upper leaf axils, have 5 free, glandular-hairy sepals and 5 free, white petals that are up to ⅜" long. The petals are much longer than the sepals and are notched less than a third of their length. Each flower has 10 stamens and a pistil with 3 styles.

Flowering time: May–July

Habitat/range: Meadows and damp, shady forest; mixed conifer, montane, and subalpine zones; 3,900–8,500'.

Comments: The plant was named for Edwin P. James, who was the naturalist on a government-funded exploration of land acquired with the Louisiana Purchase. In 1820, he and his team were the first European-Americans to climb Pikes Peak.

Similar plants: Sierra Starwort (*Pseudostellaria sierrae*), which is somewhat rare in the park, is quite similar, but its sepals are smooth (no hairs or glands) and it has only 5 stamens. Both plants look something like plants in the *Stellaria* genus, but the petals of plants in the *Stellaria* genus are divided almost to the base.

ARCTIC PEARLWORT
Sagina saginoides
Pink family (Caryophyllaceae)

Description: Arctic Pearlwort is a common, hairless perennial with numerous slender, somewhat fleshy, ascending or sprawling stems, 1–4½" long. The bright, often shiny green, narrowly linear leaves are up to ¾" long. They grow in 1 or more basal rosettes and in opposite pairs along the stems. The rosette of leaves that produces flowering stems is often accompanied by 1 or more sterile rosettes. The tiny, solitary flowers, which grow at the end of the stems and from leaf axils, have 4 or 5 styles and usually 10 stamens. The 5 ovate, somewhat blunt-tipped sepals are about the same length as the 5 white, ovate petals. The flower stalks are erect when the flowers are blooming, begin to nod as the fruit develops, and become erect again when the fruit is mature.

Flowering time: May–September

Habitat/range: Streambanks, seeps, and drainages; mixed conifer, montane, subalpine, and alpine zones; 3,500–11,000'.

Similar plants: Less common Western Pearlwort (*Sagina decumbens* ssp. *occidentalis*) is an annual that has almost identical flowers, but its stems are thread-like rather than fleshy and its stem leaves are awl shaped rather than linear. Annual Sandwort (*Minuartia pusilla*) **[inset]** also has linear, opposite stem leaves and similar flowers, but its sepals are distinctly pointed and are longer than the petals.

BOUNCING BET
(non-native)
Saponaria officinalis
Pink family (Caryophyllaceae)

Description: The stout, erect stem of this hairless perennial is 1–3' tall and is sometimes branched toward the top. Its 3-veined leaves are up to 4½" long and are elliptic to oblanceolate or ovate. The flowers, which grow in dense clusters at the stem or branch ends, have a united, green or reddish, 5-lobed calyx. The corolla has 5 white, broad-tipped petal limbs that fade to pink and often dry to dark purple. The flowers are about 1" wide and have 10 white stamens and a pistil with 2 styles.

Flowering time: June–August

Habitat/range: Roadsides and disturbed ground around developments; chaparral/oak-woodland and mixed conifer zones; up to 6,000'.

Comments: These plants spread by rhizomes and often form large colonies, several of which grow in Yosemite Valley meadows. The common name is a nickname for a washerwoman working at her scrubbing board, in reference to the plant's use in making soap. If you were to peel away the sepals, you'd find that each petal is separate, with a limb that spreads out above the calyx and a narrower claw that extends down into the calyx. *Silene* species and the species of several other genera in the Pink family look as though they might have a united corolla tube, but they too have separate petals with a limb and a claw.

SLEEPY CATCHFLY
Silene antirrhina
Pink family (Caryophyllaceae)

Description: Sleepy Catchfly, on the left, is an annual with an erect, hairless or short-hairy stem that's up to 2½' tall and is somewhat sticky above. The opposite leaves are 1–2" long and are pointed at the tip. The lower leaves are oblanceolate, and the smaller upper leaves are linear to oblanceolate. The erect flowers, which grow in open clusters, have a hairless, glandless calyx with 10 distinct veins. The 5 small, ascending to spreading, white to pinkish petal limbs have 2 rounded lobes at the tip. The 10 stamens do not extend beyond the calyx tube.

Flowering time: April–August

Habitat/range: Open, sandy or grassy areas; chaparral/oak-woodland and mixed conifer zones; up to 5,000'.

Similar plants: Sleepy Catchfly is somewhat similar to three less common catchflies in the park that also have white, 2-lobed petals. Bridges' Catchfly (*S. bridgesii*), upper right, has nodding flowers, and its calyx is glandular-hairy. Menzies' Catchfly (*S. menziesii*), middle right, has ascending to erect flowers, but it has a densely hairy calyx without distinct veins. The petals of non-native Common Catchfly, aka Windmill Pink (*S. gallica*), lower right, are often somewhat twisted and are either slightly 2 lobed or unlobed, and its calyx is glandular-hairy.

PALMER'S CATCHFLY
Silene bernardina
Pink family (Caryophyllaceae)

Description: This perennial has slender, few-branched stems that are 6–22" long and are hairy throughout and sticky-glandular above. Its opposite, linear to oblanceolate leaves are ⅜–3" long on the lower part of the stem and are reduced in size upward. Solitary, ascending to erect flowers grow at the stem end and from leaf axils. The flowers have a green or reddish, cylindric, somewhat inflated, glandular-hairy calyx that's ½–⅝" long and has 5 pointed lobes and 10 prominent veins. The 5 white to pinkish, spreading petal limbs are less than ¼" long and are deeply divided into 4 narrow, pointed lobes. The 10 stamens extend beyond the calyx.

Flowering time: June–August

Habitat/range: Dry, grassy or gravelly slopes; mixed conifer, montane, and subalpine zones; 6,000–9,000'.

Similar plants: Less common Menzies' Catchfly (*S. menziesii*) also has white petals that can have 4 lobes, but they usually have only 2. Its calyx is less than ⅜" long and has inconspicuous veins. Lemmon's Catchfly (*S. lemmonii*), which is common and widespread, also has 4-lobed, white petals, but the lobes are usually intricately curled and twisted and its flowers nod at maturity. The flowers of Menzies' Catchfly and Palmer's Catchfly are spreading, ascending, or erect at maturity.

WHITE CAMPION
(non-native)
Silene latifolia
Pink family (Caryophyllaceae)

Description: White Campion is a biennial or perennial with erect, rough-hairy stems, 1–3¼' tall, that are sometimes glandular above and sometimes branched. Its opposite leaves are ½–4" long and are lanceolate to oblanceolate. The lower leaves have a petiole, and the upper leaves are smaller and sessile. The species is dioecious, meaning that male and female flowers grow on separate plants. The fused, tubular, green or reddish calyx has 5 short-hairy sepals. The male flowers have a 10-veined calyx, and the female flowers have a larger, 20-veined calyx that becomes more inflated with maturity. The corolla has 5 white limbs that are about ½" long and have 2 broad lobes.

Flowering time: June–September

Habitat/range: Meadow borders, roadsides, and disturbed areas; mixed conifer zone; around 4,000'.

Comments: White Campion is a European native that has become naturalized throughout much of North America. It grows in disturbed areas and around meadows in Yosemite Valley and has been reported in Wawona.

Similar plants: White Campion's broad corolla lobes and its strongly inflated calyx distinguish it from other similar plants in the park.

LEMMON'S CATCHFLY
Silene lemmonii
Pink family (Caryophyllaceae)

Description: This dainty perennial has an erect stem, 6–18" tall, that's glandular above and often has small, spreading or reclining branches toward the base. The leaves, most of which are in basal clusters, are ¾–1⅜" long and are elliptic to oblanceolate. The smaller stem leaves grow in opposite pairs. The nodding flowers grow at the stem end and from leaf axils. The broadly cylindric or narrowly bell-shaped, 10-veined calyx is up to ⅜" long and has 5 fused, glandular-hairy sepals with pointed tips. The corolla has 5 white limbs that are deeply divided into 4 linear lobes, which often become curled, twisted, and tangled. The 10 stamens and 3 styles extend well beyond the calyx.

Flowering time: April–June

Habitat/range: Dry forest openings; mixed conifer and montane zones; 3,600–8,000'.

Comments: This plant was named for Sara and John Lemmon, who did extensive botanical work in Arizona and California in the late 1800s.

Similar plants: Lemmon's Catchfly is the only *Silene* species in the park that has nodding flowers with 4 petal lobes that are usually curly and twisted. Bridges' Catchfly (*Silene bridgesii*), which is much less common, also has nodding flowers that can have curly, twisted petal lobes, but each petal has only 2 lobes.

ALPINE CATCHFLY
Silene sargentii
Pink family (Caryophyllaceae)

Description: Alpine Catchfly is a small alpine perennial with relatively large flowers. Its reclining to erect stems, 4–6" long, are hairy throughout and are usually glandular above. The fleshy, tufted basal leaves are ½–1¼" long and are narrowly oblanceolate. The 1 or 2 opposite pairs of stem leaves are smaller. The flowers are mostly erect and grow at the stem end or from leaf axils. The inflated, vase- to urn-shaped calyx is up to ½" long and has 10 prominent dark veins. The corolla has 5 white, spreading limbs, and each limb has 2 deep lobes at the tip and a smaller tooth on each side. The 10 stamens extend slightly beyond the calyx.

Flowering time: July–August

Habitat/range: Dry, rocky areas; subalpine and alpine zones; 10,000–11,500'.

Comments: The showy, vase-shaped calyx, with its intricate dark veins, looks like a miniature, one-of-a-kind Tiffany vase. The family's common name isn't related to the color pink. Instead, the name refers to the fact that the petals of many plants in the family are variously notched, as though someone went at them with pinking shears.

Similar plants: Alpine Catchfly is the only *Silene* species in the park that has tightly clustered (tufted), fleshy leaves. The lateral teeth on each petal limb also set it apart.

LONG-STALKED STARWORT
Stellaria longipes ssp. *longipes*
Pink family (Caryophyllaceae)

Description: Long-stalked Starwort is a mostly hairless perennial with reclining to erect, usually unbranched stems that are 2–14" long. Its evenly spaced, opposite leaves, 1½–2" long, are linear to narrowly lanceolate with a pointed tip. The flowers grow solitary or in small groups on long, slender stalks at the stem end or from leaf axils. The 5 free, hairless, lanceolate to ovate sepals have pointed tips and membranous margins. The 5 white petals, up to ¼" long, are as long as or longer than the sepals. The petals are so deeply notched that they can be mistaken for 10 petals. Each flower has 10 or fewer stamens and a pistil with 3 styles.

Flowering time: May–August

Habitat/range: Meadows and moist ground in forest openings; mixed conifer, montane, and subalpine zones; 3,900–10,500'.

Similar plants: Long-stalked Starwort is one of three *Stellaria* species in the park with petals and sepals that are similar in length; its petals are ⅛–¼" long and are *at least* as long as its sepals. Much less common Sitka Starwort (*S. borealis* ssp. *sitchana*) has petals that are less than ¼" long, and its petals are shorter than its sepals. Non-native Common Chickweed (*S. media*) has petals that can be as long as its sepals; but, unlike the other two species, its stem has a distinct line of hairs between the sets of leaves.

SHINING STARWORT
Stellaria nitens
Pink family (Caryophyllaceae)

Description: This annual has thread-like stems that are 1–10" long. The opposite, shiny leaves, up to ⅝" long, are mostly crowded near the base of the plant. Few to several flowers grow at the branch ends and have entirely membranous bracts beneath them. The tiny flowers **[inset]** have 5 hairless sepals and 5 white petals, though some may be missing. The petals are much shorter than the sepals and are divided almost to the base.

Flowering time: March–June

Habitat/range: Streambanks and open woodlands, often at the base of large rocks; chaparral/oak-woodland and mixed conifer zones; up to 5,000'.

Similar plants: Shining Starwort is one of four *Stellaria* species in the park with hairless sepals and either no petals or petals that are much shorter than the sepals. Shining Starwort is the only one with most of its leaves crowded at the base of the plant. Crisp Starwort (*S. crispa*) is the only one with flowers that grow solitary in the leaf axils, and its leaves often have wavy margins. Subalpine Starwort (*S. umbellata*) is the only one with flowers in a loose, umbel-like arrangement and the only one, except for Shining Starwort, that has entirely membranous bracts below the flowers. Northern Starwort (*S. calycantha*) doesn't have leaves crowded at the base of the plant, and its flowers grow from the leaf axils and at the branch tips.

CALIFORNIA BASTARD TOADFLAX
Comandra umbellata ssp. *californica*
Bastard Toadflax family (Comandraceae)

Description: This common, hairless perennial has attractive green or blue-green herbage and ascending to erect stems that are 4–16" long. Its alternate, sessile leaves are ½–2" long and are lanceolate with a pointed tip. The umbel-like inflorescences are somewhat dense clusters at the branch ends and from leaf axils. The tiny flowers, which have no petals, have a green urn- or bell-shaped calyx tube with 4, 5, or 6 white, triangular lobes. The number of stamens in each flower usually matches the number of calyx lobes. The stamens are inserted between the lobes and have a tuft of hairs at their base. The pistil has 1 style with a head-like stigma.

Flowering time: April–August

Habitat/range: Dry, sometimes rocky places in full or partial sun; chaparral/oak-woodland, mixed conifer, and montane zones; up to 7,000'.

Comments: The plants are partial root parasites, obtaining water and nutrients from over 200 plant species. California Bastard Toadflax is itself parasitized. It's an alternate host to an organism called the Comandra Pine Blister Rust Fungus. The fungus is passed on to pines and can cause growth defects and even death. Native Americans have used this plant medicinally, and they ate the fruit when other foods were scarce.

SIERRA FALSE BINDWEED

Calystegia malacophylla ssp. *malacophylla*
Morning-glory family (Convolvulaceae)

Description: Sierra False Bindweed is a perennial with sprawling to ascending stems that are 4"–3¼' long and sometimes climb over plants and other objects. Its herbage is covered with dense, woolly hairs and feels incredibly soft to the touch. The arrowhead-shaped, alternate leaves are 1–2½" long and have basal lobes with 1 or 2 broad teeth. The leaf petioles can be longer or shorter than the blade. The flowers grow solitary from the leaf axils, and the 2 triangular-ovate bracts beneath the flowers mostly conceal the smaller, densely hairy calyx. The funnel-shaped corolla is ⅜–1⅜" long and has 5 broad, cream-colored, fused petals and 5 stamens that are fused to the petals. The pistil has a style with a 2-lobed stigma.

Flowering time: June–August

Habitat/range: Dry, open to shaded slopes; mixed conifer zone; 3,900–6,600'.

Comments: The showy flowers open in the morning and twist themselves closed by early afternoon. The plant is one of over 1,300 plants that are California endemics, meaning that they grow only in California.

Similar plants: Non-native, highly invasive Field Bindweed (*Convolvulus arvensis*) is somewhat similar, but its foliage is mostly hairless.

FIELD BINDWEED

(non-native)
Convolvulus arvensis
Morning-glory family (Convolvulaceae)

Description: This invasive, mostly hairless perennial has reclining or twining stems, 1–3¼' long. Its alternate, arrowhead- to heart-shaped leaves, up to 1½" long, grow on slender petioles that are shorter than the blade. The large, funnel-shaped flowers grow solitary on long stalks from the leaf axils. The flowers, up to 1" long, have 5 small, oblong sepals and 5 large, white to lavender, mostly fused petals that are twisted clockwise in bud. The 5 sepals are fused to the petals.

Flowering time: May–October

Habitat/range: Disturbed areas; chaparral/oak-woodland and mixed conifer zones; up to 5,300'.

Comments: A Eurasian native, Field Bindweed has become naturalized throughout the United States and is classified as a noxious weed in the west. It grows vine-like on the ground, often forming dense masses that crowd out native vegetation and cultivated crops. Its seeds can remain viable for 20 years, and the deep, expansive root system stores nutrients, making it possible for new plants to sprout even after the growth above the ground has been removed.

Similar plants: Sierra False Bindweed (*Calystegia malacophylla*) is somewhat similar, but its foliage is densely woolly.

CHAPARRAL DODDER

Cuscuta californica var. *californica*
Morning-glory family (Convolvulaceae)

Description: Chaparral Dodder is a parasitic plant that lacks chlorophyll and looks like yellow or orange twine tangled up in its host plant. Its leaves are tiny, inconspicuous scales. The small flowers grow in open clusters. The calyx has a fleshy base and 5 overlapping lobes. The white corolla has a cylindric to bell-shaped tube and 5 lanceolate, reflexed lobes that are longer than the tube.

Flowering time: May–August

Habitat/range: Open or partially shady, wet to dry areas; chaparral/oak-woodland, mixed conifer, and montane zones; up to 8,900'.

Comments: When a Dodder seed germinates and produces a seedling, the seedling will die unless it finds a green host plant before it uses up the meager food supply in its embryo. The plant uses chemosensory clues to grow toward the nearest host. After it attaches itself to a host, it wraps around it and inserts an appendage into the vascular tissue of the plant. Once it starts drawing in nutrients, the Dodder's root dies and the plant detaches from the ground.

Similar plants: One other variety of Chaparral Dodder and four other dodder species have been reported in the park. Distinguishing them requires dissection of the flowers and precise measurements of the flower parts.

MOUNTAIN DOGWOOD, PACIFIC DOGWOOD

Cornus nuttallii
Dogwood (Cornaceae)

Description: This deciduous shrub or small tree grows up to 65' tall, though it's usually quite a bit shorter than that in the park. Its hairy twigs are green when they're young and turn red to brownish black with age. The elliptic to obovate, opposite leaves are 2–5" long, are bright green above, and are paler and soft-hairy beneath. The small, white to greenish-yellow, 4-petaled flowers grow in a dense cluster. Immediately below them are 4–7 showy, white bracts that are 1½–2½" long and can easily be mistaken for petals. The densely packed clusters of shiny red, berry-like fruit have black or dark blue notches at the tip.

Flowering time: April–July

Habitat/range: Dry to moist, shaded forest understory; mixed conifer zone; 3,400–6,100'.

Comments: Mountain Dogwood's "flowers" are so bright and showy that the tree is held in high esteem by wildflower admirers. The bracts and flowers, measured together, can be over 5" wide. In autumn, its leaves become various shades of crimson and provide vibrant fall colors. The plant was named for Thomas Nuttall, a 19th-century botanist, ornithologist, and curator of the Harvard Botanic Gardens. About a dozen California plants and one woodpecker were named in his honor.

RED-OSIER DOGWOOD

Cornus sericea ssp. *sericea*
Dogwood (Cornaceae)

Description: Red-osier Dogwood is a deciduous shrub, 5–13' tall, with branches and twigs that are bright reddish purple when they're young and become gray green with age. Its opposite, ovate to lanceolate leaves are up to 4½" long, are bright green and sparsely hairy above, and are paler and smooth or only slightly hairy below. The inflorescence is a flat-topped cluster of small, white to pinkish flowers with 4 oval petals, 4 tiny sepals, and 4 stamens. The petals are no more than ⅛" long. The white fruit **[inset]** is round and berry-like.

Flowering time: May–July

Habitat/range: Moist, shady or partially shady places; mixed conifer and montane zones; 3,300–8,500'.

Comments: The red leaves of this shrub put on a show in the fall, but in winter, when all the leaves are gone, it still brightens the landscape with its striking red stems. The shrubs are planted to protect streambanks from erosion, and they're planted as ornamentals for their bright green foliage and white flower clusters, but especially for their bright red winter stems.

Similar plants: Less common Western Dogwood (*Cornus sericea* ssp. *occidentalis*) has petals that are ⅛" long or longer, and its leaves are densely rough-hairy on the lower surface.

CALIFORNIA MAN-ROOT

Marah fabacea
Gourd family (Cucurbitaceae)

Description: The stems of this trailing or climbing perennial grow from scratch each year and can get up to 20' long. The plant uses branched tendrils, which grow at the stem end and from the leaf axils, to support itself on nearby vegetation. The alternate leaves are roundish in outline, have 5–7 palmate lobes, are deeply indented at the base, and look a lot like maple leaves. Separate male and female flowers grow on the same plant. The flowers have a white to greenish-white, flat, wheel-shaped, 5-lobed corolla and no calyx. The male flowers, up to ⅜" wide, and a solitary female flower, up to ⅝" wide, grow together from the leaf axils, the male flowers in panicle-like clusters. The fruit **[inset]** is a round capsule that's up to 2" wide and is covered with soft spines that are less than ¼" long.

Flowering time: February–May

Habitat/range: Streamsides and shrubby, open areas; chaparral/oak-woodland zone; up to 5,400'.

Comments: This plant has been reported from one or two out-of-the-way locations in the park, but it's common west of the park in the El Portal area.

Similar plants: Sierra Man-root (*Marah horrida*) grows in Poopenaut Valley and also in the El Portal area. Its flowers have a cup-shaped tube, and its fruit is usually oblong rather than round and has stiff spines that are up to 1¼" long.

ROUND-LEAVED SUNDEW
Drosera rotundifolia
Sundew family (Droseraceae)

Description: Round-leaved Sundew is a glistening, carnivorous perennial with no stem. Its leaves, which grow in a spreading basal rosette, have a round blade, up to ½" wide, and a flat petiole, up to 2" long. Sometimes the basal rosettes are not evident due to erect or ascending leaves or the commingling of plants. The upper surface of the leaf blade is covered with bright red hairs, each tipped with a sticky gland. The erect, sometimes forked flower stalks, 2–12" long, have 2–15 flowers, up to ½" wide. The flowers have 5 sepals that are fused at the base, 5 white to pale pink petals, usually 5 stamens, and 3 styles, each with 2 branches that are divided more or less to the base.

Flowering time: June–September

Habitat/range: Sphagnum bogs; mixed conifer and montane zones; 4,500–7,600'.

Comments: The red hairs on the leaves are tipped with glands that secrete a sticky, sugary substance. The shiny red color and the possibility of a sweet meal attract insects to the leaves. Once an insect lands on a leaf, the sticky-tipped hairs trap the creature, and the plant secretes enzymes that digest it. In this fashion, the plants are able to obtain nitrogen, a nutrient that's in low supply in the acidic bogs where the plants grow. If you find Sundew plants, look for insect exoskeletons, which are all that remain of the plants' unfortunate visitors.

SUGAR STICK
Allotropa virgata
Heath family (Ericaceae)

Description: Sugar Stick is a beautiful, intricate, parasitic perennial with a narrow, unbranched flowering stalk that's up to 1½' tall and has longitudinal, red and white, candy-cane stripes. The white, leaf-like structures on the lower stalk and under each flower are bracts. The white, cup-shaped corolla has 5 petals and 10 stamens with anthers that are red at maturity.

Flowering time: June–August

Habitat/range: Shaded forest floor; mixed conifer and montane zones; 3,900–8,500'.

Comments: Sugar Stick, like several other members of the heath family, lacks chlorophyll and was previously classified as a saprophyte, a plant that gets its nourishment directly from dead organic matter. Somewhat recently, it was discovered that the plants are actually mycoheterotrophs, which means that they're parasitic on soil fungi. The roots of conifers and the mycelia (root-like structures) of fungi have developed a mutually beneficial relationship; the fungi get carbohydrates and the trees get improved nutrient and water absorption. Sugar Stick and its relatives are parasites that absorb nutrients from the root-like structures of soil fungi and are not known to provide anything in return.

PINEMAT MANZANITA
Arctostaphylos nevadensis ssp. *nevadensis*
Heath family (Ericaceae)

Description: This low-growing, densely branched shrub, up to 2' tall, forms extensive mats on rocky outcrops. Its reddish branches are hairy when young. The alternate, short-petioled leaves, ½–1½" long, are obovate or oblanceolate, are wedge shaped at the base, and often have a sharp point at the tip. The leaves are hairy when they're young and become smooth with age. The inflorescences are compact clusters with nodding or spreading flowers that are about ¼" long. The urn-shaped flowers have a small, white calyx with 5 rounded lobes and a white corolla that's broader at the base and narrow at the throat and has 5 slightly flared lobes. The berry-like fruit is reddish to brown.

Flowering time: May–July

Habitat/range: Rocky outcrops in coniferous forests; mixed conifer, montane, and subalpine zones; 6,000–10,000'.

Comments: Manzanitas are pollinated mostly by bumblebees and hummingbirds, which can access the nectar from the corolla opening. Honeybees and some native bees aren't able to get nectar or pollen from the corolla opening; so they chew little portholes at the corolla base to get at the goodies.

Similar plants: The other manzanita species in the park are upright shrubs that grow more than 3' tall.

WHITE HEATHER
Cassiope mertensiana
Heath family (Ericaceae)

Description: White Heather is a low, densely branched, evergreen shrub that's up to 1' tall and has ascending to erect, smooth or finely hairy branches. Its tiny, opposite leaves are boat shaped (concave), tightly overlapping, and sessile. The small, widely bell-shaped, nodding flowers are about ¼" long and grow from the upper leaf axils on long, slender, red stalks. The showy calyx has 4 or 5 ruby-red sepals, and the widely bell-shaped, white corolla has 5 fused petals with reflexed lobes.

Flowering time: July–August

Habitat/range: Moist areas, usually around rocks; montane, subalpine, and alpine zones; 8,000–11,800'.

Comments: Much of the appeal of this plant's flowers is the sharp contrast between the ruby-red sepals and the snowy-white corolla. The elegant little shrub was one of John Muir's favorite plants. In an essay about the High Sierra, he described the blossoms as being so beautiful that they "thrill every fiber of one's being." In the Sierra Nevada, White Heather reaches its greatest abundance in the Yosemite region, and the hardy, slow-growing shrub has been reported to live for up to 20 years.

ALPINE WINTERGREEN
Gaultheria humifusa
Heath family (Ericaceae)

Description: This low, mat-forming, slightly woody shrub has smooth to sparsely hairy, slender stems that are 4–12" long. Its alternate, leathery, evergreen leaves are up to 1" long. The leaves are round to oval, are prominently veined, and some-times have tiny teeth. The small flowers, which grow solitary from the leaf axils, have 5 fused, hairless, reddish-tinged sepals and a white to pink-tinged, bell-shaped corolla with 5 fused petals. The fruit is a bright red, berry-like capsule.

Flowering time: July–August

Habitat/range: Along streambanks and other wet places, often hidden under other vegetation; subalpine zone; 8,000–10,500'.

Comments: The mint flavoring called wintergreen comes from plants in the *Gaultheria* genus. Other *Gaultheria* species are used commercially to flavor toothpaste, mouthwash, chewing gum, and soft drinks. Alpine Wintergreen berries have the minty wintergreen flavor and can be eaten raw or made into preserves. The leaves contain the same oils as the berries and are used to make a minty tea. The plants are called wintergreen because their leaves are green throughout the winter. An easily acces-sible place to find Alpine Wintergreen is along Cathedral Creek at the Tioga Road crossing.

SIERRA LAUREL
Leucothoe davisiae
Heath family (Ericaceae)

Description: Sierra Laurel is an erect, hairless, evergreen shrub, up to 5' tall, that often forms thickets along streams. Its alternate, leathery leaves are 1¼–2½" long, are elliptic to ovate, and often have tiny teeth along the margins. Elegant, elongated inflorescences, with many nodding flow-ers, grow from the upper leaf axils. The fragrant flowers have 5 small, white sepals that are fused at the base and pointed at the tip. The white, urn-shaped corolla is up to a little over ¼" long and has 5 curled lobes. The style and 10 stamens are concealed inside the corolla.

Flowering time: June–August

Habitat/range: Shady, moist streambanks; mixed conifer zone; 3,900–6,400'.

Comments: Sierra Laurel is one of the rarest shrubs in the park, known from only five locations, one of which is along Tenaya Creek near Iron Spring. Mythological Princess Leucothoe was loved by the god Helios. In a twisted set of circumstances involving disguise and a jealous sister, Leocothoe was buried alive by order of her father, King Orcha-mus, the fifth king of Babylon. Mournful Helios turned Leocothoe's lifeless body into a sweet-scented shrub. The plant is named for Nancy Jane Davis (1833–1921), who first collected it in Nevada County, California. Sierra Laurel is cultivated as an ornamental in woodland gardens.

45

ONE-SIDED WINTERGREEN
Orthilia secunda
Heath family (Ericaceae)

Description: This evergreen perennial is 2–7" tall and has a slightly woody base. Its alternate leaves are mostly toward the base of the plant and often appear to be whorled. The glossy, sometimes leathery leaves are up to 2½" long, are ovate to elliptic, and are sometimes toothed. The inflorescence is an elongated, arching stalk with nodding flowers that are crowded in a 1-sided row toward the top. The round, vase-shaped flowers have 5 inconspicuous little sepals and 5 separate, cream-colored petals that are less than ¼" long and have irregularly toothed lobes.

Flowering time: July–September

Habitat/range: Dry to moist, shady conifer forest; mixed conifer, montane, and subalpine zones; 6,000–10,000'.

Comments: Although this plant has no minty scent, it is related to plants that are used to make wintergreen flavoring. The plant is circumboreal, growing in areas throughout the Northern Hemisphere, and the genus is monotypic, meaning that it contains only one species.

Similar plants: One-sided Wintergreen was previously included in the *Pyrola* genus, and its flowers are similar to those of plants that are still in the genus, but the *Pyrola* genus no longer includes any plants with a one-sided inflorescence.

FRINGED PINESAP
Pleuricospora fimbriolata
Heath family (Ericaceae)

Description: Fringed Pinesap is a stemless, leafless, parasitic perennial, 4–8" tall, with a stout, fleshy, cream-colored stalk that's crowded with cream-colored flowers. The 4 lanceolate sepals have fringed margins and turn yellow to brown with age. The bell- to vase-shaped corolla has 4 (or 5) separate petals that are up to ⅜" long and sometimes have fringed margins. The flowers have 8 stamens and a style with a large, yellow stigma. The fruit is a round, white to cream-colored berry.

Flowering time: June–August

Habitat/range: Dry forest floors; mixed conifer and montane zones; 4,000–8,500'.

Comments: This odd-looking plant and many of its relatives lack chlorophyll, so they can't create nutrients by photosynthesis. Instead, they parasitize soil fungi, stealing their nutrients and providing nothing in return. This plant was first described from specimens collected by Henry Nicholson Bolander (1831–1897) in the Mariposa Grove. Bolander was a botanist who worked for the California Geological Survey in the late 1800s and collected many plants in the Yosemite region. He frequently corresponded with other botanists and shared his collections with them. They showed their gratitude by naming many newly described plant species in his honor.

LESSER WINTERGREEN
Pyrola minor
Heath family (Ericaceae)

Description: Lesser Wintergreen is an evergreen perennial, 4–9" tall, with petioled leaves that grow in a basal rosette. The leaves are 1–4" long and have a thin, dark green, round to ovate blade that sometimes has shallow teeth along the margin. The smooth, green stem has numerous alternate, nodding or spreading flowers with a straight style and 10 stamens that are mostly hidden inside the corolla. The partially fused, somewhat fleshy calyx has 5 triangular sepals with pointed tips. The round to bell-shaped, white corolla has 5 separate, rounded petals that are less than ¼" long.

Flowering time: July–August

Habitat/range: Moist, mossy areas in shaded forest; mixed conifer, montane, and subalpine zones; 6,000–10,000'.

Comments: This plant has difficulty making enough food from photosynthesis in the shady places where it grows. To compensate, its roots are able to steal nutrients from fungi.

Similar plants: Much more common White-veined Wintergreen (*P. picta*) has leaves with conspicuous white veins. Bog Wintergreen (*P. asarifolia*) has pink flowers and its style, which extends beyond the corolla, is strongly curved. One-sided Wintergreen (*Orthilia secunda*) has similar flowers, but they all grow on one side of the stem.

WHITE-VEINED WINTERGREEN
Pyrola picta
Heath family (Ericaceae)

Description: This common, evergreen perennial, 5"–1½' tall, has leathery leaves that grow in a basal rosette and are 1½–5" long. The dark green leaves have an ovate to elliptic blade with conspicuous white veins. The base of the leaf blade narrows somewhat abruptly to a distinct petiole. The reddish flower stalk has numerous alternate, nodding or spreading flowers **[inset]** with 10 stamens that are partially concealed by the corolla and a conspicuous, sometimes reddish, curved style that extends beyond the corolla. The 5 partially fused, sometimes reddish sepals have pointed tips. The widely bell-shaped corolla has 5 separate, rounded petals that are cream colored, pale greenish, or pale pink and are a little over ¼" long.

Flowering time: June–August

Habitat/range: Dry, shady places; mixed conifer, montane, and subalpine zones; 3,900–9,100'.

Similar plants: Rattlesnake Plantain (*Goodyera oblongifolia*), in the orchid family, is the only other plant in the park that has a basal rosette of leathery leaves with conspicuous white veins. If you find a set of such leaves with no flower stalk, look at the base of the leaves. White-veined Wintergreen's leaves narrow somewhat abruptly to a distinct petiole. Rattlesnake Plantain's leaves narrow gradually at the base and often appear to have no petiole.

47

WESTERN AZALEA

Rhododendron occidentale
Heath family (Ericaceae)

Description: Western Azalea is a fragrant, densely branched, deciduous shrub that can grow up to 25' tall but is mostly less than 10' tall in the park. Its stems often have shredding bark, and the hairy herbage is sometimes glandular sticky. The bright green, alternate leaves are 1–4" long, are elliptic, ovate, or obovate, and are ciliate along the margins. The inflorescences, which grow at the ends of the branches, have loose clusters of 3–15 large, showy flowers. The small, partially fused, green sepals have 5 triangular, ciliate lobes. The widely funnel-shaped corolla is up to 2" long and has 5 petals that are fused about halfway up from the base. The petal lobes are white, often with pink tinting or lines, and the upper lobe has a yellow, orange, or salmon spot. The style and 5 stamens extend far beyond the corolla.

Flowering time: April–August

Habitat/range: Streambanks and meadows; mixed conifer and montane zones; 3,400–7,500'.

Comments: Western Azalea's large, gorgeous flowers and lovely fragrance make it one of the most popular plants in the park. The flower buds, which are often a bright red to rose color, and the long stamens and style contribute to the plant's showiness. The seeds of the shrub were sent to England in the mid-1800s and were used to develop garden azaleas.

WESTERN LABRADOR TEA

Rhododendron columbianum (*Ledum glandulosum*)
Heath family (Ericaceae)

Description: Western Labrador Tea is a showy evergreen shrub, up to 6' tall, with glandular twigs and smooth bark that sometimes shreds with age. Its leathery, alternate leaves, up to 3¼" long, are ovate, lanceolate, or elliptic. They sometimes have scattered glands and usually have margins that are rolled under. The flowers grow in dense, rounded, terminal clusters of 10–35, with brown bracts at the base. The slightly hairy, partially fused calyx has 5 lobes, and the widely bell- or saucer-shaped corolla has 5 white or cream, mostly separate, oval petals that are about ¼" long. The flowers have 10 long stamens and a green ovary with a single style.

Flowering time: June–August

Habitat/range: Meadow borders and rocky areas along streams and lakes; mixed conifer, montane, subalpine, and alpine zones; 5,900–10,200'.

Comments: The crushed leaves of Western Labrador Tea have a strong fragrance, and a plant with the word "tea" in its name might tempt people to use it to make tea, but Western Labrador Tea is considered extremely toxic and the plant should not be consumed in any fashion. A stimulating, though somewhat toxic tea is made from the leaves of the eastern species *Rhododendron groenlandicum*, and naturalist Henry David Thoreau reportedly said that it smells something like a cross between turpentine and strawberries.

THYME-LEAVED SPURGE

Euphorbia serpillifolia ssp. *serpillifolia*
(*Chamaesyce serpyllifolia* ssp. *serpyllifolia*)
Spurge family (Euphorbiaceae)

Description: This mostly hairless annual has reddish, reclining to ascending, diffusely forked stems. Its opposite, oblong or ovate leaves are up to ½" long, have an asymmetrical base, and are finely toothed along the margins, at least toward the tip. The inflorescences grow solitary at the leaf nodes or in small clusters on short side branches. The reddish, bell-shaped involucre has a ring of 4 oblong, reddish nectar glands with a white, scalloped fringe. Each involucre has several tiny male flowers and a single female flower, none of which have sepals or petals. The male flowers have a single stamen with a short filament and an anther with yellow pollen. The female flowers have a forked style. The ovary enlarges as the fruit develops and becomes a dangling orb **[inset]**, which is often the most noticeable feature of the inflorescence.

Flowering time: June–October

Habitat/range: Dry, open roadsides and other disturbed areas; chaparral/oak-woodland and mixed conifer zones; up to 7,000'.

Similar plants: Hairy Thyme-leaved Spurge (*Euphorbia serpillifolia* ssp. *hirtula*, previously *Chamaesyce serpyllifolia* ssp. *hirtula*) looks practically identical, but its leaves and stems are conspicuously hairy.

SPANISH LOTUS

Acmispon americanus var. *americanus*
(*Lotus purshianus* var. *purshianus*)
Pea family (Fabaceae)

Description: Spanish Lotus is a common annual with soft-hairy herbage and reclining to erect, often branched stems, 2–22" long. Its leaves have mostly 3 lanceolate to elliptic leaflets that are up to ¾" long. The small pea flowers are solitary at the branch tips. The calyx has 5 long, narrow, pointed lobes that are much longer than the corolla tube. The corolla can be completely white, but it usually has a banner petal with reddish or purplish veins and sometimes has yellow-tinged wing petals. The slender, hairless pea pods have a curved beak.

Flowering time: May–October

Habitat/range: Dry, open to somewhat shaded places; chaparral/oak-woodland, mixed conifer, and montane zones; up to 7,900'.

Comments: North American native plants that were in the *Lotus* genus have been reassigned to the *Acmispon* genus, the *Hosackia* genus, and two other genera that are not represented in California.

Similar plants: Less common Small-flowered Lotus (*Acmispon parviflorus*, previously *Lotus micranthus*) has a similar small, white or cream corolla that often has a pink banner. Its calyx lobes are shorter than the corolla tube or about the same length. Its herbage is hairless or has sparse, short hairs, and its lower leaves have 3–9 leaflets.

BOLANDER'S MILKVETCH
Astragalus bolanderi
Pea family (Fabaceae)

Description: This perennial has erect to reclining stems that are 6–17" long and are leafless toward the base. Its herbage has somewhat sparse, fine, curly or wavy hairs. The pinnate leaves are 1½–6" long and have 13–27 linear-oblong or oblanceolate leaflets that are up to ¾" long. The lower surface of the leaflets has a prominent midrib that extends to the tip as a small, hard point. The pea flowers grow in crowded, spreading clusters of 7–18 on a long stalk, and they have a green, sometimes red-lobed calyx. The narrow corolla has white to cream-colored petals, and the banner is a little over ½" long. The inflated, strongly curved pods are green, red-speckled, or solid red, and they have a small beak at the end.

Flowering time: June–September

Habitat/range: Dry, open areas; montane, subalpine, and alpine zones; 7,000–10,600'.

Comments: *Astragalus* is from a Greek word that means anklebone or dice, possibly for the rattling sound seeds can make inside inflated pods.

Similar plants: Congdon's Milkvetch (*Astragalus congdonii*) **[inset]** has similar leaves and similar white to cream-colored flowers, though the flowers usually have a reddish calyx. The plant is a foothill species that grows around El Portal. Its fruit is not inflated and is straight or only slightly curved.

WHITEWHORL LUPINE
Lupinus microcarpus var. *densiflorus*
Pea family (Fabaceae)

Description: Whitewhorl Lupine is a robust annual with erect, hairy, often branched stems that are 8–20" tall. Its leaves are palmately divided into 5–11 (typically 7–9) oblanceolate leaflets that are up to 2" long and are mostly smooth above and hairy below. The distinctly whorled inflorescence is 2–12" long and has pea flowers that are up to ¾" long. The petals are yellow in bud, become white at maturity, and fade to yellow. Roadside plantings of the species often have flowers with bright yellow petals. The upper margins of the keel are ciliate near the base. The silky-hairy, stubby pods are about ½" long and migrate to one side of the inflorescence stalk, often forming tight circles.

Flowering time: April–June

Habitat/range: Roadsides and other dry, open, grassy slopes and flats; chaparral/oak-woodland zone; up to 5,000'.

Comments: This plant is one that you're likely to see (and notice) if you approach the park from one of its three western entrances in April, May, or June. Its whorls of flowers end up, in fruit, as an interesting row of tight pea-pod rings. Many lupines are pollinated by bees and bumblebees. When the insects hang onto a lupine's wing petals, their weight causes the wing petals to spread apart, providing access to the flower's pollen.

FOREST CLOVER
Trifolium breweri
Pea family (Fabaceae)

Description: This perennial clover has reclining to ascending stems, 4–12" long, and short-hairy to long-hairy herbage. Its alternate, palmate leaves grow along the stem and have 3 obovate, toothed leaflets that are ¼–⅞" long and are often slightly notched at the tip. The umbel-like inflorescences grow from the leaf axils and have 5–15 pea flowers, up to ⅜" long, in a circular or widely spreading cluster without a whorl of bracts (involucre) at the base. The tubular calyx has 5 needle-like lobes, and the corolla is white to lavender tinged with a banner petal that's often purple veined.

Flowering time: May–August

Habitat/range: Dry forest openings and other open areas; mixed conifer zone; 3,000–6,200'.

Comments: This is one of many plants named in honor of William H. Brewer, who was a member of the famous Whitney geological survey party in California in the 1860s.

Similar plants: Carpet Clover (*Trifolium monanthum* ssp. *monanthum*) and its related subspecies are similar, but they have no more than 9 white flowers in each cluster and they have mostly basal leaves that are matted or tufted. Non-native White Sweetclover (*Melilotus albus*) is 1½–6½' tall and has an elongated inflorescence of tiny, white pea flowers that are less than ¼" long.

MOUNTAIN CARPET CLOVER
Trifolium monanthum ssp. *monanthum*
Pea family (Fabaceae)

Description: This distinctly mat-forming perennial has prostrate stems, ½–4" long, and smooth to sparsely hairy herbage. The leaves are mostly basal and have 3 obovate or broadly elliptic, toothed leaflets, up to ½" long, that are rounded or truncate at the tip. The inflorescences have a tiny, often inconspicuous set of bracts (involucre) at the base and have 1–4 flowers that are often obscured by the matted foliage. The flowers, up to ½" long, have a calyx with 5 pointed lobes and a white corolla that often has a magenta-tinged keel.

Flowering time: June–August

Habitat/range: Moist areas; mixed conifer, montane, subalpine, and alpine zones; 5,500–12,000'.

Similar plants: Two other white-flowered Carpet Clover subspecies have been reported in the park. They have tufted patches of leaves, but they aren't distinctly matted. Delicate Carpet Clover (*T. monanthum* ssp. *tenerum*) has inflorescences with 1–7 flowers and leaflets with pointed tips. Small Carpet Clover (*T. monanthum* ssp. *parvum*) has inflorescences with 1–9 flowers and leaflets that are rounded, truncate, or notched at the tip. Somewhat similar Forest Clover (*T. breweri*) has 5–15 flowers in its inflorescences. Most of its leaves grow along the stem and are definitely not tufted or matted.

WHITE LAWN CLOVER
(non-native)
Trifolium repens
Pea family (Fabaceae)

Description: White Lawn Clover is a more or less hairless perennial with creeping stems, 4–12" long, that are branched from the base and root at the nodes. Its alternate, long-petioled stem leaves have 3 obovate, finely toothed leaflets that are up to ¾" long. The leaflets are wedge shaped at the base, are often shallowly notched at the tip, and sometimes have a paler chevron along the middle. The spherical flower heads, up to 1" wide, grow on a stalk that's 1½–4" long, and they have no whorl of bracts (involucre) at the base. The flowers have a green or pinkish calyx with 5 pointed lobes and a white corolla that's up to ⅜" long.

Flowering time: March–October

Habitat/range: Meadows, lawns, and disturbed areas; chaparral/oak-woodland and mixed conifer zones; up to 6,000'.

Comments: This plant is native to Eurasia and North Africa. It was introduced as a pasture crop but escaped and has become common in open areas, especially lawns. It does well in lawns because it tolerates mowing and spreads by underground stems. White Lawn Clover is short when it grows in mowed areas, but it can get quite tall when it's not constantly mowed down, and people familiar with the mowed version may wonder what the plant is when they find it in unmowed places.

SIERRA ALPINE GENTIAN
Gentiana newberryi var. *tiogana*
Gentian family (Gentianaceae)

Description: This attractive, mostly hairless perennial has 1 or more stems that are 2–4" long. Its stems usually lie along the ground and curve up toward the end. The basal leaves form a rosette, and the stem leaves grow opposite each other. The partially fused, funnel-shaped corolla, which is usually white but sometimes pale blue, is 1–2¼" long and has 5 rounded, spreading lobes. The appendages between the lobes have triangular divisions that taper to thread-like tips, with fringed margins in between. The inside of the corolla is decorated with hundreds of green dots, and the outside has a dark stripe running down the length of each petal.

Flowering time: August–October

Habitat/range: Wet to somewhat dry meadows; montane, subalpine, and alpine zones; 7,000–12,000'.

Comments: The plant's stems and leaves are sometimes hidden by surrounding vegetation, and all you might see of the plant is the large, showy flowers. The plant was named for John Strong Newberry (1822–1892), an American physician who served as geologist, botanist, and naturalist on expeditions to the West in the 1850s. He assisted in the creation of the Geological Society of America in 1888.

WHITE-STEMMED GOOSEBERRY
Ribes inerme var. *inerme*
Gooseberry family (Grossulariaceae)

Description: White-stemmed Gooseberry is a shrub, 3–9' tall, with erect to sprawling, mostly hairless stems and branches. The leaf and branch nodes can have 1–3 spines, but there are usually some nodes with no spines. The thin, mostly hairless, broadly ovate leaves are up to 1¼" long and are palmately divided into 3 or 5 somewhat deep lobes with rounded teeth. The small, pendulous flowers grow 1–5 from leaf axils. The smooth, light green flower tube (hypanthium) is narrowly bell shaped and ends with 5 green, spreading or reflexed sepals that are rounded at the tip and often have a reddish base. The 5 white, sometimes overlapping petals extend beyond the hypanthium, and the 5 stamens have green anthers and extend beyond the petals. The smooth berries are greenish or reddish purple and are less than ½" wide.

Flowering time: May–June

Habitat/range: Streambanks and meadow edges; montane and subalpine zones; 7,500–10,500'.

Comments: The shrub was probably given the name *inerme*, which means unarmed in Latin, because some of its leaf and branch nodes have no spines. Gooseberries have spiny stems, and currants have stems with no spines. Native Americans made fishhooks with the spines of some gooseberries, and they also used gooseberry spines to remove splinters.

STICKY CURRANT
Ribes viscosissimum
Gooseberry family (Grossulariaceae)

Description: Sticky Currant is an erect shrub that's 3–5' tall and has spineless branches. Its thick, fragrant, glandular-hairy leaf blades are 1–3" wide and have a heart-shaped base and 3 or 5 rounded lobes with scalloped, irregular teeth. The erect to pendulous, glandular-hairy flowers grow 4–15 from leaf axils. The broadly cylindric flower tube (hypanthium) has a glandular-hairy ovary at its base and ends with 5 spreading to reflexed sepals that become erect as they age. The hypanthium and the sepals are cream colored or greenish and are sometimes pink or purple tinged. The 5 white to pink, overlapping petals extend beyond the hypanthium. The black or bluish berries are less than ½" wide and are smooth or glandular-hairy.

Flowering time: May–July

Habitat/range: Open to shaded slopes, meadow borders, and rocky ledges; mixed conifer, montane, and subalpine zones; 3,200–9,500'.

Comments: White Pine Blister Rust, which originated in Asia, has become established in North America and has killed many 5-needle pines in the Sierra Nevada. To complete its life cycle, the rust needs two hosts, a 5-needle pine and a currant or gooseberry shrub. Efforts to eradicate *Ribes* species from areas where 5-needle pines grow have been unsuccessful and have not reduced the amount of rust infection.

MOCK ORANGE

Philadelphus lewisii
Hydrangea family (Hydrangeaceae)

Description: This deciduous shrub is 3–10' tall and has shredding bark and many open, erect to spreading stems and branches. Its red-brown stems fade to gray with age. The light green, opposite leaves are 1–3" long, are ovate to oval, and taper to a point at both ends. The leaves have smooth or slightly toothed margins and 3 distinct parallel veins from the base to the tip. The showy flowers are about 1" wide, and they grow in clusters of 6 or more at the branch tips. The flowers have 4 or 5 sepals, 4 white petals (rarely 5), and a central cluster of stamens with bright yellow anthers. The wonderfully fragrant flowers smell much like orange blossoms, with a hint of pineapple.

Flowering time: May–July

Habitat/range: Open or shaded, moist, rocky places; chaparral/oak-woodland and mixed conifer zones; up to 4,500'.

Comments: Mock Orange, which is Idaho's state flower, is widespread but not common in the park, usually growing as an individual plant among other species. Native Americans used the strong, hard wood for bows, arrows, tobacco pipes, snowshoes, cradles, and other furniture. They mixed the leaves and bark with water to make a mild soap. The shrubs are popular in ornamental gardens, and Swallowtail Butterflies love the flower nectar.

PITCHER SAGE

Lepechinia calycina
Mint family (Lamiaceae)

Description: Pitcher Sage is an attractive, aromatic shrub that's 1–6½' tall and is branched throughout. Its opposite, lanceolate to ovate leaves are 1½–4¾" long, are somewhat woolly, are sometimes glandular, and are shallowly scalloped or sharp toothed on the margins. The flowers are about 1" long and grow solitary in the axils of the upper leaves or in small clusters at the branch ends. The soft-hairy, bell-shaped, green calyx has 5 triangular lobes that turn purplish as they age. The white or pale lavender corolla has a broad tube with a ring of hairs inside. The corolla has 5 broad lobes that can be straight or curled backward, and the lower lobe is considerably longer than the others.

Flowering time: April–June

Habitat/range: Open, grassy slopes or partially shaded shrub thickets; chaparral/oak-woodland zone; up to 3,000'.

Comments: Pitcher Sage grows along the park's western boundary in the El Portal area and may grow within the park. Because the shrub is drought tolerant, somewhat deer proof, and attracts hummingbirds, it's planted in gardens and used in landscaping. The Miwok people, who lived in the Yosemite area, used the aromatic leaves of Pitcher Sage to treat fevers and headaches.

HOREHOUND
(non-native)
Marrubium vulgare
Mint family (Lamiaceae)

Description: This invasive perennial is 7"–2' tall and has white-woolly stems. Its roundish, deep-veined leaves are ½–2" long and have scalloped margins. The flowers grow in head-like clusters in the leaf axils. The cylindric calyx has 10 narrow teeth. The white corolla is up to ¼" long and has an erect, notched upper lip and a 3-lobed lower lip.

Flowering time: May–August

Habitat/range: Disturbed areas; chaparral/oak-woodland and mixed conifer zones; up to 4,100'.

Comments: This European native has become naturalized and common worldwide. Horehound has an advantage on grazed ground because it's highly unpalatable to livestock, which may be why the weed seems to thrive around horse and mule stables. Horehound has been used medicinally at least as far back as the 1st century BC, and a study conducted in 2011 concluded that its essential oil contains potent anticancer properties. Another study in 2012 concluded that marrubin, an active compound in the plant, has antidiabetic and anti-inflammatory properties.

Similar plants: Horehound resembles several other mint family plants that grow in the park, but of the plants it resembles, it's the only one that has a calyx with 10 teeth.

MOUNTAIN PENNYROYAL
Monardella odoratissima ssp. *pallida*
Mint family (Lamiaceae)

Description: Mountain Pennyroyal is an aromatic subshrub that's 6–18" tall and usually has several stems. Its oblanceolate, green or ash-green leaves are up to 1¾" long. The flowers grow in crowded heads, and directly beneath the heads are green to reddish, lanceolate bracts that taper gradually to a pointed tip. The flowers are up to ¾" long and have a woolly, 5-lobed calyx and a 2-lipped corolla that is usually white but can be pale lavender. Each flower has 4 white stamens that extend beyond the corolla lobes.

Flowering time: June–August

Habitat/range: Dry, gravelly to sandy flats and slopes; mixed conifer, montane, subalpine, and alpine zones; 4,000–11,000'.

Comments: Mountain Pennyroyal's leaves have been used to make tea, and Indians used the plant as a remedy for upset stomach, respiratory problems, and sore throats. Its flowers are popular with bumblebees, butterflies, and hummingbirds.

Similar plants: Sierra Coyote Mint (*M. candicans*) has similar flower heads with white flowers, but it's an annual rather than a subshrub and it has narrower leaves and a single stem. It grows in the Merced River Canyon west of the park boundary but has also been reported in Yosemite Valley.

WHITE-STEMMED HEDGENETTLE
Stachys albens
Mint family (Lamiaceae)

Description: This slender perennial has an erect, square, sometimes branched stem that's 1–6½' long, and its herbage is densely cobwebby-woolly throughout. Its opposite, lanceolate to ovate, often ascending leaves are 2–6" long, have rounded or sharp teeth on the margins, and are long-petioled on the lower stem and sessile above. The flowers grow in whorls of 6–12 around the stalk, the whorls becoming more crowded toward the top. The calyx has 5 triangular lobes, and the 2-lipped corolla is white and sometimes has faint lavender markings. The erect upper lip forms a hood over 4 stamens, and the middle lobe of the 3-lobed lower lip is much larger than the 2 lateral lobes.

Flowering time: May–October

Habitat/range: Streambanks and wet meadows; chaparral/oak-woodland and mixed conifer zones; up to 7,000'.

Similar plants: Less common Sierra Mint (*Pycnanthemum californicum*) **[upper inset]** can have cobwebby herbage and is sometimes confused with White-stemmed Hedgenettle, but its flowers grow in densely crowded, head-like clusters, with many more than 12 flowers per cluster. Even less common Rigid Hedgenettle (*Stachys rigida* var. *rigida*, previously *S. ajugoides* var. *rigida*) **[lower inset]** is similar to White-stemmed Hedgenettle, but its herbage, though hairy, is not cobwebby.

LEICHTLIN'S MARIPOSA LILY
Calochortus leichtlinii
Lily family (Liliaceae)

Description: This common, bulbed perennial has an unbranched stem, up to 24" tall, and a single linear basal leaf that's 5–6" long and withers early. Its stem leaves are linear and shorter. The broadly bowl-shaped flowers, 1–5 per plant, have 3 pale green, lanceolate sepals and 3 white petals that are broadly wedge shaped and up to 1½" long. On the inside of each petal, at the base, is an oval, yellow nectar gland covered with yellow hairs; above the nectar gland is a red to purple-black spot, which is highly variable in size and shape.

Flowering time: June–August

Habitat/range: Dry, open places; montane, subalpine, and alpine zones; 6,900–10,800'.

Similar plants: Much less common Plain Mariposa Lily (*C. invenustus*) **[inset]** has a round nectar gland that's encircled by a small, but conspicuous fringed membrane, and it can have white, lavender, or purplish petals. Butterfly Mariposa Lily (*C. venustus*) and Superb Mariposa Lily (*C. superbus*) are showier than Leichtlin's Mariposa Lily and Plain Mariposa Lily. They have a conspicuous red to brownish blotch or crescent near the central area of each of their petals, and the blotch or crescent is usually surrounded by bright yellow. Their petals are often white, but they can also be a variety of other colors.

SIERRA MARIPOSA LILY

Calochortus minimus
Lily family (Liliaceae)

Description: Sierra Mariposa Lily is a low-growing, hairless perennial with an unbranched, reclining to ascending stem that's ½–2" long. Its single linear to narrowly lanceolate basal leaf is 4–8" long and is flat and strap-like. The plant has 1–8 shallow-bowl-shaped flowers with an opposite pair of leaf-like bracts below. The 3 white or pale green, lanceolate sepals are visible between the 3 white, obovate to wedge-shaped petals, which are about ½" long. The 6 stamens have white, blue, or purple anthers. Each petal has a rectangular, fringed nectar gland at its base and often has finely notched margins. The fruit is a nodding, elliptic, 3-winged capsule.

Flowering time: May–August

Habitat/range: Moist forest openings, lake and meadow margins; mixed conifer zone; 3,900–7,000'.

Comments: The flowers of plants in the *Calochortus* genus have either spreading petals (the mariposa lilies) or petals with tips that curve toward each other, forming a globe (the globe lilies). All the *Calochortus* plants in the park have spreading petals, but Fairy Lanterns aka White Globe Lilies (*Calochortus albus*) **[inset]** grow near the park's western boundary in the El Portal area and are common and widespread throughout the Sierra Nevada foothills, often growing in somewhat crowded populations on shady, grassy slopes.

BUTTERFLY MARIPOSA LILY

Calochortus venustus
Lily family (Liliaceae)

Description: This common perennial has a stiffly erect, sometimes branched stem that's 4–24" tall. Its single basal leaf is 4–8" long, is linear, and withers early. The stem sometimes has 1 or 2 smaller, alternate leaves. Each plant has 1–6 bowl- to bell-shaped flowers. The flowers have 6 stamens and 3 lanceolate sepals that taper to a curled tip. The 3 wedge-shaped petals are 1¼–2" long and can be white, magenta, purple **[upper inset]**, pink, red, or yellow **[lower left inset]**. Each petal has a dark red blotch near the center, sometimes with a paler blotch above it. Beneath the dark blotch is a hairy, rectangular or square nectar gland.

Flowering time: May–July

Habitat/range: Dry, open places, often in sandy soil; chaparral/oak-woodland and mixed conifer zones; up to 6,400'.

Similar plants: Less common Superb Mariposa Lily (*Calochortus superbus*) **[lower right inset]** is the only other showy *Calochortus* species in the park. Its petals also have a dark blotch (or crescent) near the center, but its hairy nectar gland, near the petal base, is shaped like an upside-down V. It usually has mostly white petals, but they can be lavender, purple, or yellow. The blotches on the petals of both plants are often surrounded by yellow.

BRIDE'S BONNET, QUEEN'S CUP

Clintonia uniflora
Lily family (Liliaceae)

Description: Bride's Bonnet is an elegant perennial, 5–10" tall, with an unbranched, mostly underground stem. Its 2 or 3 hairless or sparsely hairy basal leaves are 3–7" long, are oblanceolate to obovate, and have a pointed tip. The hairy flower stalk has a single erect flower (rarely 2) that has 1 or 2 linear bracts at the base. The flowers have 6 white, oblanceolate, completely free tepals that are up to ⅜" long and 6 white stamens with pale yellow anthers. The showy fruit is a round, metallic-blue berry.

Flowering time: June–July

Habitat/range: Shaded conifer forest; mixed conifer zone; 3,300–6,000'.

Comments: This plant grows in the Merced and Tuolumne Groves of Giant Sequoias and in the Carlon area. Its two common names are both so appealing that it's hard to decide which one to use. Whether or not the plant is blooming, its broad, shiny green leaves attract attention, contrasting conspicuously with their forest floor surroundings. Native Americans used the inedible berries to make a blue dye. The genus name *Clintonia* is for DeWitt Clinton (1769–1828), an American politician and naturalist who is best known as the New York governor who got the Erie Canal built.

WASHINGTON LILY

Lilium washingtonianum ssp. *washingtonianum*
Lily family (Liliaceae)

Description: Washington Lily is an eye-catching, hairless perennial with an erect stem that's 2–6½' tall. Its oblanceolate or obovate leaves are 1½–5" long, are sometimes wavy-margined, and grow along the stem in 1–8 whorls with 3–16 leaves per whorl. Each elongated inflorescence has 1–33 large, fragrant, funnel-shaped flowers that are horizontal or slightly nodding. The 6 oblanceolate, white tepals are 2½–4½" long, have pale blue-gray dots, and are slightly curved, the lower ones often less so and forming a landing place for pollinators. The bases of the tepals just barely overlap to form a tube shape. The 6 stamens extend beyond the corolla throat. The fruit is an erect, oblong capsule with 6 longitudinal ridges.

Flowering time: June–August

Habitat/range: Dry slopes in the open or in partial shade; mixed conifer zone; 3,700–6,500'.

Comments: This attractive, fragrant plant looks something like cultivated Easter lilies. It was named Lady Washington Lily by early settlers in the Western states, in honor of Martha Washington, wife of the first U.S. president, and the name got shortened somewhere along the line. In Oregon, the plant is often called Mount Hood Lily or Cascade Lily.

HOOKER'S FAIRY BELLS

Prosartes hookeri (*Disporum hookeri*)
Lily family (Liliaceae)

Description: This leggy perennial, 11–30" tall, has short-hairy herbage and stems that are sparsely branched toward the top of the plant. Its alternate, clasping leaves are 1–6" long and are ovate to heart shaped. The inflorescences, at the branch ends, have 1–3 pendent, funnel-shaped flowers with 6 white to greenish tepals that are 3/8–3/4" long and are often curled back at the tips. You sometimes have to lift the leaves to find the flowers. The 6 stamens extend slightly beyond the tepal lobes. The fruit is a shiny red berry.

Flowering time: April–June

Habitat/range: Dry to moist, shaded forest floor; mixed conifer zone; 3,900–6,000'.

Comments: This plant was named in honor of Sir Joseph Dalton Hooker (1817–1911), a British botanist and explorer in the 19th century. He was Charles Darwin's closest friend and an important ally to Darwin in his efforts to have his theory of evolution considered seriously by the scientific community. He botanized around the world, from Antarctica to Nepal, and he wrote many books, including *Flora Antarctica*, *Flora Indica*, and *Introductory Essay to the Flora of Australia*.

WHITE MEADOWFOAM

Limnanthes alba ssp. *versicolor*
Meadowfoam family (Limnanthaceae)

Description: This mostly hairless annual has erect, sometimes branched stems, 3–15" tall. Its leaves, 3/4–4" long, have 5–11 leaflets that are linear, ovate, or oblong and are often shallowly to deeply 3 lobed. The bowl- to bell-shaped flowers, which grow solitary from the leaf axils, have 10 stamens, 1/8–1/4" long, and 5 lanceolate, hairless to sparsely hairy sepals. The 5 white petals, about 1/2" long, are sparsely long-hairy and greenish toward the base and have squared-off tips that are often irregularly jagged. The petals turn pink to magenta with age and curve over the fruit as it matures.

Flowering time: April–June

Habitat/range: Vernally moist, grassy areas, margins of pools and streams; chaparral/oak-woodland and mixed conifer zones; up to 5,000'.

Similar plants: This is one of four meadowfoams that grow in the El Portal and Hetch Hetchy areas. Another subspecies of White Meadowfoam, *L. alba* ssp. *alba*, is nearly identical to ssp. *versicolor*, but its sepals are densely long-hairy. The petals of Mountain Meadowfoam (*L. montana*) also curve over the fruit as it matures, but they remain white as they age and its stamens are about 1/8" long. Unlike the other three meadowfoams, the petals of Foothill Meadowfoam (*L. douglasii* ssp. *striata*, previously *L. striata*) curve away from the fruit as it matures and they typically have more conspicuous veins.

MEADOW DEATH CAMAS

Toxicoscordion venenosum var. *venenosum*
(*Zigadenus venenosus* var. *venenosus*)
False-hellebore family (Melanthiaceae)

Description: Extremely toxic Meadow Death Camas is an erect, hairless perennial, 7–24" tall, with grass-like, mostly basal leaves. Its elongated inflorescence is a mostly unbranched raceme, 2–10" long, with 10–50 flowers, each on its own stalk. Occasionally, a plant will have a single branch with more than 1 flower at the base of the inflorescence. The broadly bell-shaped flowers have 6 white to cream-colored tepals that are less than ¼" long and have a yellowish-green nectar gland at the base. The flowers have 6 stamens, 3 styles, and a yellowish-green ovary.

Flowering time: May–August

Habitat/range: Moist to dry meadows and rocky hillsides; mixed conifer, montane, and subalpine zones; 4,000–10,000'.

Similar plants: Two other *Toxicoscordion* species have been reported in the park. Foothill Death Camas (*T. paniculatum*, previously *Zigadenus paniculatus*) also has flowers with small tepals that are less than ¼" long, but its inflorescence is a panicle with multiple branches that have more than 1 flower. The inflorescence of Giant Death Camas (*T. exaltatum*, previously *Z. exaltatus*) is also a panicle with multiple branches that have more than 1 flower, but its tepals, up to ½" long, are larger and showier than the tepals of the other two species.

CALIFORNIA CORN LILY

Veratrum californicum var. *californicum*
False-hellebore family (Melanthiaceae)

Description: California Corn Lily is a distinctive perennial, with a hollow, unbranched, hairy stem, 3–7' tall, that's densely leafy throughout. Its broad, alternate, mostly ascending leaves are 7–16" long, are sparsely hairy, and have prominent veins. The lower leaves are ovate, and the upper leaves are lanceolate to broadly linear. The inflorescence is a dense, hairy, many-flowered panicle that's 10–24" long and has stiff, spreading to erect branches. The bowl-shaped flowers have 6 elliptic to obovate, white or greenish tepals that are up to ⅝" long, are sometimes finely notched along the margins, and have a V-shaped gland at the base that turns black with age. The flowers have 3 styles and 6 showy stamens with yellow, heart-shaped anthers. The fruit is a 3-lobed capsule.

Flowering time: June–August

Habitat/range: Moist to wet meadows, streambanks, and forest edges; mixed conifer, montane, and subalpine zones; 3,600–10,500'.

Comments: This common plant is well named, with its corn-like stalks and leaves. The foliage and roots are toxic and cause female sheep that eat the plant to give birth to lambs with birth defects. Indians used the dried, powdered roots and shoots as a pesticide. Compounds in the plant are being researched as treatments for various cancers and have shown significant promise.

BUCKBEAN

Menyanthes trifoliata
Buckbean family (Menyanthaceae)

Description: This circumboreal, aquatic perennial has thick stems that grow from creeping rhizomes. Its long-petioled leaves have 3 oval to elliptic, thick, hairless leaflets that are up to 4¾" long. The funnel-shaped flowers, up to ⅝" long, grow in showy, white clusters at the end of an erect flower stalk. The flowers have 5 sepals and 5 white, spreading petals. The numerous long, crinkly, white hairs on the inner surface of the petals give the flowers a frilly look. The petal tips are pink when the flowers are in bud. The 5 stamens have white filaments and contrasting dark anthers that turn black with age. The fruit is a round, beige capsule.

Flowering time: June–August

Habitat/range: Bogs, ponds, and margins of shallow lakes; mixed conifer, montane, and subalpine zones; 5,200–9,000'.

Comments: Approaching this plant can result in wet and sometimes muddy feet, which is a reasonable price to pay for a close-up look at the decorative flowers. In Lapland (and other places), when flour was scarce, Buckbean roots were ground and mixed with flour, and the mixture was used to make bitter-tasting, edible loaves of "famine bread." This plant grows in ponds in the Tuolumne Meadows area, at the southwest end of Hodgdon Meadow, and at Lost Lake in Little Yosemite Valley, among other places.

WESTERN SPRING BEAUTY, LANCE-LEAVED SPRING BEAUTY

Claytonia lanceolata
Miner's Lettuce family (Montiaceae)

Description: This hairless, somewhat fleshy perennial has an erect stem, 2–6" long, and it has 1–6 long-petioled, linear to lanceolate basal leaves that are usually withered by the time the flowers are in bloom. The 2 opposite stem leaves are ½–3" long, lanceolate to ovate, and usually sessile. The inflorescence is a raceme of 3–15 flowers at the end of the stem. The flowers have 2 ovate sepals and 6 stamens. The 5 white petals are up to ½" long, often have pink veins, and are usually yellow or greenish yellow at the base.

Flowering time: May–July

Habitat/range: Gravelly woodland and meadows; mixed conifer and montane zones; 5,000–8,500'.

Comments: This plant reportedly grows in the area between Chilnualna Falls, Chain Lakes, and Glacier Point Road, but it hasn't been documented in the park. If you find it, please note the location and report it to yose_web_manager@nps.gov.

Similar plants: Congdon's Lewisia (*Lewisia congdonii*) is a rare plant that grows on steep, rocky, north-facing slopes near Pigeon Gulch in El Portal. It has similar leaves and similar white flowers with pink veins and its basal leaves also wither early, but its stems are much longer, up to 2' long, and it doesn't have opposite stem leaves.

ALPINE SPRING BEAUTY

Claytonia megarhiza
Miner's Lettuce family (Montiaceae)

Description: Alpine Spring Beauty is a hairless perennial with succulent leaves and spreading stems that are ½–2½" long and grow from a greatly enlarged taproot. The basal leaves are ¾–4" long and grow in an organized, crowded rosette. They have reddish margins and are roughly triangular in shape with a rounded or obtuse tip. The opposite stem leaves are ¾–1" long, are more or less linear, and have a blunt tip. Each stem ends with a raceme of 2–6 flowers. The stems often grow along the ground, with the flowers emerging near the edge of the leaf rosette. The flowers have 2 broadly lanceolate, often magenta-tinged sepals, 5 white or pale pink petals, up to ⅜" long, and 5 stamens.

Flowering time: July–August

Habitat/range: Talus and scree slopes, usually north-facing; alpine zone; 10,000–13,000'.

Comments: Alpine Spring Beauty's succulent leaves and large taproot are able to store enough water to sustain the plant through dry periods.

Similar plants: Sierra Spring Beauty (*Claytonia nevadensis*) is also strictly an alpine plant, and it has similar succulent leaves and almost identical flowers, but its leaves, though they can be crowded, don't grow in an organized rosette, and the plant grows in wet places, usually near melting snow. Both species are somewhat rare in the park.

SIERRA SPRING BEAUTY

Claytonia nevadensis
Miner's Lettuce family (Montiaceae)

Description: Sierra Spring Beauty is a hairless perennial with succulent leaves and spreading to ascending stems that are 1–4" long. Its reddish-margined basal leaves are 1–6" long, including the linear petiole, and they have an elliptic to widely ovate blade with a wedge-shaped base and a rounded tip. The pair of opposite, sessile stem leaves are less than 1" long, are ovate, and have a rounded tip. Each stem ends with a raceme of 2–8 flowers. The flowers have 5 stamens and 2 ovate, often reddish-tinged sepals with pointed tips. The 5 oblong to elliptic, white or pale pink petals are up to ⅜" long and often have pink veins.

Flowering time: July–August

Habitat/range: Streams, springs, and melting snow beds, in gravel or sand; alpine zone; 10,000–12,000'.

Similar plants: Alpine Spring Beauty (*Claytonia megarhiza*) is also an alpine plant, and it has similar succulent leaves and almost identical flowers, but its leaves grow in an organized rosette and the plant grows in drier habitats. Both plants are rare in the park. Sierra Spring Beauty grows only in the southern Cascade Range and in northern and central Sierra Nevada. Alpine Spring Beauty is more widespread, growing north into Canada and east into Colorado.

MINER'S LETTUCE
Claytonia perfoliata ssp. *perfoliata*
Miner's Lettuce family (Montiaceae)

Description: Miner's Lettuce is a succulent, hairless annual with spreading to erect, sometimes reddish stems, up to 16" long. Its long-petioled basal leaves are in a loosely organized rosette and are all about the same size. The broadly elliptic, roundish, or triangular leaf blade is up to 1½" wide and is always wider than it is long. The opposite stem leaves are fused into a roundish disk that completely surrounds the stem. The inflorescence has a leaf-like bract at its base and has 5–40 flowers. The flowers have 2 green sepals, 5 white or pinkish petals that are up to ¼" long, 5 stamens, and a style with 3 stigmas.

Flowering time: February–May

Habitat/range: Vernally moist, shaded, often disturbed places; chaparral/oak-woodland and mixed conifer zones; up to 5,500'.

Similar plants: Very similar Small-flowered Miner's Lettuce (*C. parviflora* ssp. *parviflora*) has similar fused stem leaves, but its basal leaf blades are much longer than they are wide and the blades taper gradually to a petiole. Like Miner's Lettuce, Red-stemmed Miner's Lettuce (*C. rubra*) has basal leaves that are wider than they are long, but they're in a more organized rosette and are smaller toward the center of the rosette. Their stem leaves are often only partially fused around the stem, and they usually have angled margins.

RED-STEMMED MINER'S LETTUCE
Claytonia rubra ssp. *rubra*
Miner's Lettuce family (Montiaceae)

Description: This hairless, succulent annual has spreading to erect, reddish stems that are ½–6" long. Its long-petioled basal leaves are in a somewhat flattened, often well-organized rosette, and the leaves are smaller toward the center of the rosette. The leaves have a broadly elliptic to widely triangular blade, up to ¾" wide, with a wedge-shaped base and an obtuse tip. The reddish stem leaves are fused around the stem or are more or less free on 1 side, and they usually have angled margins. The inflorescence has 3–30 flowers, and it has a leaf-like bract at its base. The tiny flowers have 2 green sepals, 5 white or pinkish petals, a style with 3 stigmas, and 5 stamens.

Flowering time: February–May

Habitat/range: Moist to dry forest floor; chaparral/oak-woodland, mixed conifer, and montane zones; up to 8,000'.

Similar plants: Miner's Lettuce (*C. perfoliata*) also has basal leaves that are wider than they are long, but their basal leaves are in an unflattened, less organized rosette and are all about the same size. Their stem leaves are completely fused around the stem, and they usually don't have angled margins. Small-flowered Miner's Lettuce (*C. parviflora*) also has fused stem leaves, but its basal leaf blades are much longer than they are wide, and the blades taper gradually to a petiole.

KELLOGG'S LEWISIA

Lewisia kelloggii ssp. *kelloggii*
Miner's Lettuce family (Montiaceae)

Description: This hairless perennial has distinctive, leathery, gray-green, spatula- or spoon-shaped leaves that are ¾–3½" long, lie flat on the ground in a dense rosette, and are often slightly notched at the tip. The flowering stems, which are usually shorter than the leaves, end with a single showy flower that's 1–1½" wide and has 5–12 white or pale pink petals. Under the petals are 2 sepals and 2 similar bracts, all with toothed margins that are sometimes glandular and sometimes rusty red.

Flowering time: June–July

Habitat/range: Dry, sandy or gravelly flats and ridges; mixed conifer and montane zones; 6,000–8,500'.

Comments: This plant was named in honor of Dr. Albert Kellogg (1813–1887), who did extensive botanical work in California and was one of the founders of the California Academy of Sciences. He specialized in the study of trees, and the California Black Oak (*Quercus kelloggii*) is one of several plants that have been named for him. Kellogg was determined that women be allowed entry into the male-dominated scientific community, and he hired Katharine Brandegee and Alice Eastwood as curators for the academy. Eastwood risked her life to rescue many of the academy's botanical collections during the fires caused by the 1906 San Francisco earthquake.

NEVADA LEWISIA

Lewisia nevadensis
Miner's Lettuce family (Montiaceae)

Description: Nevada Lewisia is a hairless perennial with several partially buried stems. It has 5–15 narrow, somewhat fleshy leaves that are 1–5" long and radiate in a loose, somewhat sprawling fashion. The leaves are often broader toward the tip and are slightly upturned along the margins, giving them a U shape in cross section. Each stem ends with a single flower (or sometimes 2 or 3). The flowers have 2 green sepals that have a pointed tip and are sometimes slightly jagged. The 5–10 white or pale pink petals are ⅜" to a little more than ¾" long. The 2 lowest petals are broader than the other petals and have a somewhat blunt tip. The rest of the petals have a more pointed tip. The flowers have 6–18 stamens and a style with 3–6 stigmas.

Flowering time: June–July

Habitat/range: Wet to dry meadows and streambanks; mixed conifer, montane, subalpine, and alpine zones; 5,900–12,000'.

Similar plants: Dwarf Lewisia (*L. pygmaea*) and Glandular Alpine Lewisia (*L. glandulosa*) look similar, but their petals are shorter (at most ⅜" long), their leaves are usually in a more organized rosette and are shorter (at most 4" long), and their sepal tips are rounded or squared off rather than pointed.

THREE-LEAVED LEWISIA
Lewisia triphylla
Miner's Lettuce family (Montiaceae)

Description: This common, distinctive perennial
has hairless herbage and 1 to several slender,
sprawling to erect stems that are ¾–2¾" long.
Its basal leaves are withered before the flowers
bloom. The stem has 2–5 (but usually 3) linear,
fleshy leaves that grow from about the same point
on one side of the stem. The flowers are about
½" wide and grow in loose clusters of 1–25. They
have 2 untoothed, ovate sepals, 5–9 white or pale
pink petals that often have purplish veins, 3–5
stamens, and a style with 3–5 stigmas.

Flowering time: June–August

Habitat/range: Moist, sandy or gravelly, open
areas and grassy meadows; mixed conifer, montane, subalpine, and alpine zones; 5,000–11,000'.

Comments: The genus was named for Meriwether
Lewis of the Lewis and Clark Expedition. In 1806,
he collected *Lewisia rediviva* in Montana in a
valley now known as the Bitterroot Valley. Indians
used the plant's roots for food and collected the
roots before the plants bloomed because the roots
become bitter afterward. Unaware of this pertinent
detail, Lewis tried eating the roots after the plants
had bloomed and described them as "nauseous to
my palate." The attractive plant grows west of the
park in the Sierra Nevada foothills.

TOAD LILY
Montia chamissoi
Miner's Lettuce family (Montiaceae)

Description: Toad Lily is a hairless, fleshy perennial with erect to sprawling stems, up to 9" long,
that root at the nodes and sometimes grow in
matted clusters. Its opposite stem leaves are ¼–2"
long and are oblanceolate, ovate, or diamond
shaped. The plant has 2–8 flowers that grow at
the stem end or from leaf axils. The flowers have
2 unequal, rounded sepals, 5 stamens, and a style
with 3 stigmas. The 5 white or pinkish petals are
¼–⅜" long and are much longer than the sepals.

Flowering time: June–August

Habitat/range: Seeps, wet meadows, and along
small streams; mixed conifer, montane, subalpine,
and alpine zones; 3,600–11,000'.

Comments: The plant was named for Adelbert von
Chamisso, a German botanist who was a member
of an 1817 Russian oceanic expedition searching
for the Northwest Passage. During the trip they
docked in San Francisco to restock. While there,
Chamisso collected California Poppy (*Eschscholzia
californica*) and named it for his friend Johann
Friedrich von Eschscholtz, the ship's surgeon.

Similar plants: Water Chickweed (*Montia fontana*)
[inset] is a less conspicuous plant that also grows
in wet places. It also has opposite leaves and 5
white petals, but its petals are less than ⅛" long
and are about the same length as the sepals.

NARROW-LEAVED MONTIA

Montia linearis
Miner's Lettuce family (Montiaceae)

Description: This hairless, succulent annual has 1 to several erect, sometimes branched stems that are 2–10" long. Its alternate, linear leaves are up to 3" long and have petioles that are enlarged and membranous. The inflorescence has 3–14 flowers mostly in a 1-sided raceme. The tiny flowers are nodding in bud and become more or less erect when they bloom. The flowers have 3 stamens, a style with 3 stigmas, and 2 roundish sepals that are slightly unequal and are white-margined near the tip. The 5 white or pale pink, somewhat unequal petals are ⅛–¼" long.

Flowering time: April–June

Habitat/range: Moist grasslands, meadows, and open woodlands; mixed conifer and montane zones; 3,900–7,500'.

Similar plants: Water Chickweed (*M. fontana*) grows in wet rather than moist places; it also has tiny flowers with 5 white petals, but its petals are less than ⅛" long and its leaves are opposite rather than alternate. Slightly more robust Toad Lily (*M. chamissoi*) also grows in wet places and has 5 small, white petals, but its petals are up to ⅜" long and its leaves are opposite rather than alternate.

SMALL-LEAVED MONTIA

Montia parvifolia
Miner's Lettuce family (Montiaceae)

Description: This distinctive plant is a hairless, leggy, sometimes mat-forming perennial with several ascending to erect stems, 2–16" long, that often become tangled with each other and with the stems of neighboring plants. Its long-petioled basal leaves and alternate stem leaves are ½–2¾" long and are oblanceolate and fleshy. The leaves get smaller and become bract-like toward the top of the stem. The flowers, which grow 2–12 in racemes at the stem ends, have 2 green, unequal, obovate sepals and 5 white or pale pink petals that are up to ⅝" long and often have conspicuous veins. Each flower has 5 stamens with pink pollen and a style with 3 stigmas. The fruit is a 3-valved capsule.

Flowering time: May–July

Habitat/range: Moist, shady sites, often near streams; mixed conifer and montane zones; 3,500–8,000'.

Comments: The genus was named for Giuseppe Monti (1682–1760), an Italian pharmaceutical chemist who studied plants to acquire knowledge about medicinal herbs. Monti was considered one of the great botanists of his time, and his works were a major source for Carl Linnaeus' botanical research. He and his son Gaetano Lorenzo Monti were among the last naturalists who defended the notion that the biblical flood was the determiner of the Earth's geological features.

SMALL ENCHANTER'S NIGHTSHADE

Circaea alpina ssp. *pacifica*
Evening Primrose family (Onagraceae)

Description: Small Enchanter's Nightshade is a perennial with an erect, slender, unbranched stem, 8–19" long, that usually has dense, stiff, flattened hairs. Its opposite, petioled leaves, 1–4" long, are ovate to more or less round, with a round to heart-shaped base and a narrow, pointed tip. The thin leaves are hairless to somewhat hairy and have smooth or slightly toothed margins. The inflorescence is an erect raceme with dense, stiff, flattened hairs and clusters of small flowers. The flowers look like they have 4 tiny petals, but they actually have 2 reflexed, unnotched, white sepals and 2 notched, white petals that are about the same size as the sepals. The flowers have 2 white stamens and a hairy, inferior ovary. The bur-like fruit has hooked hairs that adhere to fabric, fur, and feathers.

Flowering time: May–August

Habitat/range: Moist, shady forest floor, sometimes in marshy places; mixed conifer and montane zones; 3,900–8,500'.

Comments: Plants in the *Circaea* genus grow throughout the Northern Hemisphere. The genus was named for Circe, an enchantress in Greek mythology who used a plant in the genus to make magical potions. In Homer's *Odyssey*, she turned members of Odysseus' crew into swine by feeding them food laced with a transformative potion.

WHITE-FLOWERED WILLOWHERB

Epilobium lactiflorum
Evening Primrose family (Onagraceae)

Description: This perennial has somewhat clumped, unbranched stems, 6–20" long, that are ascending, or at least not perfectly erect, and have no peeling layers near the base. The stems have lines of small, stiff, appressed, nonglandular hairs below the leaves. The narrowly ovate to narrowly lanceolate leaves are up to 2" long. The flowers are few in the upper leaf axils, in nodding or erect, glandular inflorescences. The flowers have 4 sepals and 4 white, notched petals, up to about ⅜" long. The fruit is a cylindric capsule. The fruit and stalk, together, are 2¾–5¾" long, and the fruit is less than 3 times longer than the stalk.

Flowering time: June–September

Habitat/range: Damp meadows, streambanks, and lake borders; mixed conifer, montane, subalpine, and alpine zones; 4,600–11,000'.

Similar plants: Two other willowherbs have stems that are at least somewhat hairy, that are ascending (or at least not perfectly erect), and that have no peeling layers near the base. Hornemann's Willowherb (*E. hornemannii* ssp. *hornemannii*) has flowers that are pink to rose-purple or white. Its fruit and stalk, together, are 1¾–3⅛" long, and the fruit is more than 4 times longer than the stalk. Howell's Willowherb (*E. howellii*) has tiny, white petals, up to ⅛" long, and, unlike the other two willowherbs, its stem is densely glandular-hairy.

SPREADING GROUNDSMOKE
Gayophytum diffusum ssp. *parviflorum*
Evening Primrose family (Onagraceae)

Description: This erect annual, 4–24" tall, has a wispy stem that's somewhat hairy toward the top and is branched above and sometimes below. The stem usually has 0 or 1 leaf node between the branches. The ascending, alternate leaves, up to 2½" long, are linear to narrowly lanceolate and become somewhat smaller toward the top of the stem. The wide open flowers, which grow from leaf axils **[inset]**, have 4 reflexed sepals that are free or fused in pairs. The 4 white petals, up to ⅛" long, have 2 yellow spots at the base. The 8 stamens are unequal in length, and the stigma does not extend beyond the anthers. The fruit is a cylindric, somewhat knobby capsule. The stalk of the capsule is usually shorter than the capsule itself. In each of the 4 capsule chambers, the seeds are usually in 1 row and are not overlapping, but they can occasionally be in 2 overlapping rows.

Flowering time: May–August

Habitat/range: Dry, sandy places; mixed conifer, montane, and subalpine zones; 3,000–10,000'.

Similar plants: This is one of five *Gayophytum* species in the park that grow in dry places and have cylindric fruit rather than flattened fruit. The other four species can be differentiated from Spreading Groundsmoke, and from each other, as follows.

Coville's Groundsmoke (*G. eriospermum*) can be distinguished from *all* the other groundsmoke species in California by its significantly larger flowers. Its petals are ³⁄₁₆–⁵⁄₁₆" long, and the petals of all the other species are less than ³⁄₁₆" long. It's also the only species in this group, besides Zigzag Groundsmoke (below), with a stigma that extends beyond the anthers.

Zigzag Groundsmoke (*G. heterozygum*) is the only California groundsmoke species that has irregular, lumpy fruit capsules, which is due to the fact that about 50% of its seeds fail to develop, making the capsules bulge in some spots and not in others.

Much-branched Groundsmoke (*G. ramosissimum*) is the only California groundsmoke species that always has seeds in 2 overlapping rows in each of the 4 chambers, though Spreading Groundsmoke sometimes does. Its petals are truly tiny, no more than ¹⁄₁₆" long, and its capsule stalk is usually longer than the capsule. Spreading Groundsmoke's capsule stalk is usually shorter than the capsule.

That leaves Deceptive Groundsmoke (*G. decipiens*). It differs from Spreading Groundsmoke in that its stems usually have 2–8 leaf nodes between the branches, as opposed to 0 or 1.

Note: If you have difficulty arriving at a determination, keep in mind that *Gayophytum* species intergrade, which can make them difficult to identify to species. If you find a groundsmoke plant with petals less than ³⁄₁₆" long, you'll almost always need mature fruit to attempt to identify it to species.

DWARF GROUNDSMOKE
Gayophytum humile
Evening Primrose family (Onagraceae)

Description: Dwarf Groundsmoke is an erect annual, 2–12" tall, with a stem that's often branched from near the base. The plant has mostly hairless herbage, and its alternate, linear leaves are up to 1" long. The wide open flowers grow from the leaf axils, and they have 4 tiny, reflexed sepals that are free or fused in pairs. The 4 white petals are no more than $\frac{1}{16}$" long, and the longest of the 8 unequal stamens is less than $\frac{1}{16}$" long. The fruit is a flattened, sometimes knobby, erect capsule that has 4 chambers with 24–50 seeds. The capsules have a groove along the midline and sometimes have short, glandular hairs. When a capsule opens, 2 of the chambers remain attached and the other 2 split away.

Flowering time: July–August

Habitat/range: Drying margins of wet sites and snowbeds; montane, subalpine, and alpine zones; 7,000–12,500'.

Similar plants: Blackfoot Groundsmoke (*Gayophytum racemosum*) is the only other groundsmoke in the park with flattened fruit. It usually has sparsely hairy herbage. Its petals can be more than $\frac{1}{16}$" long, and its longest stamen is about $\frac{1}{16}$" long. Its fruit has 10–35 seeds, and when a capsule opens, all 4 of the chambers split away. Blackfoot Groundsmoke also grows along drying margins of wet sites.

PHANTOM ORCHID
Cephalanthera austiniae
Orchid family (Orchidaceae)

Description: Phantom Orchid is an erect perennial that's entirely white, except for a golden-yellow patch on the lip of each flower. The stem is 8–20" tall and has several scattered, leaf-like bracts that form a sheath at the base and are pointed at the tip. Up to 20 white flowers grow along the upper part of the stem. The vanilla-scented flowers have 3 sepals and 3 petals. All 3 sepals and 2 of the petals are somewhat similar, and the other petal is the lip-like part with the yellow patch. The upper sepal is between the upper 2 petals, and all 3 are fused at the base. The other 2 sepals spread out along the sides. The plants turn yellow and then brown as they age.

Flowering time: May–June

Habitat/range: Deep humus in dark woods and forests; mixed conifer zone; 4,300–6,000'.

Comments: A plant with no green parts cannot perform photosynthesis and must get its nourishment from an outside source. Phantom Orchids get their nourishment from soil fungi, which have root-like strands called mycelia. Mycelia grow into the roots of the orchid, and the orchid absorbs nutrients from the mycelia. Because the fungi receive no apparent benefit from the orchid, the relationship between the two is parasitic rather than mutualistic.

MOUNTAIN LADY'S SLIPPER
Cypripedium montanum
Orchid family (Orchidaceae)

Description: Mountain Lady's Slipper is a distinctive perennial with an erect, leafy, glandular-hairy stem that's 10–28" tall. Its alternate, sessile leaves, 2–6" long, are elliptic to ovate and have wavy margins and conspicuous veins. Several showy flowers grow at the top of the stem, each of them with a large, erect, green bract behind it. The large, white, pouch-like petal has purple veins inside. The elongated, brown to purple parts are sepals and petals. A single sepal arches over the top of the flower, and there are 2 fully fused sepals under the pouch. The 2 twisted lateral parts are the other 2 petals.

Flowering time: May–July

Habitat/range: Dry slopes and moist forest floor, usually in shade; mixed conifer zone; 4,000–5,300'.

Comments: The slipper has a fragrant scent that attracts flying insects in search of nectar. Once inside the pouch, an insect finds no nectar and, looking for an exit, it follows lines that lead toward the light of two windows in the back of the pouch. But, alas, the windows are closed. Next it climbs hairs along the back wall. On the way up, the insect bumps into the flower's stigma, which rubs off any pollen from a previously visited flower. As the insect continues on, it turns left or right toward either of two narrow exits. When it squeezes through an exit, pollen is deposited on its back.

RATTLESNAKE PLANTAIN
Goodyera oblongifolia
Orchid family (Orchidaceae)

Description: This slender perennial, 7–16" tall, has a leafless stem and a basal rosette of thick, evergreen leaves that are 1½–3½" long. The lanceolate to widely elliptic leaves taper gradually at the base to a short, sometimes indistinct petiole. The leaf blades are white along the central vein and often along the smaller lateral veins. The inflorescence is a dense, spike-like raceme with 10–48 more or less sessile flowers that sometimes spiral around the stalk. Each flower **[inset]** has 3 sepals (2 lateral sepals and 1 upper sepal) and 3 white petals (2 lateral petals and 1 lip petal). The 2 lateral petals and the upper sepal are fused and form a hood that encloses the reproductive parts and sometimes at least partially conceals the lip petal. The fruit is a hairy, ascending to erect capsule.

Flowering time: June–August

Habitat/range: Dry, shaded forest floor; mixed conifer zone; 3,000–6,000'.

Similar plants: White-veined Wintergreen (*Pyrola picta*), in the heath family, is the only other plant in the park that has a basal rosette of leathery leaves with conspicuous white veins. If you find a set of such leaves with no flower stalk, look at the base of the leaves. White-veined Wintergreen's leaves narrow somewhat abruptly to a distinct petiole. Rattlesnake Plantain's leaves narrow gradually at the base and often appear to have no petiole.

ROYAL REIN ORCHID
Piperia transversa
Orchid family (Orchidaceae)

Description: This erect, slender, hairless perennial is 5–22" tall and has narrow, sprawling, linear to widely oblanceolate basal leaves that often wither by the time the flowers bloom. The inflorescence is a more or less dense spike, 2–12" long. The small, white flowers have 3 sepals and 3 petals (2 lateral petals and 1 lip petal). The upper sepal projects forward between the 2 lateral petals, and all 3 have green or yellow-green midveins and look much alike. The lateral sepals spread outward or curve backward. The white, oblong to ovate lip is straight or bends slightly downward. The elongated spur, which is more than twice as long as the lip, is mostly horizontal and is often green toward the tip. The fruit is an ascending to erect capsule.

Flowering time: May–August

Habitat/range: Dry, open or shady places; mixed conifer zone; 3,200–6,200'.

Similar plants: Royal Rein Orchid is the only *Piperia* species in the park that has white flowers, though they can be 2-toned white and green. The park's two other *Piperia* species have green or yellow-green flowers. White Bog Orchid (*Platanthera dilatata*) is somewhat similar, but its flowers are always pure white and it grows only in wet places.

WHITE-FLOWERED BOG ORCHID
Platanthera dilatata var. *leucostachys*
(*P. leucostachys*)
Orchid family (Orchidaceae)

Description: White-flowered Bog Orchid is an erect, hairless perennial, ½–4½' tall, that is common in wet places throughout the park's middle elevations. Its alternate stem leaves are 2–13" long, are linear to elliptic or lanceolate, and become gradually smaller upward. The inflorescence is a robust, usually dense spike, 2–13" long. The bright white flowers have 3 sepals and 3 petals (2 lateral petals and 1 lip petal). The upper, hood-like sepal and the 2 lateral petals are about the same length, and the 2 petals usually curve toward each other, forming an unfused hood with the upper sepal. The lateral sepals are spreading or bend downward. The lip either spreads downward or the tip of the lip adheres to the tips of the upper sepal and lateral petals. The downward curving, greenish spur is much longer than the lip.

Flowering time: May–August

Habitat/range: Wet meadows, seeps, and streambanks, usually in the open; mixed conifer, montane, and subalpine zones; 3,900–10,200'.

Comments: What looks like a stalk between the flower and the stem is actually the flower's inferior ovary. The ovary's 180-degree twist is evidence that the flower's lip evolved from what was originally its uppermost petal.

71

HOODED LADIES' TRESSES

Spiranthes romanzoffiana
Orchid family (Orchidaceae)

Description: This elegant, mostly hairless perennial has an erect, stout stem that's 3–12" tall. Its basal and alternate lower stem leaves are linear-lanceolate and are 1–5" long. The inflorescence, 1–5" long, is a dense spike of flowers arranged in longitudinal spiraled rows. The fragrant, white to cream flowers have 3 sepals and 3 petals (2 lateral petals and 1 lip petal). The upper sepal and the 2 lateral petals are about the same length and are fused to form an open, tubular hood. The 2 ascending lateral sepals lie against the edges of the fused hood, making the hood look as though it has free tips. The downward curving lip has a pouch-like base rather than a spur, and the lip is expanded at the base and at the tip, giving it somewhat of a violin shape.

Flowering time: June–August

Habitat/range: Wet meadows, streambanks, and seeps; mixed conifer, montane, subalpine, and alpine zones; 4,000–10,400'.

Similar plants: Western Ladies' Tresses (*Spiranthes porrifolia*) also has a dense spike of spiraled flowers, but the lip of the flowers is lanceolate to ovate rather than violin shaped. Even though the upper 3 flower parts are partially fused, they are noticeably free at the tips, and the 2 lateral sepals spread outward, not converging with the upper 3 parts.

VALLEY TASSELS

Castilleja attenuata
Broomrape family (Orobanchaceae)

Description: Valley Tassels is a slender, erect annual with mostly unbranched stems, 4–20" long, and spreading-hairy, non-glandular herbage. Its alternate leaves, ¾–3" long, are more or less linear, and the upper leaves have 2 thread-like lateral lobes. The flower spike is 1–12" long and ⅜–¾" wide and is about the same width throughout. The bracts in the inflorescence have 3 narrow lobes with white or pale yellow tips. The calyx has 4 white-tipped lobes, and the narrow, 2-lipped corolla has an inconspicuous upper lip and a lower lip with 3 pouches. The lower lip is mostly white below, is usually more or less yellow at the top, and has purple dots. The stigma is hidden within the corolla.

Flowering time: March–May

Habitat/range: Dry, open, grassy places; chaparral/oak-woodland zone; up to 5,000'.

Similar plants: Pale Owl's-clover (*Castilleja lineariloba*) **[inset]** has glandular-hairy herbage. It has a similar corolla, though its yellow area is often more predominant. Its flower spike is wider, 1–1½" wide, and is often broader toward the top. Its stigma is usually visible, and its corolla is broader toward the top; the corolla of Valley Tassels is narrow throughout. Both plants are common in the foothills, mostly outside of the park, but they also grow in the park's lower elevations, such as the Wawona and Ackerson Meadow areas.

SLENDER BIRD'S-BEAK

Cordylanthus tenuis ssp. *tenuis*
Broomrape family (Orobanchaceae)

Description: This slender, lanky annual has diffusely branched stems that are 11"–2¼' long. Its herbage is glandular-hairy, especially above. The alternate leaves are ¾–2½" long, are narrowly to broadly linear, and have no lobes. The flowers are solitary or in loose clusters of 2 or 3, with 1 or 2 linear, leaf-like, unlobed outer bracts underneath. The club-shaped, flattened corolla, up to ¾" long, is partially hidden between a sheath-like calyx on one side and a calyx-mimicking inner bract on the other side. The calyx, the inner bract, and the corolla are all about the same length. The lower part of the calyx partially surrounds the corolla tube laterally, and the tip of the calyx is notched. The yellow-tipped corolla is mostly white with conspicuous maroon markings.

Flowering time: July–September

Habitat/range: Dry, open places; chaparral/oak-woodland, mixed conifer, and montane zones; up to 7,000'.

Similar plants: Stiff-branched Bird's-beak (*Cordylanthus rigidus* ssp. *rigidus*) has a similar overall appearance and also grows in dry, open areas, but its flowers are in dense, head-like clusters of 5–15 and its outer flower bracts usually have 3 lobes.

NORTHERN GRASS-OF-PARNASSUS

Parnassia palustris (*P. californica*)
Grass-of-Parnassus family (Parnassiaceae)

Description: This erect, hairless perennial, 6–20" tall, has flowering stalks that end with a solitary flower **[inset]**. Its ovate to lance-ovate, long-petioled basal leaves are 2–5½" long, including the petiole, and have parallel longitudinal veins. The calyx has 5 elliptic lobes that are reflexed in fruit. The 5 white or cream-colored petals, ¼–¾" long, are round to ovate and are distinctly veined. The flowers have 5 typical-looking stamens and 5 yellow or green, sterile stamens called staminodes. Each staminode has a broad base and many thread-like lobes at the end, each with a tiny, round nectar gland. The superior ovary has a style with a 4-lobed stigma.

Flowering time: July–October

Habitat/range: Wet streambanks and meadows; montane, subalpine, and alpine zones; 6,500–11,000'.

Comments: The infertile stamens, instead of participating in sexual reproduction, have evolved to become nectar-producing appendages that give pollinators a reason to visit the flowers.

Similar plants: Marsh Marigold (*Caltha leptosepala*), in the buttercup family (Ranunculaceae), has somewhat similar flowers and leaves and it also grows in wet places, but its flowers have 5–12 white sepals that resemble petals and its leaves are net veined.

73

SPURRED SNAPDRAGON
Antirrhinum leptaleum
Plantain family (Plantaginaceae)

Description: Spurred Snapdragon is a glandular-hairy annual with an erect stem, 3½–22" tall. Its oblanceolate to ovate stem leaves, up to 1¾" long, taper to a short petiole and are alternate above and usually opposite below. The leaves are not much reduced in size upward. The flowers, about ¼" long, are solitary and nearly sessile in most of the leaf axils. The upper lobe of the 5-lobed calyx is longer than the other lobes. The hairy, 2-lipped corolla is white to pale lavender. Its upper lip has 2 erect lobes. The 3-lobed lower lip has a swollen bulge that closes off the corolla throat and is referred to as the palate.

Flowering time: May–July

Habitat/range: Grassy, often disturbed areas; chaparral/oak-woodland and mixed conifer zones; up to 6,000'.

Comments: This plant has been reported in the Wawona and El Portal areas and seems to be a first-year pioneer after intense wildfires. *Antirrhinum* is from Greek words that mean like and nose, in reference to the snout-like bulge on the corolla's lower lip. Garden snapdragons are in the *Antirrhinum* genus. If you squeeze the sides of a Spurred Snapdragon corolla, or the corolla of a garden snapdragon, you open the dragon's mouth, and the mouth snaps shut as soon as you let go.

TINCTUREPLANT
Collinsia tinctoria
Plantain family (Plantaginaceae)

Description: The erect stem of this robust annual is 7–24" tall and is sometimes branched. Its opposite, lanceolate leaves, 1¼–3½" long, are shallowly toothed and are hairless on the upper surface and fine-hairy below. The lower leaves are sessile or short-petioled, and the upper leaves are clasping and sometimes mottled. The flowers grow in well-spaced whorls of 3–9 in an elongated, densely glandular inflorescence. The calyx is deeply divided into 5 narrow lobes. The 2-lipped corolla is white to yellowish or lavender to magenta **[upper inset]**, and the upper lip is much smaller than the lower lip. The 2-lobed upper lip curves strongly backward and has 2 darker bands. The lateral lobes of the 3-lobed lower lip have a line down the center and have various splotches and dots. The central lobe of the lower lip is keel shaped and is mostly hidden by the lateral lobes.

Flowering time: May–August

Habitat/range: Dry or damp places; chaparral/oak-woodland and mixed conifer zones; up to 6,000'.

Similar plants: Chinese Houses (*Collinsia heterophylla* var. *heterophylla*) **[lower inset]** grows near the park's western boundary in the El Portal area. When Tinctureplant has purple flowers, the plants resemble each other. However, the corolla of Chinese Houses has an erect upper lip that's only slightly smaller than the lower lip.

BRACTLESS HEDGE-HYSSOP
Gratiola ebracteata
Plantain family (Plantaginaceae)

Description: This mud-loving annual has an erect, hairless, sometimes branched stem that's 1½–7½" tall. Its opposite, lanceolate leaves are ¼–1" long, are sessile or clasping, and usually have tiny teeth along the margins. The odd little flowers, which grow on plump stalks from the leaf axils, have no bracts beneath them, as the common and scientific names suggest. Each flower has 5 lanceolate sepals. The odd-looking, 4-angled, tubular corolla is about ¼" long, is often curved, and is indistinctly 2 lipped. It has a greenish-yellow tube and 5 erect or slightly spreading, white lobes. The 2 stamens and 1 style are hidden inside the corolla.

Flowering time: April–August

Habitat/range: Wet, muddy places; chaparral/oak-woodland and mixed conifer zones; up to 6,000'.

Comments: *Gratiola* is from the Latin word *gratia*, which means grace, favor, or pleasant, in reference to the supposed medicinal properties of some plants in the genus.

Similar plants: Very similar Clammy Hedge-hyssop (*Gratiola neglecta*) also grows in muddy places, but each of its flowers has 2 bracts at the base. The bracts look a lot like the sepals and are at least as long. Bractless Hedge-hyssop grows in the Ackerson Meadow area, and both plants have been reported in the Hetch Hetchy area.

GAPING PENSTEMON
Keckiella breviflora var. *glabrisepala*
Plantain family (Plantaginaceae)

Description: Gaping Penstemon is a common shrub, 1½–6½' tall, with many ascending to erect, hairless stems that have a waxy, powdery coating. Its opposite, hairless, lanceolate leaves are ½–2" long, are nearly sessile, and sometimes have tiny teeth along the margins. The flowers grow in panicles, and they have a 5-lobed calyx that is neither hairy nor glandular. The conspicuously 2-lipped, tubular corolla is ½–¾" long, is white to purplish with purple lines, and has glandular hairs on the outer surface. The 2-lobed upper corolla lip is erect and arches forward. The 3-lobed lower lip is reflexed and has spreading, deeply divided lobes. The flowers have 2 pairs of fertile stamens and a well-developed infertile stamen (staminode).

Flowering time: May–July

Habitat/range: Rocky slopes; chaparral/oak-woodland and mixed conifer zones; up to 6,000'.

Comments: *Keckiella* is for David D. Keck. He and Philip Munz co-authored *A California Flora*, which was published in 1959 and was recognized as the authority on California plants until publication of *The Jepson Manual* in 1993.

Similar plants: The park has one other variety of Gaping Penstemon, var. *breviflora*. Its glandular-hairy calyxes distinguish it from var. *glabrisepala*. The two varieties sometimes grow together.

HAIRY PURSLANE SPEEDWELL
Veronica peregrina ssp. *xalapensis*
Plantain family (Plantaginaceae)

Description: Hairy Purslane Speedwell is an easily overlooked annual with glandular-hairy herbage and an erect, sometimes branched stem that's 3–12" long. Its opposite, sessile or short-petioled leaves are up to 1" long, are narrowly oblong to spoon shaped, and sometimes have tiny teeth along the margins. The inflorescences are leafy-bracted racemes at the stem and branch ends. The tiny flowers have 4 lanceolate sepals, 2 stamens, and 1 style. The white, 4-lobed corolla is less than ¼" wide, and its lower lobe is noticeably smaller than the other 3 lobes. The fruit is a somewhat flattened, heart-shaped, glandular-hairy capsule.

Flowering time: April–August

Habitat/range: Moist places; chaparral/oak-woodland and mixed conifer zones; up to 4,300'.

Comments: The corollas of plants in the *Veronica* genus are described as having 4 lobes rather than 4 petals. The reason may be that the upper corolla lobe could be 2 petals that are completely fused. The upper lobe is often somewhat larger than the 2 lateral lobes, and the lower lobe is usually smaller than the other lobes. Whenever you find a plant that has a 4-lobed corolla with a lower lobe that's smaller than the other 3 lobes, chances are good that the plant is a member of the *Veronica* genus.

WHITE FALSE GILIA
Allophyllum integrifolium
Phlox family (Polemoniaceae)

Description: This annual is widespread in the park's middle elevations. Its erect, sometimes branched stem is 2–10" long and is glandular-hairy. Its alternate leaves are often crowded toward the top of the stem. The lower leaves are oblong to lanceolate and are sometimes irregularly lobed. The deeply 3-lobed upper leaves have a terminal lobe that's larger than the lateral lobes. The flowers, which grow mostly in pairs, have 5 anthers and a white or blue-tinged, trumpet-shaped corolla that's about ⅜" long and has 5 lanceolate lobes.

Flowering time: June–August

Habitat/range: Open, rocky and sandy places; mixed conifer and montane zones; 3,900–8,000'.

Similar plants: Variable-leaved Collomia (*Collomia heterophylla*) **[inset]** has been reported in the Hodgdon Meadow area and around El Portal. Its trumpet-shaped corolla can be white or pink, and it has highly variable leaves. Its lower leaves are often deeply pinnately lobed, often with sharp, coarse teeth on the margins. Its upper leaves are typically toothed or lobed, but they are *not* deeply 3 lobed. The trumpet-shaped corollas of Staining Collomia (*Collomia tinctoria*) can be white, pink, or pale yellow, but its linear-lanceolate leaves are unlobed. It also grows in the mixed conifer and montane zones, but it's uncommon in the park, where it reaches the southern extent of its range.

FOOTHILL GLOBE GILIA
Gilia capitata ssp. *pedemontana*
Phlox family (Polemoniaceae)

Description: This annual has an ascending to erect, often branched stem that's 1–3' long and is either smooth or glandular. Its leaves are pinnately lobed once or twice into long, narrow segments. The lower leaves, which often form somewhat of a rosette, are divided into many segments, and the alternate stem leaves are smaller and have 3–5 segments. The inflorescences, at the stem or branch ends, are in dense, round heads, up to ⅞" wide, with many stalkless flowers. The densely white-woolly calyx has 5 lobes that gradually taper to a sharp tip and have concave sides toward the tip. The fused sepals **[inset]** have a reddish central rib and broad, colorless, membranous margins. The white to pale blue-violet, trumpet-shaped corolla is ¼–⁷⁄₁₆" long and has 5 spreading, oblong lobes. The corolla tube is mostly hidden inside the calyx, and the 5 stamens, with disk-shaped anthers, extend beyond the corolla.

Flowering time: April–July

Habitat/range: Dry, rocky places; chaparral/oak-woodland and mixed conifer zones; up to 6,500'.

Similar plants: The corollas of Mountain Globe Gilia (*Gilia capitata* ssp. *mediomontana*) are white to pale blue, are ³⁄₁₆–⁵⁄₁₆" long, and have linear rather than oblong lobes. Its calyx lobes don't have concave sides. In the park, both subspecies tend to have white rather than blue corollas.

HARKNESS' FLAXFLOWER
Leptosiphon harknessii (*Linanthus harknessii*)
Phlox family (Polemoniaceae)

Description: Harkness' Flaxflower is an easily overlooked annual. It has an erect, thread-like, hairless stem that's 2–6" long and is usually branched. Its leaves look like a whorl of linear leaves but are actually 2 opposite leaves that are deeply palmately divided into 3–5 thread-like, sometimes hairy segments that are ¼–⅝" long. The inflorescence is a solitary flower or a few flowers in a loose group. The tiny flowers are up to ⅛" long and grow on thread-like, elongated stalks. The green calyx has 5 narrow, pointed lobes with membranous margins. The funnel-shaped, 5-lobed, white or pale blue corolla sometimes just barely reaches out beyond the confines of the calyx. The 5 stamens have yellow anthers that are visible at the corolla throat.

Flowering time: July–August

Habitat/range: Open, sandy and gravelly flats; mixed conifer, montane, and subalpine zones; 3,500–10,000'.

Comments: Almost everything about Harkness' Flaxflower is tiny or thread-like, and the plant is probably more common in the park than records indicate. This plant and many of its relatives were previously in the *Linanthus* genus, which was split into two groups somewhat recently.

EVENING SNOW

Linanthus dichotomus ssp. *dichotomus*
Phlox family (Polemoniaceae)

Description: Evening Snow is a hairless annual with an erect, simple or branched, waxy stem that's 2–8" long. Its leaves look like a whorl of linear leaves but are actually 2 opposite leaves that are palmately divided into 3–7 linear segments, less than 1" long. The flowers, which grow in the forks of a branched inflorescence, are mostly closed during the day and unfurl in the late afternoon. The calyx is deeply divided into 5 linear, pointed segments that are connected by a broad, white membrane. The funnel-shaped, 5-lobed corolla, ⅝–1¼" long, is white and often has light purple shading along the margins on the lower surface.

Flowering time: April–June

Habitat/range: Dry areas; chaparral/oak-woodland and mixed conifer zones; up to 5,000'.

Comments: It's easy to overlook this plant unless you come across it toward the end of the day or in the morning. The flowers typically open in late afternoon, stay open throughout the night, and close the next morning. This behavior makes it less likely that we'll see them but more likely that they'll be seen by night-feeding moths. To attract the moths, the flowers give off a sweet scent that the moths can detect with their antennae. The white petals make the flowers visible in low light, and many plants usually grow somewhat close together in extensive areas.

GRANITE PRICKLY-PHLOX

Linanthus pungens (*Leptodactylon pungens*)
Phlox family (Polemoniaceae)

Description: This shrub is 4–14" tall, and it has glandular-hairy herbage and sprawling, branched stems that are up to 12" long. Its alternate leaves, up to ⅝" long, are palmately divided into 3–7 unequal, linear segments with needle-sharp tips. The flowers grow in clusters at the branch ends or solitary in upper leaf axils. They have a calyx with 5 sharp-tipped lobes and 6 stamens with yellow anthers. The narrowly funnel-shaped, white or pale pink corolla is up to 1" long and is often purplish below. The corolla has 5 spreading, overlapping lobes that sometimes have raggedy margins.

Flowering time: May–August

Habitat/range: Open, rocky areas; mixed conifer, montane, subalpine, and alpine zones; 4,000–12,400'.

Comments: Despite the sharp leaf lobe tips and some toxicity in the leaves, Granite Prickly-phlox is eaten by marmots, jackrabbits, pikas, and deer.

Similar plants: This plant looks a lot like plants in the *Phlox* genus, but its corolla lobes usually overlap at the base, giving the corolla a twisted look. Also, most of its leaves are alternate, and the leaves of plants in the *Phlox* genus are mostly opposite. One way to find out for sure is to touch the tip of a leaf lobe. If your experiment is painful, the plant is Granite Prickly-phlox.

MOUNTAIN NAVARRETIA
Navarretia divaricata ssp. *divaricata*
Phlox family (Polemoniaceae)

Description: Mountain Navarretia is an annual with erect to spreading, hairy or glandular-hairy stems that are up to 4" long and sometimes have spreading branches just below the inflorescence. Its alternate, thread-like leaves are ⅜–¾" long and sometimes have 1 or 2 pairs of thread-like lobes. The inflorescences have tiny flowers, less than ¼" long, that are nestled in a cluster of dense, spiny, palmately 3- to 5-lobed bracts with long, white hairs toward the base. The calyx has 5 unequal, needle-like lobes. The throat of the funnel-shaped corolla is yellowish green, and the 5 white corolla lobes are sometimes pink tipped. The 6 stamens have white anthers that do not extend well beyond the throat of the corolla.

Flowering time: June–August

Habitat/range: Dry flats and slopes; mixed conifer, montane, and subalpine zones; 3,900–8,500'.

Similar plants: Needle-leaved Navarretia (*N. intertexta*) **[inset]** has been reported from Big Meadow and the Mather area. It looks a lot like Mountain Navarretia, but it's easily distinguished by the fact that its stamens have yellow anthers that extend well beyond the corolla throat. *N. divaricata* ssp. *vividior* was reported north of Hetch Hetchy in 1941. Its corolla throat is purple rather than yellowish green, and its anthers do not extend beyond the corolla throat.

CONDENSED PHLOX
Phlox condensata
Phlox family (Polemoniaceae)

Description: This common, tightly cushion-like plant has such crowded flowers that they often conceal the rest of the plant. Its narrow, glandular-hairy, overlapping leaves, less than ¼" long, are concave on the upper surface and have 2 parallel grooves on the lower surface. The flowers, which grow solitary at the branch ends, have a glandular-hairy calyx. The trumpet-shaped corolla, up to ⅜" long, has 5 spreading lobes that are usually white but can be pale pink or lavender.

Flowering time: July–August

Habitat/range: Dry, gravelly or rocky slopes and flats; subalpine and alpine zones; 9,000–12,300'.

Similar plants: Cushion Phlox (*P. pulvinata*) and Spreading Phlox (*P. diffusa*) are similar cushion-like plants, but they don't form dense, tight cushions. Cushion Phlox is uncommon in the park. It also has glandular-hairy calyxes, but its leaves are mostly more than ¼" long and their upper surface is flat rather than concave. Spreading Phlox is common and widespread in the park. Its calyxes are not glandular, though they are hairy. Granite Prickly-phlox (*Linanthus pungens*) can be somewhat mat-forming, but unlike the *Phlox* species, the tips of its leaves are positively painful to touch. All of these matted plants can have white corollas, but they can also be various shades of pale pink, pale lavender, or pale blue.

POKE KNOTWEED

Aconogonon phytolaccifolium
(*Polygonum phytolaccifolium*)
Buckwheat family (Polygonaceae)

Description: Poke Knotweed is a robust perennial
with an erect, stout stem that's 2–6½' tall and
is sometimes hairy. Its alternate, short-petioled
leaves are 2–7" long, lanceolate to lance-ovate,
and hairless or densely hairy. The leaves are usually pointed at the tip and are rounded at the base.
The sheaths at the leaf bases are usually brown.
The inflorescences grow mostly at the stem and
branch ends, but sometimes from leaf axils. The
tiny flowers, which are in loose, mostly leafless,
panicle-like clusters, have 8 stamens and 3 styles.
The 5 rounded, white or greenish-white tepals are
unequal, the outer 2 smaller than the inner 3. The
fruit is a shiny yellow-brown, egg-shaped achene.

Flowering time: June–September

Habitat/range: Streambanks, moist meadows, and
springs; mixed conifer, montane, and subalpine
zones; 4,000–9,000'.

Similar plants: Triangular-fruited Dock (*Rumex
triangulivalvis*) and California Willow Dock (*Rumex
californicus*) are similar, robust plants, but their
stems are reclining to ascending (rather than
erect), their leaves are tapered at the base, and
their flowers have 6 tepals that turn red with age.
Their fruit is red or dark brownish red rather than
yellow brown.

WESTERN BISTORT

Bistorta bistortoides (*Polygonum bistortoides*)
Buckwheat family (Polygonaceae)

Description: This perennial is one of the most
common and most recognizable meadow dwellers
in the park. It has 1–3 erect, unbranched stems
that are 7–28" tall. Its mostly basal leaves are
3–15" long and are elliptic, lance-oblong, or oblanceolate with a rounded or tapered base. The basal
leaves have a long petiole, and the 2–4 alternate
stem leaves are petioled below, sessile above,
and gradually reduced upward. The inflorescence
is a dense, short-cylindric to egg-shaped, terminal
raceme. The small, bell-shaped flowers have 5
white to pale pink tepals that are fused at the base
and 5–8 stamens with white anthers that extend
beyond the tepals and give the flowers a frilly look.

Flowering time: June–August

Habitat/range: Wet or dry meadows and streambanks; mixed conifer, montane, and subalpine
zones; 3,900–10,000'.

Comments: This plant has an interesting aroma
and is sometimes called Dirty Socks.

Similar Plants: Much less common Western
False-asphodel (*Triantha occidentalis*), in the
false-asphodel family (Tofieldiaceae), has a similar
overall appearance. It also has tight clusters of
white flowers and it grows in similar habitats at
similar elevations, but its flowers have 6 tepals
and their stamens have bright yellow anthers.

LOBB'S BUCKWHEAT
Eriogonum lobbii
Buckwheat family (Polygonaceae)

Description: Lobb's Buckwheat is a distinctive, sometimes mat-forming perennial with flowering stems that are 2–7" long and typically lie flat against the ground. Its leaves are ¾–3" long and form a tufted rosette at the base of the plant. The round leaf blades are either densely woolly-hairy on both surfaces or are hairless on the upper surface. The blades are sometimes rusty colored, and they narrow abruptly to a well-defined petiole. The dense inflorescences are often spherical or are sometimes umbel-like. The woolly, turban- to bell-shaped involucres (the structures from which the flowers grow) have 6–10 lobe-like, reflexed teeth. The flowers have 6 white to cream-colored tepals in 2 series. The tepals have a green midrib that gives the flowers a greenish tint, and they become red as they age. The 9 stamens extend beyond the tepals.

Flowering time: June–August

Habitat/range: Dry, sandy or gravelly places; montane, subalpine, and alpine zones; 7,500–12,300'.

Comments: Plants in the *Eriogonum* genus can be difficult to identify, but Lobb's Buckwheat, with its sprawling flowering stems and round leaf blades, is easily recognizable, which contributes to its popularity. Like many plants in the *Eriogonum* genus, its flowers start out white or cream and become red with age.

NAKED BUCKWHEAT
Eriogonum nudum var. *nudum*
Buckwheat family (Polygonaceae)

Description: This common perennial is 11–40" tall and has 1 or a few slender, hairless, branched stems. Its petioled leaves, in a basal rosette, are hairless or thinly hairy on top and gray-woolly-hairy beneath. The oblong to elliptic blades are up to 2" long. The flower clusters **[inset]** in the branched inflorescences have 2–5 hairless or sparsely hairy involucres. The small flowers have 6 hairless, white or yellowish (sometimes pinkish) tepals in 2 series.

Flowering time: June–October

Habitat/range: Dry, gravelly or sandy places; chaparral/oak-woodland, mixed conifer, and montane zones; up to 7,600'.

Similar plants: Naked Buckwheat is one of the park's most common and widespread plants, and three varieties of the plant grow in the park. Var. *deductum*, which grows from the mixed conifer zone up into the subalpine zone, also has 1 or a few branched stems and branched inflorescences, but its leaf blades are no more than ⅞" long, and its flower clusters have only 1 (or sometimes 2) involucres. Var. *scapigerum*, which grows only in the subalpine and alpine zones, has an unbranched stem and a single terminal, head-like flower cluster with 3–6 crowded involucres, which makes the clusters dense and spherical. Its leaf blades are no more than ⅞" long.

OVAL-LEAVED BUCKWHEAT
Eriogonum ovalifolium var. *nivale*
Buckwheat family (Polygonaceae)

Description: This common perennial forms dense, matted cushions that are sometimes over 1' wide. Its ascending to erect flowering stems are up to 4" long and are woolly-hairy and often reddish. The long-petioled, usually erect leaves have a round blade that contracts abruptly where it meets the petiole. The slightly fleshy leaf blades are less than ⅜" wide and are covered on both sides with dense, white-woolly hairs. The roundness of the leaf blades is not readily apparent when the leaves are folded, which they usually are. The densely clustered inflorescences are nearly spherical and have 2–4 bell-shaped involucres (the structures from which the flowers grow). The small, hairless flowers have 6 white, cream, pink, or red tepals in 2 series, and the 9 stamens extend beyond the tepals.

Flowering time: July–August

Habitat/range: Dry, gravelly or sandy slopes and flats; subalpine and alpine zones; 8,000–13,200'.

Comments: This plant is common in the park's alpine fellfields and gravel flats, especially on the peaks and ridges near Tioga Pass.

Similar plants: Its densely matted cushions and round, persistently hairy leaf blades help distinguish Oval-leaved Buckwheat from the other buckwheat species that grow in the park.

REDDING'S SPURRY BUCKWHEAT
Eriogonum spergulinum var. *reddingianum*
Buckwheat family (Polygonaceae)

Description: This wispy annual has erect, hairless or glandular-hairy stems that are 3–16" tall. The stems are slender, but stiff, and are much-branched toward the top. The linear basal and stem leaves, up to 1¼" long, are bristly-hairy. The stem leaves, which are reduced in size upward, grow in whorls at the bases of the lowest branches and in sets of 2 or 3 at the bases of the upper branches. The calyx-like, turban-shaped involucres have 4 deep teeth and contain a solitary flower. The hairless to sparsely hairy flowers **[inset]** are less than ⅛" long and have 6 white tepals in 2 series. Each tepal has a greenish to reddish midrib.

Flowering time: June–August

Habitat/range: Dry, sandy or gravelly flats; mixed conifer, montane, and subalpine zones; 5,000–9,000'.

Comments: These plants are not showy individually, but they often grow in masses that can make large areas look like a misty white haze is hovering above the ground.

Similar plants: Spurry Buckwheat (*Eriogonum spergulinum* var. *spergulinum*), which is much less common in the park, has slightly larger, hairless flowers, at least some of which are more than ⅛" long.

BLACK BINDWEED
(non-native)
Fallopia convolvulus (*Polygonum convolvulus*)
Buckwheat family (Polygonaceae)

Description: Black Bindweed is a low annual with climbing or sprawling, twining stems that are 1½–3¼' long and are often branched toward the base. Its arrowhead-shaped leaves are 1¼–6" long, including the petiole. The blade is smooth on the top but sometimes rough to the touch below, and the petiole is shorter than the blade. The erect or spreading, spike-like inflorescences grow from the leaf axils. The white or greenish perianth, less than ¼" long, has 5 tepals in 2 series, and the outer 3 are somewhat indistinctly keeled. The flowers, which are sometimes pinkish at the base, have 8 stamens and 3 styles that are fused toward the tips. The fruit is a 3-angled, black achene.

Flowering time: May–October

Habitat/range: Meadows and disturbed areas; chaparral/oak-woodland and mixed conifer zones; up to 4,100'.

Comments: Native to Eurasia, this plant has become naturalized throughout much of North America and has become established in meadows and around developments in Yosemite Valley. The genus was named for Italian botanist Gabriello Fallopio (1523–1562), who was also a student of anatomy and is considered to be one of the founders of modern anatomy. The plant probably got its common name from its black fruit.

COMMON KNOTWEED
(non-native)
Polygonum aviculare ssp. *depressum*
(*P. arenastrum*)
Buckwheat family (Polygonaceae)

Description: This somewhat mat-forming annual or short-lived perennial is believed to be native to Europe. It has 3–15 much-branched stems that are sprawling to ascending. Its short-petioled leaves are ¼–2¼" long and are narrowly elliptic to oblanceolate. Its tiny flowers **[inset]** grow in groups of 1–6 in leaf axils and are closed to only half open. The perianth tube is often more than half as long as the entire perianth. The flowers have 5–7 stamens and 5 white tepals that are sometimes pink tinged.

Flowering time: May–November

Habitat/range: Disturbed places; chaparral/oak-woodland and mixed conifer zones; up to 4,600'.

Similar plants: Quite similar *Polygonum aviculare* ssp. *aviculare* may also grow in the park, but would be much less common. It has ascending to erect stems, its perianth tube is less than 40% as long as the entire perianth, and it's less trample resistant. Somewhat similar Marshpepper (*Persicaria hydropiper*, previously *Polygonum hydropiper*) is a European native that's been reported a few times in the park. It has ascending to erect stems. Its lanceolate to diamond-shaped leaves, 1⅝–4¼" long, are longer than the leaves of both *Polygonum aviculare* subspecies, and it grows along lakes, ponds, and rivers.

83

DOUGLAS' KNOTWEED
Polygonum douglasii
Buckwheat family (Polygonaceae)

Description: This common, slender annual has an erect stem, 2–30" tall, that's sharp-angled rather than round in cross section. Its alternate, short-petioled leaves, ½–2¼" long, are lance-linear to oblanceolate. The leaves are smaller upward, and the lower leaves often wither early. The flowers grow 1–3 on curved stalks from the leaf axils and at the stem or branch ends, and at least the lower buds are always nodding. The tiny flowers have 8 stamens. The perianth, which is sometimes only partially open, has 5 white or greenish-white tepals that are sometimes pink at the base.

Flowering time: June–October

Habitat/range: Meadow borders and dry, grassy areas; mixed conifer, montane, subalpine, and alpine zones; 3,900–10,500'.

Similar plants: Three similar knotweeds in the park have ascending or erect (rather than nodding) flower buds. Sawatch Knotweed (*P. sawatchense ssp. sawatchense*, previously *P. douglasii ssp. johnstonii*) **[left inset]** has 1–4 semi-open flowers in the leaf axils. The mostly open flowers of California Knotweed (*P. californicum*) **[right inset]** are solitary in leaf axils and are often surrounded by prominent bristles. Like Douglas' Knotweed, Sawatch and California Knotweed have sharp-angled stems. Yellow Knotweed (*P. ramosissimum*) has a *round* stem with conspicuous ribs and has closed flowers.

SHASTA KNOTWEED
Polygonum shastense
Buckwheat family (Polygonaceae)

Description: Shasta Knotweed is a small, sprawling to partially upright shrub with gnarled, brown, profusely branched stems that are up to 16" long. The stems are tough and scaly, but flexible. The hairless, mostly sessile, somewhat leathery leaves are up to 1" long, are lanceolate to elliptic, and are often slightly rolled under along the margins. The leaves have 2 parallel veins on the upper surface and are at least slightly folded lengthwise. The small, semi-open to open flowers grow in clusters of 2–6 from the upper leaf axils. The perianth has 5 white or pinkish, somewhat overlapping tepals with a gray or greenish midvein. The flowers have 8 stamens and a 3-lobed style. The small fruit is a 3-angled, shiny brown achene.

Flowering time: July–September

Habitat/range: Rocky, gravelly slopes and flats; subalpine and alpine zones; 8,500–11,000'.

Comments: This is the only shrubby *Polygonum* species in the park and is easy to identify. It grows on Mount Shasta and was named after the mountain, but it's more common in the Sierra Nevada.

PYGMY-FLOWER ROCK-JASMINE
Androsace septentrionalis
Primrose family (Primulaceae)

Description: This small annual or biennial grows up to 2½" tall, and its herbage usually turns reddish by the time the flowers are in bloom. Its slightly hairy, narrowly lanceolate leaves are ¼–¾" long, form a dense basal rosette, and are sometimes toothed. Several erect to spreading, leafless flower stalks emerge from the center of the leaf rosette. An umbel, with several bracts at its base, grows at the end of each stalk. The rays of the umbel can be almost as long as the flower stalks, and each ray ends with a single tiny flower, less than ¼" long. The calyx forms a conspicuous cup with 5 triangular lobes, and the white, trumpet-shaped corolla has 5 flaring, slightly notched lobes and a pale yellow throat. The flower tube is mostly hidden inside the calyx.

Flowering time: July–August

Habitat/range: Dry, rocky places; alpine zone; 10,900–12,950'.

Comments: Also called Fairy Candelabra, this small, shallow-rooted alpine plant, with its jasmine-scented flowers, emerges as soon as the snow melts and finishes its life cycle before the dry summer weather can wither its delicate foliage. To prevent self-pollination, a single flower's anthers and stigma are at different levels in the corolla tube, with the stamens considerably longer than the style or vice versa.

RED BANEBERRY
Actaea rubra
Buttercup family (Ranunculaceae)

Description: Red Baneberry is a perennial with 1 to several ascending to erect, sparsely hairy, branched stems that are up to 3' long. The plant has alternate stem leaves and no basal leaves. The 1–4 lower leaves are up to 15" long, including the long petiole, and are divided 2 or 3 times into parts of 3. The thin, lanceolate to ovate leaflets are 1–3½" long and are deeply cleft to irregularly toothed. The inflorescence is a dense, bottlebrush-like raceme. The small flowers have 3–5 whitish-green, roundish, petal-like sepals that fall away early and 4–10 white, obovate or spatula-shaped petals with a distinct claw. Each flower has many showy, white stamens and a 2-lobed stigma. The fruit is a shiny red or white berry.

Flowering time: May–August

Habitat/range: Moist, open or shaded places in deep soil; mixed conifer zone; 3,000–6,500'.

Comments: All parts of this plant are considered poisonous, causing nausea, vomiting, and dizziness if eaten. The toxins are believed to have a sedative effect on cardiac muscle tissue, which could cause cardiac arrest. Red Baneberry was considered sacred by some northern Native American tribes. They used the plant, with utmost caution, to treat coughs and colds when nothing else seemed to work.

WESTERN PASQUEFLOWER
Anemone occidentalis
Buttercup family (Ranunculaceae)

Description: This perennial has 1 to several stems that are 4–25" long and are silky-hairy when young. The silky-hairy, long-petioled basal leaves are 3-parted, and the 3 parts are pinnately dissected once or twice into narrowly linear, pointed segments. The flower stalks have a whorl of 3 short-petioled, leaf-like bracts that are similar to the basal leaves and are sometimes far beneath a solitary flower. The flowers, which have no petals, have 5–7 white, ovate to obovate, petal-like sepals that are ⅜–¾" wide and are sometimes purple tinged below. The sepals fade and wither early but remain at the base of the fruiting body. Each flower has 150–200 stamens and many styles. The styles become elongated and feathery-silky in fruit, forming a fluffy sphere **[inset]**.

Flowering time: June–July

Habitat/range: Open, rocky slopes; subalpine zone; 9,000–9,700'.

Comments: This showy plant grows only in a few out-of-the-way locations in the park, such as Upper Merced Pass Lake and Red Top.

Similar plants: Quite similar Drummond's Anemone (*Anemone drummondii*) has been found in Virginia Canyon near the park's northeastern boundary. Its sepals are smaller, ¼–⅜" wide, and its mature fruit have no elongated, feathery styles.

SIERRA COLUMBINE
Aquilegia pubescens
Buttercup family (Ranunculaceae)

Description: Sierra Columbine is an elegant perennial with 1 to several ascending to erect stems that are 8–20" long. Its herbage is covered throughout with tiny, short hairs. The long-petioled basal leaves and lower stem leaves are once or twice divided into 3 deeply cleft to scalloped leaflets. The showy, more or less erect flowers, up to 2¼" long, have 5 spreading, petal-like sepals that are white to pale yellow or pink and have pointed tips. The 5 petals have a long, often curving, white to pale yellow or pink nectar tube and an oblong, cream or yellow lobe. The flowers have 12–21 stamens that extend slightly beyond the corolla.

Flowering time: July–August

Habitat/range: Open, generally rocky slopes; subalpine and alpine zones; 9,200–12,200'.

Comments: Sierra Columbine has flowers that attract nocturnal moths. The moths can detect the pale flowers in low light and have a long proboscis that reaches the nectar at the end of the spurs. The red flowers of Crimson Columbine (*Aquilegia formosa*) are primarily pollinated by hummingbirds. Hummingbirds sometimes feed on the nectar of Sierra Columbine, and moths sometimes feed on the nectar of Crimson Columbine. When cross-pollination occurs, the plants produce offspring that have characteristics of both species.

WESTERN VIRGIN'S BOWER
Clematis ligusticifolia
Buttercup family (Ranunculaceae)

Description: This woody, climbing vine has stems that are up to 20' long. Its leaves are once pinnately divided into 5 leaflets or twice pinnately divided into up to 15 leaflets. The ovate to lanceolate leaflets are coarsely toothed or have 2 or 3 irregular lobes, and the largest leaflet is up to 3½" long. The leaf petiole and shaft have tendril-like capabilities that they use to attach to other objects. The inflorescences grow from leaf axils and have 7 to many crowded flowers without petals. The 4 white to cream, petal-like sepals, ¼–⅜" long, are variously shaped and are hairy on both surfaces. The flowers have many stamens and pistils and often have several infertile, white, petal-like, flat stamens that are narrow toward the base and slightly enlarged toward the tip. The styles become elongated and feathery-silky in fruit, forming a fluffy sphere.

Flowering time: May–August

Habitat/range: Along streams and in other wet places; chaparral/oak-woodland and mixed conifer zones; up to 4,000'.

Similar plants: This vine grows in the Wawona area. Chaparral Clematis (*Clematis lasiantha*) is similar and has been collected within the park in the El Portal area. Its leaves have only 3–5 leaflets, its inflorescences usually have only 1 or 2 flowers, and it grows in drier areas, often draping over other vegetation and reaching impressive heights.

MARSH MARIGOLD
Caltha leptosepala
Buttercup family (Ranunculaceae)

Description: Marsh Marigold is a hairless perennial with 1 to several erect stems that are 3–19" long, are green to purple, and sometimes have a solitary stem leaf. Its fleshy, long-petioled basal leaves have round to kidney-shaped, net-veined blades that are ¾–5" wide and often have toothed or scalloped margins. Usually just 1 flower grows at the end of each stem, but the stems can have 1–4 flowers. The 5–12 white to cream, petal-like sepals are up to ¾" long, are oblong to elliptic, and are sometimes blue tinged on the back. The showy flowers have 10–40 yellow stamens, 5 or more pistils, and no petals.

Flowering time: May–July

Habitat/range: Marshes, pond margins, wet meadows, and streambanks; mixed conifer, montane, and subalpine zones; 4,500–10,500'.

Comments: These common plants often grow in profusion in wet meadows. Native Americans cooked and ate the flower buds, leaves, and roots.

Similar plants: Northern Grass-of-Parnassus (*Parnassia palustris*) in the grass-of-Parnassus family (Parnassiaceae) is less common. It has somewhat similar flowers and leaves and it also grows in wet places, but its flowers have 5 white petals and its leaves have parallel veins.

HANSEN'S LARKSPUR

Delphinium hansenii ssp. *hansenii*
Buttercup family (Ranunculaceae)

Description: Hansen's Larkspur is a perennial with a stout, erect stem that's 9"–5½' tall. Its basal leaves usually wither early. The alternate, petioled stem leaves are deeply palmately cleft into 3–18 sections with narrow lobes. The inflorescence has many crowded flowers with 5 showy, petal-like sepals that are variable in color but are typically white and sometimes have green, pink, or purple spots. The spur and the back of the upper sepal are often lavender, purplish, or pink **[inset]**. The 4 small petals are usually white. The lower 2 petals are notched, are sparsely to densely hairy, and are sometimes lifted, exposing the stamens. The spur of the upper sepal contains the 2 nectar spurs of the upper petals.

Flowering time: April–July

Habitat/range: Dry, rocky places and open grasslands; chaparral/oak-woodland and mixed conifer zones; up to 5,000'.

Similar plants: Seven larkspur species grow in the park. Hansen's Larkspur and Red Larkspur (*Delphinium nudicaule*) are the only two that are positively distinctive. There are two blue-flowered species that are 2–5' tall and are fairly easy to distinguish from each other, and there are three smaller, blue-flowered species, less than 20" tall, that are often difficult to impossible to distinguish from each other.

WATER BUTTERCUP

Ranunculus aquatilis var. *diffusus*
(*Ranunculus aquatilis* var. *capillaceus*)
Buttercup family (Ranunculaceae)

Description: This aquatic, mostly hairless perennial has underwater stems that are 8–24" long and often grow in tangled masses. Most of its leaves are submersed. The alternate leaves are round to fan shaped in outline and are divided into long, thread-like segments. The flowers, which are also mostly submersed, grow solitary on long, leafless stalks. They have 5 rounded, green sepals and 5 white, clawed petals that are up to ¼" long and are usually yellow at the base. Each flower **[inset]** has numerous yellow stamens and numerous styles.

Flowering time: April–July

Habitat/range: Streams, ponds, and river edges; mixed conifer and montane zones; 3,900–7,500'.

Comments: *Ranunculus* was derived from the Latin word for little frog, in reference to the wet habitat of many buttercup species.

Similar plants: The only other plant you're likely to confuse this plant with is its close relative *Ranunculus aquatilis* var. *aquatilis* (previously *Ranunculus aquatilis* var. *hispidulus*). It has similar flowers and submersed, thread-like leaves, but it also has completely different floating leaves with a kidney-shaped blade that's divided into 3–5 segments.

WATERFALL BUTTERCUP

Ranunculus hystriculus (*Kumlienia hystricula*)
Buttercup family (Ranunculaceae)

Description: Waterfall Buttercup is a charming, hairless perennial with erect, leafless flowering stems that are 5–16" long and have 1 or 2 flowers. The blades of the long-petioled basal leaves are semicircular or kidney shaped in outline, and they have 5–7 shallow lobes that have shallow lobes of their own. The flowers have 5–9 (though usually 5) showy, petal-like, deciduous, white sepals that are ¼–⅜" long. The 5–12 somewhat inconspicuous, green to yellow-green petals are cupped around many cream to white stamens and numerous tightly packed, green pistils.

Flowering time: February–June

Habitat/range: Wet places near waterfalls and streams; chaparral/oak-woodland and mixed conifer zones; up to 6,500'.

Comments: Waterfall Buttercups thrive in steep, rocky, wet habitats, like the rock faces along the Mist Trail.

Similar plants: Western Rue-anemone (*Enemion occidentale*, previously *Isopyrum occidentale*) **[inset]** has similar flowers with 5 white, petal-like sepals, but its leaves are divided into separate leaflets, its flowers have no petals, and it grows in drier habitats. The plant is also an early bloomer, is sometimes abundant in the El Portal area, and may grow in the park.

FEW-FLOWERED MEADOWRUE

Thalictrum sparsiflorum
Buttercup family (Ranunculaceae)

Description: This delicate-looking perennial has erect, leafy stems that are 1–4' tall and are branched toward the top. Its alternate leaves are 1½–12" long and are divided into 2–4 sets of 3 leaflets, which are cleft into 3 parts that are usually lobed. The lower leaves are longer than the upper leaves, and the leaf blades are often finely glandular-hairy. The small, bisexual flowers **[inset]**, which grow in open, erect or drooping panicles, have 4 or 5 white to greenish-white, petal-like sepals and a spray-like set of 10–20 flattened stamens that are widest where the anther is attached and taper gradually to the base. The pistils mature into 6–22 compressed, beaked achenes that are curved along the inner margin and straight along the outer margin.

Flowering time: July–August

Habitat/range: Streambanks and boggy meadows; mixed conifer, montane, and subalpine zones; 4,900–10,000'.

Similar plants: The leaves of this plant are almost identical to the leaves of Fendler's Meadowrue (*Thalictrum fendleri*) and the plants are similar in stature, but Fendler's Meadowrue has unisexual flowers with wind-pollinated, male and female flowers on separate plants. Before either species blooms, their leaves can easily be mistaken for the leaves of Crimson Columbine (*Aquilegia formosa*).

MOUNTAIN WHITETHORN

Ceanothus cordulatus
Buckthorn family (Rhamnaceae)

Description: This common, dense, evergreen shrub is 1–5' tall and is usually broader than it is tall. Its pale gray to gray-green, spreading branches have rigid, thorn-like twigs, and its young stems are usually yellow-green. Its alternate, 3-veined, petioled leaves are ½–1¼" long. The leaf blades are ovate to elliptic and are sometimes slightly hairy and minutely toothed. Small, white flowers grow from leaf axils in dense clusters that are ⅜–2" long. The 5 triangular sepals are fused at the base and are united with an urn-shaped hypanthium. Attached to the hypanthium are 5 spoon-shaped petals and 5 or 6 stamens. At the center of the flower, a fleshy, yellow nectary surrounds the 3-lobed, green ovary. The fruit is a 3-parted capsule.

Flowering time: May–July

Habitat/range: Dry, open, gravelly and rocky places; mixed conifer, montane, and subalpine zones; 4,000–9,000'.

Similar plants: Chaparral Whitethorn (*Ceanothus leucodermis*) is the only other white-flowered *Ceanothus* species in the park with rigid branches, thorny twigs, and alternate leaves. The shrub is 5–13' tall, has longer flower clusters (1¼–6" long), and has white or pale blue flowers. It grows in the chaparral/oak-woodland zone in the Merced River Canyon up into Yosemite Valley.

BUCKBRUSH

Ceanothus cuneatus var. *cuneatus*
Buckthorn family (Rhamnaceae)

Description: Buckbrush is an erect, mound-like, evergreen shrub, up to 10' tall, with rigid, spreading to ascending, grayish branches and gray-brown twigs. Its opposite leaves, ½–1¼" long, are thick and leathery and sometimes grow in small clusters. The leaf blade is elliptic to obovate and has a wedge-shaped base. The upper leaf surface is hairless and somewhat shiny, and the lower surface has fine, whitish hairs. The small, white (or pale blue) flowers are intoxicatingly fragrant, and they grow in umbel-like clusters from leaf axils and at the branch ends. The 5 triangular sepals are fused at the base and are united with an urn-shaped hypanthium. The 5 spoon-shaped petals and 5 or 6 stamens are attached to the hypanthium. The 3-lobed, green ovary is surrounded by a fleshy, yellowish to greenish nectary. The fruit is a capsule with 3 segments and 3 short horns near the top.

Flowering time: March–May

Habitat/range: Dry, sandy to rocky slopes and flats; chaparral/oak-woodland and mixed conifer zones; up to 6,500'.

Similar plants: Buckbrush is similar to several other *Ceanothus* species in the park, but it is the only erect, non-mat-forming *Ceanothus* species that has opposite rather than alternate leaves.

DEER BRUSH

Ceanothus integerrimus var. *macrothyrsus*
Buckthorn family (Rhamnaceae)

Description: Deer Brush is a common, deciduous shrub, up to 13' tall, that has ascending to erect stems and flexible, green twigs that are not thorn-like. Its thin, alternate, 3-veined leaves are ¾–2½" long, widely ovate to lanceolate, usually untoothed, and sometimes sparsely hairy. The upper surface of the leaf is dull green, and the lower surface is paler. The white or pale blue flowers grow in elongated clusters at the branch ends. The 5 triangular sepals are fused at the base and are united with an urn-shaped hypanthium. The 5 spoon-shaped petals and 5 or 6 stamens are attached to the hypanthium. The green ovary is surrounded by a fleshy, yellowish to greenish nectary, and the fruit is a 3-segmented capsule.

Flowering time: May–July

Habitat/range: Dry, open areas; chaparral/oak-woodland, mixed conifer, and montane zones; up to 7,400'.

Similar plants: Two other *Ceanothus* species in the park have alternate leaves, are not mat-forming, and have twigs that are not thorny. Little-leaved Ceanothus (*C. parvifolius*), which usually has vivid blue flowers, has smaller leaves (⅜–1" long). Snowbrush Ceanothus (*C. velutinus*) is known in the park only from Virginia Canyon. It has white flowers, and its shiny, broad, roundish leaves have tiny, gland-tipped teeth along their margins.

CHAMISE, GREASEWOOD

Adenostoma fasciculatum var. *fasciculatum*
Rose family (Rosaceae)

Description: This evergreen shrub grows up to 12' tall. It has resinous foliage, reddish twigs, and grayish-brown, shredding bark. Its ascending to erect, rigid, wand-like branches grow from a basal burl. The linear to awl-shaped, needle-like leaves are up to ½" long, grow in tight bundles all along the stems and branches, and become shiny and greasy, especially in warm weather. The small flowers are crowded along open, branched inflorescences at the branch ends. The fused calyx has 5 lobes, and the corolla has 5 small, white, round to widely obovate petals. The flowers have a single pistil and 15 stamens that are arranged in 5 groups of 3. The fruit is an achene that's enclosed by the hardened hypanthium.

Flowering time: May–June

Habitat/range: Dry slopes and ridges, often in rocky, nutrient-poor, barren soil; chaparral/oak-woodland zone; up to 4,000'.

Comments: Chamise has been collected just within the park's western boundary in the El Portal area and is common and widespread throughout the Sierra Nevada foothills and in the Coast Ranges. The shrub is a major component of chaparral communities and sometimes forms dense, pure stands. Like other chaparral plants, Chamise burns easily and recovers quickly after fires, sprouting from seeds and from its basal burl.

UTAH SERVICEBERRY
Amelanchier utahensis
Rose family (Rosaceae)

Description: This deciduous shrub, 1½–15' tall, has gray to reddish-brown bark, widely spreading branches, and white-hairy twigs. Its somewhat stiff, alternate leaves, ½–2" long, are roundish to oval, are slightly hairy, and have serrate teeth from the middle to the tip. The upper leaf surface is dull green, and the lower surface is paler. Clusters of 3–6 flowers grow at the branch tips. The showy flowers have a bell-shaped hypanthium, 5 hairy sepals, and 5 white, oval to obovate petals that are about ⅜" long and are often twisted. The flowers have 2–4 styles and about 15 stamens. The berry-like, purplish-black fruit is edible.

Flowering time: April–June

Habitat/range: Open, rocky slopes and streambanks; mixed conifer, montane, and subalpine zones; 3,900–9,000'.

Comments: Native Americans highly prized the berries. They ate them fresh, but they also dried them and added them to soups and stews.

Similar plants: The twigs of less common Western Serviceberry (*Amelanchier alnifolia* var. *pumila*) are hairless, and its flowers have 4 or 5 styles. The leaves of somewhat similar Bitter Cherry (*Prunus emarginata*) and Sierra Plum (*Prunus subcordata*) are toothed along the entire margin rather than just above the middle.

MOUNTAIN MISERY, BEAR CLOVER
Chamaebatia foliolosa
Rose family (Rosaceae)

Description: Mountain Misery is a common, evergreen shrub, ½–2½' tall, that forms extensive colonies. It has numerous leafy branches and dark red-brown bark, and its glandular-hairy herbage is strongly aromatic. The feathery leaves, up to 4" long, are pinnately divided 2 or 3 times into tiny, elliptic segments. The flowers have a glandular-hairy hypanthium and 5 green, triangular, pointed sepals. The 5 white petals are ¼–⅜" long, grow opposite the sepals, and are often notched. Each flower has 35–65 yellow stamens and a single pistil. The fruit is a leathery, dark brown-black achene.

Flowering time: May–July

Habitat/range: Forest and woodland openings; mixed conifer zone; 3,000–6,500'.

Comments: The leaves of this plant are extraordinarily sticky and highly aromatic. Imagine trying to walk through knee-high shrubs with tangled branches that grab at your ankles and with foliage that makes your shoes and pant legs sticky and smelly, and you'll understand why the plant is called Mountain Misery. Some people say that they like the scent of the plants, but they might have a change of heart if they tried to hike through a patch of them. Miwok Indians call the plant Kit-kit-dizze. They make tea with the leaves and use the tea to alleviate the symptoms of colds and coughs.

SIERRAN WOOD-BEAUTY

Drymocallis lactea var. *lactea*
(*Potentilla glandulosa* ssp. *nevadensis*)
Rose family (Rosaceae)

Description: Sierran Wood-beauty is a common perennial with erect stems, 4–24" long, that are rarely glandular at the base, though they are often hairy. Its herbage is mostly smooth but can have some soft, spreading hairs. Its leaves **[lower left inset]** are 2–8" long and are pinnately divided into 7–9 obovate leaflets that are smaller toward the leaf base. The leaflets have simple teeth (rather than double teeth) along the margins. The relatively narrow, branched inflorescences are densely hairy and sometimes have a few glandular hairs. The flowers have 5 small bractlets, 5 lanceolate sepals, 20–25 yellow stamens, many pistils, and 5 cream-colored, spreading petals, ¼–½" long, that are longer than the sepals and sometimes hide them.

Flowering time: June–August

Habitat/range: More or less moist, mostly rocky places; mixed conifer, montane, subalpine, and alpine zones; 5,000–11,800'.

Similar plants: The park has five similar rose family plants with basal leaves that are pinnately divided into 5 or more leaflets with shallow, somewhat broad teeth. Four of them, including Sierran Wood-beauty, were previously treated as subspecies of *Potentilla glandulosa* and are now assigned to the *Drymocallis* genus. The other one is still in the *Potentilla* genus.

The petals of Sierran Wood-beauty are longer than its sepals, its leaflets are not double toothed, and its stem bases, though often somewhat hairy, are rarely glandular.

Yosemite Wood-beauty (*D. hansenii*, previously *Potentilla glandulosa ssp. hansenii*), which is common in the park, also has petals that are longer than its sepals, but its 7–9 leaflets are usually double toothed (meaning that some of the teeth are toothed themselves) and its stems are glandular-hairy at the base rather than simply hairy.

Two varieties of Sticky Wood-beauty, *D. glandulosa* var. *glandulosa* (previously *P. glandulosa ssp. glandulosa*) and *D. glandulosa* var. *reflexa* (previously *P. glandulosa ssp. reflexa*) are uncommon in the park. Their leaves have 5–7 leaflets. Unlike Sierran Wood-beauty and Yosemite Wood-beauty, they have flowers with petals that are shorter than or about the same length as the sepals. The two varieties can be distinguished from each other by the color and width of their petals. The petals of var. *glandulosa* **[upper right inset]** are cream to pale yellow and are at least ⅛" wide. The petals of var. *reflexa* **[lower right inset]** are bright yellow and are less than ⅛" wide.

Silverweed Cinquefoil (*Potentilla anserina ssp. anserina*) has 11–25 leaflets, and it's the only cinquefoil in the park with flower stalks that end in a solitary flower. The plant is known in Yosemite from only a single pothole west of Parsons Lodge in Tuolumne Meadows.

MOUNTAIN STRAWBERRY
Fragaria virginiana
Rose family (Rosaceae)

Description: This common perennial has runners that root at the nodes. Its stems are up to 4¾" long and end with 2 or 3 flowers. The thin, sometimes bluish-green leaves have long, hairy petioles and 3 leaflets, up to 2½" long, with 7–13 teeth from near the middle to the tip. The leaflets are mostly hairless above and somewhat hairy below, and the lateral leaflets have slightly asymmetric bases. The central leaflet is obovate, and its central tooth is shorter than the adjacent teeth. The silky-hairy hypanthium has 5 pointed bractlets at its base, and the 5 pointed sepals are broader than the bracts. The flowers have 5 white, round petals that are up to ⅜" long, 20–35 yellow stamens, and many pistils. The fragrant fruit are usually devoured by woodland creatures as soon as they become ripe.

Flowering time: May–July

Habitat/range: Meadows and forest openings; mixed conifer, montane, and subalpine zones; 3,900–10,500'.

Similar plants: Woodland Strawberry (*Fragaria vesca*) is also common in the park. Its leaflets have 12–21 teeth that begin below the middle and continue up to the tip. The central tooth of its central leaflet is not shorter than the adjacent teeth, and its leaflets are sparsely hairy on the upper surface.

CREAM BUSH, OCEAN SPRAY
Holodiscus discolor var. *discolor*
Rose family (Rosaceae)

Description: Cream Bush is a common shrub, 3–16' tall, with soft-hairy twigs and reddish, shredding bark that turns gray with age. Its ovate to elliptic leaves, up to 3¾" long, are truncate or rounded at the base. The leaf margins are toothed from the tip to below the middle, and at least some of the teeth have teeth of their own (toothed teeth). The upper leaf surface is sparsely hairy, the lower surface is densely hairy, and both surfaces have conspicuous veins. The hairy inflorescences, at the branch ends, can be up to 10" long and up to 10" wide, and they have numerous densely clustered flowers. The small flowers have a saucer-shaped hypanthium, 5 white or cream-colored, roundish petals, and 5 narrower sepals that are also white or cream colored. Each flower has 5 pistils and 15–20 stamens that are longer than the sepals.

Flowering time: June–August

Habitat/range: Moist woodland edges and rocky slopes; mixed conifer, montane, and subalpine zones; 3,900–10,000'.

Similar plants: Quite similar Small-leaved Cream Bush (*H. discolor* var. *microphyllus*, previously H. microphyllus) is also common in the park. Its leaves are wedge shaped at the base. The leaf margins are toothed mainly toward the tip, and the teeth do not have teeth of their own.

DUSKY HORKELIA

Horkelia fusca var. *parviflora*
Rose family (Rosaceae)

Description: Dusky Horkelia is a common perennial with ascending to erect, hairy stems that are
4–24" long. Its densely clustered, glandular-hairy
basal leaves, 1½–6" long, are pinnately divided
into 4–8 pairs of well-separated leaflets. The fan-
shaped to round leaflets have 5–7 lobes or teeth.
The alternate stem leaves become smaller upward.
The sometimes branched inflorescences are more
or less dense clusters of 5–20 flowers **[upper
inset]**. The hypanthium has 5 linear bractlets at its
base. The flowers have 5 lanceolate, often reddish
sepals, 10 stamens, and 10–20 pistils. The 5 white
petals, less than ¼" long, are narrowly wedge
shaped and are sometimes slightly notched.

Flowering time: June–August

Habitat/range: Dry meadow edges and forest
openings; mixed conifer, montane, subalpine, and
alpine zones; 3,900–11,000'.

Similar plants: Three-toothed Horkelia (*Horkelia
tridentata* var. *tridentata*) is less common in the
park and grows only in the mixed conifer zone. Its
flowers are similar, but its leaves **[lower inset]**
have only 2–5 pairs of leaflets and each leaflet has
2 or 3 lobes or teeth at the tip. Yosemite Mousetail
(*Ivesia unguiculata*) has similar leaves and flowers,
but its leaflets are divided all the way to the base
rather than just being toothed.

SIERRA MOUSETAIL

Ivesia santolinoides
Rose family (Rosaceae)

Description: This common, gravel-loving perennial
has densely clustered, rosetted basal leaves and
thin, sprawling to erect, usually reddish stems,
5–16" long, that are diffusely branched and mostly
hairless. Its mousetail-like, densely silvery-silky-
hairy basal leaves, 1½–4" long, are pinnately
divided into 60–80 pairs of much overlapping, tiny,
2- to 5-lobed segments. The stems have 1–3 much
smaller, alternate leaves. The open inflorescence
has widely spaced flowers on thread-like stalks.
The flowers have a shallow hypanthium with 5
tiny, green bractlets underneath. The 5 green,
lance-ovate sepals are shorter than the 5 white,
round petals, which are about ⅛" long. Each flower
has 15 stamens and a single pistil.

Flowering time: June–September

Habitat/range: Dry, gravelly slopes and flats;
mixed conifer, montane, subalpine, and alpine
zones; 6,000–11,000'.

Comments: This plant was first described from
specimens collected above Washburn Lake in
the late 1800s by Henry Nicholson Bolander
(1831–1897). Bolander did extensive plant collecting in the Yosemite region. *Ivesia* is for Eli
Ives (1779–1861), a Yale University professor who
founded the Medical Institution of Yale College
and was a pioneer in pediatric studies.

YOSEMITE MOUSETAIL
Ivesia unguiculata
Rose family (Rosaceae)

Description: Yosemite Mousetail is a rare perennial with ascending to erect, reddish stems, 6–13"
tall, and green, long-silvery-silky-hairy herbage. Its
numerous basal leaves, 2¾–6" long, are pinnately
divided into 15–25 pairs of crowded leaflets that
are divided to the base into 3–8 linear-oblong
lobes. The 3–6 alternate stem leaves are smaller.
The inflorescences **[inset]** are dense or loose clusters of 10 or fewer flowers growing at the stem
ends and from leaf axils. The shallow, purplish or
brownish hypanthium has 5 bractlets at its base.
The flowers have 5 narrowly triangular sepals,
10–15 stamens, and 3–9 pistils. The 5 white,
oblanceolate or wedge-shaped petals are about ⅛"
long and are distinctly narrowed at the base.

Flowering time: June–August

Habitat/range: Wet meadows; montane zone;
6,900–8,000'.

Comments: The species was first described from
plants collected at Westfall Meadows. The plant
also grows in Peregoy Meadow, in other meadows
along Glacier Point Road, and in the meadow
across from the Crane Flat service station.

Similar plants: The flower clusters of Dusky
Horkelia (*Horkelia fusca*) look a lot like Yosemite
Mousetail's flower clusters, but its leaflets are
toothed rather than divided all the way to the base.

PACIFIC NINEBARK
Physocarpus capitatus
Rose family (Rosaceae)

Description: Pacific Ninebark is an erect,
deciduous, multi-stemmed shrub, up to 8' tall, with
arching, spreading branches and pinkish young
twigs. Its shredding, curling bark forms brown and
gray stripes along the stems. The alternate, ovate
to more or less round, maple-like leaves, 2–5"
long, are palmately cleft into 3–5 toothed lobes
and sometimes have branched hairs on either or
both surfaces. The flowers grow in dense, round
clusters of 30–50 at the twig ends. They have 5
ovate sepals, 20–40 stamens, and 1–5 pistils with
thread-like styles and a head-like stigma. The 5
rounded, white, spreading petals are about ⅛"
long. The fruit is an inflated, bean-shaped pod
that's shiny red at first and turns brown with age.

Flowering time: May–July

Habitat/range: Streambanks and moist, north-
facing slopes; mixed conifer zone; 3,400–5,000'.

Comments: Pacific Ninebark got its common name
from the multiple layers of peeling bark on its
stems. The attractive shrub has been reported near
Happy Isles in Yosemite Valley, in the Wawona
area, and near Hodgdon Meadow. It grows easily
from seeds and cuttings and is often cultivated
as a garden ornamental. Native Americans made
arrow shafts from its branches and made cord and
rope from its stems.

BITTER CHERRY
Prunus emarginata
Rose family (Rosaceae)

Description: This common, deciduous shrub grows up to 20' tall in the park, often forms dense thickets, has no thorns, and has gray bark and reddish twigs. The alternate, mostly hairless leaves are ¾–3" long, are elliptic to narrowly obovate (rather than round), and are finely toothed along the entire margin. The somewhat flat-topped racemes have 6–12 flowers with 5 green sepals, many white stamens, and 1 pistil. The 5 round, white petals are up to 5⁄16" long. The small, red, berry-like fruit are bitter tasting.

Flowering time: April–June

Habitat/range: Rocky slopes and flats, roadsides; mixed conifer and montane zones; 4,900–8,200'.

Similar plants: Quite similar Sierra Plum (*Prunus subcordata*) has similar flowers **[upper inset]** and also has leaves that are toothed along the entire margin, but its branches are rigid and thorny, its leaves are distinctly roundish, and it has umbel-like flower clusters with 2–5 flowers. Utah Serviceberry (*Amelanchier utahensis*) is a shrub with similar white flowers, but its roundish leaves are toothed only above the middle. Toyon (*Heteromeles arbutifolia*) grows around El Portal and Wawona and has red, berry-like fruit. Its evergreen leaves also have teeth along the entire margin, but the leaves are stiff and leathery. Its similar, smaller flowers **[lower inset]** grow in clusters of 20–150.

WESTERN CHOKE-CHERRY
Prunus virginiana var. *demissa*
Rose family (Rosaceae)

Description: Western Choke-cherry is a deciduous shrub or small tree, up to 18' tall, that often forms dense thickets. It has long, flexible branches with smooth, gray-brown bark and hairy young twigs, and it has no thorns. Its alternate, oblanceolate to elliptic leaves are 1½–5" long and are finely serrated and prominently veined. The showy inflorescences are elongated, many-flowered clusters that grow at the branch ends. The flowers have a cup-shaped hypanthium, 1 pistil, 10–30 white stamens with yellow pollen, and 5 green, gland-toothed sepals. The 5 white, roundish petals are up to ¼" long. The red to black fruit are roundish and berry-like.

Flowering time: May–June

Habitat/range: Brushy, sometimes rocky slopes and flats and moist forest floor; mixed conifer and montane zones; 3,500–7,000'.

Comments: Western Choke-cherry's fruit have strong astringent properties that give them a bitter taste. However, with proper preparation, they make tasty jams, jellies, pies, and wine. Native Americans often dried the fruit and added them to stews and soups. They also added the dried fruit to mixes of other dried fruits and seeds that they used as trail food. Some Indian groups made a syrup from the fruit and used it to treat sore throats and coughs.

97

HIMALAYAN BLACKBERRY
(non-native)
Rubus armeniacus (*R. discolor*)
Rose family (Rosaceae)

Description: This robust, arching shrub, up to 8' tall, forms extensive, rounded mounds and has alternate leaves that are deciduous to semi-evergreen. The stout main stems are 5-angled, and the branches root at the tips. Its numerous, stout, sharply pointed prickles are straight or curved. The leaves on the main branches have blades that are palmately divided into 3 or 5 broad, dark green, coarsely toothed leaflets that are mostly hairless above and densely white-hairy below. Numerous flowers grow in large clusters. The flowers have 5 hairy, reflexed sepals, numerous stamens, and many pistils. The 5 white to pinkish, obovate petals are up to ⅝" long. The fruit is an edible blackberry.

Flowering time: April–July

Habitat/range: Disturbed areas; chaparral/oak-woodland and mixed conifer zones; up to 5,000'.

Comments: This Eurasian native is considered to be one of the greatest threats to the park's natural plant resources, and efforts are constantly being made to curtail its spread.

Similar plants: The park has three native *Rubus* shrubs with prickly branches and leaves that are palmately divided into mostly 3 leaflets. Unlike Himalayan Blackberry with its 5-angled main stems, their main stems are round in cross section.

CUT-LEAVED BLACKBERRY
(non-native)
Rubus laciniatus
Rose family (Rosaceae)

Description: This invasive shrub has woody, ascending or climbing, 5-angled stems, up to 10' long, with many stout, wide-based prickles that are usually strongly curved. Its alternate leaves are pinnately divided into 3–5 dark green, coarsely toothed, deeply dissected leaflets. The leaves are hairless on their upper surface and sparsely to densely hairy below. The inflorescence is a panicle-like cluster of 5–25 flowers, which have 5 prickly-hairy, leaf-like, reflexed sepals that are glandular and taper to a pointed tip. The 5 white or pinkish, obovate petals are about ½" long and usually have 3 lobes, and the flowers have many pistils and many stamens with thread-like filaments. The fruit is an edible blackberry.

Flowering time: April–July

Habitat/range: Disturbed areas; chaparral/oak-woodland and mixed conifer zones; up to 5,000'.

Comments: The fruit of this European cultivar provides food for wildlife, but the plants take over large areas, crowding out native vegetation. Like its noxious relative Himalayan Blackberry, Cut-leaved Blackberry is among the most invasive weeds in Yosemite, and the park is involved in ongoing efforts to control both species, using manual, mechanical, and targeted chemical methods.

WHITEBARK RASPBERRY
Rubus leucodermis
Rose family (Rosaceae)

Description: This common, deciduous shrub is 3½–8' tall and has erect, trailing or arching, unangled, prickly stems that are up to 7' long and have a smooth, waxy coating when they're young. Its conspicuously bicolored leaves are pinnately divided into 3 or 5 ovate to lanceolate, toothed leaflets, up to 3½" long, that are green above and densely white-hairy below. The flowers have 5 small, white petals, many stamens and pistils, and 5 sepals that spread outward when the flowers are in bloom. The fruit is an edible, red to purplish raspberry **[inset]**.

Flowering time: April–July

Habitat/range: Moist, often rocky areas; mixed conifer and montane zones; 3,000–7,500'.

Similar plants: Two other native *Rubus* species in the park have leaves with 3 or 5 leaflets and prickly stems that are round rather than angled. Both species are much less common in the park and are smaller than Whitebark Raspberry, usually less than 1' tall. The leaves of Wax-leaved Raspberry (*R. glaucifolius*) are also conspicuously bicolored, green above and white below, but its sepals are strongly reflexed when the flowers are in bloom. The leaves of California Blackberry (*R. ursinus*) are hairy and are paler on the lower surface, but they are not conspicuously bicolored. Its sepals spread outward when the flowers are in bloom.

THIMBLEBERRY
Rubus parviflorus
Rose family (Rosaceae)

Description: Thimbleberry is an erect, deciduous, shrubby perennial, 1½–6½' tall, that has no prickles or thorns. Its branches are hairless or have fine hairs with stalked glands. The leaf blades are 4–6" wide, are palmately 3 or 5 lobed, and have sharp teeth along the margins. The upper leaf surface is hairless, and the lower surface is sparsely hairy to densely gray-hairy. The leaf petioles are glandular-hairy. Open clusters of 3–7 flowers grow at the branch ends. The flowers have many stamens and pistils, a shallow hypanthium, and 5 glandular-hairy sepals that taper to a long, pointed tip. The 5 white petals are ½–1¼" long and are widely elliptic, obovate, or roundish. The delicate, red fruit is shaped like a thimble.

Flowering time: April–August

Habitat/range: Moist, partially shady places, especially woodland edges; mixed conifer and montane zones; 3,600–7,600'.

Comments: Thimbleberry's sweet fruit look a lot like raspberries. Because the fruit are too delicate to pack or ship well, the plant is rarely cultivated for commercial use. The fruit make excellent jam, which is sometimes sold as a local delicacy in areas where the plant grows abundantly.

BUTTONBUSH

Cephalanthus occidentalis
Madder family (Rubiaceae)

Description: This deciduous shrub or small tree, up to about 12' tall, has shiny young branches and older branches with brown to gray, furrowed bark. Its elliptic to ovate, petioled leaves, 2¾–8" long, grow in opposite pairs or in whorls of 3. The leaf blades are hairless above and are slightly hairy along the veins on the lower surface. The dense, ball-shaped flower clusters, up to 1⅜" wide, grow on long stalks at the branch ends. The small, fragrant, tubular flowers have a white calyx with 4 lobes, a white corolla with 4 lobes, and a conspicuously long style with a greenish-yellow stigma. The hard, dry, reddish-brown nutlets remain in rounded masses throughout the winter.

Flowering time: May–September

Habitat/range: Along streams and in marshy areas; chaparral/oak-woodland zone; up to 3,300'.

Comments: Buttonbush grows around El Portal and near the park boundary along the Tuolumne River below Hetch Hetchy reservoir, and it may grow inside the park.

Similar plants: Elk Clover (*Aralia californica*) in the ginseng (Araliaceae) family is a large perennial that grows along the trail to Poopenaut Valley near Hetch Hetchy. It has similar white, ball-shaped flower clusters, but its huge leaves are pinnately divided into large, egg-shaped leaflets.

CALIFORNIA MOUNTAIN ASH

Sorbus californica
Rose family (Rosaceae)

Description: California Mountain Ash is a deciduous shrub, up to about 12' tall, with multiple stems. The hairs in the leaf and leaflet axils and in the inflorescence are reddish brown. Its alternate leaves are pinnately divided into 7–11 hairless, oblong to elliptic leaflets, 1–1¾" long, that are usually finely sharp toothed. The leaflets are shiny green above and paler below. The small flowers grow in compact, somewhat flat-topped clusters of 25–120 on mostly hairless stalks that become red as the fruit develops. The flowers have 20 stamens, 3 or 4 styles, and 5 sepals. The 5 white petals are round and are less than ¼" long. The fruit are round and become bright red to red-orange at maturity.

Flowering time: May–June

Habitat/range: Moist places, often along streams, in sun or shade; mixed conifer, montane, and subalpine zones; 5,000–10,000'.

Comments: The leaves of this shrub turn reddish orange in autumn, contributing to the mosaic of fall colors in the mountains.

Similar plants: Less common Cascade Mountain Ash (*Sorbus scopulina*) has 7–15 leaflets that are up to 2½" long. The hairs in its leaf and leaflet axils and in its inflorescences are mostly whitish, and its flower stalks are sparsely to densely hairy.

COMMON BEDSTRAW
Galium aparine
Madder family (Rubiaceae)

Description: This common annual has sprawling stems, 4–40" long, that cling to other objects with small, hooked bristles. Its narrowly oblanceolate leaves, 1–2½" long, are in whorls of 6–8, and they have hooked bristles on the midrib and margins. The tiny flowers grow in clusters of 1–3 from the upper leaf axils. They have a white, 4-lobed corolla and no calyx. The fruit is a pair of bristly nutlets.

Flowering time: March–July

Habitat/range: Shady areas; chaparral/oak-woodland and mixed conifer zones; up to 6,000'.

Similar plants: Three other bedstraws in the park have leaves with at least 6 leaflets, flowers with 4 corolla lobes, and bristly nutlets. Sweet-scented Bedstraw (*G. triflorum*) is the only one with leaves that grow at an angle to the stem so that they're parallel to the ground. Mexican Bedstraw (*G. mexicanum* ssp. *asperulum*) and non-native Wall Bedstraw (*G. parisiense*), unlike Common Bedstraw and Sweet-scented Bedstraw, have side branches with 3 or more flowers. Mexican Bedstraw's leaves are ½–1" long. The leaves of Wall Bedstraw are less than ⅜" long and often bend upward at the tips. Non-native Carpetweed (*Mollugo verticil-lata*) **[inset]**, in the Molluginaceae family, has similar whorls of narrow leaves and small, white flowers, but its flowers have 5 petals. It grows in low-elevation disturbed areas.

TWIN-LEAF BEDSTRAW
Galium bifolium
Madder family (Rubiaceae)

Description: Twin-leaf Bedstraw is a hairless annual with ascending to erect, 4-angled stems that are 2–6" long and are sometimes branched. Its ascending to erect, lanceolate to narrowly elliptic leaves are ⅜–1" long and grow in whorls of 4, in 2 unequal pairs, on the lower stem. The uppermost leaves are usually opposite pairs. The tiny flowers usually grow solitary at the stem end and from leaf axils. The flowers have a white, usually 3-lobed corolla and no calyx. The fruit **[inset]** is a pair of nutlets with hooked bristles.

Flowering time: June–September

Habitat/range: Open conifer forest, meadows, and gravelly slopes; mixed conifer, montane, and subalpine zones; 6,000–10,500'.

Similar plants: Three-petaled Bedstraw (*Galium trifidum*) is the only other bedstraw in the park with a corolla that usually has 3 lobes. Its nutlets are smooth, and its much-branched, often tangled stems are straggling to ascending or tufted and matted. Two subspecies of the plant grow in the park. *G. trifidum* ssp. *columbianum* (previously var. *pacificum*) has straggling to ascending stems, and its leaves are mostly in whorls of 5 or 6. Much less common *G. trifidum* ssp. *subbiflorum* (previously var. *pusillum*) is a low, tufted, matted plant with leaves that are usually in whorls of 4. Both subspecies tend to grow in wet places.

NORTHERN BEDSTRAW
Galium boreale
Madder family (Rubiaceae)

Description: This fragrant, circumpolar perennial is 1–2' tall and has erect, leafy, branched stems that are 4-angled and mostly hairless. Though the plant looks somewhat shrubby, its stems are not woody at the base. The linear to narrowly lanceolate leaves are ½–1¼" long, grow in whorls of 4, and have somewhat hairy margins. The small, bisexual flowers grow in crowded, showy clusters at the branch ends. The flowers have a white, 4-lobed corolla, 4 stamens, 2 styles, and no calyx. The fruit is a pair of bristly nutlets.

Flowering time: June–August

Habitat/range: Damp meadows and roadside drainages; mixed conifer and montane zones; 4,000–6,900'.

Comments: Northern Bedstraw is easy to find along the south side of Ahwahnee Meadow when it's in bloom. The plant has also been reported in the Wawona area. Plants in the *Galium* genus are called bedstraw because species that have stems covered with stiff, hooked hairs have been used to stuff mattresses. The hooks on the stems catch onto the hooks of other stems and cling to them, which keeps the plants from becoming compacted.

Similar plants: Northern Bedstraw is the only bedstraw in the park that has showy clusters of many flowers.

SWEET-SCENTED BEDSTRAW
Galium triflorum
Madder family (Rubiaceae)

Description: Sweet-scented Bedstraw is a fragrant perennial with weak, ascending or sprawling, 4-angled stems that are 6–24" long and are mostly unbranched. Its thin, elliptic to ovate leaves, ¼–1½" long, grow in whorls of 6 and usually orient themselves parallel to the ground, which puts them at an angle to the stem. The leaves are often minutely rough-hairy along the margins and on the midrib. The bisexual flowers usually grow in loose clusters of 3 from the upper leaf axils. The small flowers have a 4-lobed, white to greenish corolla, 4 stamens, 2 styles, and no calyx. The fruit is a pair of densely hook-bristled nutlets.

Flowering time: May–July

Habitat/range: Damp, shady forest floor; mixed conifer and montane zones; 3,200–6,500'.

Comments: Sweet-scented Bedstraw is probably the most common bedstraw in the park's middle elevations. The plant's stems usually lie along the ground or crawl over nearby low vegetation, and its leaves position themselves so that they're parallel to the ground, which makes the plants both easy to identify and particularly appealing. *Galium* is from the Greek word for milk. The fact that some *Galium* species have been used to curdle milk for cheesemaking may be why the genus name was selected. The name *triflorum* refers to the fact that the flowers usually grow in groups of three.

FEATHERY FALSE SOLOMON'S SEAL

Maianthemum racemosum (*Smilacina racemosa*)
Butcher's-broom family (Ruscaceae)

Description: This fairly common perennial has an erect or arching, unbranched stem that's 1–3' long. Its alternate, sessile or clasping leaves are 2¾–8" long, are ovate to oblong-elliptic, and are sometimes finely hairy beneath. The inflorescence is a dense, sometimes zigzagged panicle with 20 or more flowers. The tiny flowers have 6 white, narrowly oblong tepals and a single style. The 6 white stamens are broad at the base and taper toward the tip. The fruit is a reddish berry.

Flowering time: April–June

Habitat/range: Moist woodland openings and streambanks; mixed conifer, montane, and subalpine zones; 3,900–10,300'.

Comments: Despite this plant's scientific name, its inflorescence is a panicle rather than a raceme. Its common name refers to the similarity of plants in the *Maianthemum* genus to the closely related "true" East Coast Solomon's Seal (*Polygonatum biflorum*), which has scars on its roots that resemble the ancient Hebrew seal of King Solomon.

Similar plants: Starry False Solomon's Seal (*Maianthemum stellatum*, previously *Smilacina stellata*) **[inset]** is less common in the park. It has 15 or fewer flowers in a simple raceme rather than a panicle (though the inflorescence is occasionally branched at the base).

ALPINE WILLOW

Salix petrophila (*S. arctica*)
Willow family (Salicaceae)

Description: Alpine Willow is a common, sprawling shrub. It forms mats that are up to 7' wide and less than 4" tall. Its leaves have an elliptic to obovate blade that's up to 1¾" long and is pale dull green on the upper surface. The leaves are long-soft-hairy when young, especially on the lower surface. Like all willows, the shrub is dioecious, which means that male and female flowers grow on separate plants. Its tiny flowers grow in crowded clusters called catkins. The male flowers, when mature, have many showy stamens with bright red anthers **[inset]**. The female flowers become fluffy white as the fruit opens and reveals the hairy-tufted seeds.

Flowering time: July–August

Habitat/range: Rocky slopes and flats; subalpine and alpine zones; 9,500–11,700'.

Similar plants: Snow Willow (*S. nivalis*, previously *S. reticulata* ssp. *nivalis*) and Tea-leaved Willow (*S. planifolia*) are two other low willow shrubs, less than 3½' tall, that grow in the subalpine and alpine zones. Unlike Alpine Willow, their leaves are shiny dark green on the upper surface. Snow Willow, which is rare in the park, is a mat-forming plant with leaves that are conspicuously net veined on the lower surface. Tea-leaved Willow, which is common in the park, doesn't form mats, and its leaves are not conspicuously net veined on the lower surface.

CALIFORNIA BUCKEYE
Aesculus californica
Soapberry family (Sapindaceae)

Description: California Buckeye is a deciduous shrub or tree, up to 40' tall. Its spreading branches give it a rounded shape. Its opposite leaves have petioles that are up to 5" long. The leaf blades are palmately divided into 5–7 oblong-lanceolate, finely toothed leaflets that are 2–6¾" long. The inflorescences are erect, elongated panicles with densely packed flowers. The flowers have a 2-lobed calyx that's often pink and 4 or 5 white to pale rose, unequal petals that are ½–¾" long. The 5–7 elongated stamens have orange anthers. The gray-green, fig-shaped, leathery fruit is 2–3" long and encloses a shiny amber-colored seed with a large, pale spot.

Flowering time: May–June

Habitat/range: Dry slopes and canyons; chaparral/oak-woodland zone; up to 5,500'.

Comments: This plant copes in its Mediterranean climate by growing leaves and flowers in the cooler, wetter months and going dormant during the hot, dry months of late summer. The plant is common in the El Portal area and has been reported in Yosemite Valley. Plants in the *Aesculus* genus have fragrant flowers that attract many kinds of insects, and they have seeds that resemble the large eyes of deer. Native Americans mashed the toxic seeds and put the mash in slow-moving or dammed-up streams to stupefy and capture fish.

LARGE BROOKFOAM
Boykinia major
Saxifrage family (Saxifragaceae)

Description: This stout perennial has fragrant foliage and erect stems that have rust-colored, glandular hairs and are 1½–3½' long. Its round to heart-shaped, 5- or 7-lobed basal leaves are 4–8" wide and have coarse, gland-tipped teeth and glandular-hairy petioles. The alternate stem leaves become smaller upward. The glandular-hairy, somewhat flat-topped inflorescences have many flowers, each with a bell-shaped, glandular-hairy hypanthium and a shiny yellow nectary at the center. The flowers have 5 triangular-lanceolate sepals with pointed tips, 5 stamens, and 1 pistil. The 5 white, elliptic to round, clawed petals are about ¼" long and are sometimes lobed **[inset]**.

Flowering time: June–August

Habitat/range: Streambanks; mixed conifer and montane zones; 3,900–7,100'.

Comments: Native Americans used the leaves and roots of this plant medicinally and sometimes put dried leaves under their caps to enjoy their pleasant fragrance.

Similar plants: Indian Rhubarb (*Darmera peltata*) has similar flower clusters and similar large leaves, and it also grows in and along streambanks in the mixed conifer zone. Its leaves grow much larger, up to 3' wide, and its flowers have 10 stamens and are pink in the center rather than yellow.

INDIAN RHUBARB

Darmera peltata
Saxifrage family (Saxifragaceae)

Description: Indian Rhubarb is a hardy perennial with erect, dark reddish flowering stalks, 1–5' tall, that are covered with stiff, brown hairs. The mostly hairless, roundish basal leaves have long petioles that attach to the lower leaf surface. The huge leaf blade, 1–3' wide, is cupped in the center and has 6–15 irregularly toothed lobes. The inflorescence is a roundish cluster of many flowers, each with 2 bright pink pistils and 10 white or pink stamens in the center. The flowers have 5 rounded to oblong, reflexed sepals and 5 white to pale pink, broadly elliptic to obovate petals that are about ¼" long.

Flowering time: April–July

Habitat/range: Streambanks and streambeds, often in water; mixed conifer zone; 3,900–6,500'.

Comments: The tall flowering stalks of Indian Rhubarb emerge from the rocks and gravel along streams and rivers before its gigantic leaves put in an appearance. The plants are often partially submerged in swift, rushing currents, but the stout stalks withstand the flow.

Similar plants: Large Brookfoam (*Boykinia major*) looks somewhat similar and also grows along streambanks in the mixed conifer zone, but its leaves are smaller, only 4–8" wide, and its flowers have 5 stamens and are yellow in the center rather than pink.

COMMON WOODLAND STAR

Lithophragma affine
Saxifrage family (Saxifragaceae)

Description: This common perennial has erect, often reddish, glandular-hairy stems that are 8–22" tall. Its basal leaves **[lower left inset]** have hairy, roundish blades, ½–1¼" long, that are divided no more than halfway to the base into 3 or 5 scalloped lobes. Its alternate stem leaves **[upper left inset]** have 3 deep lobes. Its uncrowded raceme has 3–15 flowers with a cone-shaped, hairy hypanthium that tapers to the base. The 5 white petals, up to ½" long, have 3 lobes, and the middle lobe is usually larger than the lateral lobes. The petals sometimes have a few smaller teeth along the sides.

Flowering time: March–May

Habitat/range: Grassy slopes; chaparral/oak-woodland and mixed conifer zones; up to 4,500'.

Similar plants: Bolander's Woodland Star (*L. bolanderi*) is also common in the park. Its basal leaves are also divided less than halfway to the base, but its hypanthium is shallowly rounded rather than tapered at the base and its petals are either unlobed or have more than 3 lobes. Hillside Woodland Star (*L. heterophyllum*) **[lower right inset]**, which has been reported in the park, would be the only other *Lithophragma* species in the park with basal leaves that are divided halfway or less to the base. It has 3-lobed petals and its hypanthium is conspicuously truncate (squared off) at the base.

105

BOLANDER'S WOODLAND STAR

Lithophragma bolanderi
Saxifrage family (Saxifragaceae)

Description: This common perennial has an erect, sometimes branched, often reddish stem that's 7–28" tall. The basal leaves **[upper right inset]** have roundish blades, ½–1¼" long, that are unlobed or have 3–5 shallow, scalloped lobes. The smaller stem leaves are deeply divided into narrow segments. The uncrowded, sometimes zigzagged raceme has 5–25 flowers with 5 triangular, often reddish sepals. The hypanthium is sometimes reddish and has more or less parallel sides and a rounded base. The 5 white, ovate-elliptic petals, up to ¼" long, are either unlobed or have more than 3 lobes that are often tooth-like **[lower left inset]**.

Flowering time: April–July

Habitat/range: Open, grassy areas in woodlands; chaparral/oak-woodland, mixed conifer, montane, and subalpine zones; up to 9,500'.

Similar plants: Common Woodland Star (*L. affine*) also has basal leaves that are shallowly divided, but its hypanthium tapers to a narrow base and its petals have 3 lobes. Hillside Woodland Star (*L. heterophyllum*) **[inset on page 105]** has been reported in the park, and it would be the only other *Lithophragma* species in the park with basal leaves that are divided halfway or less to the base. It has 3-lobed petals, and its hypanthium is conspicuously truncate (squared off) at the base.

BULBOUS WOODLAND STAR

Lithophragma glabrum
Saxifrage family (Saxifragaceae)

Description: Bulbous Woodland Star is a somewhat common perennial with erect, usually reddish stems, 3½–10" tall. The blades of its leaves **[inset]** are deeply divided to near the base into 3 segments with 3 or 4 rounded lobes. The similar stem leaves and the leaf bracts often have little bulb-like structures, called bulblets, in their axils. The inflorescence is a solitary flower or a raceme with 2–7 flowers, some of which are often replaced with bulblets. The sometimes raggedy-looking flowers have a bell-shaped, often reddish, glandular-hairy hypanthium. The flowers have 5 often reddish sepals and 5 white or pink petals, less than ⁵⁄₁₆" long, that are deeply divided into 3–5 narrow lobes.

Flowering time: April–July

Habitat/range: Dry, gravelly places in the open; mixed conifer, montane, subalpine, and alpine zones; 5,000–12,000'.

Similar plants: Small-flowered Woodland Star (*Lithophragma parviflorum* var. *parviflorum*) is the only other *Lithophragma* species in the park with at least some basal leaves that are divided more than halfway to the base. It has white or pink, 3-lobed petals, but its stems have no bulb-like structures and its petals are longer, ¼–⁵⁄₈" long. The plant has been reported from Mather, Hetch Hetchy, and El Portal and may grow elsewhere in the park.

106

SIERRA SAXIFRAGE

Micranthes aprica (*Saxifraga aprica*)
Saxifrage family (Saxifragaceae)

Description: Sierra Saxifrage is a perennial that has only basal leaves and grows alone or in clumps that sometimes form mats. Its hairless, obovate to elliptic, fleshy leaves are ¾–2¼" long and taper to a short, flattened petiole. The leaf blades often have purplish margins, are sometimes sparsely hairy, and occasionally have tiny teeth toward the tip. The single flowering stem is 1¼–4" long and is usually reddish and hairy throughout. The stem is sometimes glandular, but only near the base. The tiny flowers **[inset]** typically grow in a single dense, often head-like cluster of 5 or more, but there can be 1 or 2 smaller clusters nearby. The flowers have 5 ovate, spreading to erect sepals, 10 stamens with linear, flattened filaments, and 2 pistils. The 5 white, ovate or obovate petals have a narrow claw.

Flowering time: May–August

Habitat/range: Moist, gravelly flats and meadow borders; mixed conifer, montane, subalpine, and alpine zones; 6,000–12,000'.

Similar plants: Peak Saxifrage (*Micranthes nidifica*) has a similar overall appearance, but its flowers are in scattered, loose to somewhat compact clusters. Its flowering stalk is glandular-hairy throughout and is usually green rather than reddish, and its flowers have more or less reflexed sepals.

BUD SAXIFRAGE

Micranthes bryophora (*Saxifraga bryophora*)
Saxifrage family (Saxifragaceae)

Description: Bud Saxifrage is an annual that has only basal leaves and that grows by itself or in clustered groups. Its glandular-hairy, mostly sessile leaves are ¼–1½" long, linear-elliptic to oblanceolate, and sometimes toothed. The thread-like, often reddish flowering stems are 1½–10" long, densely glandular-hairy, and branched above. The small flower buds dangle from thread-like, red stalks. The buds become erect as the flowers open and begin to droop again as the fruit develops. The distinctive flowers have 5 petals, 5 reflexed sepals, a single pistil, and 10 stamens. The stamens have slender, white, flattened filaments and bright red anthers that darken with age. The white, distinctly clawed petals have triangular to broadly ovate blades with 2 yellow or green dots near the base. The flowers sometimes have 2 or 3 petals that are smaller than the others, and oddball flowers occasionally have 1 or 2 extra petals.

Flowering time: July–August

Habitat/range: Moist, open flats; montane, subalpine, and alpine zones; 6,800–11,500'.

Comments: Like many *Micranthes* species, Bud Saxifrage is protandrous, which means that its stigma remains undeveloped until the anthers no longer have pollen, which prevents self-pollination.

PEAK SAXIFRAGE

Micranthes nidifica (*Saxifraga nidifica*)
Saxifrage family (Saxifragaceae)

Description: This perennial grows alone or in clumps. Its fleshy basal leaves are 1¼–4¼" long. The ovate blade tapers to a flattened petiole and sometimes has tiny teeth along the margins. The flowering stems are 4–18" long and have scattered, loose to somewhat head-like flower clusters **[upper inset]**. The stems are glandular-hairy throughout and are usually green but can be reddish. The tiny flowers have 5 reflexed or spreading sepals and 5 white petals that are the same length as the sepals or slightly shorter.

Flowering time: June–August

Habitat/range: Open, wet meadows and moist, shady places; mixed conifer, montane, subalpine, and alpine zones; 3,900–11,000'.

Similar plants: The flowers of Sierra Saxifrage (*M. aprica*) are usually in a solitary tight cluster, and they have erect to spreading sepals. Its stem is reddish and mostly smooth, but it can be minutely glandular-hairy at the base. California Saxifrage (*M. californica*, previously *Saxifraga californica*) has been reported in Yosemite Valley, at Hetch Hetchy, and near El Portal. It has glandular-hairy, usually reddish flowering stems and scattered flower clusters, but its flowers **[lower inset]** have petals that are much larger than the sepals and its leaves are usually conspicuously toothed or scalloped.

BROOK SAXIFRAGE

Micranthes odontoloma (*Saxifraga odontoloma*)
Saxifrage family (Saxifragaceae)

Description: This attractive perennial is 8–18" tall and is uncommon in the park. It has basal leaves only and grows alone or in groups. Its leaves are 2½–28" long, including the petiole. The round, bright green leaf blades are 2¾–15" wide and are hairless above and sparsely hairy below. The triangular teeth along the margins of the blades are all about the same size, which gives the leaves a tidy appearance. The inflorescence is an open panicle. Each flower **[inset]** has 5 ovate to elliptic, reflexed sepals. The 5 white, deciduous petals are less than ¼" long and are shaped like tiny ping pong paddles, with 2 green or yellow spots near the base of the paddle blade. The 10 stamens have distinctly club-shaped filaments and bright red anthers that darken with age, and the 2-lobed pistil in the center of the flower is red toward the top and whitish near the base.

Flowering time: July–August

Habitat/range: Shady streambanks; montane, subalpine, and alpine zones; 6,200–11,000'.

Similar plants: Wood Saxifrage (*Saxifraga mertensiana*) has similar flowers and leaves, but its leaf blades have variously shaped lobes, each with 2–5 irregular teeth, and its petals have no claws and no spots. Wood Saxifrage is rare in the park and grows only in the montane zone.

BOG SAXIFRAGE, OREGON SAXIFRAGE

Micranthes oregana (*Saxifraga oregana*)
Saxifrage family (Saxifragaceae)

Description: Bog Saxifrage is a slender perennial, up to 4' tall, that has basal leaves only and grows by itself or in small groups. Its hairless to sparsely hairy, elliptic to oblanceolate, fleshy leaves are 3–10" long. The blades taper to an indistinct petiole and are smooth or sharp toothed on the margins. The stout flowering stems are glandular-hairy and are branched above. The small flowers, which grow in dense clusters at the stem and branch ends, have 2 green pistils and 10 stamens. The flowers **[inset]** are green in the center and have 5 reflexed, ovate to triangular sepals and 5 white, elliptic to obovate petals that are usually longer than the sepals.

Flowering time: June–August

Habitat/range: Bogs and wet meadows; montane and subalpine zones; 6,000–10,000'.

Similar plants: Peak Saxifrage (*M. nidifica*) and California Saxifrage (*M. californica*) grow in moist, shady places rather than in wet meadows. Peak Saxifrage is shorter, only up to 20" tall, and its leaves have a distinct petiole. California Saxifrage is also shorter, only up to 14" tall, and its leaves have a roundish blade and a distinct petiole. It grows mostly west of the park but has been reported in Yosemite Valley, near Hetch Hetchy, and in the El Portal area.

ALPINE SAXIFRAGE

Micranthes tolmiei (*Saxifraga tolmiei*)
Saxifrage family (Saxifragaceae)

Description: Alpine Saxifrage is a mat-forming, mostly hairless perennial with a woody base and sprawling stems. Its plump, crowded leaves, which are up to ⅝" long, are sessile and are elliptic to obovate. The lower leaves sometimes have long hairs along their margins. The ascending to erect, reddish flowering stems are finely glandular-hairy and are branched near the top. The inflorescence has leaf-like bracts and a cluster of 2–10 flowers, sometimes with 1 or more solitary flowers nearby. The flowers have a single 2-lobed, green pistil and 10 stamens with club-shaped filaments and red anthers that darken with age. The 5 green, ovate sepals are spreading to ascending, and the 5 white petals are linear to oblanceolate and are less than ¼" long.

Flowering time: July–August

Habitat/range: Granitic talus and scree among protective boulders; subalpine and alpine zones; 10,000–11,000'.

Comments: This plant is uncommon in the park and often grows in areas with little other vegetation. Plants in the *Micranthes* genus were assigned to the *Saxifraga* genus until DNA evidence showed that they're more closely related to plants in the *Boykinia* and *Heuchera* genera but are different enough to justify being in a genus of their own.

PYGMY SAXIFRAGE
Saxifraga hyperborea (*S. rivularis*)
Saxifrage family (Saxifragaceae)

Description: This small, attractive perennial is 1–4" tall and grows by itself or in compact or open groups. Its thin to slightly fleshy leaves are hairless to sparsely hairy. The kidney-shaped leaf blade is wider than it is long, is truncate or slightly heart shaped at the base, and is divided more than halfway to the base into 3–5 broad lobes. The slender, branched, often reddish flowering stems have a solitary flower at the end of each branch. The flowers have a U-shaped hypanthium, a pistil with 2 curved styles, and 10 stamens with thread-like filaments. The 5 elliptic to ovate sepals are sometimes purplish, and the 5 white petals are up to ¼" long, are elliptic to obovate, and often have a pinkish midvein.

Flowering time: July–August

Habitat/range: Moist, often mossy rock crevices, usually in deep shade; subalpine and alpine zones; 10,000–11,200'.

Comments: This uncommon plant is easily overlooked due to its small size and the fact that it usually grows in the deep shade of overhanging rocks. The genus name *Saxifraga* is from two Latin words that mean rock and break, and it probably got the name because plants in the genus often grow in rock crevices. The name *hyperborea* means of the far north, referring to the fact that the plant grows up into the Arctic Circle.

JIMSON WEED, SACRED DATURA
Datura wrightii
Nightshade family (Solanaceae)

Description: Jimson Weed is an annual or perennial with short-gray-hairy, foul-smelling herbage. Its widely branched stems are 1½–5' long and often grow along the ground. The alternate, ovate, long-petioled leaves are 2½–7½" long and are often irregularly lobed. The flowers have a long, tubular calyx with 5 triangular lobes. The funnel-shaped, white corolla, up to 8" long, is often lavender tinged and has 5 fused petals, each with a narrow, curled tooth on the margin. The 5 stamens have white filaments and white pollen, and the fruit is a large, spherical, densely prickly capsule.

Flowering time: May–October

Habitat/range: Open, sandy or gravelly areas, often on roadsides; chaparral/oak-woodland and mixed conifer zones; up to 4,300'.

Comments: This plant's flowers start to bloom in the evening and shrivel up during the next day. The fragrant flowers attract night-feeding moths as pollinators. Some observers believe that moths can become addicted to Jimson Weed's intoxicating nectar and avoid visiting flowers of other species. Native Americans have used the plant as a hallucinogen in ceremonies, but it should be noted that all parts of the plant contain highly poisonous alkaloids and that ingestion has caused numerous deaths.

MANY-FLOWERED TOBACCO
(non-native)
Nicotiana acuminata var. *multiflora*
Nightshade family (Solanaceae)

Description: This South American native is an annual with erect, branched stems, 1½–5' tall, and densely glandular-hairy herbage. The alternate, long-petioled leaves, 2–10" long, have an ovate to lanceolate blade. The flowers, which grow in open panicles, have a fused calyx with 5 unequal lobes, each with a dark stripe running from the tip of the lobe to the base of the calyx. The trumpet-shaped corolla, 1¼–1¾" long, has a greenish-white tube and 5 shallow, white, broadly triangular lobes. Each flower has a single style and 5 stamens that are attached near the middle of the tube.

Flowering time: May–October

Habitat/range: Open, gravelly or sandy places; chaparral/oak-woodland and mixed conifer zones; up to 4,500'.

Similar plants: Coyote Tobacco (*Nicotiana attenuata*) is a native plant that looks a lot like Many-flowered Tobacco, but its corolla tube often has a maroon tint and its calyx has mostly equal lobes with no dark stripes, or stripes toward the tip but not all the way to the base. Although both species are uncommon in the park, both of them have been found in Yosemite Valley, near Wawona, and at Ackerson Meadow. Many-flowered Tobacco has also been reported in the Hetch Hetchy area.

AMERICAN BLACK NIGHTSHADE
Solanum americanum
Nightshade family (Solanaceae)

Description: This uncommon annual to subshrub has ascending to sprawling stems, 11–32" long, and herbage with nonglandular hairs that are short and curved or more or less appressed. Its alternate, ovate leaves, up to 6" long, are wedge shaped or truncate at the base, and the margins often have wavy teeth. The small flowers **[inset]** grow in loose clusters. They have a 5-lobed calyx and a white (sometimes purple-tinged) corolla that's up to ¼" wide and has 5 deeply divided lobes. The 5 stamens have large, yellow anthers. The fruit is a toxic berry that becomes shiny black with age.

Flowering time: April–November

Habitat/range: Disturbed areas; chaparral/oak-woodland and mixed conifer zones; up to 4,000'.

Similar plants: The Eurasian native European Black Nightshade (*Solanum nigrum*) has been reported in the park, but the plants in question may have been American Black Nightshade. The only way to distinguish the two species is to carefully measure their seeds and examine their hairs. American Black Nightshade's seeds are no more than ⅟₁₆" long, and its hairs are appressed or curved and are not glandular. European Black Nightshade's seeds can be slightly more than ⅟₁₆" long, and its hairs are spreading or curved and can be glandular. Some botanists think that the plants should not be considered separate species.

SIERRA BLADDERNUT
Staphylea bolanderi
Bladdernut family (Staphyleaceae)

Description: Sierra Bladdernut is a deciduous tree or large shrub that's 6½–20' tall and has smooth, hairless herbage throughout. Its opposite, petioled leaves are divided into 3 widely ovate to round leaflets, 1–2½" long, with tiny, sharp teeth along the margins. The cylindric to bell-shaped flowers grow in long-stalked, somewhat open clusters from the leaf axils. The 5-lobed, white or greenish-white calyx is divided almost to the base, and the 5 white, narrowly oblong to oblanceolate petals are ⅜–½" long and are usually slightly longer than the calyx. The 6 white stamens extend beyond the petals and have yellow anthers. The fruit **[inset]** is a thin-walled, inflated, 3-lobed capsule, up to 2" long, that turns brown with age.

Flowering time: March–May

Habitat/range: Wooded or shrubby slopes, often near rivers and streams; chaparral/oak-woodland zone; up to 2,800'.

Comments: This uncommon plant grows only in California, in the Cascade Range, in the Klamath Range, and in central and southern Sierra Nevada. Because of its attractive flowers, shiny green leaves, and interesting fruit, Sierra Bladdernut is sometimes planted as a garden ornamental. In Yosemite, the plant grows only in the Merced River Canyon, and it's fairly easy to find near the Arch Rock entrance and around El Portal.

WILD HYACINTH, WHITE BRODIAEA
Triteleia hyacinthina
Brodiaea family (Themidaceae)

Description: Wild Hyacinth is a hairless perennial with an erect flowering stem that's 10–28" tall. Its 1–3 linear, grass-like basal leaves, 4–16" long, are keeled and are often withered by the time the flowers are in bloom. The umbel-like inflorescence has green, lanceolate bracts at its base, and it has many flowers, each on an ascending to erect stalk that's up to 2" long. The white, slightly bowl-shaped flowers are ⅜–⅝" long and have 6 tepals with spreading lobes. Each tepal has a green midvein on its lower surface. The single style is obscurely 3 lobed, and the 6 white stamens have flat filaments that are conspicuously broadened at the base. The plant is somewhat common in the park's lower elevations, and it grows in Yosemite Valley, around Wawona, and in the Hetch Hetchy area.

Flowering time: April–July

Habitat/range: Vernally wet, grassy places and dry slopes; chaparral/oak-woodland and mixed conifer zones; up to 6,200'.

Similar plants: Although it has no onion odor, Wild Hyacinth could easily be mistaken for a member of the onion genus (*Allium*). However, the onions in the park don't have stamens with filaments that are conspicuously broadened at the base (although their anthers are usually somewhat broader at the base than at the top), and most of them have a pronounced onion odor.

WESTERN FALSE-ASPHODEL

Triantha occidentalis ssp. *occidentalis*
(*Tofieldia occidentalis* ssp. *occidentalis*)
False-asphodel family (Tofieldiaceae)

Description: This uncommon perennial has an erect stem, 1–2½' tall, that's hairless below and densely glandular-hairy above. Its erect or ascending, somewhat rigid, grass-like leaves are 2–8" long and are mostly basal. The inflorescence is rounded or shaped like an elongated egg. The small flowers have 6 solid white, oblong-ovate tepals, up to ¼" long, and 3 of them are slightly narrower and longer than the other 3. The 6 white stamens extend beyond the tepals and have bright yellow anthers. The ovary is green and has 3 white styles, and the fruit is an ovoid capsule.

Flowering time: July–August

Habitat/range: Wet meadows and bogs; mixed conifer, montane, and subalpine zones; 3,900–9,900'.

Similar plants: The quite similar death camas (*Toxicoscordion*) species have tepals with distinctly contrasting, greenish-yellow nectar glands toward their base. Western Bistort (*Bistorta bistortoides*) is also similar overall, but its flowers have 5 tepals. Western False-asphodel could be mistaken for an onion, but its inflorescences have no papery bracts at the base, and all onion species have inflorescences with papery bracts at the base.

CALIFORNIA VALERIAN

Valeriana californica
Valerian family (Valerianaceae)

Description: California Valerian is a fairly common perennial with 1 or more erect to ascending stems, 10–23" long, that are hairy below and smooth above. Its oblanceolate basal leaves are 2–6" long and are usually unlobed but occasionally have 3–5 deep lobes. The spreading stem leaves, which grow in opposite pairs, have 3–9 lobes and sometimes have tiny teeth or a few large teeth on the margins. The terminal inflorescence is an umbel-like cluster of flowers that has 3 stamens and a calyx with 5–15 lobes. The funnel-shaped, white to pinkish corolla is less than ¼" long and has 5 lobes that are about the same length as the tube, which is mostly hidden within the calyx. The 6 stamens and 1 style extend well beyond the corolla throat.

Flowering time: July–September

Habitat/range: Moist to dry areas, in partial shade or in the open; montane and subalpine zones; 6,500–10,500'.

Comments: Some Native Americans boil the roots of California Valerian and eat them as a vegetable, and the roots have been used to treat stomach ailments. This plant's European relative *Valeriana officinalis* has been used for centuries as a sedative and is currently used as an ingredient in some sleep aids. Despite its somewhat disagreeable odor, the plant was used as an ingredient in perfumes in 16th-century Europe.

EUROPEAN FIELD PANSY

(non-native)
Viola arvensis
Violet family (Violaceae)

Description: European Field Pansy is an annual that's native to Europe, Siberia, and North Africa. It has an erect to reclining, branched stem that's 4–15" long. Its alternate, short-petioled stem leaves are ½–1" long and have an ovate to lanceolate blade with rounded teeth. The 2 large, leaf-like bracts at the base of the leaves are palmately divided into several lobes, with a much longer terminal lobe. The flowers have 5 lanceolate sepals and 5 stamens. The 5 white to cream-colored petals are ¼–⅝" long and are sometimes lavender tinted. The middle lower petal is yellow at the base and often has several dark nectar guides.

Flowering time: May–June

Habitat/range: Damp or dry meadows; mixed conifer and montane zones; 4,000–6,200'.

Comments: This noninvasive little violet grows in Yosemite Valley meadows and at Ackerson Meadow. The plant contains a substance that's toxic to human cancer cells, and it's being studied in the hope that it can be used to treat cancer.

Similar plants: Macloskey's Violet (*Viola macloskeyi*) is a native plant, and it's the only other violet in the park that has white petals. Since it has no stem leaves (only basal leaves), it's easily distinguished from European Field Pansy.

MACLOSKEY'S VIOLET

Viola macloskeyi
Violet family (Violaceae)

Description: This erect perennial, up to 4" tall, has leafy stolons that often form somewhat dense patches along the ground. Its long-petioled basal leaves have a thin, ovate blade that's smooth or slightly toothed along the margins and is sometimes somewhat heart shaped at the base. The flowers, which grow on long, leafless stalks, have 5 ovate to lanceolate sepals and 5 ivory-white petals that are ¼–⅝" long. The lower petal has purple nectar guides, and the 2 side petals have hairs that scrape pollen off insects as they follow the guidelines to find the nectar in the spur.

Flowering time: May–August

Habitat/range: Wet meadows, bogs, and streamsides; mixed conifer, montane, and subalpine zones; 3,400–11,000'.

Comments: Candied violets were a delicacy in the 19th century. Violet flowers, along with other edible flowers, are now sold at high-end markets to add splashes of color to salads and other dishes. This plant was named for George Macloskey (1834–1920), an Irish naturalist and educator who became the chair of biology at Princeton University.

Similar plants: European Field Pansy (*Viola arvensis*) is the only other white-petaled violet in the park. Its lower petal has a distinctive yellow patch at its base, and it has mostly stem leaves.

YELLOW FLOWERS

Alpine Gold (*Hulsea algida*)

This section contains plants with pale to bright yellow flowers, and it includes several plants with flowers that are yellow at maturity and fade to red as they age.

If you've gone through this section looking for a plant with pale yellow flowers and didn't find it, check the section for white to cream flowers, since some plants that have pale yellow flowers can also have cream-colored flowers.

If the plant you're looking for has golden-yellow flowers and you can't find it in this section, check the section for orange and red flowers.

If your plant has flowers that are partially yellow and partially another color, the plant is most likely included in the section of the color that stands out the most. For example, a plant with bicolored flowers that are vivid yellow and pale purple is most likely included in this section.

Note: The similar plants sections include plants that are not covered elsewhere in the book, as well as plants that have a separate photo unit of their own. The names of plants that have their own photo unit in the book are highlighted with green text.

FRAGRANT SUMAC

Rhus aromatica (*R. trilobata*)
Sumac family (Anacardiaceae)

Description: Fragrant Sumac is a much-branched, sprawling, deciduous shrub, 2–6' tall, with velvety twigs and lower branches that curve up at the tip. The green to blue-green leaves are divided into 3 broad-tipped leaflets that taper to a wedge-shaped base, and the middle leaflet is noticeably larger than the lateral leaflets. The spike-like flower clusters, which develop before the leaves in the spring, have small flowers with 5 yellow petals. In the fall, the small, round fruit **[inset]** and the leaves turn bright red to red-orange.

Flowering time: March–April

Habitat/range: Canyons and washes in dry to moist areas; chaparral/oak-woodland and mixed conifer zones; up to 4,000'.

Comments: Native Americans ate the fruit, and they used the pliable, fibrous stems to make baskets for holding water. The plant's foliage has a pleasant fragrance, especially when crushed, and the shrub is often planted as a garden ornamental for its fragrance and for its colorful fall leaves and berries.

Similar plants: Poison Oak (*Toxicodendron diversilobum*) has similar leaves with 3 leaflets, but the middle leaflet is about the same size as the lateral leaflets or only slightly larger and the leaflets don't have a wedge-shaped base.

CALIFORNIA WAVEWING

Cymopterus terebinthinus var. *californicus*
Carrot family (Apiaceae)

Description: California Wavewing is a woody-based perennial, 6–20" tall, with finely dissected basal leaves, up to 13" long, that tend to grow along the ground. The flowers are arranged in open, compound umbels with 3–24 rays, unequal in length, that terminate in an umbellet with several narrow, pointed bractlets at the base and numerous small flowers with 5 yellow petals and 5 yellow anthers. The oval fruit are less than ¼" long and have multiple prominent wavy wings.

Flowering time: May–June

Habitat/range: Dry areas; mixed conifer, montane, subalpine, and alpine zones; 5,000–10,500'.

Similar plants: Sierra Biscuitroot (*Lomatium torreyi*) is easily mistaken for California Wavewing, and it also grows up into the alpine zone, but its umbellets have no bractlets at the base and its finely dissected leaves are more fern-like and don't tend to hug the ground. Purple Sanicle (*Sanicula bipinnatifida*) grows near the western park boundary and has similar flowers that are yellow rather than purple in the Yosemite region. Its leaves are not finely dissected; they have broad lobes and a winged, toothed midrib. Bladder Parsnip (*Lomatium utriculatum*) is a lower-elevation plant with similar flowers and finely dissected leaves, but its stem leaves have an expanded, balloon-like base, which California Wavewing and Sierra Biscuitroot lack.

BLADDER PARSNIP, SPRING GOLD
Lomatium utriculatum
Carrot family (Apiaceae)

Description: This early-blooming perennial is 4–20" tall and has a smooth to slightly hairy stem that's usually purplish toward the base. Its alternate leaves are up to 10" long and are finely dissected into many long, narrow, sometimes thread-like segments. The base of each stem leaf widens into a pale, thin, balloon-like sheath that clasps the stem. The variably shaped compound umbels have 5–13 rays that end in a cluster of tiny flowers with 5 yellow petals. The distinctive oval to oblong fruit are about ½" long and have wings that are often wider than the fruit body.

Flowering time: February–May

Habitat/range: Grassy areas; chaparral/oak-woodland and mixed conifer zones; up to 5,000'.

Similar plants: No similar carrot family plant in the park has leaves with a conspicuously balloon-like sheathing base. However, two other plants in the park have somewhat similar yellow flower clusters and grow only in the chaparral/oak-woodland and mixed conifer zones. The basal leaves of less common Sierra Sanicle (*Sanicula graveolens*) are divided into broad segments **[upper inset]**. Turkey Pea (*Sanicula tuberosa*) grows mostly west of the park but has been reported from El Portal, Mather, and Wawona. The segments of its finely dissected leaves **[lower inset]** are usually triangular rather than linear, and its foliage smells like cilantro.

SIERRA PODISTERA
Podistera nevadensis
Carrot family (Apiaceae)

Description: This alpine plant is a cushioned perennial with a woody base and no stem. It forms low mats that are up to 2' wide. The fleshy, pale green leaves are less than ½" long and are pinnately divided into 3–7 pointed leaflets that are covered with short, whitish, rough-textured hairs. A cluster of yellow flowers grows at the end of the flower stalks, which are up to 1¼" long. Beneath the flower cluster is a cup-like structure of fused bracts. The yellow flowers fade before long and are often beige or brownish when they're encountered.

Flowering time: July–September

Habitat/range: Rocky slopes; alpine zone; 10,000–13,000'.

Comments: Alpine plants are typically slow-growing, long-lived perennials. Many of them grow in low, dense mats that absorb more of the sun's heat and minimize damage from strong, icy winds.

Similar plants: Sierra Podistera's leaves are pinnately divided only once. Gray Spring-parsley (*Cymopterus cinerarius*) is also a cushioned plant that forms low mats and grows in rocky habitats at high elevations. It has similar flower clusters and leaves, but its leaves are pinnately divided twice **[inset]**. The plant has rarely been reported in the park but may be encountered on alpine ridges.

ANNUAL DANDELION
Agoseris heterophylla var. *heterophylla*
Sunflower family (Asteraceae)

Description: This common annual is up to 16" tall. It grows from a slender taproot and has 1 or more stems or flowering stalks. Its erect to ascending, sparsely hairy leaves are linear to oblanceolate and have smooth margins or small, shallow teeth or lobes. The plant often has a few stem leaves, but most of the leaves are crowded at the base of the plant. The terminal flower heads are up to 1" wide and have many yellow ray flowers. The fruit is an oval achene with a long, slender beak that ends in a tuft of hairs (the pappus).

Flowering time: April–July

Habitat/range: Grassy places; chaparral/oak-woodland and mixed conifer zones; up to 5,000'.

Similar plants: This plant's perennial *Agoseris* relatives have a stout taproot and rarely have stem leaves. Smooth Cat's-ear (*Hypochaeris glabra*), an annual, and Rough Cat's-ear (*Hypochaeris radicata*) **[inset]**, a perennial, are non-natives that look similar, but they typically grow only in disturbed areas and their leaves tend to lie flat against the ground. Nodding Silverpuffs (*Microseris nutans*) and Lindley's Silverpuffs (*Uropappus lindleyi*) also look similar, but Nodding Silverpuffs has nodding buds (unlike the other plants discussed here), and Lindley's Silverpuffs has phyllary tips that extend beyond the ray flowers (unlike the other plants discussed here).

PALE MOUNTAIN DANDELION
Agoseris monticola (*A. glauca* var. *monticola*)
Sunflower family (Asteraceae)

Description: This stemless perennial is up to 10" tall and has 1 to several glandular-hairy flower stalks that often recline along the ground and bend upward at the tip. The leaves are oblanceolate in outline, are sparsely to densely hairy, and are arranged in a basal rosette. The leaf margins can be smooth or toothed, but they can also have conspicuous pairs of lobes. If so, the lower lobes are often angled toward the leaf base, the upper lobes are often angled toward the leaf tips, and some of the lobes spread straight outward. The flower head is ¾–1¼" wide and has 10–40 yellow ray flowers that often have a dark stripe underneath. The phyllaries are in 2–4 series and are usually rosy-purple with a green margin.

Flowering time: July–August

Habitat/range: Subalpine meadows, forest openings, and rocky slopes; montane, subalpine, and alpine zones; 6,500–11,000'.

Similar plants: Steppe Agoseris (*A. parviflora*, previously *A. glauca* var. *laciniata*) is quite similar. To tell the two plants apart, look closely at the hairs along the stalk and at the base of the flower head. If you find glandular hairs, the plant is probably Pale Mountain Dandelion; if the hairs are not glandular, it's likely Steppe Agoseris. The leaves of Spearleaf Dandelion (*A. retrorsa*) have deep, narrow lobes that point strongly backward toward the leaf base.

SPEARLEAF DANDELION
Agoseris retrorsa
Sunflower family (Asteraceae)

Description: This milky-sapped perennial has a stout stalk, 6–20" long, which grows from a basal rosette of numerous leaves that are lanceolate to oblanceolate in outline. Each leaf ends in a long, spear-like tip and has several pairs of deep, narrow lateral lobes that bend backward toward the base of the leaf. The leafless stalk ends in a dandelion-like flower head that's ¾–1½" wide and has 10–100 yellow ray flowers. The fruit is an oval achene that abruptly contracts into a long beak with a tuft of hairs at the end. Young plants usually have woolly-hairy foliage, and more mature plants are mostly hairless.

Flowering time: April–August

Habitat/range: Dry, grassy or rocky places; chaparral/oak-woodland, mixed conifer, and montane zones; up to 8,000'.

Similar plants: Large-flowered Agoseris (*Agoseris grandiflora* var. *grandiflora*) often has leaves with conspicuous pairs of lobes, but few or none of the lobes bend strongly backward. Both Spearleaf Dandelion and Large-flowered Agoseris have erect phyllaries. The leaves of the lawn pest Common Dandelion (*Taraxacum officinale*) have lobes that bend strongly backward, but its outer phyllaries curve down conspicuously toward the flower stalk, distinguishing it from plants with similar leaves and flower heads.

119

DISTINCTIVE ARNICAS

Arnicas can be difficult and sometimes virtually impossible to identify to species. Several species hybridize with other species, but even non-hybrid plants of a particular arnica species often exhibit a wide range of variation. This section highlights Yosemite arnica species with distinguishing characteristics that make them readily identifiable. All of them have 2–4 pairs of stem leaves, except for Rayless Arnica, which has 3–7 pairs. All arnica species in the park have yellow or yellow-orange flower heads.

Heart-leaved Arnica (*A. cordifolia*), top left, is the only arnica with lower leaves that have a deeply heart-shaped base.

Nodding Arnica (*A. parryi*), top right, is the only arnica with buds that droop when they're young.

Rayless Arnica (*A. discoidea*), bottom left, is the only arnica that has no ray flowers and has erect buds. (Nodding Arnica sometimes has no ray flowers, but it has nodding buds.)

Sticky-leaved Arnica (*A. ovata*, previously *A. diversifolia*), bottom right, and **Mock Leopardbane** (*A. dealbata*, previously *Whitneya dealbata*) are the only arnicas in the park whose lower stem leaves have 3 (or more) principal veins; all the other species have leaves with a single principal vein. The achenes (fruit) of Sticky-leaved Arnica have numerous fine, hairy bristles (pappus) at the tip. The achenes of Mock Leopardbane have no pappus; it's the only arnica species in North America that has achenes with no pappus.

SEEP-SPRING ARNICA
Arnica longifolia
Sunflower family (Asteraceae)

Description: This perennial is 1–2' tall, grows in dense groups, and has herbage that feels rough to the touch. Its basal leaves are withered by flowering time. The sessile stem leaves, in 5–7 pairs, are narrowly lanceolate and mostly toothless. The large flower heads have many yellow disk flowers and 8–13 yellow ray flowers. The glandular, long-hairy phyllaries have pointed tips.

Flowering time: July–August

Habitat/range: Banks of small streams and other wet areas; mixed conifer, montane, subalpine, and alpine zones; 5,000–11,000'.

Similar plants: Excluding the *Arnica* species on page 120, two other arnicas have 4–10 pairs of stem leaves, but they don't grow in dense groups and their herbage does not feel rough to the touch. The basal leaves of Clasping Arnica (*A. lanceolata* ssp. *prima*, previously *A. amplexicaulis*) are still green at flowering time, and its 5–7 pairs of stem leaves are usually conspicuously toothed. The basal leaves of Leafy Arnica (*A. chamissonis*) are usually withered by flowering time, and its 4–10 pairs of stem leaves are mostly toothless; unlike Seep-spring Arnica and Clasping Arnica, its hairy phyllaries have an extra little tuft of white hairs on the inner surface. Narrow-leaved Mule-ears (*Wyethia angustifolia*) is similar to Seep-spring Arnica and it grows in similar habitats, but its middle stem leaves are alternate.

SIERRA ARNICA
Arnica nevadensis
Sunflower family (Asteraceae)

Description: This strongly aromatic perennial is 4–10" tall and has glandular-hairy herbage. Its stem leaves, in 2 or 3 pairs, have short, distinct petioles, and the lower leaves are usually larger than the upper leaves. The mostly toothless leaf blades are elliptic to ovate and are truncate or slightly heart shaped at the base. One or a few stems end in 1–3 large flower heads with 6–15 yellow ray flowers and numerous yellow disk flowers. The achenes (fruit) have white or straw-colored pappus bristles.

Flowering time: July–August

Habitat/range: Conifer forests, meadows, and open, rocky areas; montane, subalpine, and alpine zones; 6,500–11,900'.

Similar plants: Excluding the Arnica species on page 120, two other Arnica species have 5 or fewer pairs of stem leaves. Hairy Arnica (*A. mollis*) also has strongly aromatic herbage. It has 3–5 pairs of stem leaves that are mostly sessile and are mostly untoothed, and its lower leaves are usually larger than the upper leaves. Its pappus bristles are tawny and often have amber-like deposits. The herbage of Broad-leaved Arnica (*A. latifolia*) is often not strongly aromatic. It has 2–4 pairs of toothed or serrate stem leaves that are sessile or have relatively short, broadly winged petioles. Its lower stem leaves are usually smaller than the middle stem leaves, and its achenes have white pappus.

121

SILVER WORMWOOD

Artemisia ludoviciana ssp. *incompta*
Sunflower family (Asteraceae)

Description: Silver Wormwood is a herbaceous perennial, 11–34" tall, that grows in colonies from creeping rhizomes and has many stiff, unbranched, gray to green stems. The alternate leaves are 1–3" long, are mostly greenish above, and are white-woolly beneath. The lower leaves are mostly twice divided into narrow lobes that are less than ¼" wide. Small, round, erect or nodding flower heads grow in leafy, elongated clusters along the top of the stem, and they have phyllaries with transparent margins.

Flowering time: July–September

Habitat/range: Open, dry, rocky places; mixed conifer, montane, subalpine, and alpine zones; 4,000–11,500'.

Similar plants: Silver Wormwood is one of four herbaceous (non-shrub) *Artemisia* species in the park. The lower leaves of Boreal Sagewort (*A. norvegica* ssp. *saxatilis*) are also divided into narrow lobes, but Boreal Sagewort's phyllaries have blackish-green rather than transparent margins. The leaves of Mugwort (*A. douglasiana*) can be lobed or unlobed, but when a Mugwort leaf is lobed, its terminal lobe is more than ¼" wide. Tarragon (*A. dracunculus*) is the only one in the group with narrowly linear, mostly unlobed leaves, though some can be cleft into 3 long, narrow lobes.

TIMBERLINE SAGEBRUSH

Artemisia rothrockii
Sunflower family (Asteraceae)

Description: Timberline Sagebrush is an ever-green shrub, up to 1¾' tall, with a distinct, narrow trunk and glandular, strongly aromatic herbage. The light to dark gray-green leaves are narrowly wedge shaped. The non-flowering stems have mostly 3-lobed leaves, and the flowering stems usually have unlobed leaves. The densely clustered, small flower heads **[inset]** have yellow disk flowers surrounded by shiny, hairy, straw-colored phyllaries with wide, membranous margins.

Flowering time: August–September

Habitat/range: Meadows and rocky areas; mixed conifer, montane, subalpine, and alpine zones; 6,500–10,200'.

Similar plants: Timberline Sagebrush is one of four *Artemisia* shrubs that have been reported in the park. Low Sagebrush (*A. arbuscula* ssp. *arbuscula*) is less than 1' tall and is the only one of the four that does not have a distinct trunk. Silver Sagebrush (*A. cana* ssp. *bolanderi*) is uncommon and is the only one of the four that has mostly unlobed leaves. Mountain Sagebrush (*A. tridentata*) has mostly 3-lobed leaves. Unlike Timberline Sagebrush, its silvery-hairy herbage is not glandular and is not highly aromatic. It has two subspecies; ssp. *vaseyana* is a common, flat-topped shrub that gets up to 3½' tall; ssp. *tridentata* is an uncommon, round-topped shrub that gets up to 6½' tall.

ARROWLEAF BALSAMROOT
Balsamorhiza sagittata
Sunflower family (Asteraceae)

Description: Arrowleaf Balsamroot is a hairy, aromatic perennial with several white-woolly, often leafless stems, 9–24" tall. Its basal leaves, 8–20" long, are silver-hairy above and below when young, the upper surface becoming greener and less hairy with age, the lower surface remaining silver-hairy. The leaf blades are heart shaped at the base and taper to the tip, forming a narrow arrowhead shape. Alternate stem leaves, if any, are much smaller. The large, saucer-shaped flower heads, 1–3 per stem, are up to 4" wide and have white-woolly phyllaries, 13–21 yellow ray flowers, and many yellow disk flowers.

Flowering time: May–August

Habitat/range: Openings in shrubby or forested areas; mixed conifer, montane, and subalpine zones; 3,900–9,200'.

Similar plants: Deltoid Balsamroot (*Balsamorhiza deltoidea*), which is rare in the park, also has large, arrowhead leaves, but they're more sparsely hairy and are green on both surfaces, even when they're young. The largest leaves of both balsamroots look like an arrowhead with a base that's deeply heart shaped. The leaves of plants in the *Wyethia* genus can be somewhat triangular shaped, and their leaves are truncate or slightly heart shaped at the base, but the base of their leaves are never deeply heart shaped.

CALIFORNIA BRICKELLBUSH
Brickellia californica
Sunflower family (Asteraceae)

Description: California Brickellbush is a leggy shrub that's 1½–6½' tall and has glandular-hairy stems. Its alternate, green to gray-green leaves, up to 3" long, have a triangular to ovate blade that's heart shaped or truncate at the base and scalloped to toothed along the margins. The cylindric, erect to spreading flower heads are about ¾" long, grow in clusters at the branch tips, and have only disk flowers. The dingy white corollas are much less noticeable than the long, pale yellow style branches, which extend well beyond the corolla. The green to reddish, papery phyllaries are long, narrow, and overlapping.

Flowering time: August–October

Habitat/range: Dry, rocky slopes; chaparral/oak-woodland and mixed conifer zones; up to 6,000'.

Comments: Native American groups made a bitter-tasting tea from this shrub and used it to treat fever, body aches, and flu. One Indian group from the American Southwest gave it to individuals who were near death in the theory that if it didn't kill them it might revive them.

Similar plants: Tassel-flowered Brickellbush (*Brickellia grandiflora*) **[inset]**, which is less common in the park, has similar leaves and flower heads, but it's a herbaceous perennial rather than a shrub and it has nodding flower heads.

YELLOW STAR-THISTLE

(non-native)

Centaurea solstitialis

Sunflower family (Asteraceae)

Description: Yellow Star-thistle is an invasive, gray-hairy annual, up to 3½' tall. Its rough-hairy basal leaves are 2–6" long, are pinnately lobed, and are often withered when the plant is in bloom. Its alternate, much smaller stem leaves have wavy-margined wings that extend down the stem. The flower heads are about ¾" long. They have many yellow disk flowers and a spherical involucre that's constricted at the top and has stout, sharp, straw-colored spines that are up to 1" long.

Flowering time: May–October

Habitat/range: Disturbed places, grassy slopes and flats; chaparral/oak-woodland and mixed conifer zones; up to 4,000'.

Comments: Yellow Star-thistle is native to southern Eurasia, where it grows in balance with the flora and fauna. It thrives in California in habitats much like its native habitat, but with different flora and fauna. Because Star-thistle has no natural impediments to survival in North America, it has taken over large tracts of land, especially in disturbed areas.

Similar plants: Tocalote (*Centaurea melitensis*) **[inset]**, another invasive non-native plant, can easily be mistaken for Yellow Star-thistle, but its spines are less than ½" long and are often purple tinged.

GRAY HAWKSBEARD

Crepis intermedia

Sunflower family (Asteraceae)

Description: This stout perennial is 10–23" tall and has 1 or 2 densely short-hairy stems that are branched near the middle or above. Its densely gray-hairy basal leaves are 2–16" long, elliptic to lanceolate in outline, and deeply pinnately cut, about halfway to the midvein, into numerous narrowly triangular-shaped, sometimes toothed lobes. The alternate stem leaves are similar but smaller. Each branch ends in a rounded or flat-topped cluster of 10–60 flower heads with 7–13 yellow ray flowers. The short-hairy involucre is narrowly cylindric and has lanceolate phyllaries in 2 series, several very short outer phyllaries and 7–10 much longer inner phyllaries.

Flowering time: June–August

Habitat/range: Dry slopes and ridges, open forest; mixed conifer and montane zones; 3,900–7,100'.

Similar plants: Almost identical Long-leaved Hawksbeard (*Crepis acuminata*) grows up to 10,500' and has 30–70 or more flower heads. You can distinguish it from Gray Hawksbeard by the number of ray flowers and phyllaries. The flower heads of Long-leaved Hawksbeard have 5–10 ray flowers and 5–8 inner phyllaries (and several short outer phyllaries). Nodding Silverpuffs (*Microseris nutans*) has similar flowers and sometimes has toothed or lobed leaves, but it has only about 1–6 flower heads per plant.

BLOOMER'S GOLDENBUSH

Ericameria bloomeri
Sunflower family (Asteraceae)

Description: Bloomer's Goldenbush is a strongly scented, glandular-hairy, leafy shrub, up to 2' tall, that has flexible stems and is densely branched from near the base. Its alternate, bright green leaves are up to 3" long and are narrowly linear but usually a bit broader at the tip. The flower heads, which grow in clusters along the branches and at the top of the stems, have 4–12 yellow disk flowers and 1–5 yellow, scattered ray flowers that give the flower heads a haphazard look. The narrowly bell-shaped involucre has linear, leaf-like, loosely overlapping phyllaries in 3–6 series.

Flowering time: July–October

Habitat/range: Open, sandy or gravelly places; mixed conifer, montane, and subalpine zones; 5,500–10,000'.

Similar plants: Golden-fleece (*E. arborescens*), a similar leggy-looking shrub that's much less common in the park, is usually over 4' tall and has no ray flowers. Single-headed Goldenbush (*E. suffruticosa*), the only other *Ericameria* in the park with both disk and ray flowers, has 15–40 disk flowers. Brewer's Aster (*Eucephalus breweri*) looks something like Bloomer's Goldenbush, but it's a perennial rather than a shrub and it has no ray flowers.

SHOWY RUBBER RABBITBRUSH

Ericameria nauseosa var. *speciosa*
(*Chrysothamnus nauseosus* ssp. *albicaulis*)
Sunflower family (Asteraceae)

Description: This strongly aromatic shrub grows up to 3½' tall and has many flexible, leafy, much-branched, whitish stems. The alternate, narrowly lanceolate leaves are 1–3" long, are crowded along the branches, and are dark green to grayish white. The flower heads, which grow in dense, rounded clusters at the branch ends, usually have 5 yellow disk flowers, each with an extended, 2-branched style. The cylindric, hairless or short-hairy involucre has 3–5 sets of narrow, green to yellow, overlapping, strongly keeled phyllaries.

Flowering time: August–September

Habitat/range: Dry, rocky places; mixed conifer, montane, and subalpine zones; 3,900–10,000'.

Comments: This shrub needs very little water, grows well in rocky, alkaline soils, and is often used as an ornamental plant in places where water conservation is important. The shrub is under serious consideration as a commercial source of natural rubber, in place of Brazilian Rubber Trees, which are the only other known source of natural rubber in the world.

Similar plants: Although there are a few somewhat similar shrubs in the park, Showy Rubber Rabbitbrush is the only one that has flower heads with no ray flowers and only 5 disk flowers.

SINGLE-HEADED GOLDENBUSH

Ericameria suffruticosa
Sunflower family (Asteraceae)

Description: This erect to sprawling shrub, 4–16"
tall, has densely glandular-sticky herbage and
leafy, flexible, green stems that turn red-brown
with age. The alternate, light green to gray-green
leaves, up to 1½" long, are narrowly oblanceolate
and have wavy margins. The flower heads grow
singly or in small clusters of 2 or 3 and have
several leaf-like bracts beneath them. The heads
have 15–40 yellow disk flowers and 1–8 yellow
ray flowers. The bell-shaped involucre has 2 or 3
series of lanceolate phyllaries that are more or
less equal in length, the outer ones green and the
inner ones reddish.

Flowering time: July–September

Habitat/range: Dry, rocky or gravelly slopes and
ridges; subalpine to alpine zones; 8,500–11,800'.

Similar plants: A common roadside shrub along
Tioga Road, Bloomer's Goldenbush (*E. bloomeri*), is
the only other *Ericameria* shrub in the park that has
both disk and ray flowers, but it has only 4–14 disk
flowers. White-stemmed Goldenbush (*E. discoidea*)
has no ray flowers; its distinctive white stems
are covered with dense, white-woolly hairs and it
grows mostly above the tree line. Cliff Goldenbush
(*E. cuneata* var. *cuneata*) has no ray flowers, and
its leaves are distinctly wedge shaped. It blooms in
late summer and fall and grows on rocky cliffs at
lower elevations, such as the cliffs along Big Oak
Flat Road.

GOLDEN YARROW

Eriophyllum confertiflorum var. *confertiflorum*
Sunflower family (Asteraceae)

Description: Golden Yarrow is a low shrub,
8–28" tall, with multiple stems from the base
and densely white-woolly herbage. Its alternate
leaves are up to 2" long, are rolled under along the
margins, and have 3 or 5 deep lobes or are twice
pinnately compound. The small flower heads,
which grow in clusters of 5–40 at the branch tips,
have 10–35 glandular-hairy, golden disk flowers
and 4–6 yellow ray flowers, though some plants
have flower heads with no ray flowers. The white-
woolly, bell-shaped involucre has 4–7 overlapping
phyllaries.

Flowering time: April–July

Habitat/range: Open, rocky slopes and other dry
habitats; chaparral/oak-woodland, mixed conifer,
and montane zones; up to 7,500'.

Comments: Golden Yarrow can survive in hot, dry
habitats because its dense matted hairs reflect
the sun's rays, provide insulation from the heat,
and reduce the drying effects of wind across the
plant's surfaces. Many hardy, attractive plants like
Golden Yarrow can be purchased at native plant
nurseries, and several chapters of the California
Native Plant Society have regular native plant
sales. In a state where water is often at a premium, planting natives is a good practice. They're
used to a hot, dry summer climate, don't need
rich soils, and need to be watered only sparingly,
unlike many non-native water hogs.

COMMON WOOLLY SUNFLOWER

Eriophyllum lanatum var. *integrifolium*
Sunflower family (Asteraceae)

Description: This common perennial or subshrub is 4–20" tall and has a woody base, several to many stems, and white-woolly herbage. The alternate, flat-margined leaves are ½–1½" long and are wedge shaped in outline. The leaf margins can be smooth, toothed, or lobed with 3–5 variously shaped lobes. Each stem ends with a single flower head, which has many bright yellow disk flowers and usually 8 ray flowers with golden-yellow rays that are less than ½" long. The bell-shaped to hemispheric involucre usually has 8 strongly keeled phyllaries.

Flowering time: July–August

Habitat/range: Dry, open places; mixed conifer, montane, and subalpine zones; 5,000–10,300'.

Similar plants: Three *Eriophyllum lanatum* varieties grow in the park, and Common Woolly Sunflower is the most common of the three. Large-flowered Woolly Sunflower, var. *grandiflorum*, has 10–15 bright yellow (but not golden-yellow) ray flowers that are more than ½" long. Golden Woolly Sunflower, var. *croceum*, has 13 golden ray flowers that are less than ½" long. A somewhat similar plant, Congdon's Woolly Sunflower (*Eriophyllum congdonii*), grows west of the park on rocky ridges and scree slopes in the El Portal area. It also has white-woolly foliage and toothed or lobed leaves, but it's an annual and doesn't have a woody base.

YOSEMITE WOOLLY SUNFLOWER

Eriophyllum nubigenum
Sunflower family (Asteraceae)

Description: Yosemite Woolly Sunflower, one of the rarest plants in Yosemite, is an annual with stiff, leafy stems that are 2–6" long and usually have a few ascending to erect branches. Its herbage is densely gray-woolly throughout. The alternate leaves are less than 1" long, are spatula shaped to oblanceolate, and sometimes have a few teeth or short lobes near the tip. The tiny flower heads, which are solitary or in small clusters at the branch tips, have 3–16 yellow disk flowers and 4–6 yellow ray flowers that turn red with age. The disk and ray flowers just barely peek out from the top of the phyllaries.

Flowering time: June–August

Habitat/range: Open, gravelly and rocky areas; mixed conifer and montane zones; 5,500–9,000'.

Comments: Yosemite Woolly Sunflower grows at only a few sites in the Yosemite region, mainly in the Little Yosemite Valley area, but also at Chilnualna Falls. The plant is found only in Mariposa County and is listed as rare but not particularly endangered by the California Native Plant Society.

BREWER'S ASTER

Eucephalus breweri (*Aster breweri*)
Sunflower family (Asteraceae)

Description: This perennial is up to 3' tall and has several stems that are often branched. Its herbage can be smooth, glandular-hairy, or white-woolly-hairy. The alternate stem leaves are up to 2" long and are lanceolate, ovate, or linear. The flower heads **[inset]**, which grow solitary at the branch tips, have numerous yellow disk flowers with extended yellow styles, and they have no ray flowers.

Flowering time: July–September

Habitat/range: Open coniferous forest and subalpine meadows; mixed conifer, montane, and subalpine zones; 4,600–10,500'.

Comments: This is one of many plants that used to be in the *Aster* genus. A 1994 worldwide study of plants assigned to the *Aster* genus revealed that Eurasian members of the group are substantially different from North American members. By rules of scientific nomenclature, the Eurasian plants, which were named long before the North American plants, got to keep the *Aster* genus name. That meant that about 180 North American plants had to be assigned to other genera. Half of them, about 90 species, are now in the *Symphyotrichum* genus.

Similar plants: Bloomer's Goldenbush (*Ericameria bloomeri*) looks similar, but it's a shrub rather than a perennial and its flower heads almost always have at least a few ray flowers.

WESTERN GOLDENROD

Euthamia occidentalis
Sunflower family (Asteraceae)

Description: Western Goldenrod is a perennial, 2–4' tall, with smooth, erect to ascending stems that are leafy throughout and much-branched toward the top. Its alternate, sessile leaves are linear, gland-dotted, and often rough to the touch along the margins, and they're larger toward the middle of the stem. The small flower heads, which grow in somewhat flat-topped clusters at the branch ends, have 6–15 yellow disk flowers and 15–25 yellow ray flowers. The narrow, pointed-tipped phyllaries are in 3 or 4 graduated series, like layered shingles on a roof.

Flowering time: July–September

Habitat/range: Streambanks and moist meadows; chaparral/oak-woodland and mixed conifer zones; up to 4,500'.

Comments: Powdered dry leaves of this plant have been used as an antiseptic powder, and boiled stems and leaves have been made into an antiseptic lotion.

Similar plants: Western Goldenrod is related to plants in the *Solidago* genus, and it was once assigned to that genus. It has narrow, untoothed and unscalloped leaves that are several times longer than they are wide; members of the park's *Solidago* genus have broader leaves, and their lower leaves are often scalloped or toothed.

WHITNEY'S GOLDENBUSH

Hazardia whitneyi var. *whitneyi*
Sunflower family (Asteraceae)

Description: Whitney's Goldenbush is a perennial or subshrub with several ascending stems, 8–20" long, that are slightly soft-hairy and have stalked glands toward the top. Its thick, rough, glandular leaves are 1–2" long, widely oblong to spatula shaped, and conspicuously sharp toothed along the margins. The lower leaves are tapered to the base, and the upper leaves are occasionally clasping. The flower heads are solitary or variously clustered, and they have leafy bracts at the base that blend in with the phyllaries. The heads have 13–30 yellow disk flowers and 5–18 ray flowers with yellow rays that are about ½" long. The bell-shaped involucre has leathery, sharp-pointed phyllaries in 4–6 loosely graduated series.

Flowering time: July–September

Habitat/range: Dry, sometimes rocky forest openings; mixed conifer, montane, and subalpine zones; 4,000–10,500'.

Comments: The genus was named for Barclay Hazard (1852–1938), an amateur California botanist. The genus has 11 species, all of which grow only in western North America.

Similar plants: Western Dwarf Mountain Ragwort (*Senecio fremontii*) has similar flower heads and distinctly toothed leaves, but its herbage is neither hairy nor glandular.

BIGELOW'S SNEEZEWEED

Helenium bigelovii
Sunflower family (Asteraceae)

Description: This common perennial has smooth to sparsely hairy herbage and 1 to several stems, 1–4¼' long, that are sometimes branched. Its thick, alternate stem leaves are 3–9" long and are narrowly lanceolate to oblanceolate. The leaves rapidly reduce in size upward. The larger lower leaves taper to a long, wavy-winged petiole that extends down the stem, and the upper leaves clasp the stem. The flower heads **[inset]** are solitary on long stalks and have a large sphere of 250–500 yellow or reddish-brown disk flowers surrounded by 13–30 ray flowers with yellow, 3-lobed rays that are up to 1" long and are often reflexed.

Flowering time: June–September

Habitat/range: Wet meadows and streambanks; chaparral/oak-woodland, mixed conifer, montane, and subalpine zones; up to 10,000'.

Comments: The powdered, dried leaves and flower heads of some *Helenium* species were used to make a snuff that was inhaled to cause sneezing and was thought to help cure colds.

Similar plants: The immature flower heads of Bigelow's Sneezeweed look something like the mature flower heads of Orange Sneezeweed (*Hymenoxys hoopesii*), but Orange Sneezeweed has longer, narrower, raggedy-looking ray flowers, and its leaves don't have a winged petiole.

CALIFORNIA SUNFLOWER
Helianthus californicus
Sunflower family (Asteraceae)

Description: California Sunflower is a perennial, up to 11½' tall, with smooth, hairless, waxy stems. Its mostly alternate, narrowly lanceolate leaves are up to 8" long, taper at both ends, and are mostly toothless. The lower leaf surface is gland-dotted and rough to the touch. The stem has 3–10 long-stalked flower heads. Each head has 50 or more yellow disk flowers that darken with age and 12–21 ray flowers with bright yellow rays that are up to 1¼" long. The long, narrow, pointed phyllaries bend backward and curl as the flower head ages.

Flowering time: July–August

Habitat/range: Streambanks and wet meadows; chaparral/oak-woodland and mixed conifer zones; up to 6,000'.

Similar plants: Three other plants in the park have similar flower heads, but they grow only in dry habitats. The weedy native Common Sunflower (*H. annuus*) has oval phyllaries that abruptly narrow to a long, slender tip. Bolander's Sunflower (*H. bolanderi*) has lanceolate phyllaries. California Helianthella (*Helianthella californica* var. *nevadensis*) has lanceolate phyllaries, and, unlike the other plants in this group, most of its leaves are basal. All four of the plants in this group are reported only occasionally in Yosemite, and they grow only in the chaparral/oak-woodland and mixed conifer zones.

SHAGGY HAWKWEED
Hieracium horridum
Sunflower family (Asteraceae)

Description: This shaggy-looking perennial is 4–14" tall and has 1 or a few stems that are branched above. Its gray to gray-green herbage is covered with dense, long, soft, white or brownish hairs. The alternate, oblong to spatula-shaped leaves are 1–4" long, and the upper leaves clasp the stem. Many flower heads, about ⅜" long, grow in relatively loose clusters at the stem and branch ends. Each head has 6–14 yellow ray flowers that are squared-off at the tip and have 5 tiny, pointed teeth. The cylindric to narrowly bell-shaped involucre has long hairs that are black at the base.

Flowering time: July–September

Habitat/range: Dry, rocky places; mixed conifer, montane, subalpine, and alpine zones; 5,000–10,800'.

Comments: Somehow, it always seems a treat to come across Shaggy Hawkweed, no matter how many times you've seen it before. It's difficult to resist the urge to run your hands along the hairy foliage, which is pleasantly soft to the touch. The plants often grow from rock crevices in areas where nothing else seems to grow. The unappealing (some would say misleading) name *horridum* means bristly, which might refer to the plant's impressive hairiness, though the hairs are undeniably soft rather than bristly.

SLENDER HAWKWEED

Hieracium triste (*H. gracile*)
Sunflower family (Asteraceae)

Description: Slender Hawkweed is a perennial with 1 to several slender, short-hairy stems, 4–11" tall, that are sometimes branched toward the top. The basal leaves form a rosette, and a few smaller, alternate leaves sometimes grow along the stem. The mostly hairless leaves are 1–4" long, are spatula shaped to oblanceolate, taper gradually to a petiole, and usually have smooth margins. The glandular-hairy flower heads, which grow in an open raceme, have a bell-shaped involucre (often with black, gland-tipped hairs) and 20–60 ray flowers with yellow rays that are less than ¼" long.

Flowering time: July–August

Habitat/range: Damp, partially shaded forest openings, often near streams; montane, subalpine, and alpine zones; 7,800–10,800'.

Comments: *Hieracium* is Greek for hawk. Pliny the Elder, the Roman naturalist, believed that hawks fed on Meadow Hawkweed (*Hieracium caespitosum*), a European native, to strengthen their vision. That plant has somehow found its way to North America. In Idaho, Montana, Oregon, and Washington, the plant is considered a noxious weed, but it hasn't been reported in California yet. We resent the intrusion of undesirable non-native plants, but we should keep in mind that a considerable number of our native plants have become unwelcome pests in other countries.

ALPINE GOLD

Hulsea algida
Sunflower family (Asteraceae)

Description: This gorgeous perennial is a favorite of many alpine hikers. It grows up to 15" tall and has 1–5 unbranched stems. Its soft-hairy herbage is strongly sticky-glandular and aromatic. The linear to oblanceolate, trough-like leaves are up to 4" long and have coarse teeth along the margins. The large, solitary flower heads, up to 1½" wide, have many golden disk flowers, 20–60 bright yellow ray flowers, and glandular-hairy phyllaries.

Flowering time: July–August

Habitat/range: Talus slopes and rocky flats; alpine zone; 10,500–13,100'.

Comments: The climate in the alpine zone is so harsh, soil is so scarce, and the growing season is so short that most plants are small. Alpine Gold is a notable exception. According to the California Department of Fish and Wildlife, bighorn sheep munch on Alpine Gold flower heads early in the alpine season and leave the leaves and roots for food in the fall.

Similar plants: Yellow Daisy (*Erigeron linearis*) grows in similar clusters and has flower heads that look almost identical to Alpine Gold's flower heads, but its leaves are not toothed. The plant is known from only one location in the park, along the rocky slopes between the Great Sierra Mine and Middle Gaylor Lake in the Gaylor Lakes basin.

131

SHORT-LEAVED HULSEA
Hulsea brevifolia
Sunflower family (Asteraceae)

Description: Short-leaved Hulsea is a perennial with 1–5 stems that are 1–2' tall and are branched from the base. Its glandular-hairy herbage is strongly aromatic. The alternate, oblong to spatula-shaped leaves are up to 2½" long, sessile or slightly clasping, and coarsely toothed toward the tip. The flower heads, which are solitary at the branch tips, have many yellow disk flowers and 10–23 ray flowers with yellow rays that are about ½" long. The involucre has lanceolate, sometimes reflexed phyllaries that taper to the tip.

Flowering time: June–August

Habitat/range: Dry forest openings in gravelly soils; mixed conifer and montane zones; 5,200–8,200'.

Comments: Renowned botanist Henry Bolander collected the first herbarium specimen of this plant in the Mariposa Grove of Big Trees in 1866.

Similar plants: Red-rayed Hulsea (*Hulsea heterochroma*) **[inset]** has similar alternate, toothed leaves and also has glandular-hairy, strongly aromatic foliage. Its ray flowers are shorter and narrower and are usually red or rust colored. The plant is rare in the park, known from only a few locations in the mixed conifer and montane zones, but it sometimes grows in large populations following wildfires.

ORANGE SNEEZEWEED, OWL'S-CLAWS
Hymenoxys hoopesii (*Dugaldia hoopesii*)
Sunflower family (Asteraceae)

Description: This perennial has 1–4 erect stems, 17–40" tall, that are branched toward the top and are usually red-purple toward the bottom or throughout. Young plants have herbage with long, soft hairs. The lower leaves are up to 1' long and are oblong or oblanceolate. The upper leaves are smaller and are linear to lanceolate. The flower heads are about 1¼–2" wide and grow at the branch ends, either solitary or in somewhat flat-topped clusters of 2–12. Each head has 100–330 yellow disk flowers and 14–26 yellow, wavy, raggedy ray flowers. The narrow, spreading phyllaries are in 2 series, the inner ones smaller than the outer ones.

Flowering time: July–September

Habitat/range: Meadows and streambanks; subalpine zone; 8,500–10,800'.

Comments: Botanists change the scientific names of plants when new information becomes available. This plant was originally named *Helenium hoopesii* in 1864. In 1900, it was renamed *Dugaldia hoopesii*, and in 1994 it was given its current name.

Similar plants: The immature flower heads of Bigelow's Sneezeweed (*Helenium bigelovii*) look something like the mature flower heads of Orange Sneezeweed, but Bigelow's Sneezeweed has ray flowers with 3 conspicuously large lobes at the tip.

YOSEMITE TARWEED

Jensia yosemitana (*Madia yosemitana*)
Sunflower family (Asteraceae)

Description: Yosemite Tarweed is a small, slender annual. Its erect stem is 2½–6" long and is glandular and sometimes branched toward the top. Its soft-hairy leaves are ½–2" long and are linear or somewhat broader at the tip. The lower leaves are often crowded toward the base of the stem and are mostly opposite. The upper leaves are alternate and sometimes have stalked glands. The small flower heads **[inset]** have 1–7 yellow disk flowers and 2–8 yellow, 3-lobed ray flowers. The hairy, top-shaped involucre has nonglandular phyllaries that wrap around each ray flower ovary, making the phyllaries bulge outward.

Flowering time: May–July

Habitat/range: Moist to wet, open, sandy or grassy places and seeps; mixed conifer and montane zones; 3,400–7,500'.

Similar plants: Two other plants in the park have similar small flower heads with bulging phyllaries, but their phyllaries are glandular and feel sticky. To tell those two plants apart, you'll probably need magnification. Tiny Tarweed (*Hemizonella minima*, previously *Madia minima*), which is about the same size as or smaller than Yosemite Tarweed, has black glands on its phyllaries. Small Tarweed (*Madia exigua*), which can grow taller than the other two plants, has yellow glands on its phyllaries.

CALIFORNIA GOLDFIELDS

Lasthenia californica ssp. *californica*
Sunflower family (Asteraceae)

Description: This slender annual has an erect, somewhat hairy stem that's 2–15" long. Its opposite leaves are up to 2¾" long, are linear to narrowly oblanceolate, and grow mostly along the stem. The hemispheric to bell-shaped involucre has 4–13 lanceolate phyllaries that often become strongly keeled with age. The small flower heads have many golden disk flowers and 6–13 bright yellow ray flowers. The pappus, if any, consists of 1–7 linear bristles that are clear to brown.

Flowering time: March–May

Habitat/range: Open, grassy hillsides and flats; chaparral/oak-woodland zone; up to 3,500'.

Comments: Although goldfields haven't been reported in the park, you'll probably notice large, bright yellow, low-growing patches of them if you're traveling toward any of the three western park entrances when the plants are in bloom.

Similar plants: Needle Goldfields (*Lasthenia gracilis*) and Foothill Sunburst (*Pseudobahia heermannii*) also grow near the park's western boundary. Needle Goldfields have 2–6 (but usually 4) opaque, white, lance-ovate pappus scales, but both goldfield species sometimes have no pappus, making them difficult to distinguish. Foothill Sunburst has similar flower heads, but its leaves are alternate and are conspicuously lobed.

133

SIERRA TIDYTIPS
Layia pentachaeta ssp. *pentachaeta*
Sunflower family (Asteraceae)

Description: Sierra Tidytips is an annual with an ascending to erect stem that's 2–40" long and branched toward the top. Its glandular herbage has a pleasant lemony scent or an unpleasantly acrid scent. The alternate, sessile leaves are up to 4¼" long, linear to lanceolate or oblanceolate, and once or twice irregularly pinnately lobed. The flower heads are up to 2¼" wide and grow solitary or in loose clusters of 2–5 at the branch ends. Each flower head has 7–125 yellow disk flowers, 4–14 yellow, distinctly 3-lobed ray flowers, and a hemispheric involucre with 4–14 narrow phyllaries.

Flowering time: March–May

Habitat/range: Grassy slopes and flats; chaparral/oak-woodland zone; up to 5,100'.

Comments: This plant grows around El Portal, near Mather, and along the road to Hetch Hetchy, but it's more common in the foothills west of the park. Plants in the *Layia* genus usually have distinctively 3-lobed ray flowers. Several species have yellow ray flowers with crisply delineated white tips, which is probably why the plants are called tidytips.

Similar plants: Elegant Madia (*Madia elegans*) has similar flower heads with yellow, 3-lobed ray flowers, and it grows in similar habitats, but its leaves are unlobed.

ELEGANT MADIA, COMMON MADIA
Madia elegans
Sunflower family (Asteraceae)

Description: The erect stems of this common, strongly scented annual are 8–32" tall and are often densely glandular. Its linear to broadly lanceolate leaves are up to 5" long. The lower leaves are opposite and somewhat crowded, and the upper leaves are alternate and more widely spaced. The flower heads are up to 2" wide, grow in loose clusters, and have many yellow or maroon disk flowers and 5–22 yellow, 3-lobed ray flowers that are often maroon at the base. The involucre has sticky-hairy phyllaries that wrap around each ray flower ovary, making the phyllaries bulge outward.

Flowering time: March–August

Habitat/range: Open, grassy places and disturbed areas; chaparral/oak-woodland and mixed conifer zones; up to 7,100'.

Comments: You can pass by a patch of these plants in the morning and see many bright yellow flower heads. Pass by the same patch a few hours later and the flower heads will seem to have vanished. The ray flowers furl to protect themselves from the midday heat.

Similar plants: Much less common Bolander's Madia (*Kyhosia bolanderi*, previously *Madia bolanderi*) has similar leaves and flower heads, but its basal leaves are in a dense, tufted cluster, and its ray flowers are never maroon at the base.

SLENDER TARWEED

Madia gracilis
Sunflower family (Asteraceae)

Description: This common, aromatic annual has an erect, branching stem that can vary impressively in height, from 4"–3¼' tall. The stem, leaves, and phyllaries are covered with soft, spreading hairs and stalked resin glands. The linear, alternate, sessile leaves are up to 4" long. The small flower heads **[inset]**, which grow at the stem and branch tips, have several yellow disk flowers with dark purple anthers and 3–10 yellow ray flowers with 3 lobes at the tip. The involucre is urn shaped or pinched at the top, and the phyllaries wrap around the achenes, causing them to bulge outward.

Flowering time: April–August

Habitat/range: Open or partially shaded slopes or flats in many habitats; chaparral/oak-woodland, mixed conifer, and montane zones; up to 8,000'.

Comments: If you're used to seeing Slender Tarweed when it's less than a foot tall, you might think you've found a different plant if you come across one that's 3 feet tall. The flower heads are also variable, the ray flowers sometimes barely poking out beyond the phyllary tips and sometimes spreading wide open.

Similar plants: Much less common Mountain Tarweed (*Madia glomerata*) is similar in stature and foliage, but its flower heads grow in dense clusters and have 0–3 ray flowers.

PINEAPPLE WEED

Matricaria discoidea (*Chamomilla suaveolens*)
Sunflower family (Asteraceae)

Description: Pineapple Weed is a sweet-scented, mostly hairless annual, 1–6" tall, with stems that are branched from the base. The alternate leaves are divided 1–3 times into linear segments. Its distinctive cone-shaped flower heads are about ⅜" wide, grow in loose clusters, and have disk flowers only. The cup-shaped involucre has membranous-margined phyllaries in 2 or 3 unequal series.

Flowering time: February–August

Habitat/range: Open, disturbed areas, often in well-trampled walkways where little else grows; chaparral/oak-woodland and mixed conifer zones; up to 6,000'.

Comments: Pineapple Weed is a weedy native of northwestern North America that has spread into eastern and southwestern North America. Until somewhat recently, it was classified as a non-native plant in California. The flower heads look something like tiny pineapples, but the plant's common name comes from the pineapple scent of its crushed leaves and flower heads. Myrcene, one of the main chemical compounds in the plant, is used in the production of perfumes. Pineapple Weed is related to Chamomile (*Matricaria chamomilla*), a European native that doesn't grow in the park. Chamomile has been used as a medicinal tea for centuries. Besides its calming effects, the tea is said to have many healing properties.

NODDING SILVERPUFFS

Microseris nutans
Sunflower family (Asteraceae)

Description: This common, taprooted perennial is 4–28" tall and has milky sap and 1 or more stems. The narrowly lanceolate or oblanceolate leaves are up to 1' long, grow mostly at the base of the plant or on the lower stem, and sometimes have 2–4 pairs of lobes or teeth along the margins. About 1–6 flower heads grow solitary on long stalks, and the heads are pendant when they're in bud. The mature flower heads are about 1" wide and have 13–75 yellow ray flowers. The phyllaries are often black-hairy, and the inner, long-tapered phyllaries are much longer than the outer, uneven phyllaries.

Flowering time: June–August

Habitat/range: Moist, rocky meadows and openings in coniferous woodlands; mixed conifer, montane, and subalpine zones; 5,200–10,300'.

Similar plants: Yosemite plants in the *Crepis* genus have similar flower heads, but they have more than 10 flower heads per plant and the flower heads are erect when they're in bud. Lindley's Silverpuffs (*Uropappus lindleyi*) **[inset]** has similar leaves and flower heads, but its buds are erect and its phyllary tips extend conspicuously beyond the tips of the ray flowers. It grows in the Hetch Hetchy area, in Yosemite Valley, and on mostly south-facing slopes in the Merced River Canyon. Some *Agoseris* species look similar, but none of them have nodding buds.

WOOLLY GROUNDSEL

Packera cana (*Senecio canus*)
Sunflower family (Asteraceae)

Description: Woolly Groundsel is a perennial with herbage that's densely woolly or gray-hairy when the plant is young and less so later on. Its solitary stem is 4–12" long and grows from a tufted rosette of basal leaves, although plants often grow in clusters that make it look as though there are multiple stems per plant. The basal and lower stem leaves are up to 3" long and have a petiole about as long as the blade. The round, ovate, or elliptic blade has flat margins and is squared off or tapers at the base. The 8–15 or more flower heads, in more or less flat-topped clusters, have many golden disk flowers and 8–10 (or 13) yellow ray flowers that are up to ½" long. The heads have 13 or 21 narrow, green or yellowish phyllaries. Plants with no ray flowers do occur, but rarely.

Flowering time: June–August

Habitat/range: Dry, rocky areas; montane, subalpine, and alpine zones; 6,900–11,800'.

Comments: The matted, silvery-white hairs on young Woolly Groundsel plants act like a down jacket, insulating the plants from cold air.

Similar plants: Hoary Groundsel (*Packera werneriifolia*) also has densely clustered basal leaves, but its narrower leaves are usually rolled under along the margins and it has only 1–5 (rarely up to 8) flower heads per stem.

ALPINE GROUNDSEL

Packera pauciflora (*Senecio pauciflorus*)
Sunflower family (Asteraceae)

Description: Alpine Groundsel is a distinctive perennial that's 6–16" tall, has 1–3 stems, and is mostly hairless. The succulent, long-petioled basal leaves have an oval to kidney-shaped blade that usually has a heart-shaped base. The lower stem leaves have pinnately lobed margins, and the upper stem leaves are sessile or clasping and have toothed, ear-like lobes. The flower heads, which are in open to compact clusters, have 0, 8, or 13 bright yellow ray flowers, up to ¼" long, and 60–80 or more bright orange disk flowers that look like glowing embers when they're young and become yellow with age. The 13 or 21 phyllaries are red or green at the base and have red tips.

Flowering time: July–August

Habitat/range: Damp meadows and riparian areas; subalpine and alpine zones; 8,500–10,500'.

Comments: This plant's ray flowers and phyllaries exhibit the Fibonacci sequence (1, 1, 2, 3, 5, 8, 13, 21, etc.), in which each number is the sum of the previous two numbers. Although Leonard Fibonacci described the sequence in 1202, it was only recently determined that the pattern is common in nature because of its extraordinary efficiency. The sequence is based on the "golden ratio" or "divine proportion," which could conceivably describe the arrangement of everything in nature, from the structure of atoms to patterns in the universe.

CLEFTLEAF GROUNDSEL

Packera subnuda var. *subnuda*
(*Senecio cymbalarioides*)
Sunflower family (Asteraceae)

Description: This hairless perennial is 4–12" tall and has a single stem (or rarely 2 or 3). Its succulent leaves are mostly basal and have a petiole that's longer than the blade. The blade is roundish or elliptic, has a scalloped margin, and is tapered or squared off at the base. The smaller, alternate stem leaves clasp the stem and are sometimes deeply toothed. The stem usually has a single flower head that often has 2 large bractlets at the base. Each flower head has 40–60 yellow disk flowers and 13 yellow ray flowers that are up to almost ½" long. The 13 or 21 hairless phyllaries are green or reddish tipped.

Flowering time: July–September

Habitat/range: Moist to marshy meadows, streambanks, and lakeshores; subalpine and alpine zones; 8,200–11,500'.

Comments: These plants sometimes look like little sunbursts hovering above meadow grasses. You may have to push some grass aside to get a look at the plant's basal leaves.

Similar plants: A few other Yosemite *Packera* and *Senecio* species also have somewhat scalloped leaves and grow in wet meadows, but Cleftleaf Groundsel is the only one with a single stem that usually ends with a solitary flower head.

137

HOARY GROUNDSEL

Packera werneriifolia (*Senecio werneriifolius*)
Sunflower family (Asteraceae)

Description: Hoary Groundsel is a compact perennial, 2½–8" tall, with 1–5 mostly leafless stems and herbage that's usually white-woolly when the plant is young. The tightly clustered basal leaves are up to 1½" long, are narrowly oblanceolate to elliptic, are tapered at the base, and usually have margins that are rolled under. The alternate stem leaves, if any, are much smaller and bract-like. The flower heads, 1–5 per stem, have 30–50 yellow disk flowers and 8 or 13 yellow ray flowers with rays that are up to ⅜" long. The involucre has 13 or 21 hairy, green or reddish phyllaries.

Flowering time: July–August

Habitat/range: Dry fellfields and rocky slopes; subalpine and alpine zones; 10,200–12,200'.

Comments: These little alpine plants grow close to the ground, which protects them from the wind and allows them to warm up more quickly on sunny days. Most alpine plants are perennials. The short alpine growing season makes it difficult for plants to sprout from seed, grow to maturity, flower, and produce their own seeds in a single season.

Similar plants: Woolly Groundsel (*Packera cana*) also grows at high elevations and has clustered basal leaves, but its leaves are more spatula shaped, the leaf blades are flat along the margins, and it has 8–15 or more flower heads per stem.

BOLANDER'S MOCK DANDELION

Phalacroseris bolanderi
Sunflower family (Asteraceae)

Description: This meadow-loving, hairless perennial has milky sap and usually has a solitary, leafless stalk that's up to 16" long. The leaves, all of which grow at the base of the plant, are 2½–8" long and are linear or somewhat broader toward the tip. The solitary flower heads are about 1" wide and have green, lanceolate, somewhat equal phyllaries and many yellow ray flowers that wither and become raggedy and reddish with age.

Flowering time: June–August

Habitat/range: Wet to boggy meadows; montane zone; 5,600–8,500'.

Comments: Bolander's Mock Dandelion likes its feet in water. It lives only in wet meadows, where its leaves are often hidden among grasses and other dense vegetation. Fortunately, its flower stalks grow just long enough to lift its distinctive, bright golden-yellow flower heads above the surrounding vegetation. The plant was named in honor of Henry N. Bolander (1831–1897), who collected many plants in Yosemite and became California State Botanist in 1864.

Similar plants: Some other composites in the park look somewhat similar and grow in moist habitats, but none of those composites grow only in wet to boggy meadows.

ALPINE FLAMES
Pyrrocoma apargioides
Sunflower family (Asteraceae)

Description: Alpine Flames is a common perennial with 1–7 reclining to erect stems that are 2–8" long, smooth to slightly hairy, and often reddish tinged. The leathery basal leaves are 1–4" long and grow in a rosette. The leaves are narrowly lanceolate or oblanceolate and usually have irregular, sharp or spine-tipped teeth on the margins. The alternate stem leaves are linear and much smaller. The flower heads, which usually grow solitary at the stem ends, have many yellow disk flowers and 11–40 yellow ray flowers with rays that are up to ⅝" long. The narrowly bell-shaped involucre has 3 or 4 series of oblong to lanceolate, leathery, hairless phyllaries.

Flowering time: July–September

Habitat/range: Dry to moist meadows, forest openings, and rocky slopes; subalpine and alpine zones; 7,900–12,500'.

Comments: This plant tends to hug the ground to protect itself from the precarious weather of high elevations. Renowned botanist Henry N. Bolander collected the plant's type specimens at Soda Springs in Tuolumne Meadows in 1866, and the specimens now reside in the Smithsonian Institution's National Museum of Natural History in Washington, D.C. In plant collecting, type specimens are plants that are used to name and describe a new species.

SILKY RAILLARDELLA
Raillardella argentea
Sunflower family (Asteraceae)

Description: Silky Raillardella is an appealing perennial with a crowded rosette of basal leaves that are up to 3" long and look silver due to their dense silvery-silky hairs. The oblong or oblanceolate leaves are sometimes minutely glandular. The cylindric to bell-shaped flower heads grow solitary on a leafless stalk, are about 1" long, and have 7–26 yellow disk flowers and no ray flowers. The linear, pointed-tipped phyllaries are green to dark brown, coarse-hairy, and somewhat glandular.

Flowering time: July–August

Habitat/range: Dry, rocky or gravelly flats; subalpine and alpine zones; 9,000–12,000'.

Similar plants: Green-leaved Raillardella (*Raillardella scaposa*) looks a lot like Silky Raillardella, but its sparsely hairy leaves are unmistakably green rather than silver. Both plants are somewhat common, and they grow in similar habitats and at similar elevations.

Note: If you paused at this page because you're trying to identify a small, high-elevation composite with yellow disk flowers and no ray flowers, but the plant you're examining has divided leaves with many lobes, you've probably found Cut-leaved Daisy (*Erigeron compositus*), which often has white (or pale pink) ray flowers and just about as often has no ray flowers at all (see page 15).

CALIFORNIA CONE-FLOWER
Rudbeckia californica
Sunflower family (Asteraceae)

Description: This lofty perennial has a hairless, leafy, usually unbranched stem that's up to 5' tall. The alternate leaves are up to 2' long, broadly lanceolate to elliptic, and hairy on the lower surface. The lower stem leaves have a petiole and are often coarsely toothed or lobed. The smaller upper leaves are mostly sessile and toothless. The distinctive flower heads **[upper inset]**, which are usually solitary, have 8–21 yellow ray flowers that are 1–2½" long and an elongated cone or column of many green to yellow disk flowers.

Flowering time: July–August

Habitat/range: Meadows and other moist places; mixed conifer and montane zones; 5,500–7,000'.

Comments: California Cone-flower is common in meadows around Crane Flat. It also grows in meadows along Glacier Point Road and in the Mariposa Grove, but there are no reports of it growing in Yosemite Valley.

Similar plants: Non-native Black-eyed Susan (*Rudbeckia hirta* var. *pulcherrima*) has a flower head **[lower inset]** that has a small cone of disk flowers and looks much like the flower head of an immature California Cone-flower. Its densely hairy stem makes it easy to distinguish from California Cone-flower. In the park, Black-eyed Susan is known to grow only in Yosemite Valley meadows.

RAYLESS RAGWORT
Senecio aronicoides
Sunflower family (Asteraceae)

Description: Rayless Ragwort is a herbaceous perennial with a single stem, 1–3' tall, and mostly basal leaves **[left inset]**. Its herbage is cobwebby-woolly when young and becomes less so with age. The leaves, 3–10" long, are sometimes purplish below, and they have a triangular to ovate, often irregularly toothed blade that tapers to a long petiole. The little flower heads **[right inset]**, which grow in somewhat flat-topped clusters of 6–30 or more, have 40–75 yellow disk flowers and either no ray flowers or rarely 1 or 2. The 8 to 13 narrow main phyllaries often have purplish-black tips.

Flowering time: May–July

Habitat/range: Dry ground in forest openings; mixed conifer and montane zones; 3,900–8,000'.

Comments: Purple coloration on a leaf's lower surface reflects light back through the green upper portion of the leaf, giving the chlorophyll a second chance to utilize the sun's energy.

Similar plants: Lambs-tongue Ragwort (*Senecio integerrimus*) has 5–12 ray flowers per flower head, though the rays can be inconspicuous when the flower heads are developing or when the rays are withering with age. Otherwise, the two species have a lot in common. They both have a tall solitary stem and mostly basal, long-petioled leaves that are often purple on the lower surface.

CLARK'S RAGWORT
Senecio clarkianus
Sunflower family (Asteraceae)

Description: This herbaceous perennial is rare in the park. It has a single erect stem, 2–4' tall, and evenly distributed, alternate leaves, up to 6¼" long. The distinctive leaves are sharply cleft or deeply pinnately lobed. The flower heads, which grow in somewhat flat-topped clusters of 8–20, have 35–45 yellow disk flowers and 8 or 13 narrow yellow ray flowers with rays that are usually about ½" long. The bell-shaped involucre has linear phyllaries that are often curled backward at the tips.

Flowering time: July–September

Habitat/range: Wet meadows; mixed conifer and montane zones; 3,900–7,600'.

Comments: Galen Clark (1814–1910) was Yosemite's first park ranger, though the title was park guardian in those days. He started the job in 1864 and kept on for 24 years. Much earlier, Clark lived with his wife in Missouri. After she died, he moved to California. In 1853, at the age of 39, he got tuberculosis, and doctors predicted that he had six months to live. They prescribed rest and outdoor air to relieve his symptoms. He moved to Wawona, spent time exploring, and grew to love the area. He recovered from his illness and was eventually instrumental in crafting legislation that put Yosemite Valley and the Mariposa Grove under the protection of the U.S. government. Mount Clark and the Clark Range are named for the remarkable man.

DOUGLAS' THREADLEAF GROUNDSEL
Senecio flaccidus var. *douglasii*
Sunflower family (Asteraceae)

Description: This is the only shrubby *Senecio* species in the park. The fast-growing plant is 3–4' tall, has many woody stems, and is leafy throughout. The leaves are white-woolly when young and become hairless above with age. They are about equal in size all along the stems, are pinnately divided into linear or thread-like segments with curled-under edges, and often intertwine, forming tangled clumps. The flower heads, which grow in loose, flat-topped clusters of 3–10, have 40–50 yellow disk flowers and 8, 13, or 21 yellow ray flowers with rays about ½" long. The involucre has 13 or 21 sometimes black-tipped inner phyllaries and often has well-developed outer phyllaries, some of them up to half as long as the inner phyllaries.

Flowering time: June–November

Habitat/range: Dry, open, sandy or rocky areas; chaparral/oak-woodland and mixed conifer zones; up to 5,000'.

Comments: All *Senecio* species contain varying amounts of an alkaloid that's toxic to humans and livestock. Long-term ingestion can cause irreversible liver damage. In England and Wales, Tansy Ragwort (*Senecio jacobaea*) has poisoned so many cattle that it's responsible for more economic loss than all other poisonous plants combined.

WESTERN DWARF MOUNTAIN RAGWORT

Senecio fremontii var. *occidentalis*
Sunflower family (Asteraceae)

Description: This herbaceous perennial has succulent, hairless stems, up to 1' long, that arch upward from the base and are often purple tinged. The plant has basal leaves, but most of the small, thick, glossy leaves are alternate along the stem. The leaves are broader at the tip, are truncate or tapered at the base, and usually have sharply pointed teeth of various sizes and shapes along the margins. The flower heads have 35–40 yellow disk flowers and 8 yellow ray flowers that vary in width; sometimes the rays are broad and overlapping, but they're usually thin, somewhat twisted, and well spaced. The involucre has 8 or 13 inner phyllaries and a few somewhat inconspicuous outer phyllaries.

Flowering time: July–September

Habitat/range: Rocky sites; subalpine and alpine zones; 9,000–12,500'.

Comments: This plant is uncommon in the park. A somewhat accessible place to find it is along the Mount Hoffmann Trail near May Lake.

Similar plants: Rocky Mountain Groundsel (*Packera streptanthifolia*, previously *Senecio streptanthifolius*) also has succulent, hairless leaves with toothed or scalloped margins, but its stem leaves are few and are much smaller than its basal leaves.

LAMBS-TONGUE RAGWORT

Senecio integerrimus var. *major*
Sunflower family (Asteraceae)

Description: Lambs-tongue Ragwort is a herbaceous perennial with a single erect stem, 1–3' tall, and mostly basal leaves. Its herbage is hairy when young and becomes less so with age. The oval to lance-oblong lower leaves taper to a petiole, are often toothed, and are sometimes purplish on the lower surface. The stem leaves become smaller and sessile upward. The flower heads, which grow in more or less flat-topped clusters of 6–12, have 35–45 yellow disk flowers and 5, 8, or 13 (rarely 0) yellow ray flowers, with rays about ¼" long. The 13 or 21 linear main phyllaries are usually green tipped or are rarely minutely black tipped.

Flowering time: May–August

Habitat/range: Dry to moist areas, forest openings, rocky flats and slopes; mixed conifer, montane, and subalpine zones; 3,900–10,500'.

Similar plants: Columbia Ragwort (*Senecio integerrimus* var. *exaltatus*) is practically identical to Lambs-tongue Ragwort, but it has lanceolate, distinctly black-tipped phyllaries (and also, on rare occasions, has no ray flowers). Rayless Ragwort (*Senecio aronicoides*) also has a tall, solitary stem and mostly basal leaves, and it can easily be mistaken for Lambs-tongue Ragwort and Columbia Ragwort, but its flower heads either have no ray flowers or they have 1 or 2 somewhat inconspicuous ray flowers.

SIERRA RAGWORT
Senecio scorzonella
Sunflower family (Asteraceae)

Description: This herbaceous perennial is 8–20"
tall and usually has a single stem. Its herbage
is somewhat hairy, but not woolly, and often
becomes completely hairless with age. The basal
and alternate lower leaves are up to 6" long, are
lanceolate or oblanceolate, taper to a winged petiole, and have at least minutely toothed margins.
The alternate middle and upper leaves are smaller
and bract-like. The small flower heads grow in
somewhat tightly packed clusters of 10–30. They
have 10–20 yellow disk flowers and 0–7 yellow
ray flowers, though Yosemite plants usually have
no ray flowers. The bell-shaped involucre has
several small, inconspicuous outer phyllaries and
about 13 inner phyllaries that are green with black
tips and are sometimes hairy.

Flowering time: July–August

Habitat/range: Open woodlands and moist to wet
meadows; mixed conifer, montane, subalpine, and
alpine zones; 6,000–10,800'.

Similar plants: Yosemite has several other plants
in the *Senecio* genus and the closely related *Packera* genus that have mostly basal leaves. Sierra
Ragwort is the only one in the group that has many
densely crowded flower heads with fewer than 8
ray flowers, and most Sierra Ragwort plants in the
park have flower heads with no ray flowers.

ARROWLEAF RAGWORT
Senecio triangularis
Sunflower family (Asteraceae)

Description: Water-loving Arrowleaf Ragwort
is a herbaceous perennial with 1 or more mostly
unbranched, sometimes sparsely hairy stems that
are 1½–5' long. Its alternate, strongly toothed
leaves are shaped like an elongated triangle and
are usually squared off or heart shaped at the
base. The leaves are more or less evenly distributed along the stem and gradually become smaller
and more sessile toward the top of the stem. The
flower heads are about 1¼" wide and grow in
somewhat flat-topped clusters of 10–30. They
have 35–45 yellow disk flowers and 5–13 narrow,
yellow ray flowers. The cylindric to narrowly bell-
shaped involucre has 8, 13, or 21 narrow, usually
green-tipped (sometimes dark-tipped) inner phyllaries and a few much smaller outer phyllaries.

Flowering time: June–September

Habitat/range: Damp places and streambanks;
mixed conifer, montane, subalpine, and alpine
zones; 3,900–11,000'.

Comments: Arrowleaf Ragwort often grows in the
company of Giant Mountain Larkspur, Monkshood,
Crimson Columbine, and Alpine Lily. The colors,
textures, and shapes of the plants contrast and
blend harmoniously in the dappled sunlight of their
habitat.

143

COMMON GROUNDSEL, OLD-MAN-IN-THE-SPRING

(non-native)
Senecio vulgaris
Sunflower family (Asteraceae)

Description: This extremely common, weedy annual, up to 1½' tall, usually has a single stem that's simple or branched from below and leafy throughout. Its herbage is slightly succulent and is typically hairless, except when the plant is young. The lower leaves, up to 4" long, have short petioles and are pinnately divided into toothed lobes that are blunt and notched at the end and curve under along the margins. The upper leaves are sessile or clasp the stem. The short-stalked flower heads, which grow in small clusters, have many tightly packed yellow disk flowers. The involucre has narrow, green, distinctly black-tipped phyllaries.

Flowering time: February–July

Habitat/range: Disturbed areas; chaparral/oak-woodland and mixed conifer zones; up to 4,300'.

Comments: *Senecio* was derived from a Latin word for old man, referring to the white, hairy pappus on the achenes of plants in the genus. *Senecio vulgaris* is called Old-man-in-the-spring because it often has white seed heads when spring arrives. This Eurasian native has become a worldwide weed. It can quickly take over patches of bare ground before other plants begin to grow, and it can produce two generations in a single year.

MEADOW GOLDENROD, WEST COAST CANADA GOLDENROD

Solidago elongata (*S. canadensis* ssp. *elongata*)
Sunflower family (Asteraceae)

Description: This perennial is the common goldenrod of Yosemite Valley and middle-elevation meadows. It has densely leafy stems, 1–5' tall, and herbage with stiff, short hairs, at least toward the top of the plant. Its alternate, lanceolate leaves are 2–6" long and are well distributed along the stem. The lower leaves are usually toothed, and the largest leaves are midway up the stem. Hundreds of tiny flower heads are crowded in a somewhat diamond-shaped inflorescence with ascending to downward-curving branches. The heads have 5–12 yellow disk flowers and 8–15 yellow ray flowers.

Flowering time: June–October

Habitat/range: Meadows, meadow borders, and moist thickets; mixed conifer zone; 3,400–6,500'.

Similar plants: Meadow Goldenrod's slender leaves are more than 4 times longer than they are wide. California Goldenrod (*S. velutina*) also grows in the mixed conifer zone and has toothed leaves, but its broader leaves are less than 4 times longer than they are wide and it grows in grasslands or woodland borders rather than in meadows. Alpine Goldenrod (*S. multiradiata*) has a short inflorescence and grows only above 8,000'. Western Goldenrod (*Euthamia occidentalis*) has linear, untoothed leaves.

ALPINE GOLDENROD, NORTHERN GOLDENROD
Solidago multiradiata
Sunflower family (Asteraceae)

Description: Alpine Goldenrod is a familiar sight in Yosemite's higher-elevation meadows. The plant is a perennial with a stem that's up to 16" long, though it's usually shorter than that in the park. Its herbage has short, stiff, appressed hairs, especially toward the top. The basal and alternate lower stem leaves are up to 5" long, are elliptic to spatula shaped, have a ciliate petiole, and are sometimes toothed or scalloped along the margins. The lanceolate to ovate upper stem leaves get progressively smaller toward the top of the stem. The flower heads grow in dense, flat- to round-topped clusters at the stem tip, and smaller clusters grow from the leaf axils. Each head has 12–35 yellow disk flowers and 13–18 short, yellow ray flowers with rays that are less than ¼" long.

Flowering time: July–September

Habitat/range: Slopes and meadows; subalpine and alpine zones; 8,500–12,500'.

Comments: This common plant usually grows in the company of its equally common neighbors, Lemmon's Paintbrush (*Castilleja lemmonii*) and Brewer's Lupine (*Lupinus breweri*).

Similar plants: Alpine Goldenrod is somewhat similar to other goldenrods in the park, but it is the only one that grows in the subalpine and alpine zones.

CALIFORNIA GOLDENROD
Solidago velutina ssp. *californica*
(*S. californica*)
Sunflower family (Asteraceae)

Description: California Goldenrod is a perennial, 8–46" tall, with stems that often grow in clumps from creeping rhizomes. It has soft-hairy herbage and alternate leaves. The blades of the lower leaves are oblanceolate to obovate, are toothed, and taper to a short petiole. The smaller, sessile upper leaves **[inset]** are elliptic and toothless. The tiny flower heads grow in a spike-like cluster. They have 4–17 yellow disk flowers and 6–13 yellow ray flowers.

Flowering time: June–September

Habitat/range: Grasslands and woodland margins; mixed conifer zone; 3,200–4,900'.

Similar plants: California Goldenrod's leaves are somewhat broad and are less than 4 times longer than they are wide. Meadow Goldenrod (*S. elongata*) also has toothed leaves and grows in the mixed conifer zone, but its leaves are lanceolate and are more than 4 times longer than they are wide. Unlike California Goldenrod, it grows in meadows and along meadow borders. Western Goldenrod (*Euthamia occidentalis*) has flowers that resemble the *Solidago* species and it also grows in the mixed conifer zone, but its leaves are linear and toothless. Alpine Goldenrod (*S. multiradiata*) has similar but shorter inflorescences, and it grows only in the subalpine and alpine zones, above 8,000'.

PRICKLY SOW THISTLE
(non-native)
Sonchus asper ssp. *asper*
Sunflower family (Asteraceae)

Description: Prickly Sow Thistle is an invasive annual. Its stout, ribbed stem is up to 4' tall, is often purplish, and is mostly unbranched, except in the inflorescence. The alternate, pinnately lobed leaves are 2¼–12" long and have teeth along the margins that are prickly to the touch. The clasping upper stem leaves are conspicuously lobed at the base. The lobes are rounded and are strongly curved or coiled downward. The flower heads grow from the upper leaf axils and at the stem end. The prickly involucre is broad at the base, narrows toward the tip, and has 27–50 phyllaries in several series. Each flower head has 80–250 small, yellow ray flowers with long, white pappus hairs.

Flowering time: March–September

Habitat/range: Disturbed areas; chaparral/oak-woodland and mixed conifer zones; up to 8,000'.

Similar plants: Quite similar Common Sow Thistle (*Sonchus oleraceus*) has clasping upper stem leaves with pointed lobes that are straight or curve downward only slightly, and the teeth along the margins of its leaves are soft to the touch. Prickly Lettuce (*Lactuca serriola*) has similar flower heads, but it has distinctive pinnately lobed leaves **[inset]** that often twist to face sideways. All three plants are European natives that have become noxious weeds throughout much of North America.

COMMON DANDELION
(non-native)
Taraxacum officinale
Sunflower family (Asteraceae)

Description: This milky-sapped, stemless perennial has a basal rosette of leaves that are up to 1' long. The leaves are oblanceolate to obovate in outline and are irregularly pinnately toothed or lobed. With age, the leaves develop larger lobes that curve conspicuously toward the leaf base. The flower heads are ¾–2" wide, grow at the end of unbranched, hollow flower stalks, and have 40–150 yellow ray flowers. The involucre has lanceolate outer phyllaries that are strongly reflexed at maturity and are shorter than the inner phyllaries.

Flowering time: all year

Habitat/range: Many habitats, especially disturbed places; chaparral/oak-woodland, mixed conifer, montane, and subalpine zones; up to 9,700'.

Comments: This common lawn weed originated in Eurasia but is now found throughout the world. The flower heads are used to make wine, and the greens are used in salads.

Similar plants: Native Spearleaf Dandelion (*Agoseris retrorsa*), native Annual Dandelion (*Agoseris heterophylla*), and non-native Smooth Hawksbeard (*Crepis capillaris*) **[inset]** are similar, but they all have phyllaries that are erect or curl only slightly backward at the tip.

YELLOW SALSIFY

(non-native)
Tragopogon dubius
Sunflower family (Asteraceae)

Description: Yellow Salsify (pronounced SAL-suh-fee) is an annual or biennial European native that usually has a single stem. The stem is 1–2½' long and is often branched from near the base. The linear-lanceolate leaves are up to 8" long, are slightly hairy when young, and become hairless and waxy with age. The large flower head is 1½–2¼" wide, is solitary at the stem end, and has 50–180 lemon-yellow ray flowers. The 8–13 narrow phyllaries extend well beyond the tips of the ray flowers, giving the flower heads a distinctive look. The flower stalk is inflated at the base of the phyllaries, and the eye-catching seed heads are up to 4" wide.

Flowering time: May–September

Habitat/range: Disturbed sites, trailsides in woodlands and grasslands, and open areas in coniferous forests; chaparral/oak-woodland, mixed conifer, and montane zones; up to 8,000'.

Comments: Although this plant can be prolific in disturbed or open habitats, it rarely squeezes out much other vegetation, regardless of the habitat or the degree of disturbance. Yellow Salsify has several other common names, including Goat's Beard, in reference to the fluffy seed heads, and Oyster Plant, for its edible, oyster-flavored root.

NARROW-LEAVED MULE-EARS

Wyethia angustifolia
Sunflower family (Asteraceae)

Description: This robust perennial has a single stem that's 1–3' tall, rough-hairy, and usually unbranched. Its narrowly lanceolate basal leaves are about the same length as the stem. The leaves taper at both ends, are sparsely to densely hairy on both surfaces, and are often slightly toothed. The alternate stem leaves become smaller toward the top of the stem. The stem ends with 1 to several large, long-stalked flower heads that have many yellow disk flowers and 8–21 yellow ray flowers with rays that are ½–1¾" long. The more or less equal phyllaries **[inset]** are coarsely ciliate.

Flowering time: April–August

Habitat/range: Moist meadows and dry, open slopes; mixed conifer zone; 3,900–6,500'.

Comments: These plants often grow in colonial patches in moist meadows, but they also grow solitary or in small groups on dry, open slopes. *Wyethia* was named for Nathaniel Jarvis Wyeth (1802–1856), who was a businessman, a Western explorer, and a plant collector. He spent a lot of time in Oregon, where he established a route that became part of the Oregon Trail.

Similar plants: Seep-spring Arnica (*Arnica longifolia*) also has long, narrow leaves and grows in colonies in wet places, but its stem leaves grow in opposite pairs.

WOOLLY MULE-EARS
Wyethia mollis
Sunflower family (Asteraceae)

Description: Woolly Mule-ears is a herbaceous perennial, 16–34" tall, with unbranched stems. Its glandular herbage is densely gray-woolly early on and becomes more or less hairless and greener with age. The tufted basal leaves, which are still green when the plant is in bloom, are up to 2' long, including the petiole. The leaf blades are broadly lanceolate to ovate and are rounded at the base. The alternate, short-petioled stem leaves are much smaller. The 1–3 large flower heads have 35–150 yellow to orange disk flowers and 6–15 ray flowers with yellow rays that are ½–1¾" long. The heads have 1–3 leafy bracts below them. The bell-shaped involucre has 12–22 somewhat equal phyllaries.

Flowering time: June–August

Habitat/range: Meadows and dry to wet, open areas; mixed conifer, montane, and subalpine zones; 3,900–10,400'.

Comments: Native Americans roasted the plant's seeds and combined them with other ingredients to make a valuable flour mixture called pinole.

Similar plants: Hall's Mule-ears (*Wyethia elata*), which is rare in the park, lacks a tuft of basal leaves when it's in bloom, and its leaves are truncate at the base. Balsamroots (*Balsamorhiza* species) are similar to Woolly Mule-ears, but their largest leaves are deeply heart shaped at the base.

AMERICAN WINTERCRESS
Barbarea orthoceras
Mustard family (Brassicaceae)

Description: This common biennial, up to 2' tall, has stout stems that are branched toward the top. The tips of the plant's sepals and the tips of its basal leaves are hairy, but the rest of its herbage is hairless. The basal leaves are up to 5" long, are sometimes toothed, and usually have 2–4 small pairs of lateral lobes and a much larger, ovate terminal lobe. The clasping middle and upper stem leaves are lobed at the base and are often deeply pinnately lobed along the sides. The flowers, which grow in rather dense racemes, have 4 yellow-green sepals, 4 bright lemon-yellow petals that are about ¼" long, and a stout style. The fruit are straight, narrow, erect or ascending siliques, up to 1¾" long.

Flowering time: May–September

Habitat/range: Damp meadows, seeps, streambanks, and moist woodland; chaparral/oak-woodland, mixed conifer, montane, subalpine, and alpine zones; up to 11,200'.

Similar plants: Very similar Common Wintercress (*Barbarea vulgaris*), a Eurasian native, has been reported once in Yosemite Valley and once in Aspen Valley. Its sepals and basal leaf lobes are hairless, and its style is slender rather than stout. The plant has become naturalized throughout most of North America, and it often has green leaves in the dead of winter, providing animals with a source of food when there is little else to eat.

BLACK MUSTARD
(non-native)
Brassica nigra
Mustard family (Brassicaceae)

Description: This invasive, branched annual is
1½–4' tall and has sparsely to densely stiff-hairy
herbage. The lower leaves are 4–8" long and are
deeply pinnately lobed; the large terminal lobe and
the 2–4 small lateral lobes have toothed margins.
The sessile upper stem leaves are tapered at the
base. The flowers, in an elongated raceme, have 4
erect to ascending sepals and 4 yellow petals that
are about ½" long. The 4-sided siliques (fruit) are
up to ¾" long and press close to the stem.

Flowering time: April–September

Habitat/range: Disturbed areas; chaparral/oak-
woodland and mixed conifer zones; up to 4,900'.

Comments: The plant got its common name from
its dark seeds, which are used, along with the
seeds of other *Brassica* species, to make prepared
mustards, curries, and other condiments.

Similar plants: Non-native Field Mustard (*Brassica
rapa*) also has erect to ascending sepals, but it
has clasping upper stem leaves with 2 lobes at
the base. Shortpod Mustard (*Hirschfeldia incana*)
and Charlock (*Sinapis arvensis*) are also non-native
mustard plants with 4 yellow petals. Their sepals
are reflexed or spreading. The fruit of Shortpod
Mustard press close to the stem; the fruit of Charlock are spreading and then ascending.

MOUNTAIN TANSYMUSTARD
Descurainia incana
Mustard family (Brassicaceae)

Description: This hairy biennial is 10"–4' tall and
has a much branched stem. Its basal and lower
stem leaves are widely lanceolate to ovate in
outline and are 1-pinnately lobed; the primary
lobes have segments of various shapes along
the margins. The upper stem leaves are smaller
and have narrower lobes. The inflorescence is an
elongating cluster of tiny flowers with 4 yellowish sepals and 4 bright yellow petals. The linear,
erect, pointed fruit (siliques) are up to ⅜" long and
sometimes press close to the stem.

Flowering time: May–September

Habitat/range: Many open habitats;
chaparral/oak-woodland, mixed conifer, montane,
subalpine, and alpine zones; up to 11,500'.

Similar plants: Native Cut-leaved Tansymustard
(*D. incisa*) and non-native Flixweed (*D. sophia*) are
the only other *Descurainia* species in the park with
linear fruit, but their fruit are spreading to ascending rather than erect. The leaves of Cut-leaved
Tansymustard are only 1-pinnately lobed. Flixweed's leaves are 2- to 3-pinnately lobed. Sierra
Tansymustard (*D. californica*) has spindle-shaped
fruit that are broadest in the middle, and the seeds
in the fruit are in 2 rows. Western Tansymustard
(*D. pinnata*) has club-shaped fruit that are broadest
at the tip, and the seeds in the fruit are in 1 row.
Both plants are natives.

SLENDER DRABA
Draba albertina
Mustard family (Brassicaceae)

Description: Slender Draba is an annual, biennial, or short-lived perennial. Its stems are 2–12" long, are sometimes branched, and are hairy below and hairless above. The oblanceolate to obovate basal leaves, which form a rosette, are up to 1½" long, are toothless or minutely toothed, and are ciliate along the margins. The alternate stem leaves, if any, are similar to the basal leaves. The flowers, which grow in an open raceme, have 4 sepals and 4 yellow, spatula-shaped or oblong petals that are about ⅛" long. The fruit are narrowly elliptic or lanceolate, flattened, hairless siliques.

Flowering time: June–August

Habitat/range: Moist meadows and forest openings; montane, subalpine, and alpine zones; 6,800–12,000'.

Comments: Slender Draba is widespread and common in the park's middle and upper elevations. *Draba* is Greek for sharp or acrid, for the medicinal taste of the leaves, which were once believed to have a beneficial effect as a poultice; *albertina* may be for the Canadian Province of Alberta, where the plant also grows.

LEMMON'S DRABA
Draba lemmonii
Mustard family (Brassicaceae)

Description: Lemmon's Draba is one of the most widespread and showy of Yosemite's alpine wildflowers. Its basal leaves, which form dense, compact cushions, are often bright green and are less than 1" long. The leaves are hairy on both surfaces, have distinctly ciliate margins, and *do not* have a prominent midrib on the lower surface. The hairy, leafless stems, up to 4" long, have dense clusters of up to 30 flowers with 4 bright yellow petals, about ¼" long. The odd flattened fruit are up to ½" long and become twisted as they mature.

Flowering time: July–August

Habitat/range: Damp to wet talus areas, rock crevices, and rocky meadows; subalpine and alpine zones; 8,500–13,000'.

Comments: This plant and many others were named for Sara and John Lemmon, who did extensive botanical work in Arizona and California in the late 1800s.

Similar plants: The park has two other high-elevation drabas with yellow petals and tufted basal leaves. Cushion Draba (*D. densifolia*) also has leaves with distinctly ciliate margins, but the lower surface of each leaf has a prominent midrib. The leaves of Few-seeded Draba (*D. oligosperma*) are densely hairy all over, but they have no distinct line of ciliate hairs along the margins.

SANDDUNE WALLFLOWER
Erysimum perenne (*E. capitatum* var. *perenne*)
Mustard family (Brassicaceae)

Description: This eye-catching perennial or biennial has rough-hairy herbage and usually a single
stem that's 1¼–2' long and is sometimes branched.
Its basal leaves are 1–3" long, are spoon shaped
to widely oblanceolate, taper to a petiole, and are
sometimes toothed. The alternate stem leaves are
short-petioled or sessile. The flowers are crowded
in a head-like cluster at the stem top. They have
a tubular calyx with 4 yellowish-green sepals that
bulge at the base. The 4 yellow, obovate petals are
less than ¼" wide and taper to the base. The narrow fruit (siliques), 1½–5½" long, are spreading to
ascending and are constricted between the seeds,
making the fruit look slightly lumpy.

Flowering time: June–September

Habitat/range: Open, rocky areas; montane, subalpine, and alpine zones; 6,500–13,100'.

Comments: At alpine elevations, the basal leaves
of this plant turn brown but remain in place, help-
ing to protect the root crown from the elements.

Similar plants: Closely related Western Wallflower (*Erysimum capitatum* var. *capitatum*) looks
a lot like Sanddune Wallflower, but Western
Wallflower's orange or bright yellow petals are
broader, ¼–⅜" wide, its fruit are not constricted
between the seeds, and it doesn't grow in the
subalpine and alpine zones.

CURVEPOD YELLOWCRESS
Rorippa curvisiliqua
Mustard family (Brassicaceae)

Description: Aptly named Curvepod Yellowcress is
a hairless or sparsely hairy annual or biennial with
reclining to ascending stems that are 4–16" long
and usually have a few branches toward the top.
The early withering basal leaves, which sometimes
form a rosette, are pinnately lobed or divided; the
lobes are linear to oblong or ovate and are sometimes toothed. The similar, alternate stem leaves
are gradually reduced upward and have 2 lobes
at the base. The flowers, in an elongated raceme,
have 4 ascending sepals and 4 yellow, spreading
petals that are less than ⅛" long and are slightly
shorter than the sepals. The oblong to linear fruit
(siliques) are up to ½" long and curve upward.

Flowering time: May–September

Habitat/range: Moist or wet meadows and
streambanks; mixed conifer, montane, and subalpine zones; 3,900–10,500'.

Comments: The *Rorippa* genus formerly included
several species of watercress, which are now in
the *Nasturtium* genus. Both genera have plants
with peppery-tasting foliage.

Similar plants: Bluntleaf Yellowcress (*Rorippa curvipes*) has similar leaves and similar flowers with
yellow petals, but its petals are erect rather than
spreading and it has egg- or pear-shaped fruit.

TUMBLE MUSTARD
(non-native)
Sisymbrium altissimum
Mustard family (Brassicaceae)

Description: Tumble Mustard is a large annual with a widely branching stem, 1–5' tall. Its lower leaves, 2–7½" long, are pinnately lobed with 4–6 pairs of oblong to lanceolate lobes. The upper leaves are dissected into thread-like segments. The flowers **[inset]**, in elongated racemes, have 4 sepals and 4 cream-colored to yellow petals, about ¼" long, with a narrow claw. Its linear, ascending fruit (siliques) are 1½–4" long.

Flowering time: May–July

Habitat/range: Meadows and dry to moist disturbed areas; chaparral/oak-woodland and mixed conifer zones; up to 5,000'.

Comments: After a Tumble Mustard plant dies, it breaks off at the stem base and rolls wherever the wind takes it, leaving seed pods behind, which explains how it quickly spread across the country after it became established in the eastern states.

Similar plants: The upper leaves of London Rocket (*S. irio*) and Hedge Mustard (*S. officinale*) are not divided into linear segments. London Rocket also has linear, ascending fruit, and they can be up to 1½" long. Hedge Mustard's fruit, less than ¾" long, press against the stem. All three plants are European natives that have become naturalized throughout much of North America.

DOBIE POD
Tropidocarpum gracile
Mustard family (Brassicaceae)

Description: Dobie Pod is a common, early blooming annual. It usually has several reclining to ascending stems that are 4"–1½' long and are branched toward the top. Its basal leaves are 1½–5" long and are pinnately divided into 3–8 linear or oblong, irregularly toothed segments. The alternate upper leaves are similar but smaller. The small flowers, which grow in a raceme with leafy bracts, have 4 greenish-yellow or purplish, spreading sepals and 4 yellow, egg- to spoon-shaped petals that are less than ¼" long. The linear, ascending fruit (siliques) are about 1" long and are strongly flattened.

Flowering time: March–May

Habitat/range: Grassy slopes, open fields, and roadsides; chaparral/oak-woodland and mixed conifer zones; up to 4,500'.

Similar plants: Tansymustards (*Descurainia* species) and Yellowcresses (*Rorippa* species) have similar leaves and inflorescences and they also have small flowers with 4 yellow petals, but they have cylindric rather than flattened fruit.

CHAPARRAL HONEYSUCKLE
Lonicera interrupta
Honeysuckle family (Caprifoliaceae)

Description: Chaparral Honeysuckle is an erect shrub with a stiff, woody trunk and long, vine-like, climbing or sprawling branches that are often twining. Its herbage is hairless or has short, soft hairs. The opposite, elliptic to round leaves are ¾–1¼" long, and the upper 1–3 pairs are fused around the stem. The flowers grow in whorls on long, unbranched or few-branched, leafless flowering shoots. The 5-lobed calyx tightly encloses the ovary. The cream-yellow to bright yellow corolla is about ⅜" long and is strongly 2 lipped and deeply divided. The upper lip is divided into 4 lobes, and the lower lip is curved under. The 6 stamens and the style extend well beyond the corolla. The fruit is a shiny, bright red berry.

Flowering time: May–July

Habitat/range: Dry, often rocky, brushy slopes and flats; chaparral/oak-woodland and mixed conifer zones; up to 5,500'.

Comments: Children teach other children how to harvest drops of nectar from garden honeysuckles. They pinch the flower right above the calyx and pull just hard enough to separate the corolla from the calyx, without severing the style. Then they slowly pull the style through the tube. The stigma pulls the nectar out of the tube and delivers it as a tiny droplet.

TWINBERRY HONEYSUCKLE
Lonicera involucrata var. *involucrata*
Honeysuckle family (Caprifoliaceae)

Description: This deciduous shrub is 2–5' tall and has sparsely hairy, glandular herbage. Its opposite leaves are 1–5" long, are elliptic to oval, and have a short petiole. The flowers grow in pairs from leaf axils on somewhat long stalks. Directly beneath the flowers are 2 pairs of leaf-like bracts. The ovate outer bracts are partially united. The smaller inner bracts are densely glandular, are often deeply 2 lobed, and more or less enclose the ovaries. The bracts are green when they're young and turn dark red with age. The hairy, yellow corollas are up to ⅜" long, are cylindric to narrowly bell shaped, and have 5 lobes. The fruit is a pair of round, black berries.

Flowering time: June–August

Habitat/range: Streambanks and other moist places; mixed conifer, montane, and subalpine zones; 5,500–10,200'.

Comments: Although the long tube of the flowers makes the nectar inaccessible to most insects, hummingbirds and butterflies reach it easily. Twinberry Honeysuckle's fruit have been reported to be poisonous, mildly toxic, bitter, unpalatable, and even edible. Some Native American tribes called the plant crow food, because only the crow spirit was crazy enough to eat the bitter fruit.

153

LANCE-LEAVED STONECROP
Sedum lanceolatum
Stonecrop family (Crassulaceae)

Description: This succulent perennial is up to 8" tall and has reddish stems and leaves. Its fleshy basal and stem leaves are up to 1" long and are similar in shape and size. They're linear or narrowly lanceolate to ovate and are almost cylindric in cross section, but slightly flattened. The leaves are densely crowded at the base and are alternate along the stem, where they're often withered by the time the flowers are in full bloom. The yellow, star-shaped flowers grow in tight clusters of 3–24 at the end of the stem. They have 5 sepals and 5 petals that are up to ⅜" long. The sepals are red tinged, and sometimes the petals are too.

Flowering time: June–August

Habitat/range: Granite outcrops, rocky soils, in the open or in shade; mixed conifer, montane, subalpine, and alpine zones; 4,500–12,000'.

Comments: Stonecrops are popular green-roof plants. The green roof of Ford's truck plant in Dearborn, Michigan, is covered with 138,000 square feet of *Sedum*, and the green roof of Nintendo's American headquarters in Redmond, Washington, has 75,000 square feet of *Sedum*.

Similar plants: This is the only stonecrop in the park with somewhat cylindric leaves and the only one with stem leaves that are the same shape and size as the basal leaves.

SIERRA STONECROP
Sedum obtusatum ssp. *obtusatum*
Stonecrop family (Crassulaceae)

Description: Sierra Stonecrop is a succulent perennial with an erect, reddish stem, up to 8" tall, that grows from a basal rosette of spoon-shaped leaves that are up to 1¼" long. The alternate stem leaves are smaller. The leaves are either shiny or they're covered with a white, waxy powder that rubs off, and they can be green to blue-green, tinged with red, or solid red. The inflorescence is an erect, sometimes flat-topped cluster of numerous star-shaped flowers with widely oval petals, up to ⅜" long, that are fused at the base for at least ¼ of their length. The yellow petals fade with age and become pale pink to cream colored.

Flowering time: June–July

Habitat/range: Rock crevices and gravelly flats; mixed conifer, montane, subalpine, and alpine zones; 4,000–11,000'.

Similar plants: Broad-leaved Stonecrop (*Sedum spathulifolium*) has similar leaves, but its leaves form distinct, decorative rosettes and its petals are separate all the way to the base. Sierra Mock Stonecrop (*Sedella pumila*, previously *Parvisedum pumilum*) has similar stem leaves, but it has few or no leaves at the base of the plant and most of its leaves are withered by the time it blooms. It has starburst yellow flowers and red flower buds, and it often grows in large, sometimes bright red and yellow patches in the Hetch Hetchy area.

WOODLAND PINEDROPS
Pterospora andromedea
Heath family (Ericaceae)

Description: This tall, sticky-glandular perennial has no stem and no leaves and grows up to 5' tall. The flowering stalk and all visible plant parts other than the corolla are pink, red, or rusty red. The narrow bracts that grow along the stalk and below each flower wither early. The pendent flowers have 5 separate, narrow sepals and a cream to yellow, urn-shaped corolla, up to ⅜" long, with 5 short, recurved lobes. The 10 stamens are hidden inside the corolla. The brown, dried-out flowering stalks remain erect long after the seeds are dispersed.

Flowering time: June–August

Habitat/range: Forest floor in thick humus; chaparral/oak-woodland, mixed conifer, and montane zones; up to 8,500'.

Comments: Woodland Pinedrops and several of its relatives lack chlorophyll and were once classified as saprophytes, plants that get their nourishment from dead organic matter. Somewhat recently, it was discovered that they're actually mycohet-erotrophs, plants that are parasitic on soil fungi. The roots of conifers and the mycelia (root-like structures) of fungi have developed a mutually beneficial relationship; the fungi get carbohydrates and the trees get improved nutrient and water absorption. The roots of Woodland Pinedrops absorb nutrients from strands of mushroom mycelia, and they provide nothing in return.

BROAD-LEAVED STONECROP
Sedum spathulifolium
Stonecrop family (Crassulaceae)

Description: Broad-leaved Stonecrop is a succulent perennial, up to 9" tall, that produces multiple mats of attractive basal rosettes from a system of underground stems. The basal leaves are spatula shaped, and the stem leaves are smaller and elliptic to oblong. The inflorescence is a flat-topped cluster of small, star-shaped flowers with widely spreading, yellow petals that are a little over ¼" long and are completely separate to the base.

Flowering time: May–July

Habitat/range: Moist, rocky outcrops, in the open and in shade, often along streams; chaparral/oak-woodland and mixed conifer zones; up to 6,200'.

Comments: Stonecrops are named for their habit of cropping up in a bed of stones. The plants do prefer rocky habitats, and many *Sedum* species are popular rock garden plants. The leaves are rich in healing vitamins A and C and have been used to treat burns, bites, and wounds.

Similar plants: Sierra Stonecrop (*Sedum obtusatum*) has similar leaves, but its basal leaves aren't in distinct rosettes and its petals are united at the base for at least ¼ of their length.

SILVER-LEAVED LOTUS

Acmispon argophyllus var. *fremontii*
(*Lotus argophyllus* var. *fremontii*)
Pea family (Fabaceae)

Description: Silver-leaved Lotus is a perennial with reclining to erect, much-branched stems, up to 2' long, and silvery-silky-hairy herbage. Its leaves are irregularly pinnately to somewhat palmately divided into 3–7 obovate to lance-elliptic leaflets that are less than ½" long and have pointed tips. The circular inflorescence has 8–15 pea flowers that face outward. The densely shaggy-hairy calyx has 5 narrow lobes, and the attractive yellow corolla is up to ½" long and turns reddish to brown with age. The small, curved, 1-seeded pods are also silky-hairy.

Flowering time: April–July

Habitat/range: Dry, often rocky slopes; chaparral/oak-woodland and mixed conifer zones; up to 5,600'.

Comments: This is one of the park's showiest small plants, with its silvery leaves and its rings of soft yellow flowers in a nest of long, silky hairs. *Acmispon* is from a Greek word for hooked point, possibly for the hook-tipped pea pods.

Similar plants: Sierra Nevada Lotus (*Acmispon nevadensis*) has a similar circular inflorescence with yellow flowers that face outward, but its calyx has short hairs and its foliage is not silvery looking.

SIERRA NEVADA LOTUS

Acmispon nevadensis var. *nevadensis*
(*Lotus nevadensis* var. *nevadensis*)
Pea family (Fabaceae)

Description: Sierra Nevada Lotus is a slightly mat-forming perennial with reclining to ascending stems and short-hairy herbage that becomes less hairy with age. Its leaves are irregularly pinnately or somewhat palmately divided into 3–5 oblong to obovate, green or grayish-green leaflets that are up to ½" long. The circular cluster of 5–12 pea flowers all face outward. The short-hairy, sometimes reddish-tinged calyx has 5 pointed lobes, and the yellow corolla, up to ⅜" long, is often red in bud and turns brownish with age. The small, strongly curved pea pods have 1 or 2 seeds.

Flowering time: May–August

Habitat/range: Dry, open or partially shady areas; chaparral/oak-woodland, mixed conifer, and montane zones; up to 7,500'.

Comments: Sierra Nevada Lotus is a pioneer in areas that have recently burned. The plant is common in Yosemite Valley, around Wawona, and in the Hetch Hetchy area.

Similar plants: Silver-leaved Lotus (*Acmispon argophyllus*) has a similar circular inflorescence of yellow pea flowers, but its calyx is densely shaggy-hairy and its leaves are densely silvery-silky.

BISHOP LOTUS

Acmispon strigosus (*Lotus strigosus*)
Pea family (Fabaceae)

Description: This annual has reclining to ascending stems, 2–12" long, and herbage that often has stiff, appressed hairs. The leaves have 4–9 leaflets that are up to ½" long and are slightly offset from each other. The leaflets are narrowly oblong, elliptic, or slightly oblanceolate, but their sides are mostly parallel to each other. The pea flowers grow solitary or in pairs from the leaf axils. The 5 awl-shaped teeth on the calyx are almost as long as the calyx tube. The small, yellow corolla is up to ⅜" long and turns reddish as it ages. The pea pods are mostly straight and are covered with stiff hairs.

Flowering time: March–June

Habitat/range: Dry, open slopes and rocky areas; chaparral/oak-woodland and mixed conifer zones; up to 5,100'.

Similar plants: This is one of three similar yellow-flowered *Acmispon* species that grow in the park's lower elevations or around its western boundary, but it's the only one of the three that has leaves with up to 9 leaflets. The other two have leaves with mostly 4 leaflets, and their leaflets are distinctly broader above or below the middle. Hill Lotus or Foothill Deervetch (*A. brachycarpus*, previously *Lotus humistratus*) **[upper inset]** has leaves with long, dense, soft hairs. Chilean Trefoil (*A. wrangelianus*, previously *L. wrangelianus*) **[lower inset]** has leaves that are sparsely hairy.

STREAMBANK BIRD'S-FOOT TREFOIL

Hosackia oblongifolia var. *oblongifolia*
(*Lotus oblongifolius* var. *oblongifolius*)
Pea family (Fabaceae)

Description: This attractive perennial has sprawling to ascending stems, 8–20" long, and hairless to soft-hairy herbage. Its pinnate leaves have 5–11 elliptic to oblong, more or less opposite leaflets that are up to 1" long. Each inflorescence is a circular cluster of 2–6 pea flowers, up to ½" long. The calyx has 5 narrow lobes, and the corolla has white wing petals and a yellow banner petal that sometimes has reddish veins. The linear, shiny green pods, up to 2" long, are often red-mottled.

Flowering time: May–September

Habitat/range: Open, moist forest, wet meadows, and streambanks; mixed conifer and montane zones; 3,400–7,600'.

Comments: This plant used to be in the *Lotus* genus. North American native plants that were in the *Lotus* genus are now in the *Acmispon* genus, the *Hosackia* genus, and two other genera not represented in California. The Eurasian natives remain in the *Lotus* genus.

Similar plants: Deerweed (*Acmispon glaber* var. *glaber*, previously *Lotus scoparius*) is similar, but it has stiff, straight stems, 3–6 leaflets (mostly 3 on the upper leaves), and a solid yellow corolla. Deerweed grows in the foothills and has been reported inside the park boundary near Arch Rock.

BURCLOVER

(non-native)
Medicago polymorpha
Pea family (Fabaceae)

Description: Burclover is a mostly hairless annual with reclining, ascending, or mat-forming stems that are 4–18" long and are branched from the base. Its conspicuous, green bracts at the leaf base have long, narrow, pointed teeth. The pinnate leaves have 3 wedge-shaped leaflets with tiny, pointed teeth. The inflorescences, which grow at the end of the branches or from leaf axils, have 2–6 yellow pea flowers that are less than ¼" long. The distinctive coiled seedpods **[inset]** have several rows of curved or hooked spines.

Flowering time: March–July

Habitat/range: Disturbed places; chaparral/oak-woodland and mixed conifer zones; up to 4,500'.

Comments: Even though this plant is not a native, it's also called California Burclover because it's so widespread and common throughout the state.

Similar plants: Non-native Black Medick (*Medicago lupulina*) has a somewhat elongated inflorescence with 10–20 flowers and its fruit is not prickly. Non-native Little Hop Clover (*Trifolium dubium*) often grows in extensive patches, like a low ground cover. It has 5–10 flowers, its leaf bracts have no teeth, and its fruit is mostly concealed by the sepals. Both plants grow in disturbed areas in the same zones as Burclover.

SOURCLOVER

(non-native)
Melilotus indicus
Pea family (Fabaceae)

Description: Sourclover is a mostly hairless annual with much-branched, spreading to erect stems, 4"–2' long. Its pinnate leaves have 3 oblanceolate to wedge-shaped leaflets, ½–1¼" long, with small teeth along the upper margins. The slender, compact inflorescences, ½–4" long, grow at the branch ends and from leaf axils, and they have numerous tiny, yellow pea flowers, less than ⅛" long. The fruit is a small, egg-shaped pod.

Flowering time: April–October

Habitat/range: Disturbed areas; chaparral/oak-woodland and mixed conifer zones; up to 5,600'.

Comments: *Melilotus* species are native to Europe and Asia but are now found worldwide. Their sweet smell comes from a fragrant organic chemical called coumarin in their tissues. The pleasant fragrance of hay and newly mown grass is caused by the release of coumarin from plant tissues.

Similar plants: Sourclover looks like a miniature version of non-native Yellow Sweetclover (*M. officinalis*), which has yellow flowers that are about ¼" long and stems that are 1¾–6½' long. Another related non-native plant, White Sweetclover (*M. albus*) looks like a white-flowered version of Yellow Sweetclover, but with smaller flowers, less than ¼" long.

ALPINE GOOSEBERRY
Ribes lasianthum
Gooseberry family (Grossulariaceae)

Description: This spreading shrub is 1–3' tall and has stout, sparsely hairy branches with 1–3 spines, up to ⅜" long, at the leaf and branch nodes and no prickles between the nodes. Its thin, roundish, sparsely glandular-hairy leaves are about ¾" wide and are somewhat deeply divided into 3 or 5 blunt lobes with a few teeth that are usually rounded. The erect to pendulous flowers, which are less than ½" long, grow in groups of 2–4 from leaf axils. The cylindric, hairy, lemon-yellow flower tube (hypanthium) ends with 5 lemon-yellow sepals that are reflexed or erect. The 5 yellow petals extend beyond the flower tube and conceal the 6 stamens. The red berries are about ¼" wide and are mostly smooth.

Flowering time: June–July

Habitat/range: Open, rocky areas; montane and subalpine zones; 6,500–10,000'.

Comments: Although people eat currants and gooseberries and often use them to make jellies, jams, and pies, the berries of some species are unpalatable and the berries of others are toxic. Currants have branches with no spines, and gooseberries have spiny branches. Native Americans made fishhooks with the spines of some gooseberries, and they also used gooseberry spines to remove splinters.

TINKER'S PENNY
Hypericum anagalloides
St. John's Wort family (Hypericaceae)

Description: Tinker's Penny is a low, mat-forming annual or perennial with slender, sprawling stems that root from the lower nodes. Its opposite, somewhat clasping upper leaves, ¼–½" long, are elliptic to round and have tiny gland dots. The lower leaves are smaller and linear. The flowers, which grow in small clusters at the branch tips, have 15–25 stamens and 5 lanceolate to ovate, unequal sepals. The 5 golden-yellow petals are less than ¼" long and are about the same size as the sepals.

Flowering time: May–September

Habitat/range: Meadows and other wet places; mixed conifer, montane, and subalpine zones; 3,800–10,500'.

Comments: If you come across little spots of gold in a marshy mountain meadow, you're likely to have found Tinker's Penny. The stems of *Hypericum* species were used by the Celts and Saxons in solstice rituals to ward off evil spirits, and people carried the plants in their pockets to guard against lightning and witches. The family got its common name from the fact that one or more species are in full bloom around June 24th, the day that honors John the Baptist.

SCOULER'S ST. JOHN'S WORT

Hypericum scouleri (*H. formosum* var. *scouleri*)
St. John's Wort family (Hypericaceae)

Description: This attractive, hairless perennial is 8–28" tall and has a few slender, erect stems that are usually branched toward the top. Its more or less clasping leaves are ½–1¼" long, are ovate to elliptic, and have blunt tips. The leaf margins are dotted with black glands. Each stem has 3–25 flowers. The 5 oblong to ovate, black-dotted sepals are usually blunt at the tip. The 5 obovate, yellow petals are less than ½" long and have black dots along the edges. The many stamens are fused at the base into 3 clusters.

Flowering time: June–September

Habitat/range: Wet meadows and streambanks; mixed conifer and montane zones; 3,000–7,500'.

Similar plants: This native looks a lot like non-native, highly invasive Klamathweed (*H. perforatum*), which can grow in wet or dry habitats. Klamathweed's leaf margins are also dotted with black glands, but its leaves are mostly oblong. The lower surface of its leaves have conspicuous clear dots. If Scouler's St. John's Wort has clear dots on its lower leaf surfaces, the dots are inconspicuous. Aaron's Beard (*H. calycinum*), which is native to Turkey, is a related ornamental ground-cover shrub with similar, but much larger flowers. The shrub has been planted around developments in Yosemite Valley and Wawona, but it doesn't seem to have escaped.

HARTWEG'S IRIS

Iris hartwegii ssp. *hartwegii*
Iris family (Iridaceae)

Description: This showy perennial is 2–12" tall and has a single unbranched stem with 1 or 2 flowers at the end. Its 1–3 basal leaves are up to ½" wide and are longer than the stem, and 1–4 smaller leaves grow alternate along the stem. The flowers are pale to deep yellow, cream colored, or lavender. The spreading, somewhat spatula-shaped sepals, which are the outer 3 petal-like parts, are 1½–2¾" long. The 3 shorter, narrower, ascending to erect petals grow alternate the sepals. The 3 petal-like style branches are upturned and are deeply notched at the tip, and they have a stigma on the lower surface, just below the notch. Each style branch arches over a sepal, and a stamen is hidden between them.

Flowering time: May–July

Habitat/range: Dry forest openings; mixed conifer zone; 3,000–7,000'.

Similar plants: When Hartweg's Iris has lavender flowers, it could be mistaken for Western Blue Flag (*Iris missouriensis*), which grows in moist to wet places, often in colonies. Hartweg's Iris grows alone or in small groups in dry forest openings. So, if you find an iris in the park with pine needles nearby, it's likely to be Hartweg's Iris.

ELMER'S GOLDEN-EYED GRASS

Sisyrinchium elmeri
Iris family (Iridaceae)

Description: Elmer's Golden-eyed Grass is endemic to California. The hairless perennial is 4–11" tall and has tufted, leafless, unbranched stems that are flattened and narrowly winged. Its linear, grass-like basal leaves are sheathed and overlapping at the base and are about half as long as the stem. The flowers, which grow from a pair of sheathing bracts at the top of the stem, have 3 stamens with golden anthers, a 3-branched style, and 6 yellow, narrowly oval tepals that are about ⅜" long.

Flowering time: June–August

Habitat/range: Wet meadows; mixed conifer, montane, and subalpine zones; 3,000–8,500'.

Comments: Members of the *Sisyrinchium* genus have the word "grass" in their common names because of their grass-like leaves. The leaves of Elmer's Golden-eyed Grass are often obscured by other vegetation in the wet meadows where the plants grow. However, the plants always seem to grow just tall enough to make their flowers visible among the surrounding vegetation.

COMMON BLADDERWORT

Utricularia macrorhiza (*U. vulgaris*)
Bladderwort family (Lentibulariaceae)

Description: This aquatic perennial has submerged stems and suspended leaves that are pinnately divided into 30–160 ultimate, thread-like segments. The leaves often look like tangled masses under the surface of the water, and they have numerous small, carnivorous bladders on their margins. Several bright yellow flowers with red markings are held above the water surface on an erect, leafless stalk. The snapdragon-like, 2-lipped flowers, up to ¾" long, have an upper lip with no lobes, a lower lip with 3 shallow lobes, and a curved, horn-like spur under the lower lip.

Flowering time: July–September

Habitat/range: Quiet, acidic waters; mixed conifer, montane, and subalpine zones; 5,200–8,600'.

Comments: Bladderworts often grow in nitrogen-poor water, and they compensate by capturing and digesting nitrogen-rich aquatic organisms.

Similar plants: This plant grows in ponds around Tuolumne Meadows and at several other locations in the park. Flat-leaved Bladderwort (*U. intermedia*), which grows at Lost Lake in Little Yosemite Valley, is similar but has fewer than 20 ultimate leaf segments. Two other species, Humped Bladderwort (*U. gibba*) and Lesser Bladderwort (*U. minor*) grow in the Miguel Meadow area in the highlands north of Hetch Hetchy Reservoir.

NORTHWESTERN YELLOW FLAX
Sclerolinon digynum
Flax family (Linaceae)

Description: Northwestern Yellow Flax is an erect annual, 2½–8" tall, with stems that are branched toward the top. Its opposite leaves are up to a little over ½" long, are erect or ascending, and are broadly oblong to elliptic. The lower leaves are toothless, and the upper leaves often have sharp, saw-like teeth. The inflorescences are in clusters at the branch ends, with leafy, often saw-toothed bracts at the base. The flowers have 5 unequal sepals with gland-toothed margins, 5 stamens opposite the sepals, and 2 partially fused styles. The 5 bright yellow, oblong petals are about ⅛" long. The fruit is a hard-sided capsule.

Flowering time: June–July

Habitat/range: Vernally moist, grassy areas; mixed conifer zone; 3,400–4,900'.

Comments: This small, slender plant is often overlooked among the grasses and other meadow plants where it grows, but it is distinctive, with its bright yellow flowers and its ascending pairs of leaves. The plant grows in the Wawona area and in Hodgdon Meadow, Big Meadow, and Ackerson Meadow. *Sclerolinon* was derived from Greek and Latin words that mean hard flax, for the tough little fruit. The genus is monotypic, meaning that it has only one species.

BUSHY BLAZING STAR
Mentzelia dispersa
Blazing Star family (Loasaceae)

Description: This erect annual, 3–18" tall, has hairy herbage, alternate leaves, and whitish or reddish stems that are branched from the base. Its lower stem leaves are 1–4" long, are lanceolate, have a short petiole, and are usually lobed or toothed. Its ovate upper leaves are ½–1¼" long, are sessile, and are sometimes lobed or toothed. The small flowers are less than ½" wide, grow in clusters from leaf axils near the branch ends, and have leafy, ovate bracts at their base. Each flower has 5 triangular sepals, 5 petals that are yellow throughout or have an orange basal spot, many unequal stamens, and 1 pistil. The fruit is an elongated, slender capsule.

Flowering time: May–August

Habitat/range: Dry, sandy or rocky areas; chaparral/oak-woodland and mixed conifer zones; 2,900–6,500'.

Comments: Bushy Blazing Star is somewhat uncommon in the park, but it's a fire follower that can grow abundantly in recently burned areas. Exposure to smoke helps the seeds germinate. The seeds of some *Mentzelia* species were a staple food source for Native American tribes in the Great Basin. They ground the seeds into a substance much like peanut butter. To encourage growth of the plants, they spread seeds in brushy areas and burned the areas to get the seeds to germinate.

GIANT BLAZING STAR
Mentzelia laevicaulis
Blazing Star family (Loasaceae)

Description: Giant Blazing Star is an eye-catching perennial, up to 3¼' tall, with erect, whitish to pale pink stems that are usually hairy and sometimes branched. Its alternate leaves are green to gray green and are covered with small, hooked hairs that adhere to fabric and fur. The lower, oblanceolate leaves, up to 9½" long, are usually pinnately lobed. The shorter upper leaves are lanceolate to ovate and toothed. The large, showy flowers have 5 green, lanceolate sepals and many long, yellow stamens. The 5 bright yellow, lanceolate petals, 1½–3¼" long, are pointed at the tip. The inferior ovary matures into a hairy, cylindric capsule. The flowers often close by late afternoon.

Flowering time: May–October

Habitat/range: Sandy or rocky areas; chaparral/oak-woodland, mixed conifer, montane and subalpine zones; up to 9,800' (outside the park).

Comments: Although this striking plant isn't known to grow in the park, it's common just east of Tioga Pass along Highway 120. It also grows along Highway 49 in the foothills west of the park.

Similar plants: Sierra Blazing Star (*Mentzelia crocea*) grows in the Merced River Canyon near the western park boundary and may grow within the park. Its showy, bright yellow flowers are also eye-catching, but the petals are shorter, ¾–1½" long.

CALIFORNIA BOG ASPHODEL
Narthecium californicum
Bog Asphodel family (Nartheciaceae)

Description: This showy, hairless perennial has a single erect stem, 7–24" long. Its grass-like basal leaves are 4–12" long, have parallel veins, and are densely overlapped at the base. The stem has 3–6 much smaller, alternate leaves. The flowers grow in an open to somewhat dense raceme at the stem end. They have 6 yellow, linear-lanceolate tepals that are up to ⅜" long and 6 yellow stamens with densely hairy filaments and orange or brown anthers. The fruit is a 3-lobed, lance-shaped capsule.

Flowering time: July–August

Habitat/range: Wet meadows and streambanks; mixed conifer, montane, and subalpine zones; 4,000–8,000'.

Comments: California Bog Asphodel is rare in Yosemite and has been reported only in Tenaya Canyon, on the face of Clouds Rest, near Le Conte Falls, and at Waterwheel Falls, locations that mark the southernmost reaches of its range. The plant is more common in Northern California. The related plant European Bog Asphodel (*Narthecium ossifragum*) has similar bright yellow flowers, and its orange fruit have been used as a food-coloring agent, substituting for much more expensive saffron. The plant is also known as Maiden's Hair, in reference to its use as a hair dye in the 17th century.

YELLOW POND LILY

Nuphar polysepala (*N. lutea* ssp. *polysepala*)
Waterlily family (Nymphaeaceae)

Description: Yellow Pond Lily is a hairless, aquatic perennial that forms floating masses in still water. Its long-petioled leaves, floating on or held above the water, have an oblong to ovate blade, 4–16" long, with a heart-shaped base. The attractive flowers are 2–4" wide and have 5–9 yellow or yellow-green, spirally arranged, petal-like sepals that are rounded and concave. The 10–20 spoon-shaped petals are mostly hidden by the numerous, crowded, yellow stamens that encircle the plant's large stigma.

Flowering time: May–August

Habitat/range: Ponds and slow streams; mixed conifer and montane zones; 4,000–8,200'.

Comments: These showy plants grow in Siesta Lake, right next to Tioga Road about a mile west of the turnoff to White Wolf. According to several sources, Native Americans buried the seeds of Yellow Pond Lily and allowed them to ferment. Then they dried and roasted them and ground them into flour. They also roasted the seeds until they popped open and ate them like popcorn. Some groups dried the roots and ground them into flour, and other groups considered the roots poisonous. The mashed roots were used externally to relieve pain. Plants in the waterlily family are considered to be among the closest living relatives of the first flowering plants.

CONTORTED SUNCUP

Camissonia contorta
Evening Primrose family (Onagraceae)

Description: This common annual has coarse-hairy herbage and an ascending to erect stem, 1–12" long, that's often branched from near the base and becomes shreddy with age. Its alternate, blue-green, sessile leaves, up to 1½" long, are linear to narrowly elliptic and are finely toothed. The leaves are tapered at the base and become gradually smaller upward. The flowers grow from leaf axils and have 8 unequal stamens. The 4 small sepals are fused at the tips in pairs. The 4 roundish, yellow petals, ⅛–³⁄₁₆" long, sometimes have red dots at the base. The fruit is a cylindric capsule.

Flowering time: March–June

Habitat/range: Dry, open areas; chaparral/oak-woodland and mixed conifer zones; up to 7,200'.

Similar plants: Three similar suncups grow in the park. Grassland Suncup (*C. lacustris*) is rarely reported in the park. It also has linear leaves that taper to the base, but they're more green than blue-green, and its petals are ³⁄₁₆" to slightly more than ¼" long. Yosemite Suncup (*C. sierrae* ssp. *sierrae*) and Mono Hot Springs Suncup (*C. sierrae* ssp. *alticola*) have leaves that are lanceolate to narrowly ovate or elliptic and are rounded or obtuse at the base. Yosemite Suncup has 2 red dots at the base of each petal and grows in the Hetch Hetchy area and near Wawona. Mono Hot Springs Suncup has no red dots and is rare in the park.

YELLOW EVENING PRIMROSE

Oenothera elata ssp. *hirsutissima* (*O. hookeri*)
Evening Primrose family (Onagraceae)

Description: This robust biennial is 1–8' tall and has an erect, glandular-hairy, often reddish stem and densely hairy herbage. Its alternate leaves are 1½–10" long, oblanceolate to lanceolate or elliptic, and sometimes toothed. The lower leaves are larger and have a petiole. The upper leaves become sessile and are gradually reduced in size upward. The inflorescence is a spike with large flowers that open in the evening. The flowers have 4 reflexed, hairy, sometimes glandular sepals that are green or red tinged. The 4 yellow, broadly obovate petals are 1–2" long and are notched at the tip. The flowers have 8 yellow stamens and a yellow style that extends well beyond the stamens and has a deeply 4-lobed stigma. The fruit is a straight capsule that's up to 2½" long.

Flowering time: June–September

Habitat/range: Moist meadows and disturbed areas; chaparral/oak-woodland, mixed conifer, montane, and subalpine zones; up to 9,000'.

Comments: Yellow Evening Primrose's flowers unfold as evening approaches and wilt by the next morning, turning orange or red. The plant is often pollinated by nocturnal moths, like other plants with fragrant flowers that are open during the night. During the twilight hours, carpenter bees also pollinate the flowers.

CLUSTERED BROOMRAPE

Aphyllon fasciculatum (*Orobanche fasciculata*)
Broomrape family (Orobanchaceae)

Description: Clustered Broomrape is a glandular-hairy, parasitic plant that produces one or more sometimes branched, mostly subterranean stems, 2–8" long, from a thick, fleshy root. The entire plant is typically yellowish, though it can also be more or less purple. The inflorescence is a somewhat flat-topped raceme of 5–20 flowers on stalks that are 1¼–6" long and get shorter upward on the raceme. The flowers have a partially fused calyx with 5 narrowly triangular lobes. The 2-lipped, yellow or purple-tinged corolla has an arching tube that's somewhat constricted toward the base. The corolla lobes, 2 upper and 3 lower, are rounded and are mostly straight or slightly curled back.

Flowering time: April–July

Habitat/range: Dry, sandy or rocky places, usually in the open; chaparral/oak-woodland, mixed conifer, montane, and subalpine zones; up to 10,600'.

Comments: This plant is thought be parasitic primarily on the roots of *Artemisia* (sagebrush) species, but it's also believed to parasitize plants in the *Eriodictyon* (yerba santa), *Eriogonum* (buckwheat), and *Galium* (bedstraw) genera. A European broomrape plant parasitizes a broom (a shrub in the pea family) and causes knobs to grow on the plant's roots. The "rape" in broomrape is from the Latin word rapum, which means knob, in reference to the knobs that form on the broom's roots.

CUT-LEAVED OWL'S-CLOVER
Castilleja lacera
Broomrape family (Orobanchaceae)

Description: This annual has an erect stem, 4–15" tall, that's sometimes branched, and its herbage is glandular-bristly above and spreading-hairy below. The lower leaves are narrowly lanceolate, and the upper leaves are pinnately cut into 3–7 narrow lobes. Its spike-like inflorescence, 1–5" long, has ovate, green bracts that are palmately cut into 3–7 lance-linear lobes. The green calyx is divided into 4 thread-like, unequal lobes. The deep yellow corolla has an erect beak at the top, with the stigma and 1–3 black or brown dots usually visible. The much inflated, 3-lobed lower lip, up to ⅜" wide, has 2 purple or brown dots at the base.

Flowering time: April–July

Habitat/range: Grassy areas; chaparral/oak-woodland, mixed conifer, montane, and subalpine zones; up to 8,500'.

Comments: *Castilleja* is for Domingo Castillejo (1744–1793), a Spanish botanist and surgeon.

Similar plants: Cut-leaved Owl's-clover plants always have some flowers with a lower lip that's more than ¼" wide. Slender Owl's-clover (*Castilleja tenuis*) looks a lot like Cut-leaved Owl's-clover. Its flowers also have a yellow corolla with an inflated lower lip, but the lower lip is always less than ³⁄₁₆" wide. It's less common in the park and grows in moist flats and meadows.

PINEWOODS LOUSEWORT
Pedicularis semibarbata
Broomrape family (Orobanchaceae)

Description: Pinewoods Lousewort is a low-growing perennial. Its fern-like leaves, 2–9" long, are mostly in a basal rosette and are pinnately cleft into 11–25 lanceolate to ovate, toothed or lobed segments. The short inflorescence has hairy, often toothed bracts, some of them longer than the flowers. The ciliate calyx has 5 linear, unequal lobes that are sometimes toothed. The club-like, 2-lipped, yellow corolla, ⅝–1" long, has soft hairs and is red tinged or purple tipped. The upper corolla lip is hooded, and the lower lip has 3 more or less equal, rounded lobes.

Flowering time: May–July

Habitat/range: Dry, open or shaded slopes and flats; mixed conifer, montane, subalpine, and alpine zones; 5,000–11,500'.

Comments: As a result of DNA studies, plants in the *Pedicularis*, *Castilleja*, *Cordylanthus*, and *Orthocarpus* genera were moved from the snap-dragon family (Scrophulariaceae) to the broomrape family. The plants are hemiparasites (partial parasites). They have specialized roots called haustoria that drill into the roots of other plants to steal water and essential minerals. The plants do have chlorophyll and can produce their own food, but they do much better when they can get some of their nutrients from other plants.

CREEPING WOOD-SORREL

(non-native)

Oxalis corniculata

Oxalis or Wood-sorrel family (Oxalidaceae)

Description: This low-growing perennial has hairy, sprawling stems, up to 20" long, that creep along the ground and root at the nodes. Its alternate stem leaves grow on petioles that are up to 2½" long. The blades are palmately divided into 3 broad, heart-shaped leaflets, up to ¾" wide, that fold closed at night or when they're overexposed to sunlight. The inflorescence is an uncrowded cluster of 2–7 flowers that grow from leaf axils. The flowers have 5 narrow sepals and 5 yellow, oblong to spoon-shaped petals, about ¼" long. The fruit is a hairy, cylindric capsule that's up to 1" long.

Flowering time: May–July

Habitat/range: Meadows and open, disturbed places; chaparral/oak-woodland and mixed conifer zones; up to 4,200'.

Comments: This plant has become naturalized practically worldwide. Its place of origin is up for question though it is considered to be an Old World plant. The plant first became established in the park in Ahwahnee Meadow and has spread to other developed areas in Yosemite Valley. Members of the *Oxalis* genus have herbage that contains oxalic acid. People chew on the leaves, which have a refreshing lemony taste. The leaves are rich in vitamin C, and they can be infused in hot water to make a nutritious, lemon-flavored drink.

GOLDEN EARDROPS

Ehrendorferia chrysantha (*Dicentra chrysantha*)

Poppy family (Papaveraceae)

Description: Golden Eardrops is an erect, hairless perennial that's 1½–6' tall and has a lanky, hollow stem. Its herbage has a waxy coating throughout. The basal and alternate stem leaves, 6–12" long, are pinnately dissected 2 or 3 times into narrow, lobed segments. The inflorescence, 7–29" long, is a terminal panicle of 5 to many flowers. The golden-yellow flowers are about ½" long and have 2 small, bract-like, deciduous sepals and an oblong corolla with 4 petals in 2 unlike pairs. The lanceolate outer petals are pouched at the base and spread out toward the top. The narrower inner petals have expanded tips that are united over the stigma, and each petal has a noticeable crest.

Flowering time: April–August

Habitat/range: Dry, rocky slopes and burned areas; chaparral/oak-woodland and mixed conifer zones; up to 5,000'.

Comments: Golden Eardrops is one of many plants that thrive in recently burned areas. The seeds must be in the soil for at least a year before they germinate, but they sometimes need a stimulus of some sort to begin the process. It was once thought that the heat from fire got the seeds going, but more recently it's been determined that the plant's seeds, like the seeds of many other fire followers, require exposure to smoke to start germinating.

TUFTED POPPY
Eschscholzia caespitosa
Poppy family (Papaveraceae)

Description: Tufted Poppy is an erect, hairless annual, 2–12" tall, with several stems that grow from a tuft of leaves. The basal and alternate stem leaves are finely dissected into many narrow segments. The flowers have 2 sepals that are united into a long, pointed cap, which is shed as the petals unfurl. The 4 bright yellow to gold petals, ⅜–1" long, are wedge to fan shaped, and the flowers have many stamens.

Flowering time: March–June

Habitat/range: Dry, grassy areas; chaparral/oak-woodland and mixed conifer zones; up to 5,500'.

Comments: Tufted Poppies and California Poppies (*Eschscholzia californica*) have large, bright gold flowers in early spring, but the flowers that bloom later on are smaller and more yellow than gold. Both species often grow in masses and are fire followers. Tufted Poppy is the more common species of the two in the Yosemite area.

Similar plants: California Poppies look a lot like Tufted Poppies, but, unlike Tufted Poppies, California Poppies have a pink to purplish, disk-shaped rim at the base of the petals. Bush Poppy (*Dendromecon rigida*) grows near the western park boundary. It has similar flowers, mostly with yellow petals, but the plant is a shrub that often climbs over other vegetation and it has undivided leaves.

CREAM CUPS
Platystemon californicus
Poppy family (Papaveraceae)

Description: This cheery little annual, 2–12" tall, has multiple stems from the base and long, soft-shaggy-hairy herbage. Its opposite, mostly sessile leaves, up to 3½" long, are linear to lanceolate or narrowly oblong and have smooth margins. Solitary flowers grow from leaf axils or at the stem ends. The showy, nodding flower buds are pinkish and covered with long hairs. The flowers have 3 hairy, green sepals and many flat, cream-colored or yellow stamens. The 6 broadly oval petals are ¼–¾" long. The petals are yellow or cream colored and often have a deeper yellow patch at the base or the tip (or both).

Flowering time: March–May

Habitat/range: Open, grassy slopes and flats; chaparral/oak-woodland zone; up to 3,200'.

Comments: Cream Cups grow in the El Portal area, and in years of good rain they play a major role in the spring wildflower displays in the Sierra Nevada foothills. Though they haven't been reported in the park, they may reach the lower park boundary. The plants produce two types of seeds, some naked and others with a protective outer coat. The naked seeds get going early, and their plants may die from a late freeze or lack of water. The seeds with a protective coat act as a backup plan; they germinate only if conditions are right, and they can remain dormant in the soil for years if need be.

SKUNKY MONKEYFLOWER

Diplacus mephiticus (*Mimulus mephiticus,*
Mimulus nanus var. *mephiticus*)
Lopseed family (Phrymaceae)

Description: Skunky Monkeyflower is an annual
with erect stems, up to 6" tall, and glandular-hairy
herbage with a strong skunky smell. Its opposite, sessile leaves, up to 1¼" long, are linear to
oblanceolate and are often crowded toward the
top of the stem. The flowers grow on a stalk that's
much shorter than the calyx. The 5-lobed calyx is
sometimes reddish. The yellow or magenta corolla
is usually distinctly 2 lipped, and it has 5 spreading, nearly equal lobes with rounded tips. The 2
lobes of the upper lip are often slightly overlapping. The lower lip of a yellow corolla has reddish
dots and lines toward the throat. The lower lip of
a magenta corolla **[inset]** has 2 elongated, yellow
patches that are outlined with magenta and have
magenta dots.

Flowering time: June–August

Habitat/range: Dry, gravelly slopes; montane,
subalpine, and alpine zones; 6,000–11,400'.

Similar plants: This is the only yellow-flowered
monkeyflower in the park with a flower stalk that
is distinctly shorter than the calyx. When Skunky
Monkeyflower has a magenta corolla, the crowded
or overlapping upper corolla lobes set it apart fairly
well from the other Yosemite monkeyflowers with
magenta corollas, but to make sure, rub a leaf and
smell your fingers. If your fingers smell like skunk,
the plant is Skunky Monkeyflower.

PANSY MONKEYFLOWER

Diplacus pulchellus (*Mimulus pulchellus*)
Lopseed family (Phrymaceae)

Description: This charming little plant is a
compact, low-growing annual with soft-hairy
herbage. Its opposite, sessile leaves are up to
1⅜" long, are oblanceolate to elliptic, are rounded
at the tip, and are ciliate along the margins. The
small, tubular flowers grow on a tiny stalk that's
much shorter than the calyx. The fused, hairless
calyx has 5 prominent ribs and 5 unequal, rounded
lobes, and the slender corolla tube is much longer
than the lobes. The distinctly 2-lipped corolla has
a pale lavender to magenta, 2-lobed upper lip.
The 3-lobed lower lip is either all yellow or the
outer lobes match the upper lip. The central lobe
is yellow with reddish dots, and the throat is dark
magenta inside.

Flowering time: April–July

Habitat/range: Moist meadows and vernally wet
depressions; chaparral/oak-woodland and mixed
conifer zones; up to 6,000'.

Comments: This rare monkeyflower is a Yosemite
National Park special status species. The plant is
endemic to California and has been reported from
only three Sierra Nevada counties, Calaveras,
Tuolumne, and Mariposa. The name *pulchellus* is
derived from a Latin word that means beautiful,
and though the flowers are small, they are undeniably beautiful.

YELLOW AND WHITE MONKEYFLOWER
Erythranthe bicolor (*Mimulus bicolor*)
Lopseed family (Phrymaceae)

Description: This eye-catching annual has erect or ascending stems, 1½–10½" long, and fine, short-hairy, often glandular herbage throughout. Its opposite, linear to oblanceolate leaves, up to 1¼" long, are sessile or nearly so and are often sharply toothed. The flower stalk is as long as or longer than the 5-lobed calyx, which is strongly ridged and often has red dots. The corolla is not distinctly 2 lipped, and it has 5 equal, spreading lobes that are distinctly notched at the tip. The 2 upper lobes are usually white, the 3 lower lobes are yellow, and the middle lower lobe is speckled with red dots.

Flowering time: April–June

Habitat/range: Moist, grassy areas; chaparral/oak-woodland and mixed conifer zones; up to 6,000'.

Comments: When much more common Seep-spring Monkeyflower (*Erythranthe guttata*) is nowhere in the vicinity, populations of this plant tend to have a solid yellow corolla **[inset]**.

Similar plants: When these plants have an entirely yellow corolla, they might be mistaken for other yellow monkeyflowers in the park that also aren't distinctly 2 lipped. The monkeyflowers it might be confused with do not have corolla lobes that are distinctly notched, and they have broader, often slimy-feeling or skunky-smelling leaves.

MANY-FLOWERED MONKEYFLOWER
Erythranthe floribunda (*Mimulus floribundus*)
Lopseed family (Phrymaceae)

Description: This common, erect to sprawling annual has branched stems, 2–20" long, and has long-soft-hairy, glandular herbage that feels slimy to the touch. Its opposite, toothed, petioled leaves have a broadly lanceolate to ovate blade that's up to 1¾" long and is truncate or heart shaped at the base. The calyx, which is less than ⅓" long, has 5 equal lobes, and the flower stalk is longer than the calyx. The yellow corolla **[inset]** is not distinctly 2 lipped. It has 5 equal, rounded, spreading lobes, and the lower 3 lobes usually have red to maroon spots or splotches and few or no lines.

Flowering time: April–August

Habitat/range: Moist places; chaparral/oak-woodland, mixed conifer, montane, and subalpine zones; up to 8,500'.

Similar plants: Many-flowered Monkeyflower is one of three monkeyflowers in the park with slimy-feeling foliage and a yellow corolla that is not distinctly 2 lipped. Sand-loving Monkeyflower (*E. arenaria*, previously *M. arenarius*) has been reported near Wawona. It also has a corolla with red dots and a calyx that's less than ⅓" long, but its leaf blades are rounded or tapered at the base. Musk Monkeyflower (*E. moschata*), which is widespread and common in the park, has a corolla with thin lines (and sometimes tiny dots), and its calyx is more than ⅓" long.

SEEP-SPRING MONKEYFLOWER

Erythranthe guttata (*Mimulus guttatus*)
Lopseed family (Phrymaceae)

Description: Seep-spring Monkeyflower is a common, much-studied perennial with an erect, branched or unbranched stem, 2¼–26" long, and smooth to hairy herbage. Its opposite leaves, up to 5" long, are petioled below and become smaller and sessile upward. The blade is ovate to round, has rounded teeth along the margins, and is often irregularly small lobed or dissected at the base. The inflorescence is a raceme with ovate to heart-shaped bracts and 3–20 flowers, each on a stalk that's longer than the calyx but usually shorter than the corolla. The 5-lobed, bell-shaped, sometimes red-dotted calyx becomes inflated as the fruit develops. The distinctly 2-lipped, yellow corolla has an upper lip with 2 lobes and a lower lip with 3 lobes. The lower lip almost always has reddish dots, and 1 dot is often larger than the others.

Flowering time: March–August

Habitat/range: Streambanks and other perpetually wet places; chaparral/oak-woodland, mixed conifer, montane, and subalpine zones; up to 8,200'.

Similar plants: Seep-spring Monkeyflower, Large Mountain Monkeyflower (*E. tilingii*) and Coralline Monkeyflower (*E. corallina*) are the only three perennial monkeyflowers in the park with a distinctly 2-lipped, yellow corolla and with a flower stalk that's as long as or longer than the calyx. Seep-spring Monkeyflower is the only one of the three that has bracts in its inflorescences and that has at least some leaf blades that are lobed or cleft at the base. Large Mountain Monkeyflower and Coralline Monkeyflower have inflorescences without bracts. Their leaf blades are often toothed or scalloped, but they aren't lobed or cleft at the base.

Seep-spring Monkeyflower used to be described either as an annual without a rhizome (underground stem) or as a perennial with a rhizome. Somewhat recently the species was split. Seep-spring Monkeyflower is now defined as a perennial only, and species status was given to several "new" annuals. Two of those annuals have been reported to grow in or near the park. One of them, Snouted Monkeyflower (*Erythranthe nasuta*), has small, mostly closed, self-fertilizing flowers. The other one, Small-leaved Monkeyflower (*Erythranthe microphylla*), has small, open flowers that are pollinated by insects. The monkeyflower shown in the photo to the right may be a diminutive example of Seep-spring Monkeyflower, or it may be Small-leaved Monkeyflower. The only way to know for sure would be to uproot the plant to see if it has an underground stem or a simple root. Since uprooting plants in the park is justifiably prohibited, the best resolution is to settle for an either/or determination.

CUT-LEAVED MONKEYFLOWER
Erythranthe laciniata (*Mimulus laciniatus*)
Lopseed family (Phrymaceae)

Description: Cut-leaved Monkeyflower is a distinctive annual, 1½–15" tall, with hairless to sparsely hairy herbage. Its opposite leaves, ¼–2" long, are petioled below and sessile above, and most of them are pinnately lobed, with irregular, rounded lobes. The tubular flowers, which grow from the middle and upper leaf axils, have a stalk that's much longer than the calyx. The fused, often reddish calyx has 5 distinct ribs, dark red spots, and 5 unequal, pointed lobes. The calyx becomes conspicuously inflated as the fruit matures. The deciduous, yellow corolla is distinctly 2 lipped. The upper lip has 2 arched or ascending lobes. The middle lobe of the 3-lobed lower lip is larger than the lateral lobes and has a showy, variably shaped red patch, along with smaller red dots.

Flowering time: May–August

Habitat/range: Moist to wet places in sun or partial shade; mixed conifer and montane zones; 3,000–6,500'.

Similar Plants: This is the only monkeyflower in the park that has distinctly lobed leaves, although its close relative Seep-spring Monkeyflower (*Erythranthe guttata*) sometimes has small lobes at the base of its ovate to round leaves.

MUSK MONKEYFLOWER
Erythranthe moschata (*Mimulus moschatus*)
Lopseed family (Phrymaceae)

Description: This rhizomed perennial has erect to ascending stems that are 2–12" long. Its herbage is sparsely hairy to densely glandular-soft-hairy and feels slimy to the touch. Its opposite leaves, up to 3" long, are oblong to ovate. The lower leaves contract somewhat abruptly to a short petiole and have a rounded to wedge-shaped base. The flower stalk is much longer than the calyx, and the calyx is more than ⅓" long. The yellow corolla, which is not distinctly 2 lipped, has 5 equal lobes, and the lower lobes usually have brownish parallel lines and sometimes have tiny dots in the throat.

Flowering time: June–August

Habitat/range: Seeps, streambanks, and moist, sandy slopes; mixed conifer, montane, and subalpine zones; 4,000–10,000'.

Similar plants: Musk Monkeyflower is one of three similar monkeyflowers in the park with foliage that feels slimy to the touch and a yellow corolla that is not distinctly 2 lipped. The other two are annuals (without rhizomes). They both have corollas with red dots and few or no lines and a calyx that's less than ⅓" long. They can be distinguished from each other by their leaves. The leaves of Many-flowered Monkeyflower (*E. floribunda*) have a truncate or heart-shaped base. The leaves of Sand-loving Monkeyflower (*E. arenaria*, previously *M. arenarius*) have a rounded or tapered base.

PRIMROSE MONKEYFLOWER
Erythranthe primuloides (*Mimulus primuloides*)
Lopseed family (Phrymaceae)

Description: Primrose Monkeyflower is a common perennial with mostly sessile leaves, up to 2" long, that are crowded near the base and form a more or less distinct rosette. The oblong to obovate leaves are hairless or have dense, long, soft hairs on the upper surface, and they have irregular, shallow teeth along the margins. The tubular flowers grow on an erect, thread-like stalk that's longer than the calyx and corolla combined. The fused, hairless calyx is sometimes reddish and has 5 ribs and 5 equal, pointed lobes. The deciduous, yellow corolla is not distinctly 2 lipped. It has 5 broad, spreading, equal lobes with notched tips, and the lower 3 lobes often have red dots or splotches.

Flowering time: June–August

Habitat/range: Wet meadows, seeps, and stream-banks; montane, subalpine, and alpine zones; 4,000–12,000'.

Similar plants: The only other yellow monkey-flower in the park with a basal rosette of leaves is Candelabrum Monkeyflower (*Erythranthe pulsiferae*, previously *Mimulus pulsiferae*). The plant grows in the mixed conifer zone and has been reported in the park only following intense wildfires, after which it seems to disappear. Unlike Primrose Monkeyflower, it has leaves up to the top of the stem, in addition to its basal rosette.

SUKSDORF'S MONKEYFLOWER
Erythranthe suksdorfii (*Mimulus suksdorfii*)
Lopseed family (Phrymaceae)

Description: This small, erect annual, up to 2½" tall, has glandular-short-hairy herbage that is often reddish. Its opposite, toothless, mostly sessile leaves, up to ⅞" long, are linear, lanceolate, or oblanceolate. The tubular flowers, which grow from leaf axils, have a stalk that's about the same length as the calyx or longer. The narrowly funnel-shaped, often reddish calyx has 5 prominent ribs and 5 equal lobes. The deciduous, tiny, yellow corolla is usually not distinctly 2 lipped. It has 5 equal, spreading, notched lobes and often has reddish dots or splotches.

Flowering time: June–August

Habitat/range: Moist, sandy or gravelly slopes or well-developed soil along meadow borders; subalpine and alpine zones; 8,000–12,000'.

Similar plants: Suksdorf's Monkeyflower has the smallest corolla of all the yellow monkeyflowers in the park, although Downy Monkeyflower (*Mimetanthe pilosa*, previously *Mimulus pilosus*) **[inset]** runs a close second. Its tiny corolla is also not distinctly 2 lipped, but the corolla lobes have no notches and the middle lobe of the lower lip almost always has 2 matching red or maroon dots. Downy Monkeyflower got its name from its densely soft-shaggy-hairy foliage. The plant is rare in the park, doesn't grow above the montane zone, and often appears only after wildfires.

LARGE MOUNTAIN MONKEYFLOWER

Erythranthe tilingii (*Mimulus tilingii*)
Lopseed family (Phrymaceae)

Description: This common perennial has reclining stems that are 2–15" long. Its densely to sparsely hairy herbage feels distinctly slimy to the touch. The opposite, ovate to elliptic leaves, up to 1¼" long, have scalloped or sharp-toothed margins. The lower leaves have short petioles, and the upper leaves are sessile. The flowers, which grow from the upper leaf axils, have a stalk that's longer than the calyx, and the calyx usually has red dots. The distinctly 2-lipped, yellow corolla has an upper lip with 2 erect or ascending lobes and a lower lip with red-dotted, bulging ridges and 3 spreading to drooping lobes.

Flowering time: July–September

Habitat/range: Wet rock crevices, seeps, streambanks, and wet meadows; montane, subalpine, and alpine zones; 6,500–11,800'.

Similar plants: The park has two other perennial monkeyflowers with distinctly 2-lipped, yellow corollas and flower stalks that are longer than the calyx. Neither has herbage that feels slimy. Much less common Coralline Monkeyflower (*E. corallina*) has nonglandular, more or less hairy leaves. Seep-spring Monkeyflower (*E. gutatta*) is quite common. At least some of its leaf blades are lobed or cleft at the base. The leaf blades of the other two monkeyflowers can be toothed or scalloped, but they are not lobed or cleft at the base.

FROSTED BUCKWHEAT

Eriogonum incanum
Buckwheat family (Polygonaceae)

Description: Frosted Buckwheat is a common, mat-forming perennial with male and female flowers on separate plants. Its woolly-hairy stems are up to 8" long. Its spatula-shaped leaves are up to 1½" long, and the petiole and blade are about the same length. Both surfaces of the leaves have dense, woolly hairs that don't rub off. On plants with female flowers and young plants with male flowers, the inflorescences are head-like. On mature plants with male flowers, the inflorescences become open and umbel-like. The woolly involucres, which contain the flowers, have 5–8 erect, short teeth. The flowers have 6 bright yellow to reddish tepals.

Flowering time: July–September

Habitat/range: Dry, gravelly places; montane, subalpine, and alpine zones; 7,000–12,000'.

Similar plants: Less common Marum-leaved Buckwheat (*E. marifolium*) is also mat-forming and has similar flowers. Its leaves are also densely hairy above and below, but the upper leaf surface loses its hairiness with age, and you can rub hairs off with your fingers **[inset]**. Sulphur Buckwheat (*E. umbellatum*) also has yellow flowers, but its involucres have long, reflexed lobes rather than erect teeth. Mount Rose Buckwheat (*E. rosense*), which is rare in the park, is also matted and has yellow flowers, but unlike the rest of the plants in this group, its stems and leaves are glandular-hairy.

MOUNT ROSE BUCKWHEAT
Eriogonum rosense var. *rosense*
Buckwheat family (Polygonaceae)

Description: Mount Rose Buckwheat is a perennial with densely matted, prostrate stems, along with leafless, ascending to erect flowering stems that are densely glandular-hairy. Its oblanceolate to elliptic leaves are up to 1¾" long and have a petiole that's about the same length as the blade. Both surfaces of the leaves are covered with white, woolly, glandular hairs that are densely matted and often tangled. The small flowers in the head-like inflorescences have a sparsely hairy, glandular involucre (the structures from which the flowers grow) with 5–8 teeth. The flowers have 6 bright yellow to reddish tepals.

Flowering time: July–September

Habitat/range: Open, sandy, gravelly, or rocky areas; alpine zone; 10,900–13,100'.

Comments: This plant is somewhat rare in the park, having been found mostly around Mount Dana and Mount Gibbs and in the Gaylor Lakes basin.

Similar plants: Several other *Eriogonum* species in the park have matted leaves that are densely hairy and have similar-shaped blades, but Mount Rose Buckwheat is the only one of the group with stems that are glandular-hairy rather than simply hairy.

SULPHUR BUCKWHEAT
Eriogonum umbellatum var. *furcosum*
Buckwheat family (Polygonaceae)

Description: This erect subshrub is 8–24" tall and has hairless or sparsely hairy stems. Its elliptic or oblong leaves are in loose rosettes on the lower stems, are up to 1" long, and are densely white-woolly below and mostly green and sparsely hairy above. The umbel-like inflorescence is branched, with rays that are branched again, each ray usually terminating with a solitary involucre. The involucres have deeply divided, long, reflexed lobes (rather than teeth). The small flowers **[inset]** have 9 stamens and 6 bright yellow tepals in 2 series.

Flowering time: June–September

Habitat/range: Dry, gravelly areas; mixed conifer, montane, and subalpine zones; 3,400–10,000'.

Similar plants: Two other varieties of *Eriogonum umbellatum* are rare in the park. Var. *nevadense* is much like var. *furcosum*, but its inflorescence rays have no additional branches. Var. *covillei* also has inflorescence rays with no additional branches; unlike the other two varieties, the plant is densely matted. All three varieties have an involucre with deeply divided, reflexed lobes. The only other yellow-flowered buckwheat in the park that can have a similar, long-lobed involucre is Nevada City Buckwheat (*E. prattenianum* var. *prattenianum*), which is known only from the Merced Lake area. Its flower stems have a whorl of leafy bracts near the middle and a solitary involucre at the end.

COMMON PURSLANE
(non-native)
Portulaca oleracea
Purslane family (Portulaceae)

Description: Common Purslane is an annual that has become naturalized almost worldwide. It has hairless, succulent herbage and sprawling, branching stems that are up to 1¾' long. Its obovate to spatula-shaped leaves are up to 1" long, can be alternate or almost opposite, and are clustered at the branch tips and nodes. The leaf tips are truncate or rounded. The flowers grow solitary or in clusters at the branch ends and from leaf axils, usually with several crowded leaves below them. The flowers have 2 fused sepals and usually 5 petals, though the petal number can vary between 4 and 7. The bright yellow petals, less than ¼" long, are often notched, and the flowers have 5–12 stamens and a short style with 3–6 branches.

Flowering time: April–October

Habitat/range: Disturbed areas; chaparral/oak-woodland and mixed conifer zones; up to 6,000'.

Comments: This weedy little succulent has been reported only a few times in the park, around developments in Yosemite Valley and near El Portal, but it probably often goes unnoticed and unreported. It frequently grows in seams and cracks in asphalt and concrete. Its nutritious, edible stems, leaves, and flowers have a slightly sour, salty flavor and are eaten cooked or raw in salads.

WATER PLANTAIN BUTTERCUP
Ranunculus alismifolius var. *alismellus*
Buttercup family (Ranunculaceae)

Description: This common, hairless perennial has a sprawling to erect, slender stem that's 4–12" long and up to ⅛" wide, and the stem does not root at the nodes. The elliptic to ovate blade of its basal leaves is ¾–2" long and is unlobed and untoothed. The blade tapers to a distinct petiole that's up to 3" long and is usually longer than the blade. The alternate stem leaves, if any, are lanceolate and sessile. The flowers have 5 yellow-green sepals, many stamens, and numerous pistils. The 5–8 shiny yellow petals are about ¼" long.

Flowering time: May–August

Habitat/range: Wet meadows and streambanks; mixed conifer, montane, subalpine, and alpine zones; 4,000–12,000'.

Similar plants: Another variety of Water Plantain Buttercup grows in the park, var. *alismifolius*. It differs from var. *alismellus* in that its leaves have tiny, serrate teeth, its stem is stouter (up to ⁵⁄₁₆" wide), and its leaf blade tapers gradually to a more or less indistinct petiole. It also has stems that don't root at the nodes. Creeping Buttercup (*Ranunculus flammula*) has similar, unsegmented leaves and in other respects looks much like the two varieties of Water Plantain Buttercup, but its stems creep along the top of muddy ground, forming new roots and plants at the stem nodes.

ALKALI BUTTERCUP

Ranunculus cymbalaria
Buttercup family (Ranunculaceae)

Description: Alkali Buttercup is a hairless perennial with stems that spread along the ground and root at the nodes. Its ascending to erect flowering stems are 2–12" long. The broadly oblong, ovate, or heart-shaped blades of its long-petioled basal leaves are ⁵⁄₁₆–1¼" wide and have shallow, rounded teeth. Each flower **[inset]** has 5 greenish-yellow sepals that are visible between the petals and often resemble them. The flowers have 5 glossy yellow petals, up to ¼" long, numerous stamens, and many pistils on a cylindric receptacle. The fruit is an achene with a straight, conic beak and no spines.

Flowering time: June–August

Habitat/range: Muddy, sometimes alkaline places; subalpine zones; around 8,600'.

Comments: In Yosemite, this little buttercup is known to grow only in the Soda Springs area of Tuolumne Meadows, near Parsons Lodge.

Similar plants: Prickle-fruited Buttercup (*Ranunculus muricatus*), a Eurasian native, also grows in moist to wet habitats. Its flowers and leaves are similar to those of Alkali Buttercup, and its herbage is mostly hairless. Unlike Alkali Buttercup, at least some of its leaves are divided into 3 distinct segments and its achenes have a curved beak and numerous spines.

ALPINE BUTTERCUP

Ranunculus eschscholtzii var. *oxynotus*
Buttercup family (Ranunculaceae)

Description: Alpine Buttercup is an elegant, hairless perennial with 1 or more stout, erect or reclining stems that are 1–6" long. Its long-petioled basal and lower stem leaves are up to 1⅝" long and have 2 types of blades. The most common type is kidney shaped and has 5–9 more or less equal, rounded lobes. The other type has a truncate base and is divided into 3 segments, the outer 2 segments with lobes or teeth and the middle segment without lobes or teeth. The smaller upper stem leaves are deeply lobed or divided. The saucer-shaped flowers are ½–1" wide, and they have 5 spreading, often reddish-tinged sepals and 5 (or occasionally 6–8) luminous yellow petals. Each flower has many yellow stamens and numerous greenish pistils on a receptacle that becomes cone shaped with age.

Flowering time: July–August

Habitat/range: Open, rocky slopes and scree; subalpine and alpine zones; 7,800–11,500'.

Comments: This high-elevation wildflower is a treat to find because it's one of only a few showy alpine plants that grow in a habitat dominated by small, often well-camouflaged plants. Sky Pilot (*Polemonium eximium*), Alpine Gold (*Hulsea algida*), Sierra Columbine (*Aquilegia pubescens*), and Rock Fringe (*Epilobium obcordatum*) are some other alpine showstoppers.

CREEPING BUTTERCUP
Ranunculus flammula var. *ovalis*
Buttercup family (Ranunculaceae)

Description: This mostly hairless perennial has slender, sprawling or ascending stems that are 4–18" long. The stems creep along the top of muddy ground and form new roots and new plants at the nodes. The long-petioled lower leaves are up to 2½" long, and they have a linear, lanceolate, or oblanceolate blade that tapers to a petiole that's usually longer than the blade. The flowers [inset] have 5 greenish-yellow, spreading or slightly reflexed sepals, numerous yellow stamens, and numerous greenish pistils. The corolla has 5 or 6 shiny yellow, obovate petals that are up to ¼" long.

Flowering time: June–August

Habitat/range: Muddy ground, sometimes in shallow water; mixed conifer, montane, and subalpine zones; 3,300–8,700'.

Comments: Light that shines on buttercup petals is reflected by two layers under the petal surface, which makes the petals extra glossy. The shiny petals are a beacon to pollinators, but they can be troublesome for photographers.

Similar plants: Water Plantain Buttercup (*Ranunculus alismifolius*) is the only other buttercup in the park that has undivided, unlobed, and untoothed leaves. Its flowers and leaves are similar to those of Creeping Buttercup, but its stems do not creep along the ground and root at the nodes.

DELICATE BUTTERCUP
Ranunculus hebecarpus
Buttercup family (Ranunculaceae)

Description: This delicate, inconspicuous little annual has been reported in Yosemite Valley and Hodgdon Meadow. The plant has slender, erect stems, 3–12" tall, and hairy herbage. The blades of its long-petioled basal and lower stem leaves are heart to kidney shaped in outline and are up to 1" long and up to 1⅜" wide. The leaves have 3 deeply divided segments that are unlobed or have 2–4 lobes. The long-stalked flowers have numerous stamens and pistils and 5 hairy sepals. The 0–5 yellow petals are less than ⅛" long and are shed early on. Chances are slim of finding a Delicate Buttercup flower with all 5 petals still attached. The disk-shaped achenes have a hooked beak and are covered with tiny, hooked bristles.

Flowering time: March–May

Habitat/range: Grasslands and open to shady woodlands; chaparral/oak-woodland and mixed conifer zones; up to 4,000'.

Similar plants: Woodland Buttercup (*Ranunculus uncinatus*) also has hairy herbage, leaves with 3 deeply divided, lobed segments, and tiny flowers. Its petals are slightly larger, just a sliver over ⅛" long. Its leaves are sometimes completely divided into 3 separate segments, and its achenes have a hooked beak but no bristles. The plant has been reported in the park only along Wawona Road, in the Mariposa Grove, and at Foresta.

PRICKLE-FRUITED BUTTERCUP

(non-native)
Ranunculus muricatus
Buttercup family (Ranunculaceae)

Description: Prickle-fruited Buttercup is a weedy Eurasian annual or biennial with sprawling to erect, hairless stems that are 7–19" long. The petioles of its basal and lower stem leaves are 1¼–6" long. The hairless or sparsely hairy leaf blades, up to 2" long, are semicircular to kidney shaped in outline and are divided into 3 distinct, toothed segments. The smaller upper leaves are more shallowly lobed. The flowers have 5 reflexed sepals, 5 bright yellow petals that are about ¼" long, and numerous stamens and pistils. The fruit is a spherical cluster of 10–20 flattened achenes with a curved beak and numerous stout, curved spines.

Flowering time: March–June

Habitat/range: Streambanks, seeps, and drainages, often near developments; chaparral/oak-woodland and mixed conifer zones; up to 4,000'.

Comments: This common weed is not particularly invasive and has been reported in Yosemite Valley, near Wawona, and at Hetch Hetchy.

Similar plants: Alkali Buttercup (*Ranunculus cymbalaria*) is similar in several respects, but its leaves are only shallowly lobed, and it's known to grow in the park only at Soda Springs in Tuolumne Meadows.

WESTERN BUTTERCUP

Ranunculus occidentalis var. *occidentalis*
Buttercup family (Ranunculaceae)

Description: This common perennial has erect or reclining, usually branched stems, 12–27" long, with long, soft hairs, at least below. Its hairy basal leaves are divided or cleft into 3 wedge-shaped, toothed segments. The alternate stem leaves are smaller and are deeply divided into 3 narrow segments or leaflets. The flowers have 5 greenish-yellow sepals that are abruptly curved backward at the middle and 5 or 6 (occasionally 7) glossy yellow petals that are ⅛–¼" wide. Each flower has many yellow stamens and many tightly packed, green pistils.

Flowering time: March–June

Habitat/range: Grassy slopes and meadows; chaparral/oak-woodland and mixed conifer zones; up to 5,900'.

Similar plants: This plant is common in the park's lower elevations and grows in Yosemite Valley and in Wawona Meadow. Another variety of Western Buttercup, var. *ultramontanus*, has been reported in Wawona, Big Meadow, and Mather. It looks a lot like var. *occidentalis*, but its petals are less than ⅛" wide, and its stem is almost always sprawling rather than erect. California Buttercup (*Ranunculus californicus* var. *californicus*) has been reported to grow in Mather, El Portal, and Wawona. It also looks a lot like Western Buttercup, but its flowers have 9–17 petals.

STRAIGHT-BEAKED BUTTERCUP
Ranunculus orthorhynchus var. *orthorhynchus*
Buttercup family (Ranunculaceae)

Description: Straight-beaked Buttercup is a perennial with coarse-hairy, erect to ascending stems that are 6–20" long and are branched near the base. The basal and lower stem leaves are 1¼–5" long, are ovate to semicircular in outline, and are pinnately divided into 3–7 leaflets or segments that are lobed or toothed. The upper stem leaves are much smaller and are deeply cleft or compound. The flowers have 5 greenish-yellow, reflexed sepals that are covered with soft, spreading hairs and 5 or 6 glossy yellow petals that are ¼–¾" long and are usually reddish on the back. Each flower has many yellow stamens and numerous greenish pistils.

Flowering time: May–July

Habitat/range: Wet meadows and boggy or marshy areas; mixed conifer zone; 3,900–6,500'.

Comments: This buttercup is relatively uncommon in the park, but it does grow near Crane Flat, in Wawona Meadow, in Big Meadow, in Ackerson Meadow, and near the Mather ranger station. *Ranunculus* is from a Latin word that means little frog, for the wet habitat of many species.

Similar plants: This is the only wet-habitat buttercup in the park that has only 5 or 6 petals and has pinnately compound leaves, at least some of which have 5–7 leaflets.

SHRUBBY CINQUEFOIL
Dasiphora fruticosa (*Potentilla fruticosa*)
Rose family (Rosaceae)

Description: This distinctive, many-branched, deciduous shrub is 8–30" tall and usually grows in a sprawling mound. Its arching stems are densely leafy and soft-hairy when they're young, and they develop shredding bark with age. The leathery, alternate leaves, up to 1¼" long, are pinnately or somewhat palmately divided into 3–7 linear to narrowly elliptic leaflets that taper to a pointed tip. The leaves are sometimes silky-hairy, are green above and paler below, and have margins that are curled under. The flowers grow in groups of 1–6 at the twig ends. They have 5 triangular sepals that form a star under the 5 pale to bright yellow, round petals, which are up to ⅜" long. The flowers have 20–25 stamens and many pistils with club-shaped styles. The fruit is a cluster of achenes covered with long hairs.

Flowering time: June–August

Habitat/range: Meadows, streambanks, and rocky places; subalpine and alpine zones; 8,500–11,500'.

Comments: Shrubby Cinquefoil grows throughout the Northern Hemisphere. The hardy shrub is commonly planted as a garden ornamental, even at low elevations, and is often available in native plant nurseries. Like most rose family plants, its foliage has astringent properties and is used to treat sunburn and poison oak rashes.

LARGE-LEAVED AVENS
Geum macrophyllum var. *perincisum*
Rose family (Rosaceae)

Description: Large-leaved Avens is a perennial with ascending to erect, bristly-hairy, unbranched stems that are 1–3½' long. The bracts at the base of the alternate leaves are large and leaf-like. The lower leaves are 4–16" long. The blades are oddly pinnately divided, with 2–4 often offset pairs of main leaflets along the side, interspersed with much smaller leaflets. The much larger, 3- or 5-lobed terminal leaflet is 3–4" long, roundish in outline, and irregularly toothed. The upper stem leaves are undivided or are divided into oblanceo-late to obovate, toothed segments. Open clusters of 3–16 flowers grow at the stem ends. The flowers have 5 reflexed sepals; 5 yellow, rounded, deciduous petals that are about ¼" long; many yellow stamens; and many greenish pistils. The fruit **[inset]** are dense, rounded clusters of achenes, each with an elongated style.

Flowering time: June–August

Habitat/range: Meadows and streambanks; mixed conifer, montane, and subalpine zones; 3,300–10,500'.

Comments: The petals of Large-leaved Avens look uniformly yellow to us, but if we illuminated them with ultraviolet light, we'd see a dark area at the base of each petal. The dark areas are visible to insects in sunlight and act as nectar guides.

CLUB-MOSS MOUSETAIL
Ivesia lycopodioides var. *lycopodioides*
Rose family (Rosaceae)

Description: This common perennial has densely clustered basal leaves and sprawling to erect stems, 1¼–6" long. The cylindric, bright green basal leaves are ½–2¾" long and are pinnately divided into 10–35 pairs of congested, deeply divided leaflets. The head-like flower clusters have 3–20 flowers with 5 stamens, 5–15 pistils, and 5 triangular, yellowish-green sepals. The 5 yellow, obovate petals are up to ⅛" long. The petals and sepals are about the same length and are about the same width at their widest points.

Flowering time: July–August

Habitat/range: Dry, rocky slopes and flats; subalpine and alpine zones; 9,500–12,400'.

Similar plants: The park has another variety of *I. lycopodioides* and two other mousetail species that have yellow petals and bright green leaves with 10 or more pairs of leaflets. *I. lycopodioides* var. *megalopetala* looks much like var. *lycopodioides*, but it grows only in damp to wet meadows and its petals are ⅛–³⁄₁₆" long. Less common Gordon's Mousetail (*I. gordonii* var. *alpicola*) grows in rocky places. Its petals are narrowly oblanceolate and are shorter and much narrower than the sepals. Sky Mousetail (*I. shockleyi*) has been reported once on Mount Gibbs in 1916. Its densely matted leaves, with only 5–10 pairs of leaflets, distinguish it from the other yellow-flowered mousetails in the park.

181

GRANITE MOUSETAIL

Ivesia muirii
Rose family (Rosaceae)

Description: Granite Mousetail is a distinctive little perennial with densely clustered, rosetted basal leaves and ascending to erect, purplish stems, 2–6" long. The silvery-silky, mousetail-like basal leaves, ¾–2" long, are pinnately divided into 25–40 pairs of much overlapping, 3- to 5-lobed, indistinct leaflets, and the stems usually have a single bract-like leaf. The inflorescence is a head-like, terminal cluster of 10–20 flowers that have a cup-shaped hypanthium with 5 tiny bractlets at its base. The flowers have 5 stamens, 1–4 pistils, and 5 yellowish-green, triangular sepals. The 5 yellow, linear to narrowly oblong, deciduous petals are less than ⅛" long and are about the same length as the sepals.

Flowering time: July–August

Habitat/range: Dry, gravelly flats; subalpine and alpine zones; 9,500–12,000'.

Comments: John Muir collected this plant's type specimen on Mount Hoffmann in 1872 and sent it to Asa Gray, who described the species and named it for Muir. In plant (and animal) collecting, a type specimen is the specimen (or more often a group of specimens) used to describe and name a new species or genus. *Ivesia* is for Eli Ives (1779–1861), a Yale University professor who was elected President of the American Medical Association in 1860.

BREWER'S CINQUEFOIL

Potentilla breweri
(*P. drummondii* ssp. *breweri*)
Rose family (Rosaceae)

Description: This common perennial has sprawling to ascending stems that are 4–24" long. Its white-hairy leaves have a cottony-hairy petiole that's usually shorter than the leaf blade, which is 1–7" long. The pinnately divided leaves have 7–15 crowded leaflets that are cleft more than halfway to the midvein. Open clusters of 3–15 flowers grow at the stems ends. The flowers have 5 small bractlets at the base, 5 sepals, 15–25 yellow stamens, and multiple pistils. The 5 bright yellow petals are up to ⅜" long.

Flowering time: July–August

Habitat/range: Damp to wet meadows and rocky areas; montane, subalpine, and alpine zones; 7,000–12,500'.

Similar plants: Yosemite has two other cinquefoil species with basal leaves that are pinnately divided into 5 or more deeply cleft leaflets. Both species have petioles that are mostly longer than the leaf blades. Drummond's Cinquefoil (*P. drummondii*) is also common in the park. It has green (not white-hairy) leaves on a hairless or short-hairy petiole, and the leaves have 5–9 uncrowded leaflets. Less common Bruce's Cinquefoil (*P. bruceae*, previously *P. drummondii* ssp. *bruceae*) has gray-hairy leaves on a long-hairy petiole, and the leaves have 5–7 somewhat crowded, overlapping leaflets.

FAN-LEAVED CINQUEFOIL
Potentilla flabellifolia
Rose family (Rosaceae)

Description: Fan-leaved Cinquefoil is a common perennial with ascending to erect stems, 4–12" long, that are hairless or have sparse, usually nonglandular hairs. Its mostly basal leaves are smooth or slightly hairy, are roundish in outline, and have 3 leaflets. The terminal leaflet has 7–15 teeth, of variable sizes, that are cleft about ¼ of the way to the midvein. The stems end with 1–5 flowers that have 5 small bractlets at the base, 5 pointed sepals, 15–25 yellow stamens, and many pistils. The 5 shallowly notched, yellow petals are up to ⅜" long.

Flowering time: June–September

Habitat/range: Damp to wet meadows and streambanks; mixed conifer, montane, subalpine, and alpine zones; 6,000–11,500'.

Comments: Cinquefoil is French for five leaves. The *Potentilla* genus got the name cinquefoil because several European and North American *Potentilla* species have leaves with five leaflets.

Similar plants: Gray's Cinquefoil (*Potentilla grayi*) is the only other cinquefoil in the park that has basal leaves with only 3 leaflets. Its leaves have a central leaflet with mostly 7 teeth that are all about the same size. The plant is less common in the park and grows only in the montane and subalpine zones.

SLENDER CINQUEFOIL
Potentilla gracilis var. *fastigiata*
Rose family (Rosaceae)

Description: This common perennial has hairy stems that are 10–22" long. Its basal leaves are 2½–12" long and are palmately divided into 5–9 oblanceolate leaflets with 13–23 evenly spaced teeth that extend to the base of the leaflet and are cleft halfway or less to the midvein. The inflorescences have few to many showy flowers with 5 small bractlets at the base, 5 pointed sepals, 10–15 stamens, and many pistils. The 5 yellow, shallowly notched petals are less than ⅜" long.

Flowering time: June–August

Habitat/range: Dry meadows and open forest; mixed conifer, montane, subalpine, and alpine zones; 3,900–11,200'.

Similar plants: The park has three other cinquefoils with basal leaves that are palmately divided into 5 or more leaflets. Quite similar *P. gracilis* var. *flabelliformis*, which is rarely reported in the park, has leaflets that are cleft more than ¾ of the way to the midvein. Blue-leaved Cinquefoil (*P. glaucophylla* var. *glaucophylla*, previously *P. diversifolia*) grows in the subalpine and alpine zones and is uncommon. Its leaflets have only 3–9 teeth, and the teeth do not extend all the way to the base of the leaflets. Silky Cinquefoil (*P. pseudosericea*) has distinctive, densely silver-hairy leaves. The plant is rare in Yosemite and grows only in a few scattered locations in the alpine zone.

SILKY CINQUEFOIL
Potentilla pseudosericea
Rose family (Rosaceae)

Description: This tufted or matted alpine perennial has reclining to ascending, densely soft-hairy stems that are 1-6" long. Its leaves are up to 2½" long and are mostly basal or grow toward the lower part of the stems. The leaves are more or less palmately divided into 5–9 leaflets that are cleft halfway or more to the midrib into linear segments. Both leaf surfaces are covered with dense, silvery hairs. The upper leaf surface has appressed hairs, and the lower surface has conspicuously matted, shaggy hairs. The inflorescence is a cyme with 3–10 flowers that have a cup-shaped hypanthium. The flowers have 5 bractlets, 5 sepals, 5 petals, 20 stamens, and many pistils. The yellow, obovate petals are less than ¼" long. The bractlets, sepals, and hypanthium have dense, silvery hairs.

Flowering time: June–August

Habitat/range: Rocky slopes and flats; alpine zone; 10,900–12,200'.

Similar plants: Silky Cinquefoil is one of three cinquefoil plants in the park that have palmately divided basal leaves with at least 5 leaflets, but it's the only one of the three with leaves that are silvery-hairy and look more silver than green, at least on the lower surface. The plant is rare in the park and is known from only a few scattered locations, mostly in alpine fellfields.

CREEPING SIBBALDIA
Sibbaldia procumbens
Rose family (Rosaceae)

Description: Creeping Sibbaldia is a common, easily overlooked perennial with woody, creeping stems that are often matted, forming a low ground cover. Its long-petioled, mostly basal leaves are divided into 3 wedge-shaped leaflets that typically have 3 teeth or lobes at the tip and are sometimes sparsely hairy. The leaves are bright green to blue-green and look something like strawberry leaves. The tiny, star-like flowers, which grow in silky-hairy clusters at the stem ends, have 5 linear bractlets, 5 green sepals, 5 yellow petals, and 5 yellow stamens. The triangular sepals are only about ⅛" long, but they're much longer and wider than the narrow bractlets and petals.

Flowering time: June–August

Habitat/range: Moist, rocky places; montane, subalpine, and alpine zones; 7,500–12,400'.

Comments: This hardy little plant is circumpolar in the Northern Hemisphere. In western North America it grows from high-elevation temperate areas up into the Canadian Arctic. Linnaeus named the plant in 1753 in honor of Scottish botanist, Robert Sibbald (1641–1722). Though the flowers are small and inconspicuous, the plants often grow in rocky areas with little other vegetation, and the strawberry-like leaves are usually what first draw the attention of hikers and plant hunters.

WOOLLY MULLEIN

(non-native)
Verbascum thapsus
Figwort family (Scrophulariaceae)

Description: This erect biennial has densely woolly-hairy herbage and a coarse, sometimes branched stem that's 1–8' tall. Its oblanceolate basal leaves are 4–15" long and often form an impressively large rosette. The alternate, sessile stem leaves are 2–12" long. The inflorescence is a long, dense, spike-like raceme. The flowers **[left inset]** have a 5-lobed calyx, a yellow corolla, up to 1" wide, 5 stamens, and a single pistil.

Flowering time: May–September

Habitat/range: Roadsides and other disturbed areas; chaparral/oak-woodland, mixed conifer, montane, and subalpine zones; up to 8,500'.

Comments: This invasive Eurasian native was introduced to Virginia in the mid 1700s for its medicinal uses. The plant quickly spread across the country, and it's now a common weed along roadsides throughout much of the park. The plant grows a basal rosette of leaves the first year, grows a flowering stem the next year, and then dies.

Similar plants: Somewhat similar Moth Mullen (*Verbascum blattaria*) **[right inset]** has hairless leaves and larger, showier flowers. The plant is also an introduced Eurasian native and has been reported occasionally in Yosemite Valley meadows, but it isn't considered particularly invasive.

ROUGH-STEMMED PRETTY FACE

Triteleia ixioides ssp. *scabra*
Brodiaea family (Themidaceae)

Description: This hairless perennial has an erect, rigid, usually rough-surfaced flowering stem that's 8–20" tall, and it has 1 or 2 linear, grass-like basal leaves that are 4–20" long. Its open, umbel-like inflorescence has green, lanceolate bracts at the base and has many flowers on upcurved stalks that are ⅜–3½" long. The flowers have 6 straw-colored to pale yellow tepals that are ½–1" long. Each tepal has a reflexed lobe and a green, brown, or purple midvein on its lower surface. The 6 unequal stamens closely surround the single pistil and have cream or yellow (occasionally blue) anthers and broad, flattened filaments with 2 long, pointed appendages that are straight or curve outward. The stigma is weakly 3 lobed.

Flowering time: April–July

Habitat/range: Gravelly or sandy openings; chaparral/oak-woodland, mixed conifer, and montane zones; up to 7,200'.

Similar plants: Mountain Pretty Face (*T. ixioides* ssp. *anilina*) also has 2 sets of unequal stamens with broad, flattened filaments, but their filament tip appendages are short and are straight or curve inward, and their anthers are usually blue, though they are sometimes cream colored. Sierra Pretty Face (*T. montana*) has 6 equal stamens with thread-like filaments. All three plants are fairly common throughout much of the park.

SIERRA PRETTY FACE

Triteleia montana
Brodiaea family (Themidaceae)

Description: Sierra Pretty Face is a hairless perennial with an erect, rigid flowering stem that's 2–10" tall and is smooth or minutely roughened. The 1 or 2 linear, grass-like basal leaves are 4–12" long and are often withered by the time the flowers bloom. The open, umbel-like inflorescence has green bracts at the base and has many flowers on upcurved stalks that are up to 1⅛" long. The 6 yellow to golden-yellow tepals are up to ¾" long, have spreading lobes, and have a brown midvein on the lower surface. The 6 equal stamens have thread-like filaments and cream to blue anthers, and the single pistil is weakly 3 lobed.

Flowering time: June–July

Habitat/range: Dry forest openings; mixed conifer, montane, and subalpine zones; 3,900–8,500'.

Similar plants: Rough-stemmed Pretty Face (*T. ixioides* ssp. *scabra*) and Mountain Pretty Face (*T. ixioides* ssp. *anilina*) do not have thread-like, equal stamens. Instead, they have 2 sets of unequal stamens that have broad, flattened filaments and 2 filament tip appendages. All three plants are common throughout much of the park.

STREAM VIOLET

Viola glabella
Violet family (Violaceae)

Description: Stream Violet is a mostly hairless perennial with erect or ascending stems, up to 12" long. Its 2 or 3 bright green, kidney- or heart-shaped basal leaves are 1–3½" wide and have scalloped teeth along the margins. Its stem leaves grow toward the top of the stem and are similar but slightly smaller. The flowers, which grow on long stalks from the upper leaf axils, have 5 lance-linear sepals and 5 stamens. The 5 petals, ¼–⅝" long, are deep lemon-yellow on both surfaces. The lower 3 petals (or all 5 petals) have dark nectar guides, and the 2 lateral petals are bearded at the base.

Flowering time: March–July

Habitat/range: Shady, moist to wet places, usually along streams; mixed conifer and montane zones; 3,280–8,000'.

Comments: Most violets have dark lines called nectar guides on their lower petal. Insects follow the lines to locate the flower's nectar. The hairs at the base of the two lateral petals scrape pollen from insects, and the pollen falls directly onto the stigma below.

Similar plants: Delta-leaved Pine Violet (*Viola lobata* ssp. *integrifolia*) has similar leaves that are mostly toward the top of the stem, but it grows in dry habitats and the upper petals of its flowers are dark red-brown on the back.

PINE VIOLET
Viola lobata ssp. *lobata*
Violet family (Violaceae)

Description: Pine Violet is a common, slightly hairy perennial with 1–3 erect stems that are 4–16" tall. Most of its alternate leaves are crowded toward the top of the stem, near the flowers. The leaf blades are up to 4" wide and are ovate to kidney shaped. The basal leaves are unlobed or palmately lobed. The stem leaves are simply lobed or are deeply palmately cleft into 3–12 long lobes, some of which occasionally have a few teeth. The flowers grow solitary from leaf axils. They have 5 lanceolate sepals and 5 stamens. The 5 petals are up to ⅝" long and are lemon yellow, except that the upper 2 petals (and sometimes the lateral 2) are maroon to brown on the back. The lower 3 petals (or all 5 petals) have maroon nectar guides, and the 2 side petals are bearded at the base.

Flowering time: April–July

Habitat/range: Shady, dry areas or in the open, often along roadsides; mixed conifer zone; 3,300–6,600'.

Similar plants: Fan Violet (*V. sheltonii*) is the only other violet in the park with deeply divided leaves, but its leaves are divided into wedge-shaped segments that are again divided into multiple lobes. Closely related Delta-leaved Pine Violet (*V. lobata* ssp. *integrifolia*) also has leaves that are mostly toward the top of the stem, but its broadly triangular, unlobed stem leaves are simply toothed.

MOUNTAIN YELLOW VIOLET
Viola pinetorum ssp. *pinetorum*
Violet family (Violaceae)

Description: This common perennial has spreading to erect, leafy stems that are 2½–9" long, and its herbage is either green and mostly hairless or is covered with short, white hairs that make the herbage look gray-green. Its long-petioled leaves have linear to lanceolate (rarely ovate) blades that are often purple tinted on the lower surface and often have jagged to irregularly toothed margins. The stem leaf blades are 1¼–3¼" long, and at least some of them are 1½ or more times longer than they are wide. The flowers grow on leafless stalks from the leaf axils. They have 5 lanceolate sepals, 5 deep lemon-yellow petals that are ¼–¾" long, and 5 stamens. The upper 2 petals are red- to purple-brown on the back, the lower 3 petals have dark brown nectar guides, and the 2 side petals are bearded at the base.

Flowering time: June–August

Habitat/range: Dry to vernally moist forest floor, in the open or in shade; mixed conifer, montane, and subalpine zones; 5,500–10,500'.

Similar plants: *Viola purpurea* ssp. *mesophyta* is the only other violet in the park with stem leaf blades that are 1½ or more times longer than they are wide. The plant is not as common as Mountain Yellow Violet, and its stem leaf blades are shorter, only ⅝–1⅞" long.

GOOSEFOOT VIOLET

Viola purpurea ssp. *integrifolia*
Violet family (Violaceae)

Description: This perennial, up to 3¾" tall, has a short, erect stem that's mostly buried. Its long-petioled leaves are purple tinted below. The basal leaves have ovate to round, sparsely short-hairy blades, up to 1¼" long, that are sometimes shallowly toothed and are less than 1½ times longer than they are wide. The stem leaves are lance-oblong to ovate and are usually untoothed. The flowers, which grow from the leaf axils, have 5 lanceolate sepals and 5 yellow petals, about ½" long. The upper 2 petals are red- to purple-brown on the back, the lower 3 have dark nectar guides, and the 2 side petals are bearded at the base.

Flowering time: May–August

Habitat/range: Open coniferous forests; mixed conifer and montane zones; 4,000–8,000'.

Similar plants: Three other *Viola purpurea* subspecies in the park have basal leaf blades that are less than 1½ times longer than than they are wide. The subspecies are variable and they intergrade, which can make identification difficult. Ssp. *venosa* also has a mostly buried stem, but its leaves are toothed and mostly hairless. The stems of ssp. *quercetorum* and ssp. *purpurea* are not mostly buried. The leaves of ssp. *quercetorum* are generally gray-green and are usually not purple tinted. The leaves of ssp. *purpurea* are distinctly purple tinted below.

FAN VIOLET

Viola sheltonii
Violet family (Violaceae)

Description: Fan Violet is a mostly hairless perennial that's 1–8" tall and has 1 to several reclining to erect stems. Its bright green to blue-green leaves are 1–2½" wide, roundish in outline, and deeply palmately divided into 3 (occasionally 5) fan-shaped leaflets that are again deeply divided into lobed segments with rounded tips. The flowers grow from the leaf axils on long, leafless stalks. They have 5 lanceolate sepals, 5 lemon-yellow petals, ⅜–⅝" long, and 5 stamens. The lower 3 petals have dark nectar guides, and the 2 side petals are bearded at the base. The backs of the upper 2 petals are dark veined or are solid brown-purple.

Flowering time: April–July

Habitat/range: Dry, open to shady places; mixed conifer zone; 3,600–4,300'.

Comments: Sweet Violet (*Viola odorata*) is a cultivated violet that's been used in the perfume industry for its flirtatious scent, which comes and goes. The flowers have a chemical substance called ionone, which has an on-again, off-again effect on the human sense of smell.

Similar plants: Pine Violet (*Viola lobata* ssp. *lobata*) is the only other violet in the park that has deeply divided leaves, but its leaves are divided only once into 3–12 lobes.

CALIFORNIA WILD GRAPE
Vitis californica
Grape family (Vitaceae)

Description: This deciduous, high-climbing vine has stout, woody, sparsely branched stems with shredding bark. The stems, which can grow up to 50' long, have 2- to 3-branched tendrils that cling to nearby objects. The alternate, long-petioled leaves have a broad, roundish blade, 2¾–6" long, with a densely soft-hairy lower surface and a shiny green, sparsely hairy to hairless upper surface. The blade usually has 3 or 5 lobes, has sharp or blunt teeth along the margins, and is deeply indented at the base. The inflorescences are panicles of head- or umbel-like clusters that grow opposite the leaves. The tiny, unisexual flowers have 5 green sepals and 5 yellow petals that are attached to each other at the tips. The fruit is a berry that becomes purple or black at maturity.

Flowering time: May–June

Habitat/range: Streamsides and perennial springs, often in canyons; chaparral/oak-woodland and mixed conifer zones; up to 4,500'.

Comments: This showy vine grows in Yosemite Valley, at Hetch Hetchy, and around El Portal. The edible grapes, which ripen in September, are an important source of food for birds, and the foliage provides dense protective cover. In the fall, the leaves turn decorative shades of yellow and orange. Winemakers worldwide use this robust plant as a rootstock for their wine grapes.

PUNCTURE VINE
(non-native)
Tribulus terrestris
Caltrop family (Zygophyllaceae)

Description: Puncture Vine is an invasive annual with sprawling, hairy stems that are often reddish and are usually branched. Its stems spread radially from the root crown, forming flat patches that can be more than 3' in diameter. The opposite, pinnately compound, hairy leaves are up to 1¾" long and have 6–12 ovate to elliptic, opposite leaflets. The small flowers, which grow solitary from the leaf axils, have 5 sepals and 10 stamens. The 5 deciduous, oblong to obovate petals are lemon yellow. The 5-lobed fruit [inset] splits into 5 lumpy nutlets, each with 2–4 stout, needle-sharp spines.

Flowering time: April–October

Habitat/range: Dry, disturbed areas, often along walkways and on roadsides; chaparral/oak-woodland and mixed conifer zones; up to 4,000'.

Comments: This Mediterranean native has become a noxious weed throughout much of the United States. The nutlets are shaped so that their spines point upward, and they can easily flatten bicycle tires. We unwittingly disperse the plants when the nutlets adhere to our automobile tires and shoe treads. Two weevil species have been introduced as biological control agents in an attempt to limit the spread of the plant.

190

RED AND ORANGE FLOWERS

Spicebush (*Calycanthus occidentalis*)

Plants in this section have flowers that range from dark red to pale orange. The section includes plants with flowers that are greenish at first but quickly become red with age and remain red until they wither, such as plants in the buckwheat family (Polygonaceae).

If you've looked through this section for a plant that has orange flowers and you didn't find it, check the yellow flowers section. Some plants, such as poppies, have petals that can range from bright orange to bright yellow.

The section for yellow flowers includes many plants with flowers that are yellow at maturity and turn red as they age. The section for white flowers includes plants with flowers that are white at maturity and become red with age.

Note: The similar plants sections include plants that are not covered elsewhere in the book, as well as plants that have a separate photo unit of their own. The names of plants that have their own photo unit in the book are highlighted with green text.

ORANGE DANDELION

Agoseris aurantiaca var. *aurantiaca*
Sunflower family (Asteraceae)

Description: This stemless, milky-sapped perennial grows up to 20" tall and usually has a single flower stalk that could easily be mistaken for a stem. The narrow, lance-shaped leaves are arranged in a basal rosette, and they have smooth margins or small, scattered teeth or lobes. The leafless stalk ends in an attractive orange flower head that's about 1¼" wide and has ray flowers only. The outer tips of the rays are squared off and have 5 small, pointed lobes. The fruit is a smooth, spindle-shaped achene with a long, slender beak that ends in a tuft of white hairs (the pappus) that are designed to catch the wind for seed dispersal.

Flowering time: July–August

Habitat/range: Dry to moist, mostly grassy places and talus slopes; mixed conifer, montane, and subalpine zones; 6,000–10,500'.

Comments: Orange Dandelions are uncommon in Yosemite, so they're a treat to find. Their flower heads are shaped much like those of several other dandelion-like composites that grow in the park, but their brilliant orange color clearly sets them apart.

COMMON FIDDLENECK

Amsinckia intermedia (*A. menziesii* var. *intermedia*)
Borage or Waterleaf family (Boraginaceae)

Description: Common Fiddleneck is an erect perennial, 7–32" tall, with a simple or widely branched stem and bristly-hairy herbage. Its alternate leaves are linear to lanceolate. Many flowers grow in a dense, 1-sided inflorescence that's shaped like a shepherd's crook or the neck of a fiddle. The orange, trumpet-shaped flowers are ⁵⁄₁₆–⁷⁄₁₆" long and have red or orange blotches near the throat. The flowers open from the bottom upward as the inflorescence uncoils. The maturing fruit, farther down the stem, is a set of 1–4 bumpy nutlets.

Flowering time: March–June

Habitat/range: Open, grassy slopes and flats, roadsides, and disturbed areas; chaparral/oak-woodland and mixed conifer zones; up to 4,300'.

Comments: Fiddlenecks are sometimes called Saccato Gordo, which is Spanish for fat grass. The plant's nutlets provide nutritious food for wild animals, but all parts of the plant can be toxic to cattle and horses.

Similar plants: Menzies' Fiddleneck (*Amsinckia menziesii*, previously *A. menziesii* var. *menziesii*), has rarely been reported in the park. It looks almost identical, but its flowers are yellow and are smaller, ⅛–¼" long.

WESTERN HOUND'S TONGUE
Cynoglossum occidentale
Borage or Waterleaf family (Boraginaceae)

Description: Western Hound's Tongue is a perennial with rough-hairy leaves and 1 to several erect, leafy, hairy stems, up to 20" tall. The oblanceolate basal leaves are up to 6" long and taper at the base to a winged petiole. The smaller stem leaves are sessile or clasping. The flowers **[upper inset]** grow in clusters at the top of the stem. The corolla is less than ¾" wide and has a long tube and 5 erect to slightly spreading lobes. The corolla is often pale pink in bud, turns maroonish red at maturity, and becomes blue as it begins to wither. The fruit is a set of 4 bumpy, bristly nutlets.

Flowering time: May–July

Habitat/range: Dry openings in conifer forests; mixed conifer zone; 4,500–6,000'.

Comments: *Cynoglossum* is Greek for dog's tongue. The plant got its common name and its genus name for the shape of the leaf blade of some species.

Similar plants: Grand Hound's Tongue (*Cynoglossum grande*) has been reported near the western park boundary, and it might grow within the park. It has a similar set of basal leaves and looks somewhat similar in general, but its stem is usually solitary and is hairless and its bright blue flowers **[lower inset]** have outspread lobes that turn pink with age.

WESTERN WALLFLOWER
Erysimum capitatum var. *capitatum*
Mustard family (Brassicaceae)

Description: This tall, showy biennial or short-lived perennial has sparsely hairy herbage and usually a single stem that's sometimes branched and is 5"–3½' long. Its basal leaves are 1–4" long and are linear, spoon shaped, or oblanceolate. The leaves taper to a petiole and are usually toothed. The alternate stem leaves are shorter and narrower. The flowers are crowded in a head-like cluster at the top of the stem. They have a tubular calyx with 4 green or sometimes orange-tinted sepals that bulge at the base. The 4 orange (sometimes bright yellow), obovate petals are ¼–⅜" wide and taper to the base. The narrow fruit (siliques) are 1½–4½" long, are spreading to ascending, and are not constricted between the seeds.

Flowering time: March–September

Habitat/range: Roadsides, forest openings, and dry, rocky places; chaparral/oak-woodland, mixed conifer, and montane zones; up to 7,800'.

Similar plants: Closely related Sanddune Wallflower (*Erysimum perenne*) looks a lot like Western Wallflower, but Sanddune Wallflower's yellow petals are narrower, less than ¼" wide, and its fruit are constricted between the seeds, making the fruit look slightly lumpy. Unlike Western Wallflower, it grows up into the subalpine and alpine zones.

193

WESTERN SPICEBUSH
Calycanthus occidentalis
Sweet-shrub family (Calycanthaceae)

Description: Western Spicebush is a deciduous, rounded shrub, 3–10' tall, with fragrant foliage. Its opposite, often glossy leaves are 2–6" long and are rounded at the base and pointed at the tip. The showy, red to reddish-purple flowers are about 2" wide, and they appear after the leaves have fully matured in the spring. The lotus-shaped flowers have numerous spirally arranged tepals that are somewhat fleshy. The enlarged, urn-shaped fruit capsule **[inset]** is woody and has conspicuous veins.

Flowering time: April–August

Habitat/range: Along streams and on moist canyon slopes; chaparral/oak-woodland and mixed conifer zones; up to 4,500'.

Comments: This plant's leaves have a spicy fragrance, the scraped bark has a strong camphor odor, and the aromatic flowers smell like red wine to some people and like bubble gum to others. The dried-out, woody capsules are conspicuous on the leafless shrubs in the fall and winter. Western Spicebush grows only in western states. Carolina Spicebush (*Calycanthus floridus*) grows in eastern states and closely resembles Western Spicebush. Both plants are cultivated in gardens.

DOUBLE HONEYSUCKLE
Lonicera conjugialis
Honeysuckle family (Caprifoliaceae)

Description: This slender shrub is 2–6' tall and has soft-hairy herbage. The thin, opposite leaves are ¾–3" long, have a short petiole, are elliptic to round, and often have a pointed tip. The bright to dark red flowers grow in pairs in leaf axils toward the branch ends, and they sometimes have tiny bracts beneath them. The tubular corolla is up to ¼" long and is conspicuously 2 lipped; the upper lip is erect and has 4 shallow lobes, and the lower lip is curved under. The stigma and 5 stamens extend beyond the corolla. The fruit **[inset]** is a partially to completely fused pair of bright red, somewhat translucent berries.

Flowering time: June–July

Habitat/range: Streambanks and moist, forested areas; mixed conifer, montane, and subalpine zones; 3,500–10,000'.

Comments: Double Honeysuckle is a good example of the double nature of plants in the *Lonicera* genus, with its paired leaves and flowers and fused pair of ovaries. The name *conjugialis* is from a Latin word that means joined together.

Similar plants: Twinberry Honeysuckle (*Lonicera involucrata*) sometimes has red bracts beneath its flowers and its corolla is red toward the base, but its flowers are radially symmetrical rather than 2 lipped.

ROSE CAMPION

(non-native)
Lychnis coronaria
Pink family (Caryophyllaceae)

Description: Rose Campion is a perennial with densely silky-hairy to woolly-hairy herbage and several stout, erect stems that are 1¼–3¼' long. Its lower leaves are 2–4" long, are oblanceolate, and have winged petioles. The 5–10 opposite pairs of stem leaves are sessile and become smaller upward. The flowers, which grow at the branch ends, have a tubular calyx with 5 woolly, fused sepals that are twisted at the tip. The 5 broad, spreading petal limbs are bright red, magenta, or red-purple and have 2 shallow lobes.

Flowering time: June–August

Habitat/range: Open or shady areas around developments; mixed conifer zone; 3,600–4,300'.

Comments: This popular garden plant is native to southeastern Europe and has become naturalized in several western states and most of the eastern states. In Yosemite Valley and around Mather it has escaped cultivation and seems to be spreading.

Similar plants: Sweet William (*Dianthus barbatus*) is another garden plant that has escaped and has become naturalized near developed areas in the park. It has similar flowers that also vary in color, but its herbage is green and mostly hairless and its petals have conspicuously jagged edges and often have white bands.

INDIAN PINK

Silene laciniata ssp. *californica* (*S. californica*)
Pink family (Caryophyllaceae)

Description: This eye-catching perennial has a reclining to erect stem, ½–2' long, that's hairy or glandular-hairy and sometimes branched at the base. The opposite leaves, 1–4" long, are oblanceolate to ovate, sessile or petioled, and reduced in size upward. The flowers are solitary or in few-flowered clusters. The glandular-hairy, tubular calyx, ½–1" long, has 5 narrowly triangular lobes. The bright red petals have 5 spreading limbs, up to ⅝" long, that have 4–6 deep lobes. The 10 stamens and 3 styles extend beyond the calyx.

Flowering time: March–June

Habitat/range: Dry, open or shady slopes and flats, often along roadbanks; chaparral/oak-woodland and mixed conifer zones; up to 4,600'.

Comments: Indian Pink's brilliant red petals make it one of the showiest plants in the park. Hummingbirds and butterflies, both with good color vision, are attracted to the red petals and are the plant's primary pollinators. Since bees don't perceive the color red, they don't visit the flowers. Pollen production requires energy, and any pollen that doesn't result in more members of a species is wasted pollen, and thus wasted energy. Flowers that attract specific pollinators are more likely to have their pollen passed on to a member of their own species since the next plant the pollinator visits is likely to be a plant of the same species.

CANYON LIVEFOREVER
Dudleya cymosa ssp. *cymosa*
Stonecrop family (Crassulaceae)

Description: This gorgeous perennial is up to 1½'
tall and grows along rocky flats and canyon walls.
The thick, succulent leaves are arranged in an
attractive basal rosette, up to 8" wide. The broad,
green to gray-green leaves are wider toward the
base, taper to a pointed tip, and often turn rusty
colored with age. The reddish flower stems are
topped with a somewhat flat-topped, crowded,
candelabra-like cluster of 4–20 flowers that are up
to ½" long and can be bright red, orange, or yellow.

Flowering time: April–June

Habitat/range: Rock crevices; chaparral/oak-
woodland, mixed conifer, and montane zones; up
to 8,000'.

Comments: These plants grow in dry areas. When
precious moisture is available, the plants store it in
their succulent grayish-green leaves, which reflect
some of the sun's desiccating rays. Most plant
species open their leaf pores (stomata) during the
day to absorb carbon dioxide, which they use along
with water and sunlight to produce carbohydrates
in the process called photosynthesis. With the
stomata open, the plants lose significant amounts
of water. Canyon Liveforever keeps its stomata
closed during the day, which allows the plant to
conserve tremendous amounts of water. In the
cool of the night, it opens the stomata, absorbs
carbon dioxide, and converts it to nutrients.

WESTERN ROSEROOT, LEDGE STONECROP
Rhodiola integrifolia ssp. *integrifolia*
(*Sedum rosea* ssp. *integrifolium*)
Stonecrop family (Crassulaceae)

Description: Western Roseroot is an attractive
perennial, up to 8" tall, with several stout stems.
The green to blue-green, alternate, ovate leaves
are up to 1" long and are equally distributed in
a rather crowded fashion around the stem. The
smooth, succulent leaves curve up toward a
pointed tip and often become rusty colored with
age. The tiny flowers, which grow in dense terminal clusters of 7–50, have 4 or 5 bright red to deep
purple, fleshy petals that are less than ¼" long.

Flowering time: May–July

Habitat/range: Rocky or gravelly areas, meadow
margins, and along streams; montane, subalpine,
and alpine zones; 6,000–13,000'.

Comments: Carl Linnaeus gave this plant its scientific name in 1753. Linnaeus was born in Sweden
in 1707. As a child, he became fascinated with
plants. In college, he devised a method for giving
every living thing a binomial name, the method still
in use today. Linnaeus used the arrangement of
male and female flower parts to classify plants, a
method that was attacked by critics for its sexual
nature. One critic, botanist Johann Siegesbeck,
called it "loathsome harlotry." In response, Linnaeus assigned the name *Sigesbeckia orientalis* to
a small, ugly weed that was used to treat syphilis.

SNOW PLANT

Sarcodes sanguinea
Heath family (Ericaceae)

Description: This brilliant showstopper is a parasitic perennial. Its thick flowering stalk is ½–1' tall and is fleshy and glandular-hairy throughout. The plant has no stem and no leaves. The parts that look like red leaves are actually bracts. They grow at the base of each of the bright red flowers that cover the upper part of the stalk. The urn- to bell-shaped flowers are up to ¾" long and have 5 separate, red sepals and 5 red petals that are fused at the base.

Flowering time: May–July

Habitat/range: Dry, open or shaded areas in thick humus; mixed conifer and montane zones; 3,900–8,000'.

Comments: This might be the brightest red plant in the world, and it can be fun to witness the reactions of people when they encounter it for the first time. The common name suggests that the plants emerge from under snow. They do sometimes bloom when there's still some snow around, and they might occasionally come up through a bit of snow, but they typically emerge from snowless duff. The plant and several of its relatives in the heath family lack chlorophyll and cannot use photosynthesis to manufacture nutrients. Instead, they get their nourishment by absorbing it from soil fungi.

BROAD-LEAVED LOTUS

Hosackia crassifolia var. *crassifolia*
(*Lotus crassifolius* var. *crassifolius*)
Pea family (Fabaceae)

Description: This robust, usually hairless perennial has sprawling to erect stems that are 2–5' long. Its pinnate leaves have 9–15 oval, ovate, or obovate leaflets that are offset or opposite and up to 1¼" long. Each inflorescence has 12–20 tubular pea flowers, up to ¾" long, in a tight cluster. The calyx, which has 5 pointed lobes, is green at first and soon turns reddish. The somewhat closed corolla is white or pale yellow at first and then quickly acquires reddish to magenta streaks. The linear, hairless pea pods are up to 3" long.

Flowering time: May–August

Habitat/range: Woodland or forest openings, roadsides, and disturbed places; mixed conifer zone; 2,900–6,400'.

Comments: The genus was named for Dr. David Hosack (1769–1835), a botanist, college professor, and physician, one of the first to use a stethoscope. He purchased land near New York City, and in 1801 he created Elgin Botanical Garden, the first public botanical garden in the United States. He established a private medical practice in New York City, and Alexander Hamilton and his family were among his patients. In 1804 he attended the duel between Hamilton and Aaron Burr. He treated Hamilton's gunshot wound but was unable to save him, and Hamilton died the next day.

SULPHUR PEA
Lathyrus sulphureus
Pea family (Fabaceae)

Description: Sulphur Pea is a hairless perennial with sprawling or climbing, angled stems that are 1½–3¼' long. Its pinnate leaves have prominent, leafy bracts at their base. The leaves have a coiled, often branched tendril at the tip and 6–12 opposite or alternate, elliptic to ovate leaflets, up to 1¾" long. The flower stalks, which grow from the leaf axils, have 10–15 pea flowers in an elongated raceme or a more tightly packed cluster, with the flowers growing mostly toward one side of the stalk. The calyx has 5 lobes, the upper 2 wider and shorter than the lower 3, and the lobes are often curved toward each other. The yellowish-white to bronze-orange corolla is up to ½" long, and the banner petal sometimes has red markings. The smooth pea pods resemble culinary snow peas.

Flowering time: April–July

Habitat/range: Openings in chaparral, woodland, and forest or along meadow borders; chaparral/oak-woodland and mixed conifer zones; up to 5,300'.

Comments: Peas (*Lathyrus* species) and vetches (*Vicia* species) are often hard to tell apart, but you can use a hand lens to distinguish peas from vetches. Hold the keel away from the style and look at the tip of the style. If it has a row of hairs like a tiny toothbrush, it's a pea. If it has a ring or tuft of hairs, it's a vetch.

MOUNTAIN GOOSEBERRY
Ribes montigenum
Gooseberry family (Grossulariaceae)

Description: This much-branched shrub is 1–3' tall and has short, glandular hairs throughout. Its spreading to reclining stems have 1–5 short spines at the leaf and branch nodes and have prickles in between. The leaves are up to 1" wide and have 5 deep lobes with pointed or rounded, irregular teeth. The pendulous inflorescences grow from leaf axils and have 3–8 flowers that are up to about ⅜" wide. The short, saucer- to bell-shaped flower tube (hypanthium) is green, has stalked, sometimes red glands, and ends with 5 rounded, variously colored sepals (green, yellowish, or cream with red tinges). The 5 red, fan-shaped petals are smaller than the sepals and have a yellow, pink, or red nectary beneath them. The 5 stamens grow opposite the sepals. The red, glandular-bristly berries are less than ½" wide.

Flowering time: June–July

Habitat/range: Open, often rocky places; montane, subalpine, and alpine zones; 6,500–11,800'.

Comments: The shrub's peripheral branches often touch the ground, where they can root and start a whole new cloned plant. Eventually, younger plants will encircle the parent plant. At some point the parent plant will die, and its "offspring" will create their own clones, a process that can eventually result in a thicket up to 20 feet wide.

SIERRA GOOSEBERRY

Ribes roezlii var. *roezlii*
Gooseberry family (Grossulariaceae)

Description: Sierra Gooseberry is a shrub, up to 4' tall, with branches that have 1–3 spines at the nodes and no prickles in between. Its roundish leaves are up to 1" wide and have 3 or 5 lobes with rounded teeth. The upper leaf surface is dark green and mostly hairless, and the lower surface is paler and short-soft-hairy. The pendulous flowers, up to ½" long, grow 1–3 from leaf axils. The flowers have a glandular-hairy, inferior ovary and a cylindric, red to maroon flower tube (hypanthium) that ends with 5 matching-colored, reflexed sepals. The 5 white, erect petals extend beyond the hypanthium and are rolled inward along the sides. The 5 stamens have dark anthers and extend beyond the petals, and the 2 styles extend beyond the anthers. The glandular-hairy berries **[inset]** become bright red at maturity and have long, red spines.

Flowering time: May–June

Habitat/range: Shady places; chaparral/oak-woodland, mixed conifer, montane, and subalpine zones; up to 9,000'.

Similar plants: The flowers of Bitter Gooseberry (*Ribes amarum*) look a lot like Sierra Gooseberry's flowers, but Bitter Gooseberry's leaves are glandular-hairy (and sticky to the touch) and Sierra Gooseberry's leaves, though hairy, are not glandular. Bitter Gooseberry grows around the park's western boundary.

ALPINE LILY

Lilium parvum
Lily family (Liliaceae)

Description: This showy, hairless perennial has an erect stem, 1¼–5½' tall. Its elliptic leaves are 1½–6" long and grow in 2–5 whorls with 3–13 leaves per whorl. The elongated inflorescence has 1–26 spreading to erect, attractive, bell-shaped flowers. The 6 tepals are up to 1⅝" long and are somewhat curled backward, though the lower tepals are often straighter and serve as landing platforms for pollinators. Toward their base, the tepals are yellow to orange with red or orange dots, and they're darker orange, red-orange, or red toward the tip. The 6 stamens extend beyond the corolla throat. The fruit is an erect, oblong capsule.

Flowering time: June–September

Habitat/range: Marshy areas, wet meadows, and seeps; mixed conifer, montane, and subalpine zones; 4,000–9,500'.

Similar plants: The larger flowers of Leopard Lily (*Lilium pardalinum* ssp. *pardalinum*) **[inset]** are similarly colored and decorated, but they're nodding rather than spreading to erect. Their tepals are so strongly curved that they often touch at the tips, and their anthers are almost as long as the tepals. Although Leopard Lilies are uncommon in the park, if you drive down the road toward Hetch Hetchy Reservoir in July to early August, you're likely to find a large colony of the plants blooming in a drainage ditch right beside the road.

NARROW-PETALED WAKEROBIN, GIANT TRILLIUM

Trillium angustipetalum
False-hellebore family (Melanthiaceae)

Description: This distinctive, musty-scented perennial has 1 or more erect stems that are 7–27" tall and grow from a rhizome. The 3 large, broadly ovate, sessile leaves are 3–10" long, grow in a whorl around the stem, and are often mottled with brown blotches or with blotches that have contrasting shades of green. A single flower grows at the center of the leaf whorl, and it has 3 green to reddish-purple, lanceolate sepals and 3 erect, linear, dark red to maroon petals that are 2–4½" long.

Flowering time: April–July

Habitat/range: Damp, shady places; mixed conifer zone; 3,900–5,100'.

Comments: Plants in the *Trillium* genus are called wakerobin because they show up early in the spring along with migrating robins. *Trillium* seeds have a fleshy, protein-rich appendage that seems to have evolved solely to attract ants. When the ants find seeds, they chew off and eat appendages until they're full. Then they grab another seed and haul it off to their nest, where the fleshy material will soon be eaten. If the ants leave the seed in the nest, it will be safe from seed-eating rodents and birds and will sometimes be in a suitable habitat for germination and growth the next spring.

SCARLET PIMPERNEL

(non-native)
Lysimachia arvensis (*Anagallis arvensis*)
Myrsine family (Myrsinaceae)

Description: This attractive, hairless annual has trailing stems that are 2"–1¼' long and are usually much branched. Its opposite, ovate to oval leaves, up to ¾" long, are sessile. The flowers, which grow solitary in leaf axils, have a green, 5-lobed calyx, divided nearly to the base, and 6 stamens with yellow anthers. The wheel-shaped corolla has 5 broad, mostly free, bright orange or salmon (rarely blue) petals that are usually darker at the base and are about ¼" long. The fruit is a spherical capsule.

Flowering time: March–June

Habitat/range: Open, grassy meadows and disturbed areas; chaparral/oak-woodland and mixed conifer zones; up to 4,000'.

Comments: The flowers of this European native close in cloudy weather, probably to keep rain from rinsing their pollen away, and they seem to pop out of nowhere as soon as the sun comes back out. That characteristic inspired the writer of a famous novel to name her aristocratic British hero (and her novel) after the plant. During the Reign of Terror following the French Revolution, the unlikely hero became notorious for his ability to pop out of nowhere and rescue French aristocrats from the guillotine in the nick of time, earning him the nickname Scarlet Pimpernel.

CALIFORNIA FUCHSIA

Epilobium canum ssp. *latifolium*
Evening Primrose family (Onagraceae)

Description: California Fuchsia is a much admired, semi-woody perennial to subshrub that grows up to 3' tall and has hairy, somewhat glandular-sticky herbage. Its green to grayish, lanceolate to ovate leaves are up to 2½" long and are sometimes minutely toothed. The leaves are opposite toward the bottom of the stem and alternate above. The brilliant red to orange-red, funnel-shaped corollas are up to about ⅝" long and have 4 fused petals with reflexed, notched tips. The 8 stamens and the style, with its 4-lobed stigma, are also red and extend well beyond the corolla. The fruit is a linear, 4-angled capsule.

Flowering time: August–November

Habitat/range: Dry, rocky places; chaparral/oak-woodland, mixed conifer, and montane zones; up to 8,200'.

Comments: Like most plants with red tubular flowers, California Fuchsia is pollinated by hummingbirds, and it's sometimes called Hummingbird Trumpet. The late-blooming plant grows at low to middle elevations in the Coast Ranges and the Sierra Nevada, and it provides food for fall migrating hummingbirds at a time when there are few other hummingbird-suitable plants in bloom. The plant used to be in the genus *Zauschneria*, a challenging name to learn and one that at least a few botanists gave up somewhat reluctantly.

SPOTTED CORALROOT

Corallorhiza maculata var. *occidentalis*
Orchid family (Orchidaceae)

Description: Because this attractive perennial lacks chlorophyll, it has no green parts. Its red to yellowish-purple stem is 7–22" long, and its herbage is hairless throughout. Up to 40 flowers grow along the upper part of the stem. The flowers have an elongated inferior ovary, 3 sepals, and 3 petals. The most conspicuous part of the flower is the lower petal, which is called the lip. It has 2 rounded lateral lobes and a much larger white central lobe that is distinctly broader at the tip. The lip often has red or purple spots and is slightly toothed. The 3 sepals are arranged like the top of a cross, with each of the 2 similar upper petals between an arm and the top of the cross. The stamens and style are fused into a whitish-yellow column with purple spots. The fruit is a pendant capsule that turns brown with age. The plant's dead stem remains intact long after the growing season has passed.

Flowering time: May–August

Habitat/range: Shady forest floor; mixed conifer and montane zones; 4,000–8,500'.

Similar plants: A less common variety of Spotted Coralroot, *Corallorhiza maculata* var. *maculata*, also grows in the park. Its lip petal has more or less parallel sides and is *not* broader at the tip.

STRIPED CORALROOT

Corallorhiza striata
Orchid family (Orchidaceae)

Description: Striped Coralroot is an erect, hairless perennial, 6–20" tall, without chlorophyll. Its stem is red-brown to more or less purple, or sometimes yellow. Up to 40 flowers grow toward the top of the stem. The flowers have an inferior ovary, 3 sepals, and 3 petals. The lower petal, called the lip, hangs straight down. The lip is darker and broader than the other petals and the sepals, and it has thicker stripes and upward curving margins. The 3 sepals and 2 similar petals are curved forward and are cream to pale yellow with reddish to purplish stripes. The 2 upper petals are between the upper and lateral sepals. The stamens and style are fused into a yellow column that sometimes has purple spots, and the fruit is a pendant capsule.

Flowering time: May–July

Habitat/range: Shady forest floor; mixed conifer and montane zones; 4,000–7,900'.

Comments: This striking plant is less common than its close relative Spotted Coralroot (*Corallorhiza maculata*). Sometimes you get lucky and find both plants growing together. Both species lack chlorophyll and must get their nutrients from soil fungi, which have long strands called mycelia that spread throughout the soil and grow into the roots of other plants. Coralroots absorb nutrients from the mycelia and are not known to provide anything in return.

WAVY-LEAVED PAINTBRUSH

Castilleja applegatei ssp. *pallida*
Broomrape family (Orobanchaceae)

Description: This somewhat shrubby perennial, 4–9½" tall, often has branched stems and has glandular-hairy herbage. Its narrow, sessile leaves, ¾–2½" long, have distinctly wavy margins and often have 3 lobes. The inflorescence has a series of bracts with orange-red tips, and the bracts are much showier than the paler, tubular corolla. The upper bracts have 3–5 lobes, and the calyx is divided into 4 lanceolate lobes with orange-red tips. The narrow upper lip of the 2-lipped corolla is green to yellowish and has red margins, and the shorter lower lip is green and mostly hidden by the calyx.

Flowering time: June–August

Habitat/range: Dry, rocky places; montane, subalpine, and alpine zones; 6,500–11,200'.

Similar plants: The park has three Wavy-leaved Paintbrush subspecies, and they all have orange-red inflorescences. They are the only dry-habitat paintbrushes in the park that have leaves with conspicuously wavy margins. Ssp. *pallida* is less than 10" tall, and many of its leaves have 3 lobes. Ssp. *disticha* and ssp. *pinetorum* have mostly unlobed leaves. Ssp. *disticha* can get up to 31" tall, its calyxes are less than ¾" long, and it grows in the mixed conifer and montane zones. Ssp. *pinetorum* can get up to 24" tall, its calyxes are ⅝–1" long, and it grows from the chaparral/oak-woodland zone into the subalpine zone.

GIANT RED PAINTBRUSH
Castilleja miniata ssp. *miniata*
Broomrape family (Orobanchaceae)

Description: Giant Red Paintbrush has 1 or more stout, sometimes branched stems, 1–2½' tall, and its herbage is long-soft-hairy toward the top of the plant. Its alternate leaves, 1–2½" long, are lanceolate and sessile. The leaves are broader and softer than the leaves of the other paintbrush plants in the park, and the lower leaves have no lobes. The inflorescence, 1–6" long, has bracts with bright red tips, and the upper bracts have 2 slender lobes. The calyx is divided into 4 red, lanceolate lobes. The narrow upper lip of the 2-lipped corolla is yellow-green with red margins, and the lower lip is dark green and mostly hidden by the calyx.

Flowering time: May–September

Habitat/range: Wet meadows, seeps, and streambanks; mixed conifer, montane, subalpine, and alpine zones; 5,400–11,000'.

Similar plants: Giant Red Paintbrush's lower leaves are unlobed. Coast Paintbrush (*C. affinis* ssp. *affinis*) looks more like Giant Red Paintbrush than any of the other paintbrushes in the park, but most of its leaves are usually lobed. Woolly Paintbrush (*C. foliolosa*) has similar inflorescences, but its foliage is densely woolly-hairy. Coast Paintbrush and Woolly Paintbrush grow in dry habitats in the chaparral/oak-woodland zone. They've both been reported in the park, but they grow mostly in the foothills west of the park.

MOUNTAIN PAINTBRUSH
Castilleja peirsonii (*C. parviflora*)
Broomrape family (Orobanchaceae)

Description: This meadow-dwelling, somewhat uncommon perennial is 3–14" tall and often has clustered stems. Its herbage is mostly hairless or has long, nonglandular hairs and short, glandular hairs. The sessile leaves are ¾–2" long, are lanceolate to oblong, and usually have 3–5 narrow, pointed lobes. The inflorescence is 1–6" long and has calyxes and a series of 3- to 5-lobed bracts that are red or orange toward the top and are much showier than the pale, tubular corolla. The calyx is unequally divided into 4 linear lobes. The upper lip of the 2-lipped corolla extends well beyond the calyx lobes and is yellowish green with reddish margins. The tiny, dark green lower corolla lip is hidden by the calyx.

Flowering time: July–August

Habitat/range: Damp to wet meadows, often near lakes or ponds; subalpine and alpine zones; 8,500–10,500'.

Similar plants: Most of Mountain Paintbrush's leaves are lobed. Somewhat similar Giant Red Paintbrush (*C. miniata*) also grows in wet habitats, but most of its leaves are unlobed, though the uppermost leaves are sometimes lobed. Wavy-leaved Paintbrush (*C. applegatei*) has orange-red inflorescences and has leaves that can be lobed or unlobed, but it grows only in dry places and its leaves have conspicuously wavy margins.

203

SCARLET MONKEYFLOWER

Erythranthe cardinalis (*Mimulus cardinalis*)
Lopseed family (Phrymaceae)

Description: Scarlet Monkeyflower is a striking perennial with erect, branching stems, 1–3' long, and downy-hairy, sometimes glandular, pale green herbage. Its opposite leaves, up to 3" long, are oval, oblong, or ovate and are coarsely toothed. The lower leaves are petioled and the upper leaves are sessile. The flowers, which grow in pairs, have a stalk that is considerably longer than the calyx. The distinctly 2-lipped, bright scarlet to orange-red corolla has a wide open, yellow throat with contrasting dark stripes. The 2 lobes on the upper lip are arched forward, and the 3 broader lobes on the lower lip are spreading or reflexed. The style and stigma extend well beyond the corolla throat.

Flowering time: April–October

Habitat/range: Seeps, springs, streamsides, and road drainages; chaparral/oak-woodland and mixed conifer zones; up to 6,000'.

Comments: Cardinal means of the greatest importance. The word has long been used as the title of senior officials of the Roman Catholic Church, who incidentally wear red robes. Because of the robes, the word cardinal eventually became associated with the color red. Scarlet Monkeyflower, like many other plants with red, tubular flowers, is pollinated almost exclusively by hummingbirds.

BEAKED PENSTEMON

Penstemon rostriflorus
Plantain family (Plantaginaceae)

Description: This eye-catching, somewhat shrubby perennial has several erect stems, 1–3¼' tall, and sometimes grows in dense clumps. Its foliage is smooth to slightly hairy. The opposite stem leaves, ¾–2¾" long, are linear to lanceolate. The lower leaves have a short petiole, and the upper leaves are sessile. The 1-sided inflorescence is glandular-hairy and has many scarlet, tubular, 2-lipped flowers, up to 1½" long. The gaping flowers are sparsely glandular, inside and out, and have a hood-like, 2-lobed upper lip with slightly flaring lobes and a lower lip with 3 reflexed lobes.

Flowering time: June–August

Habitat/range: Dry slopes and flats; mixed conifer, montane, and subalpine zones; 3,900–10,500'.

Comments: Beaked Penstemon's flowers look like miniature, brilliant red Humpback Whales. *Penstemon* is Greek for 5 stamens, which all plants in the genus have. If you look into a penstemon flower, you'll see 4 obvious stamens, 2 on each side. You'll also see a style with an enlarged stigma and another skinny, nondescript part that looks like it could also be a style, but which is actually a sterile stamen with no anther, stamen number 5. If you're driving (or riding) along Tioga Road and you see small, bright red, tubular flowers, it's either this plant or Scarlet Gilia (*Ipomopsis aggregata*), which is in the phlox family.

SCARLET GILIA

Ipomopsis aggregata ssp. *aggregata*
(*I. aggregata* ssp. *formosissima*)
Phlox family (Polemoniaceae)

Description: Scarlet Gilia is an attractive, short-lived perennial with an erect, often branched stem that's 1–2½' tall and is hairless to glandular-hairy. Its basal leaves are 1¼–2" long, are pinnately dissected into 9–11 linear lobes, and are often withered at blooming time. The alternate, smaller stem leaves have 5–7 lobes with narrow pointed tips. The inflorescences are 1-sided, compact clusters of 3–7 flowers at the stem and branch ends. The calyx has 5 pointed lobes and membranous margins. The bright red to red-orange corolla is ¾–1⅜" long, and it has an elongated tube and 5 lanceolate lobes that are spreading or curved backward and are sometimes mottled with small, white or yellow blotches. The 5 unequal stamens extend well beyond the corolla throat and have white, yellow, or slightly bluish anthers.

Flowering time: June–September

Habitat/range: Forest openings and dry, sandy flats; montane zone; 6,000–8,000'.

Similar plants: Closely related *Ipomopsis aggregata* ssp. *bridgesii* is less common. It has clusters of 1–5 flowers with blue anthers. At least some of the lobes of its upper stem leaves are blunt or rounded, and its corolla is often more deep pink than red. The two subspecies sometimes grow in the same vicinity.

GRAND COLLOMIA

Collomia grandiflora
Phlox family (Polemoniaceae)

Description: This showy annual has a stout, erect, leafy stem that's 4–40" long. Its stem is sometimes slightly hairy and glandular and is usually unbranched. The alternate, lanceolate to linear leaves are 2–4" long and are unlobed. The lower leaves are sometimes slightly hairy and minutely toothed. The stem ends with a head-like cluster of long-tubed, trumpet-shaped corollas that are up to 1¼" long and have 5 spreading lobes. Robust plants often have inflorescences that grow from the upper leaf axils. The corollas are usually salmon colored, but they can be white or other subdued orangish hues. Like many other phlox family plants, the flowers have blue anthers.

Flowering time: April–July

Habitat/range: Dry, open areas; mixed conifer and montane zones; 3,600–7,500'.

Comments: Grand Collomia's flowers are often a distinctive soft salmon color, but, like many plants in the phlox family, the corollas can vary in color from plant to plant and even on the same plant. Corolla color variation can make identification of some phlox family species a bit complicated, but Grand Collomia is fairly easy to recognize because it almost always has at least one salmon-colored corolla in every flower cluster.

HAIRY-FLOWERED BUCKWHEAT

Eriogonum hirtiflorum
Buckwheat family (Polygonaceae)

Description: Hairy-flowered Buckwheat is a small, inconspicuous, greenish or reddish annual that's 2–6" tall. Its mostly erect stem has numerous, sparsely glandular, spreading, forked branches. The leaves are hairless except for their ciliate margins. The obovate to spatula-shaped basal leaves are up to 1" long and taper to a winged petiole. The lanceolate stem leaves, at the lower branch nodes, are smaller and sessile. The tiny, turban-shaped, sparsely hairy involucres are sessile or have thread-like stalks, and they grow in the branch forks and at nodes along the branches. The involucres have 4 erect teeth, and each involucre contains 2 flowers. The tiny flowers have 6 reddish tepals with stiff, hooked hairs on the back.

Flowering time: June–October

Habitat/range: Dry, sandy and gravelly areas; chaparral/oak-woodland and mixed conifer zones; up to 7,300'.

Comments: This inconspicuous little plant blends in with its surroundings and is easily overlooked. In Yosemite, it's been collected along the South Fork of the Tuolumne River and at Badger Pass, and it's been reported in the El Portal area. All things considered, Hairy-flowered Buckwheat is a good candidate for an inconspicuous plant hunt.

ALPINE MOUNTAIN SORREL

Oxyria digyna
Buckwheat family (Polygonaceae)

Description: The stems of this erect perennial are 2½–20" tall and are sometimes branched toward the top. Its hairless herbage is somewhat fleshy and is often reddish tinged. The alternate, mostly basal leaves are 1–8" long, including the petiole. The leaves have a round or kidney-shaped blade, and the petiole is much longer than the blade. The nodding, reddish or greenish flowers **[inset]** grow in compact panicles. The small perianth has 2 spreading outer tepals that are slightly larger than the 2 inner tepals. Each flower has 6 stamens and 2 styles with red, fringed stigmas. The elliptic, flattened fruit is pinkish or reddish and has 2 wings.

Flowering time: July–September

Habitat/range: Moist rock crevices and boulder edges; subalpine and alpine zones; 9,000–12,900'.

Comments: Native Americans ate the tangy leaves of this plant raw or cooked. The leaves contain ascorbic acid, giving them a citrus flavor and giving those who eat them a dose of vitamin C. The leaves also contain oxalic acid, which adds to the tangy taste, but it can limit absorption of calcium and cause stomach upset.

Similar plants: The park has several plants with similar inflorescences, but Alpine Mountain Sorrel is the only one with round or kidney-shaped leaf blades.

SHEEP SORREL
(non-native)
Rumex acetosella
Buckwheat family (Polygonaceae)

Description: This weedy perennial has several ascending to erect, slender stems that are 4–16" long, and it has male and female flowers on separate plants. The mostly basal leaves are lanceolate, oblong, or linear. The blade is ¾–2½" long, and the petioles of the lower leaves are usually longer than the blades. The lower leaf blades have 2 lobes at the base, and the upper leaves are usually unlobed. The panicle-like inflorescence is a slender, interrupted set of whorled flower clusters at the end of the stem. The tiny, drooping flowers have 6 tepals in 2 sets, the inner 3 larger than the outer 3. The tepals are yellowish when young and turn reddish with age. The fruit is a 3-angled, brown achene.

Flowering time: March–August

Habitat/range: Disturbed areas; chaparral/oak-woodland and mixed conifer zones; up to 7,300'.

Comments: This invasive plant is a Eurasian native that's become naturalized throughout most of the Northern Hemisphere. The plant is used culinarily as a tart salad green and as a curdling agent for making cheese.

Similar plants: Several other plants in the buckwheat family have inflorescences similar to those of Sheep Sorrel, but its distinctive 2-lobed leaf blades make it easy to identify.

CURLY DOCK
(non-native)
Rumex crispus
Buckwheat family (Polygonaceae)

Description: Curly Dock is an invasive Eurasian perennial with hairless herbage and erect stems, 1¼–4½' tall, that are often branched above the middle. The alternate, long-petioled leaves are mostly crowded toward the base of the stem. The lanceolate to lance-linear leaf blade is 6–12" long and has conspicuously wavy margins. The tiny flowers grow in densely packed, leafy panicles at the stem and branch ends, and the lower half of the panicle occasionally has small gaps. The perianth has 6 tepals in 2 sets, 3 inconspicuous outer tepals and 3 inner tepals that are roundish and sometimes slightly heart shaped at the base. The tepals are greenish yellow when the plant is young and turn red with age **[inset]**. The tubercles (swollen protrusions) at the center of each inner tepal are less than a third as wide as the tepals.

Flowering time: April–September

Habitat/range: Disturbed places; chaparral/oak-woodland and mixed conifer zones; up to 4,600'.

Similar plants: Clustered Dock (*Rumex conglomeratus*), another invasive Eurasian native, has similar leaves and greenish flower clusters that turn red with age, but its flower clusters are widely spaced throughout and its tubercles are about half the width of the tepals. Both plants grow in and around meadows in Yosemite Valley and at Mather.

207

ALPINE SHEEP SORREL

Rumex paucifolius
Buckwheat family (Polygonaceae)

Description: Alpine Sheep Sorrel is a hairless perennial with clustered, slender, erect stems, 3–16" tall, that are sometimes branched in the inflorescence. The plants are generally dioecious, with unisexual male and female flowers on separate plants, but a plant can also have some bisexual flowers. The mostly basal leaves have a lanceolate or ovate-lanceolate blade that's 1¼–3" long. The leaf petiole is about the same length as the blade. The alternate, linear stem leaves are much smaller. The narrow, elongated inflorescences, which grow at the stem end and from leaf axils, have crowded clusters of small flowers. The perianth has 6 tepals in 2 sets, 3 inconspicuous outer tepals and 3 somewhat round inner tepals. The greenish tepals turn red with age.

Flowering time: July–September

Habitat/range: Moist places; subalpine and alpine zones; 8,500–12,100'.

Comments: This plant is a common component of the subalpine zone and is the only *Rumex* species that ascends into the alpine zone. In alpine fellfields, the plants are dwarfed.

Similar plants: The park has three somewhat similar *Rumex* species that are invasive Eurasian natives, but they don't grow above the mixed conifer zone.

TRIANGULAR-FRUITED DOCK

Rumex triangulivalvis
(*R. salicifolius* var. *triangulivalvis*)
Buckwheat family (Polygonaceae)

Description: This stout, hairless perennial has leafy, often branched stems, 8–38" long, that are erect or ascending or grow toward or along the ground. Its alternate, greenish-yellow leaves are narrowly lanceolate, are sometimes wavy margined, and are tapered at the base. The narrow, elongated inflorescences grow at the stem and branch ends and from leaf axils. The small, densely crowded flowers **[inset]** have 6 tepals, but only the inner 3 tepals are noticeable. They are triangular shaped and are fused together around the ovary, forming a 3-winged flower. A spindle-shaped protrusion, called a tubercle, grows in each of the 3 flattened areas between the wings. The flowers are greenish at first and turn brownish red with age.

Flowering time: June–September

Habitat/range: Moist, often disturbed areas along meadows and roads; mixed conifer, montane and subalpine zones; 4,000–10,500'.

Similar plants: California Willow Dock (*Rumex californicus*, previously *R. salicifolius* var. *denticulatus*) is practically identical, but its flowers either have no tubercles or just a single inconspicuous tubercle. Somewhat similar Poke Knotweed (*Aconogonon phytolaccifolium*) has white flowers, and its leaves are rounded at the base rather than tapered.

CRIMSON COLUMBINE
Aquilegia formosa
Buttercup family (Ranunculaceae)

Description: Crimson Columbine is an attractive perennial with 1 to several ascending to erect, sometimes openly branched stems that are 1–4' long and are hairless or sparsely hairy above. Its long-petioled basal leaves and lower leaves are divided once or twice into broad leaflets that are up to 1¾" long and are variously toothed and lobed. The upper stem leaves are smaller and sometimes have 3 deep lobes. The sparsely hairy, sometimes glandular, pendent or nodding flowers are about 1½" long and become erect in fruit. The 5 spreading, petal-like, red sepals are elliptic or lanceolate, and the 5 petals have a long, straight, red nectar tube and a yellow, often squared-off lobe. The flowers have 10–18 stamens that extend well beyond the corolla.

Flowering time: May–August

Habitat/range: Streambanks, seeps, and other moist places; chaparral/oak-woodland, mixed conifer, montane zones, subalpine, and alpine zones; up to 10,800'.

Comments: As might be expected, the flowers are pollinated primarily by hummingbirds. Sierra Columbine (*Aquilegia pubescens*) has similar flowers that are white, and it hybridizes with Crimson Columbine, producing offspring with characteristics of both species.

RED LARKSPUR
Delphinium nudicaule
Buttercup family (Ranunculaceae)

Description: Red Larkspur is a perennial with an erect stem that's 7–20" tall. The blade of the long-petioled leaves has 3–10 broad segments with shallow lobes. The inflorescence is an open raceme with 3–10 flowers on long, ascending stalks. The flowers have 5 showy, petal-like, scarlet to orange-red (rarely yellow) sepals. The 4 smaller, notched petals are yellowish with red tips, and the upper 2 petals are much larger than the lower 2 petals. The upper sepal forms a spur that contains the 2 nectar spurs of the upper petals.

Flowering time: May–June

Habitat/range: Dry to moist forest or chaparral; montane zone; 3,300–8,200'.

Comments: Although Red Larkspur has been reported to grow at Porcupine Flat, in the Gin Flat area, and between Aspen Valley and White Wolf, there are no verified records of it in the park. If you find the plant in the park, please note its exact location and report it to yose_web_manager@nps.gov.

Similar plants: Of the seven larkspur species that grow in the park. Red Larkspur and Hansen's Larkspur (*Delphinium hansenii*), with its white flowers, are the only two that are positively distinctive. The other five larkspur species have blue or blue-purple flowers.

BOLANDER'S BEDSTRAW

Galium bolanderi

Madder family (Rubiaceae)

Description: This common perennial has erect to ascending, often tangled, 4-angled stems, 5–16" long, that are woody at the base and are hairless except for occasional, unhooked hairs on the angles. Its linear to narrowly elliptic leaves, ¼–1" long, are in whorls of 4, usually in 2 unequal pairs, and are sometimes coarse-gray-hairy. The plants are dioecious, with male and female flowers growing on separate plants. The tiny flowers grow from leaf axils, the male flowers in clusters and the female flowers solitary. The flowers have a 4-lobed, dark red or yellowish corolla and no sepals. The fruit is a hairless to densely hairy, dark purple berry.

Flowering time: May–August

Habitat/range: Dry, rocky places; chaparral/oak-woodland and mixed conifer zones; up to 6,000'.

Similar plants: Bolander's Bedstraw is one of three bedstraws in the park that have 4-lobed corollas, leaves in whorls of 4, and stems that are woody at the base. Sequoia Bedstraw (*G. sparsiflorum*) has greenish corollas, and it's the only one of the three with leaves that are oval to round. Climbing Bedstraw (*G. porrigens* var. *tenue*), which has linear leaves and a reddish or yellowish corolla, is the only one of the three that has stems and leaves with hooked hairs that allow it to climb up into or over any object it encounters, including itself. Its distinctive fruit is 1 or 2 pearly-white berries.

CALIFORNIA FIGWORT, CALIFORNIA BEE PLANT

Scrophularia californica

Figwort family (Scrophulariaceae)

Description: This leafy perennial is 2¾–4½' tall and has erect, 4-angled stems. Its petioled leaves grow in pairs at right angles to each other, and the triangular leaf blades have irregular teeth along the margins. The blades of the larger leaves are 3–7" long. The inflorescences are elongated, open panicles. The small, urn-shaped flowers **[inset]** grow on a straight or slightly downward-curving stalk. They have a 5-lobed calyx, 4 fertile stamens, a red staminode, and a style with a head-like stigma. The 2-lipped corolla has an erect, 2-lobed, red upper lip and a smaller, 3-lobed, paler red or yellow-green lower lip with a reflexed middle lobe.

Flowering time: March–July

Habitat/range: Damp, partially open to shady areas; chaparral/oak-woodland, mixed conifer, and montane zones; up to 8,300'.

Comments: This plant is uncommon in the park, but it has been reported at the lower end of Yosemite Valley, near Foresta, around El Portal, and along the Grand Canyon of the Tuolumne.

Similar plants: Desert Figwort (*Scrophularia desertorum*) has been reported along Tioga Road near Tuolumne Meadows and around Tioga Pass. Its corolla is usually distinctly bicolored, with a red upper lip and a cream-colored lower lip, and its flower stalks are slightly upward curving.

PINK, ROSE, AND MAGENTA FLOWERS

Sierra Primrose (*Primula suffruticosa*)

This section contains plants with flowers that range from pale pink to deep magenta.

If you looked through this section for a plant with somewhat pale red flowers and you couldn't find it, check the section for red and orange flowers. If you were looking for a plant with pink flowers and couldn't find it, check the section for white to cream flowers, since many plants have flowers that can be pink or white.

A plant you're looking for in this section could have flowers that are mid-range between pink and pale purple, in which case the plant could be in the section for blue, purple, and lavender flowers.

Many monkeyflowers have flowers in the pink to purple range, but since most of them tend to be rose to pink and it's useful to see them together, all of the pink to purple monkeyflowers are included in this section.

Note: The similar plants sections include plants that are not covered elsewhere in the book, as well as plants that have a separate photo unit of their own. The names of plants that have their own photo unit in the book are highlighted with green text.

SIERRA ONION, DUSKY ONION
Allium campanulatum
Onion family (Alliaceae)

Description: This bulbed perennial, 3–12" tall, is common and widespread throughout the park below the alpine zone, although it's often overlooked when it grows in pink-tinged granitic gravel. The plant's 2 or 3 narrow basal leaves are less than ¼" wide, are about the same length as the flower stalk, and are usually withered by the time the flowers are in bloom. The smooth, leafless stem is topped by a loose, long-stalked flower cluster that looks like a miniature fireworks display with many bursts of rose to purple, star-shaped blossoms. The 6 tepals, which are about ¼" long, have a purple crescent at their base and often have a dark midvein.

Flowering time: June–August

Habitat/range: Dry, gravelly or sandy areas; chaparral/oak-woodland, mixed conifer, montane, and subalpine zones; up to 10,000'.

Comments: Sierra Onion is easy to identify, with its starburst flower cluster. Other onion species can be difficult to identify, and some even require microscopic examination of the pattern on their bulb's papery outer covering. Onions look like they have 6 petals, but they actually have 3 outer segments and 3 inner segments, all of which are essentially identical and are collectively called tepals; the same is true of plants in several other families.

SWAMP ONION
Allium validum
Onion family (Alliaceae)

Description: Swamp Onion is the most common onion in Yosemite. It's a robust, bulbed perennial, up to 3½' tall, that often grows in large colonies, and it's the only onion in Yosemite that grows in wet meadows. The plants have such a strong onion odor that you can often smell them from a considerable distance. The 3–6 strap-like basal leaves are about ½" wide and are still green when the flowers are in bloom. The flowers are arranged in tight, upright clusters at the end of a long, smooth, leafless stem. They have 6 pale to bright magenta or rose-colored tepals that are up to ⅜" long.

Flowering time: June–August

Habitat/range: Swampy meadows and stream-banks; montane, subalpine, and alpine zones; 6,500–11,200'.

Comments: The name *validum* is from a Latin word that means strong, which in this case refers to the plant's particularly strong onion odor. The *Allium* genus includes several ornamentals and many plants that are cultivated for food, such as onions, shallots, leeks, and chives. Garlic (*Allium sativum*), which is native to central Asia, has a long history of human culinary and medicinal use, dating back at least 7,000 years. Also known as the Stinking Rose, the plant has played a role in myth and literature for its reputed ability to ward off vampires.

SPREADING DOGBANE

Apocynum androsaemifolium
Dogbane family (Apocynaceae)

Description: This bushy perennial has ascending to erect, reddish stems that are 6–16" long and are diffusely branched. The opposite, often drooping, short-petioled leaves are elliptic to oval and are usually smooth on top and hairy beneath. Clusters of flowers grow at the end of the stem and from the axils of the upper leaves. The bell-shaped, pale to bright pink flowers are up to ⁵⁄₁₆" long and have 5 fused petals with flared lobes. The fruit is a pair of erect or pendant, cylindric pods with numerous seeds, each with a tuft of silky hairs that catch the wind.

Flowering time: June–August

Habitat/range: Open areas and rocky places; mixed conifer, montane, and subalpine zones; 3,300–8,200'.

Comments: This plant is widely distributed throughout North America and is a vigorous pioneer after fires. It grows from Alaska south to Mexico and all the way to the East Coast. Although Native Americans used the stems to make baskets, rope, and other items, they used its close relative Indian Hemp (*Apocynum cannabinum*) much more extensively. Spreading Dogbane is poisonous; the genus name is Greek for "away from dog," for a similar European plant's ancient use as a dog poison.

PURPLE MILKWEED

Asclepias cordifolia
Dogbane family (Apocynaceae)

Description: This eye-catching perennial has an ascending stem that's 1–3' long and contains milky sap. Its smooth to slightly hairy herbage is sometimes purple tinged. The large leaves grow opposite each other in pairs and are often purple tinged. The leaves are shaped like an arrowhead and have a heart-shaped base that clasps the stem. The umbel flower heads grow from leaf axils and at the stem end. The intricate flowers have 5 reddish-purple, reflexed petals that are fused at the base and 5 paler parts called hoods. The large, lanceolate fruit is 4–5½" long and opens along the side to release seeds that have lots of long, silky hairs.

Flowering time: June–September

Habitat/range: Open, grassy or rocky areas and meadow borders; chaparral/oak-woodland and mixed conifer zones; up to 6,500'.

Comments: Milkweed plants have a toxic milky sap. Even so, Monarch butterfly caterpillars feed on the plant with no ill effects. The toxicity is passed on to the adult butterflies, making them distasteful to predators. Like other members of the dogbane family, the fibrous milkweed stems have been used to make twine, rope, and baskets.

Similar plants: Purple Milkweed is the only broad-leaved milkweed species in the park with herbage that is hairless or only sparsely hairy.

SHOWY MILKWEED

Asclepias speciosa
Dogbane family (Apocynaceae)

Description: Showy Milkweed is a stout perennial, 1–4' tall, with soft-hairy foliage. The gray-green, opposite leaves are lanceolate, elliptic, or oval and are rounded to heart shaped at the base. The umbel flower heads grow from leaf axils and at the end of the stem. The intricate flowers have 5 pink to rose-purple, reflexed petals that are fused at the base and 5 paler, lanceolate parts called hoods, which enclose a long, narrow "horn" that curves toward the center of the flower. The weird, woolly, warty fruit is 2–4" long and opens along the side to release seeds with myriad long, silky hairs that catch the wind.

Flowering time: May–July

Habitat/range: Meadows to dry, gravelly and rocky places; chaparral/oak-woodland and mixed conifer zones; up to 6,500'.

Similar plants: Narrow-leaved Milkweed (*A. fascicularis*) grows up the Merced River Canyon into Yosemite Valley and has been reported in several other locations in the park. It has similar flowers with pink or cream-colored petals and paler hoods, but its leaves are much narrower and its foliage is mostly hairless. California Milkweed (*A. californica*), which grows near the western park boundary and may grow in the park, is similar in many respects, but its foliage is conspicuously densely white-woolly and the hoods on its flowers have no horn.

WESTERN SNAKEROOT

Ageratina occidentalis
Sunflower family (Asteraceae)

Description: This showy perennial has many erect or ascending, green or purple, somewhat hairy stems that are 6–28" long and grow from a woody base. The sharp-toothed, triangular or ovate leaves are mostly alternate, are dotted with sticky glands, and are pointed at the tip. The flower heads are up to ⅜" long and are densely clustered at the stem and branch tips. The heads have hairy, sometimes glandular phyllaries and 9–12 pale pink to purple disk flowers with conspicuous, linear style branches that extend well beyond the corolla, giving the flowers a frilly or raggedy appearance.

Flowering time: July–September

Habitat/range: Rocky places; mixed conifer, montane, and subalpine zones; 3,200–10,000'.

Comments: Western Snakeroot is used by the Zuni people of western New Mexico as one of the ingredients in "schumaakwe cakes," which they apply externally to treat swelling and rheumatism. The plant resembles *Ageratum*, a genus of garden plants after which it was named.

Similar plants: Somewhat similar Mountain Spiraea (*Spiraea splendens*), in the rose family, has tidy, umbrella-shaped flower clusters. Western Snakeroot's flower clusters have scattered, less organized flower heads.

ANDERSON'S THISTLE

Cirsium andersonii
Sunflower family (Asteraceae)

Description: Anderson's Thistle is an attractive perennial with 1 to several purplish-red, sparsely branched stems, 1–3' tall, that are smooth or cobwebby and have no spines. The basal leaves grow in a rosette and are pinnately divided into lobed, sparsely spiny divisions. The alternate, clasping stem leaves are reduced above and are less deeply divided. The cylindric flower heads are up to 2" long and are solitary or well separated in groups of 2 or 3. They have numerous spine-tipped phyllaries and bright rose-magenta disk flowers that are the same color as the long styles.

Flowering time: June–October

Habitat/range: Woodland and forest openings; mixed conifer, montane, and subalpine zones; 4,000–10,500'.

Similar plants: Anderson's Thistle is the only native thistle in the park that has a narrow flower head with bright rose-magenta flowers. Two highly invasive non-native thistles with smaller, narrower, paler pink flower heads have been reported around the park's western border, Italian Thistle (*Carduus pycnocephalus*) **[inset]** and Slender-flowered Thistle (*Carduus tenuiflorus*). Unlike Anderson's Thistle, they have conspicuously spiny stems and crowded flower head clusters. Italian Thistle has 2–5 flower heads per cluster; Slender-flowered Thistle has 5–20 flower heads per cluster.

CALIFORNIA THISTLE

Cirsium occidentale var. *californicum*
Sunflower family (Asteraceae)

Description: This biennial thistle is 1–6' tall and has stems that are mostly leafy below and branched above. Young stems and leaves are covered with dense, finely matted hairs that often become less dense with age. The basal and lower stem leaves are 4–16" long, are green to gray on top and gray beneath, and have wavy, pinnate lobes tipped with slender yellow spines. The upper, alternate, clasping stem leaves are smaller and less deeply lobed. The flower heads, which are mostly solitary on long stalks, have numerous narrowly tubular, pale pink to rose disk flowers with a paler extended style. The involucre is ½–2" wide and has spreading, spine-tipped phyllaries that can be densely cobwebby.

Flowering time: April–July

Habitat/range: Woodland and forest openings, rocky and disturbed places; chaparral/oak-woodland and mixed conifer zones; up to 7,000'.

Similar plants: This native thistle's pale pink to rose flowers are less showy than the flowers of the other two tall thistles in Yosemite, Anderson's Thistle (*C. andersonii*), a native with bright rose-magenta flowers in a narrow flower head, and Bull Thistle (*C. vulgare*), a noxious non-native plant with brilliant pink to magenta flowers in a flower head shaped like an hourglass.

BULL THISTLE

(non-native)

Cirsium vulgare

Sunflower family (Asteraceae)

Description: This invasive biennial thistle, 20"–6½' tall, has a stout, hairy, sometimes branched stem with distinctive spine-tipped wings that extend down from the base of the leaves. The coarsely toothed basal leaves are up to 16" long, have stout spines, and are arranged in a rosette. The deeply lobed, alternate stem leaves become smaller upward and are armed with stiff, sharp spines. The leaves are bristly-hairy on top and white-woolly below, and the leaf lobes are distinctively spear shaped. The flower heads are up to 1¾" long and are shaped like an hourglass. The rounded lower part of the hourglass has numerous whorls of green phyllaries that are cobwebby at the base and have long, spiny tips. The upper part of the hourglass is a dense, showy cluster of long, tubular, bright pink to magenta disk flowers.

Flowering time: June–September

Habitat/range: Moist, undisturbed meadows and disturbed areas around developments and along roads; chaparral/oak-woodland and mixed conifer zones; up to 6,500'.

Comments: Native throughout most of Europe, western Asia, and northwestern Africa, Bull Thistle is an unwelcome, invasive plant in North America, where it now grows in every state, including Alaska and Hawaii.

NARROW-LEAVED WIRE-LETTUCE

Stephanomeria tenuifolia

Sunflower family (Asteraceae)

Description: This hairless perennial has 1–5 or more green stems that are 8–20" long and have slender branches. Its alternate, linear to thread-like leaves are often mostly withered by flowering time. The lower leaves are 2–3" long, and the upper leaves become smaller and bract-like toward the top of the stem. The flower heads, which are solitary at the branch tips, have 4 or 5 small ray flowers with pale to dark pink, spreading rays. The cylindric involucre has 5 or 6 narrow inner phyllaries and several shorter outer phyllaries.

Flowering time: July–August

Habitat/range: Dry, open areas; mixed conifer, montane, and subalpine zones; 5,200–9,200'.

Comments: This plant's small leaves reduce water loss by having less surface area where evaporation can occur, but they also have less surface area for photosynthesis. The plant's green stems and branches assist in the photosynthetic process.

Similar plants: The flower heads of Woodland Wire-lettuce (*S. lactucina*) [inset] also grow solitary at the branch tips, but they have 7–10 ray flowers, and the plant's stem leaves are well developed and are not significantly smaller at the top of the plant. The flower heads of Wand Wire-lettuce (*S. virgata*) have 5 or 6 ray flowers, and they grow along the branches, not just at the branch tips.

WAND WIRE-LETTUCE

Stephanomeria virgata ssp. *pleurocarpa*
Sunflower family (Asteraceae)

Description: Aptly named Wand Wire-lettuce is a mostly hairless annual with alternate leaves and a single stem that's up to 6½' long and has long stiff, wand-like branches. Its lower leaves are 4–8" long, are pinnately lobed, and are withered by flowering time. The upper leaves are smaller and bract-like. The stalkless flower heads, which grow from nodes along the branches and at the branch tips, have 5 or 6 pale to dark pink or white ray flowers. The cylindric involucre has 6–9 narrow inner phyllaries and several shorter outer phyllaries.

Flowering time: June–November

Habitat/range: Dry, open, sandy or gravelly areas; chaparral/oak-woodland and mixed conifer zones; up to 6,000'.

Comments: The name Wire-lettuce probably refers to the fact that this plant's flower heads look like the flower heads of plants in the *Lactuca* genus, the genus of cultivated lettuces. The plant is also called Twiggy Wreath Plant, probably because its stiff stems would make good wreaths.

Similar plants: The stem leaves of Woodland Wire-lettuce (*S. lactucina*) are well developed, and they are not significantly smaller toward the top of the plant. Narrow-leaved Wire-lettuce (*S. tenuifolia*) has flower heads that grow solitary at the branch tips, and they have 4 or 5 ray flowers.

PINK STICKSEED

Hackelia mundula
Borage or Waterleaf family (Boraginaceae)

Description: Pink Stickseed is a perennial with soft-hairy foliage and several ascending to erect stems that are up to 3' long. The narrow basal leaves are 2¼–9" long. The alternate stem leaves are sessile and become gradually smaller upward. The inflorescences have spreading branches and clusters of showy flowers that are more than ½" wide. The pink, 5-lobed corollas have a ring of white or pink, tooth-like appendages at the throat. The fruit is a small, pendulous nutlet covered with slender, barbed prickles.

Flowering time: June–July

Habitat/range: Dry to moist forest openings; montane and subalpine zones; 6,800–9,000'.

Comments: Pink Stickseed is a particular favorite of some Yosemite visitors. The stickseeds got their name from their barbed fruit, which hitch a ride on fabric and fur, a simple way for the plants to get their seeds dispersed and a strategy that's used by plants in several plant families.

CREEPING SNOWBERRY, TRIP VINE

Symphoricarpos mollis
Honeysuckle family (Caprifoliaceae)

Description: Creeping Snowberry is a sprawling shrub that roots at the stem nodes and has soft-hairy herbage. The opposite, deciduous leaves, up to 1¼" long, have an elliptic to oval blade that sometimes has a few shallow lobes along the margins. The tiny, bright pink to red, broadly bell-shaped flowers grow in small clusters from the upper leaf axils and have 2 fused, leaf-like bracts beneath them. The corolla lobes are hairy inside. The white fruit **[inset]** is round and berry-like.

Flowering time: June–August

Habitat/range: Shady areas and woodland openings; mixed conifer and montane zones; 3,500–8,000'.

Comments: When these plants are in fruit, it's obvious why they're called snowberry. The plants live up to their common names too. Their stems creep along the ground and root at the nodes, often creating arched stem segments attached to the ground at both ends, an arrangement that can easily trip unsuspecting hikers.

Similar plants: Common Snowberry (*Symphoricarpos albus* var. *laevigatus*) has been reported in the Hetch Hetchy area, in the Merced River Canyon, and in the Tuolumne Grove. It has similar pink, broadly bell-shaped flowers, but its stems are erect rather than sprawling.

ROUND-LEAVED SNOWBERRY

Symphoricarpos rotundifolius var. *rotundifolius*
Honeysuckle family (Caprifoliaceae)

Description: This shrub has slender, reclining to erect stems, 2–4' long, and the older stems have shredding bark. The opposite, short-petioled leaves, up to ¾" long, have elliptic to round, often lobed blades that are paler and more prominently veined underneath. The flowers grow singly or in pairs from the upper leaf axils and have 2 fused bractlets at their base. The small calyx has 5 triangular lobes that are often reddish. The funnel-shaped corolla is up to ⅜" long and is hairy inside. It has a pink tube and 5 erect to spreading lobes that are usually paler than the tube. The white fruit is round and berry-like.

Flowering time: June–August

Habitat/range: Dry, open, rocky areas; montane and subalpine zones; 7,000–10,000'.

Comments: Snowberries do well in cold climates, and they're common garden plants in northern latitudes. In the summer the plants have attractive flowers, and in the winter the stems have clusters of fruit that persist through most of the cold season. Clippings of stems with berry clusters are often used in flower arrangements.

Similar plants: Creeping Snowberry (*S. mollis*) and Common Snowberry (*S. albus* var. *laevigatus*) have pink corollas that are broadly bell shaped rather than funnel shaped.

GRASS PINK

(non-native)
Dianthus armeria ssp. *armeria*
Pink family (Caryophyllaceae)

Description: Grass Pink is an annual to perennial with an erect stem that's ½–2' tall. Its basal
leaves are up to 2" long and are lanceolate to
oblanceolate, and its stem leaves are somewhat
linear. The inflorescence is a cluster of flowers at
the stem end. The long-tapered flower bracts are
about as long as the sepals. The flowers have a
slender, hairy calyx with 5 long-tapered tips. The 5
bright pink or rose petals have limbs that are about
¼" long, are often sprinkled with white dots, and
have irregular teeth.

Flowering time: March–July

Habitat/range: Meadows and disturbed areas;
chaparral/oak-woodland and mixed conifer zones;
up to 5,500'.

Comments: Grass Pink is native to most of Europe
and is a popular garden plant. It grows around
Wawona and in Ackerson Meadow and has been
reported in Yosemite Valley.

Similar plants: Hairy Pink (*Petrorhagia dubia*)
[inset] has a broad set of bracts that enclose the
developing flowers; the bracts are often reddish
or brownish. Each bright pink petal limb has 2
rounded lobes and darker pink veins. The plant is
native to Southern Europe and Northern Africa, has
become naturalized in California, and grows in the
El Portal area.

GREENLEAF MANZANITA

Arctostaphylos patula
Heath family (Ericaceae)

Description: This erect, much-branched shrub,
3–8' tall, has densely hairy to glandular-hairy
stems. Its alternate, flat, glossy green leaves,
1–2½" long, are round to ovate, are hairless, and
often have a pointed tip. The inflorescences are
dense, branched clusters of nodding or spreading
flowers. The urn-shaped flowers are about ¼" long
and have a small calyx with 5 rounded lobes. The
pink to magenta or white corolla is broader at the
base and narrow at the throat and has 5 flared
lobes. The berry-like fruit is red to brown.

Flowering time: April–June

Habitat/range: Dry, open, often rocky slopes
and flats; mixed conifer and montane zones;
3,900–8,900'.

Comments: Most shrubs add a new layer of bark
each year, building up a thick outer layer that can
protect them from hazards, such as fire. Manzanitas have thin, red bark that peels off each year.
The cambium layer is close to the surface under
the bark, and even a low intensity fire around the
base will kill some manzanita species.

Similar plants: Pinemat Manzanita (*Arctostaphylos nevadensis*) is the only other manzanita in the
park that has smooth, shiny green leaves. It's a
low-growing shrub that doesn't get more than 2'
tall.

219

MARIPOSA MANZANITA

Arctostaphylos viscida ssp. *mariposa*
Heath family (Ericaceae)

Description: This erect, much-branched shrub,
3–13' tall, has smooth, reddish, shredding bark
and densely glandular-hairy twigs. Its alternate,
dull gray-green leaves are up to 2" long, ovate to
roundish, sparsely short-glandular-hairy, and rough
to the touch. The nodding or spreading flowers
grow on sticky-hairy stalks in dense, branched
clusters. The urn-shaped flowers **[inset]** have a
small, white to pink, glandular-hairy calyx with
5 rounded lobes and a pink to magenta or white
corolla that's broader at the base, narrow at the
throat, and has 5 flared lobes.

Flowering time: February–April

Habitat/range: Dry, open areas; chaparral/oak-
woodland and mixed conifer zones; up to 6,000'.

Comments: Anna's Hummingbirds stay year-round
in the park's lower elevations rather than flying
south for the winter. This shrub starts blooming in
February, and its nectar helps the hummingbirds
make it through the winter.

Similar plants: Quite similar, but less common
Whiteleaf Manzanita (*A. viscida* ssp. *viscida*) also
has dull leaves, but they're not rough to the touch.
Much less common Indian Manzanita (*A. mewukka*
ssp. *mewukka*) also has dull leaves, but, unlike any
of the other manzanita species in the park, it has a
distinctive burl at the base of its trunk-like stems.

PRINCE'S PINE, PIPSISSEWA

Chimaphila umbellata
Heath family (Ericaceae)

Description: Prince's Pine is a somewhat woody,
evergreen perennial with a stout stem that's ½–1'
tall. Its thick, waxy leaves are 1–3" long and grow
in several whorls around the stem. The leaves are
lanceolate to oblanceolate, prominently toothed,
shiny green above, and yellowish green below.
The slightly glandular-hairy inflorescence is a
loose cluster of 1–10 nodding to ascending flowers
at the end of the stem. The flowers have 5 oval,
green to maroon sepals and 5 round, concave,
white petals that are about ¼" long. The petals
are tinged with pink and are more or less strongly
curved backward. The ring of shiny red stamens
resembles a ruby-jeweled crown. The fruit is a
5-celled capsule.

Flowering time: June–August

Habitat/range: Dry conifer forest; mixed conifer
zone; 3,900–6,500'.

Comments: Native Americans made a poultice
from the leaves of Prince's Pine to relieve pain
and inflammation, and they made a tea of the
leaves to treat urinary infections. Herbalists still
recommend Prince's Pine for urinary problems. The
leaves, with their wintergreen-mint flavor, have
been used as an ingredient in old-fashioned root
beer. *Chimaphila* is from Greek words that mean
to love winter weather, for the fact that the plant's
evergreen leaves persist throughout the winter.

BOG LAUREL
Kalmia polifolia
Heath family (Ericaceae)

Description: This mat-forming, evergreen shrub, up to 2½' tall, has erect or ascending, smooth or sparsely hairy stems. Its mostly opposite, linear to ovate or oblong leaves, up to 2" long, are usually curled under along the margins, are dark green on top, and are paler and finely hairy beneath. The flowers, which grow in loose terminal clusters, have 5 oblong, reddish-tipped sepals. The saucer-shaped, rose to magenta corolla, up to ½" wide, has 5 fused petals with shallow, rounded lobes and 10 stamens that are shorter than the corolla lobes.

Flowering time: June–August

Habitat/range: Moist meadows and alpine slopes; mixed conifer, montane, subalpine, and alpine zones; 5,400–11,400'.

Comments: When Bog Laurel's flowers open, their anthers are trapped in depressions on the corolla. The anthers mature as the flowers unfold, and when the flowers are completely open, the anthers are held in spring-like tension. When a large enough insect lands on the flower, the anthers spring out of their pockets like ancient catapults, dusting the insect with pollen.

Similar plants: The stamens of Mountain Heather (*Phyllodoce breweri*) extend well beyond the corolla lobes, and its leaves are needle-like and much more crowded on the stem.

MOUNTAIN HEATHER
Phyllodoce breweri
Heath family (Ericaceae)

Description: Mountain Heather is an erect to spreading, hairless to glandular-hairy shrub, 4–14" tall, that often produces large mats. Its alternate, evergreen, needle-like leaves are ¼–⅝" long, are crowded toward the branch ends, and are strongly rolled under along the margins. The leaves are yellowish green when they're young and become darker green with age. The inflorescences are somewhat umbel-like, with crowded flowers on glandular-hairy stalks at the branch ends. The widely cup- to saucer-shaped flowers have 5 sepals that are fused at the base and a style and 10 stamens that extend well beyond the corolla lobes. The corolla is about ⅜" long and has 5 fused, pink to magenta petals.

Flowering time: July–August

Habitat/range: Moist, open to shady, rocky places; montane, subalpine, and alpine zones; 7,000–11,800'.

Comments: Mountain Heather is common in moist areas throughout the subalpine zone in the park. It often forms large mats, climbing over boulders and lining rocky areas soon after the snow melts.

Similar plants: Bog Laurel (*Kalmia polifolia*) has flowers that look much like those of Mountain Heather, but it doesn't have needle-like leaves and its stamens do not extend beyond the corolla lobes.

DWARF BILBERRY

Vaccinium cespitosum
Heath family (Ericaceae)

Description: Dwarf Bilberry is a low-growing, deciduous shrub with reclining to erect stems that are less than 4" long. The thin, alternate leaves are up to 1" long, are oblong or obovate with a tapered base, and have tiny, sharp teeth along the margins. The nodding flowers are about ¼" long and grow solitary from leaf axils. The fused calyx is unlobed or has minuscule lobes. The narrowly urn-shaped, pink or whitish, fused corolla has 5 spreading lobes. The fruit is a round, bluish-black berry with a powdery coating.

Flowering time: May–July

Habitat/range: Moist meadows or meadow margins; montane, subalpine, and alpine zones; 7,500–12,100'.

Comments: Dwarf Bilberry often covers large expanses of ground in moist, high-elevation meadows. The berries are eaten by rodents, birds, and bears. The bears chew off large bunches of the plant and eat everything. You might have to look closely to see the plant's tiny flowers and berries. The plant is showy only when its leaves change color in the fall. First they become red, yellow, and orange, with a bit of green accent. Later they turn bright orange-red.

Similar plants: Western Bog Blueberry (*Vaccinium uliginosum*) is a similar low-growing shrub, but its leaves are mostly toothless.

BOG WINTERGREEN

Pyrola asarifolia ssp. *asarifolia*
Heath family (Ericaceae)

Description: This showy, evergreen perennial is 6–22" tall and is known from only a few locations in the park. Its petioled leaves are 2–6" long and grow in a basal rosette. The leaves have a round, ovate, or elliptic blade that's shiny green above and duller light green to purplish below. The leaf blade margins sometimes have obscure, shallow, rounded teeth. The smooth, green or red stem has alternate, nodding or spreading flowers with 10 stamens that are hidden inside the corolla and a conspicuously curved style that extends beyond the corolla. The partially fused calyx has 5 triangular sepals. The broadly bell-shaped corolla is about ¼" long and has 5 rounded, rose to magenta petals.

Flowering time: July–September

Habitat/range: Moist forest floor, streambanks, and bogs; mixed conifer and montane zones; 3,900–6,600'.

Similar plants: The park has two similar *Pyrola* species that typically have white flowers, but their flowers can sometimes be pink. Lesser Wintergreen (*P. minor*) has a straight style. White-veined Wintergreen (*P. picta*) also has a strongly curved style, but its leaves have conspicuous white veins.

WESTERN BOG BLUEBERRY
Vaccinium uliginosum ssp. *occidentale*
Heath family (Ericaceae)

Description: This hairless, deciduous shrub has trailing to erect stems that are 1–2' long. Its somewhat thick, alternate, untoothed leaves are up to ⅞" long, are ovate to elliptic, and are paler below. The tiny, nodding flowers, which grow 1–4 in the leaf axils, have a green to bluish, fused calyx with 4 or 5 rounded lobes. The urn-shaped, fused corolla is pink, rose, or white and has 4 (sometimes 5) short lobes that curve backward. The fruit is a round, bluish-black berry with a powdery coating.

Flowering time: June–July

Habitat/range: Bogs and wet meadows; mixed conifer, montane, subalpine, and alpine zones; 5,900–11,000'.

Comments: Western Bog Blueberry grows throughout the Northern Hemisphere. In the Arctic it grows at sea level, and farther south it can grow up to 12,000'. Rodents, birds, and bears eat the berries. The plants grow in boggy, nitrogen-poor places, and they parasitize the root-like structures of fungi to get the nitrogen they need to survive.

Similar plants: Somewhat similar Sierra Huckleberry (*Vaccinium shastense* ssp. *nevadense*), a plant first described in 2015, is uncommon in the park, and its stems can get up to 5½' long. Its leaves have tiny teeth along the margins, its calyx has no lobes, and it grows in shady forests rather than in wet places.

WESTERN REDBUD
Cercis occidentalis
Pea family (Fabaceae)

Description: Western Redbud is a showy, deciduous shrub or tree that's 6–20' tall and has many spreading to erect stems and hairless herbage. Its glossy, somewhat leathery leaves emerge after the shrub is in full bloom. The round to kidney-shaped leaf blades are 1–4" wide and have a heart-shaped base. The flowers are about ½" long and grow in tight clusters along the woody branches. The broadly bell-shaped, 5-lobed calyx is somewhat squared off at the base and is often more brightly colored than the petals, which can be pink to purple but are mostly magenta. The flat, dangling pea pods are 2–3½" long.

Flowering time: March–May

Habitat/range: Dry slopes and flats; chaparral/oak-woodland and mixed conifer zones; up to 5,300'.

Comments: Local Indian groups used Western Redbud's branches and stems to make thread and to weave baskets, and it was the most common plant used to incorporate the color red into basket patterns. The plant is more common in the lower foothills, but it does grow around the park's western boundary, it's been planted at several locations in Yosemite Valley, and it grows along Tioga Road about a mile east of the Big Oak Flat entrance.

223

EVERLASTING PEA
(non-native)
Lathyrus latifolius
Pea family (Fabaceae)

Description: Everlasting Pea is a robust, hairless perennial with sprawling stems that are 2–6½' long. Its stems are flattened, and both the stems and the flattened leaf petioles have winged margins. The alternate leaves have 2 leafy bracts at the base and 2 lanceolate to ovate leaflets that are 1½–3" long. A somewhat stout, often branched tendril grows from the junction of the leaflets. The large, showy pea flowers, which grow in clusters from the leaf axils, have a green, 5-lobed calyx and a pink, magenta, or white corolla, up to 1" long. The hairless, flattened pea pods are about 2" long.

Flowering time: April–October

Habitat/range: Disturbed places along roads and around developments; chaparral/oak-woodland and mixed conifer zones; up to 4,000'.

Comments: Everlasting Pea is native to the Mediterranean area and was brought to North America long ago as an ornamental plant. The plant now grows along roadsides and in vacant fields in most, if not all, of the lower 48 states.

Similar plants: Jepson's Pea (*Lathyrus jepsonii* var. *californicus*) has been reported from Big Meadow, where it may no longer grow. It's also a robust plant and has similar flowers, but most of its leaves have 4–16 leaflets.

HARLEQUIN LUPINE
Lupinus stiversii
Pea family (Fabaceae)

Description: Harlequin Lupine is an eye-catching annual with sparsely hairy herbage and ascending to erect, branched stems, up to 1½' tall. Its leaves are palmately divided into 6–8 leaflets that are ½–2" long. The leaflets are broad and rounded at the tip and taper evenly to the base. The inflorescence is 1–3" long and has roughly 3–12 flowers that are up to ¾" long and grow in a dense spiral. The yellow banner petal often turns orange in the center with age, and the wing petals are pink to magenta. The keel is ciliate on the upper and lower margins from the middle to the base. The mostly hairless, somewhat flattened pods are ¾–1" long.

Flowering time: April–July

Habitat/range: Woodland clearings and open, often rocky areas; chaparral/oak-woodland and mixed conifer zones; up to 6,500'.

Comments: Because lupines often grow in nitrogen-poor soil, they were once thought to be harmful to soil, and they were given the name lupine, Latin for wolf, for their supposed nutrient-devouring nature. Lupines, like many other plants in the pea family, have nitrogen-fixing bacteria in their root nodules and are able to convert unusable nitrogen in soil to useable nitrogen. When the plants die back to the ground, their now useable nitrogen is released into the soil where it can be absorbed by other plants.

ROSE CLOVER
(non-native)
Trifolium hirtum
Pea family (Fabaceae)

Description: This annual clover has an ascending to erect stem, 3–11" long, and soft-hairy herbage. Its leaves have 3 leaflets, up to 1" long, that are broadest toward the tip and sometimes have a reddish or pale green chevron across the middle. The densely packed, rounded flower heads have 1 or 2 leaves that grow directly beneath them. The flowers, up to ⅝" long, have a pink or rose corolla and a tubular, feathery-hairy calyx with linear lobes that are much longer than the tube.

Flowering time: April–June

Habitat/range: Disturbed areas; chaparral/oak-woodland and mixed conifer zones; up to 6,000'.

Comments: Rose Clover was brought to the U.S as a forage plant. Scientists developed a strain that ended up having bristle-tipped hairs on the fruit-bearing calyx, which could then attach itself to fabric and fur. That accidental outcome caused the plant to become a highly invasive weed throughout much of California in only 10 to 15 years.

Similar plants: Non-native Red Clover (*Trifolium pratense*) is the only other clover in the park with 1 or 2 leaves directly beneath the flower head. Its leaflets are broadest at the middle or toward the base, and it often has assymetrical flower heads. The plant is not particularly invasive.

LONG-STALKED CLOVER
Trifolium longipes ssp. *hansenii*
(*T. longipes* var. *nevadense*)
Pea family (Fabaceae)

Description: Long-stalked Clover is a common perennial with sprawling to erect stems, 2–16" long, and palmate leaves with 3 leaflets. Its oblong to linear-lanceolate, minutely toothed leaflets, ½–2" long, are at least 2½ times longer than they are wide and are hairy below and mostly smooth above. The flower stalks are 1–4" long and are often soft-hairy toward the top. The flower head is a sphere of densely clustered flowers with no whorl of bracts (involucre) beneath it. The flowers, up to ¾" long, have a hairy calyx with 5 thread-like lobes and a narrow corolla that's pink, rose, or white.

Flowering time: June–September

Habitat/range: Wet meadows; mixed conifer, montane, and subalpine zones; 5,000–10,200'.

Comments: Some clover flower heads have an involucre, or whorl of bracts, beneath them and others don't, a characteristic that is used in botanical keys to distinguish species. The involucre is a set of fused bracts shaped like a bowl or a flat wheel. The bracts are variously toothed.

Similar plants: Much less common Cow Clover (*Trifolium wormskioldii*) is a similar wet meadow dweller. Unlike Long-stalked Clover, it has a conspicuous whorl of bracts at the base of its flower heads and its leaves and calyxes are hairless.

SMALL-HEADED CLOVER
Trifolium microcephalum
Pea family (Fabaceae)

Description: This petite annual has reclining to erect stems that are 7–12" long and are branched from the base. Its herbage is covered with long hairs. Its long-petioled, palmate leaves have 3 oval, obovate, or oblanceolate, toothed leaflets that are up to ¾" long and have a notched tip. The compact, round flower head is less than ⅜" wide and has many tiny pea flowers that are up to ¼" long. The shallowly bowl-shaped involucre (whorl of bracts beneath the flower head) has 7–10 triangular lobes with web-like margins. The hairy calyx has 5 long, bristle-tipped lobes, and the corolla is pink to lavender.

Flowering time: April–August

Habitat/range: Moist, grassy areas; chaparral/oak-woodland, mixed conifer, and montane zones; up to 8,000'.

Similar plants: Rancheria Clover (*Trifolium albopurpureum*) **[inset]** also likes moist, grassy habitats. Its small flower heads, which have no whorl of bracts beneath them, are oval rather than round and have a distinctive fuzzy, grayish-purple appearance. The appealing little native has not been reported in the park, but it grows in the foothills to the west and may eventually find its way into the park's lower elevations, if it hasn't already. Small-headed Clover grows in Yosemite Valley and in the Mather and Wawona areas.

CANCHALAGUA, CHARMING CENTAURY
Zeltnera venusta (*Centaurium venustum*)
Gentian family (Gentianaceae)

Description: Canchalagua is an elegant, hairless annual with an erect stem that's 1¼–15" tall and is often branched toward the top. Its opposite leaves are up to 1" long, are mostly along the stem, and are narrowly ovate to oblong. The showy flowers grow in more or less open, umbel-like inflorescences. The narrow, tubular calyx is fused at the base and has 5 long, narrow lobes. The tubular corolla is ½–1¼" long and has 5 widely spreading lobes that are pink to brilliant magenta or sometimes pure white. The corolla throat has white splotches, often with a pink to magenta, irregular ring below. The extended stamens have bright yellow anthers.

Flowering time: May–August

Habitat/range: Dry to moist grasslands, meadows, and rocky areas; chaparral/oak-woodland and mixed conifer zones; up to 6,000'.

Comments: This plant can be tiny and sometimes has only one or two flowers, but it can be also be over a foot tall and profusely branched. The genus was named for Swiss botanists Louis and Nicole Zeltner, who studied the gentian family, and *venusta* is from a Latin word that means charming or handsome. Members of the *Zeltnera* genus have been used to treat stomach ailments.

WAX CURRANT

Ribes cereum var. *cereum*
Gooseberry family (Grossulariaceae)

Description: Wax Currant is a much-branched shrub, up to 4½' tall, with glandular-hairy young twigs and no spines at the leaf and branch nodes. Its spicy smelling, round to kidney-shaped leaves, up to 1½" wide, are truncate or heart shaped at the base. The leaves are palmately divided into 3 or 5 shallow lobes that have toothed margins. The upper leaf surface is often glandular-hairy, and the lower surface is mostly hairless. The pendulous, glandular flowers are up to ⅜" long and grow in groups of 3–7 from leaf axils. The green bracts at the base of the flowers are broad at the tip and have several prominent teeth or lobes. The narrow flower tube (hypanthium) is pale pink or occasionally white, and it has 5 spreading or recurved sepals attached at the end. The 5 tiny, white to pink petals are hidden within the hypanthium. The fruit is a small, red berry.

Flowering time: May–July

Habitat/range: Dry, open, sometimes rocky slopes and forest edges; montane, subalpine, and alpine zones; 6,000–11,800'.

Similar plants: Pink Wax Currant (*Ribes cereum* var. *inebrians*) looks a lot like Wax Currant, but the bracts below its flowers are pointed and they have smooth margins or 1 or 2 lateral teeth. It grows almost exclusively in the alpine zone and is more common there than variety *cereum*.

SIERRA CURRANT

Ribes nevadense
Gooseberry family (Grossulariaceae)

Description: This attractive shrub is 3–6½' tall and has loose, spreading branches with no spines and no prickles. Its roundish leaf blades are 1–3" wide and have a deeply notched base and 3 or 5 lobes with toothed margins. The leaves have tiny gland dots on both surfaces, and they're hairless above and sometimes slightly hairy below. The pendulous, crowded flowers, up to about ⅜" long, grow in clusters of 8–20 from leaf axils, and they have glandular bracts at their base that are pink, red, or greenish. The flower tube (hypanthium) is pink to rose and ends with 5 erect, pink to red sepals. The 5 shorter, white petals are somewhat hidden by the sepals. The sparsely glandular-hairy berries, about ¼" wide, are blue-black with a waxy coating that makes them look white.

Flowering time: May–July

Habitat/range: Forest margins; chaparral/oak-woodland, mixed conifer, montane, and subalpine zones; up to 8,500'.

Comments: This shrub and many other shrubs in the gooseberry family have a hypanthium and sepals that are much showier than their petals. Although people eat currants and gooseberries and often use them to make jellies, jams, and pies, the berries of some species are unpalatable and the berries of others are toxic.

227

NETTLE-LEAVED HORSEMINT
Agastache urticifolia
Mint family (Lamiaceae)

Description: This common, fragrant perennial has several erect, square stems that are 2–5' tall and are branched toward the top. The opposite, sometimes slightly hairy, petioled leaves have a lanceolate to triangular blade that's ¾–3" long and has scalloped teeth on the margins. The flowers are about ½" long and grow in dense, sessile whorls that form a spike at the end of the stem. The spikes look purplish when the calyx tips are purplish, and the spikes sometimes have a raggedy appearance. The 2-lipped calyx has 5 pointed lobes. The tubular, 2-lipped, pale pink or white corolla has an erect, 2-lobed upper lip and a larger, drooping, 3-lobed lower lip. Extending well beyond the corolla are 4 stamens in 2 unequal pairs.

Flowering time: June–August

Habitat/range: Wet meadows, roadside drainages, and streambanks; mixed conifer and montane zones; 3,900–8,900'.

Comments: *Agastache* is from a Greek word that means many spikes, for the numerous spike-like inflorescences. The name *urticifolia* refers to the similarity of the plant's leaves to the leaves of plants in the *Urtica* genus, the stinging nettles. Though the leaves are similar, they lack the stinging hairs that make stinging nettles notorious.

BULL MALLOW
(non-native)
Malva nicaeensis
Mallow family (Malvaceae)

Description: This invasive annual or biennial has a reclining to ascending, sparsely hairy stem, 7"–2' long. Its alternate leaves, up to 4¾" wide, are round to kidney shaped and have 5 or 7 shallow lobes with rounded teeth. The flowers grow 1–4 from leaf axils. Each flower has 3 widely lanceolate to ovate bractlets beneath it, and the lower half of each bractlet is fused to the calyx. The flowers have 5 broadly lanceolate sepals that are fused at the base and 5 oblanceolate, shallowly notched, pink to blue-violet petals, up to ½" long, that turn blue as they dry. The petals are much longer and broader than the sepals. The fruit is a cheese-wheel-shaped, strongly net-veined capsule with 7–10 segments.

Flowering time: March–June

Habitat/range: Disturbed places; chaparral/oak-woodland and mixed conifer zones; up to 4,000'.

Similar plants: Little Mallow (*M. parviflora*) has been reported in the park. Its 3 bractlets are free from the calyx and are linear to thread-like, and its petals and sepals are about the same length. Common Mallow (*M. neglecta*) has not been reported in the park but is to be expected. Its 3 bractlets are free from the calyx and are widely linear, and its petals are about twice as long as its sepals. The three non-native plants are quite similar and have become widespread weeds in California.

CREEPING CHECKERBLOOM

Sidalcea reptans
Mallow family (Malvaceae)

Description: Creeping Checkerbloom is a perennial with stems that are 8–20" long and are densely bristly-hairy in the lower-middle portion. The stems trail along the ground and root at the nodes. The toothed to lobed leaves, ¾–3" wide, are mostly at the base of the plant and are roundish in outline. The hairs on the stems and leaves are simple rather than branched (not stellate). The open, elongated, few-flowered inflorescence is sometimes glandular-sticky. The bowl-shaped flowers have 5 pink to lavender petals, ½–¾" long. The stamens are fused into a column that encloses the style.

Flowering time: June–August

Habitat/range: Moist meadows and dry places; mixed conifer and montane zones; 4,400–7,500'.

Similar plants: The stems of Waxy Checkerbloom (*S. glaucescens*) have a white powdery coating; its stems are not densely bristly-hairy and they don't root at the nodes. Dwarf Checkerbloom (*S. asprella* ssp. *asprella*, previously *S. malviflora* ssp. *asprella*) grows near the park's western boundary in the El Portal area and may grow in the park. Its leaves are well distributed on the stems rather than mostly at the base. It also has bristly-hairy stems that root at the nodes, but the lower part of its stems and the underside of its leaves have at least some hairs that are branched (stellate), looking like tiny spokes of a wheel with no rim, under magnification.

RED MAIDS

Calandrinia menziesii (*C. ciliata*)
Miner's Lettuce family (Montiaceae)

Description: This showy annual has reclining to ascending, spreading stems that are 2–16" long. Its alternate, fleshy leaves are ½–4" long and are linear to narrowly oblanceolate. The leaves are either smooth or have long, stiff hairs, especially along the margins. The inflorescence is a leafy, few-flowered raceme. The 2 ovate, overlapping, keeled sepals often have ciliate hairs on the midrib and the margins. The 5 broad petals are up to ⅝" long, are magenta to reddish purple, and have white streaks at the base. The flowers have a 3-branched style and 3–15 stamens with bright yellow pollen.

Flowering time: February–May

Habitat/range: Grassy areas, meadow borders, and disturbed areas; chaparral/oak-woodland and mixed conifer zones; up to 5,000'.

Comments: Magenta Maids would be a more suitable name for this early bloomer. The plant grows in scattered locations in Yosemite, but it often forms large, bright magenta patches in plowed fields in the Central Valley. Although the plant is a native, it has a tendency to grow in disturbed areas. *Calandrinia* is for Jean Louis Calandrini, a 16th-century Swiss botanist, and *menziesii* is for Archibald Menzies, a Scottish botanist and surgeon who explored California with Captain Vancouver in the late 18th century.

229

ONE-SEEDED PUSSYPAWS
Calyptridium monospermum
Miner's Lettuce family (Montiaceae)

Description: This common perennial has a thick base that produces a single leaf rosette and 2 or more flowering stems. Its stems tend to lie on the ground from the evening to the morning and become more erect during the day. The spatula-shaped, fleshy leaves are ½–3" long and are usually dark green and glossy. The stem leaves, if any, are much smaller. Each stem ends with a dense, umbel-like, pink or white flower cluster. The 2 round, pink to white, papery sepals enclose and almost conceal the 4 rose to white petals and the 3 stamens, which have pink or rose anthers.

Flowering time: May–August

Habitat/range: Dry, sandy areas in the open; chaparral/oak-woodland, mixed conifer, montane, subalpine, and alpine zones; up to 12,000'.

Similar plants: The leaf rosette of One-seeded Pussypaws has a distinct central point from which all the leaves radiate, and from which 2 or more stems are produced. Common Pussypaws (*Calyptridium umbellatum*) has multiple, often crowded leaf rosettes that grow from the branches of an underground base, and each rosette produces only a single stem. If you're examining a plant to determine which of the two it is, and you can make out a distinct central point where the bases of all the stems and leaves meet, the plant is One-seeded Pussypaws.

COMMON PUSSYPAWS
Calyptridium umbellatum
Miner's Lettuce family (Montiaceae)

Description: Common Pussypaws is a common perennial with a thick, underground, woody base that produces 2 or more basal leaf rosettes, each with only a single flowering stem. The multiple leaf rosettes are often crowded and overlap each other. The stems usually lie against the ground from the evening to the morning and become more erect during the day. The spatula-shaped, fleshy basal leaves are ½–2¾" long, and the plants rarely have stem leaves. A dense, umbel-like, pink, red, or white flower cluster grows at the end of each stem. The 2 somewhat round, pink to white, papery sepals enclose the 4 white petals and almost conceal them. The 3 stamens have pink, rose, or yellow anthers.

Flowering time: May–August

Habitat/range: Dry, sandy or gravelly areas in the open; chaparral/oak-woodland, mixed conifer, montane, subalpine, and alpine zones; up to 13,000'.

Similar plants: One-seeded Pussypaws (*Calyptridium monospermum*) produces only a single leaf rosette, and 2 or more stems grow from the center of the rosette. If you're examining a plant to determine which of the two it is, and you're unable to find a distinct central point where the bases of all the stems and leaves meet, the plant is Common Pussypaws.

YOSEMITE LEWISIA
Lewisia disepala
Miner's Lettuce family (Montiaceae)

Description: This rare perennial has a basal leaf rosette with many fleshy, cylindric leaves that are up to ¾" long. Each flower is solitary on a stem that's shorter than the leaves. If you look closely at a flower, you'll notice that 2 of the petals, across from each other, look a bit different from the others, varying slightly in shape and color. Those "petals" are actually 2 sepals. The rest are 5–9 pale rose-pink to magenta petals, ½–¾" long. The flowers have 5 stamens with bright yellow anthers.

Flowering time: February–June

Habitat/range: Open domes in granitic gravel; mixed conifer and montane zones; 4,900–9,200'.

Comments: One of the easiest places to find the plant is on Turtleback Dome, which is accessible from a gated road that steeply climbs about a half mile to several park buildings at the top of the dome. The turnoff for the road is about two miles south of Tunnel View along Wawona Road. The trick is to get there at the right time, which is usually in March or April. The plant also grows on many other domes above Yosemite Valley, such as Mount Watkins and North Dome.

Similar plants: Yosemite Lewisia is the only *Lewisia* species in the park with 2 sepals that mix in with the petals and are almost identical to them.

GLANDULAR ALPINE LEWISIA
Lewisia glandulosa
Miner's Lettuce family (Montiaceae)

Description: Glandular Alpine Lewisia is a hairless, low-growing perennial with a dense rosette of fleshy, linear to narrowly lanceolate leaves that are ¾–4" long, are somewhat flattened, and often have upturned tips. Its flowering stems, which barely rise above the leaves, have 1 or 2 pairs of bracts with red, gland-tipped teeth. The flowers are about ½" wide and have 2 green to reddish sepals, which also have red, gland-tipped teeth. Each flower has 6 stamens, a style with 4 stigmas, and 6–8 pink or white petals, often with reddish midveins.

Flowering time: July–August

Habitat/range: Moist rock cracks, granitic sand, and wet meadows; subalpine and alpine zones; 8,700–12,500'.

Similar plants: The leaves and petals of Dwarf Lewisia (*L. pygmaea*) are about the same length as those of Glandular Alpine Lewisia, but it has no red glands on its bract and sepal margins. Its flowers, which are also pink or white, have 4–8 stamens and a style with 3–6 stigmas. Nevada Lewisia (*L. nevadensis*) has longer leaves (up to 5⅛" long) and longer petals (up to a little more than ¾" long). Its sepal tips are pointed and its petals are white.

PACIFIC STARFLOWER

Lysimachia latifolia (*Trientalis latifolia*)
Myrsine family (Myrsinaceae)

Description: This distinctive perennial has an erect, unbranched stem, 2–12" tall, and smooth, hairless herbage. Its short-petioled leaves grow in a whorl of 4–7 at the top of the stem. The ovate leaf blades, 1–3½" long, are tapered at both ends. The flowers grow from the axils of the whorled leaves, on a stalk that's shorter than the leaves. The calyx has 7 (or 5–9) narrow lobes, and the pink to rose corolla, up to ⅝" wide, has 7 (or 5–9) lobes that are fused just at the base and taper to a pointed tip. Each flower has 7 (or 5–9) stamens. The fruit is a somewhat spheric, 5-valved capsule.

Flowering time: May–July

Habitat/range: Shaded places; mixed conifer zone; 4,500–5,600'.

Comments: According to reports, this plant grows near Tuolumne Grove and is to be expected in the vicinity of Crane Flat and Hodgdon Meadow. However, the plant hasn't been documented in the park. If you find the plant in Yosemite, please report it to yose_web_manager@nps.gov and provide precise location information.

Similar plants: Young Mountain Dogwood plants (*Cornus nuttallii*) can easily be mistaken for Pacific Starflower plants before they've grown flower stalks, but Mountain Dogwood's leaves are at least sparsely hairy, especially on the lower surface.

FIREWEED

Chamerion angustifolium ssp. *circumvagum*
(*Epilobium angustifolium* ssp. *circumvagum*)
Evening Primrose family (Onagraceae)

Description: Fireweed is a conspicuous perennial, up to 8' tall, that has unbranched, leafy stems and often grows in colonies, spreading by rhizomes. The plant is hairless below to densely stiff-hairy above. The alternate, narrowly lanceolate leaves are sometimes sparsely toothed. Numerous showy flowers, up to 1¼" wide, open first at the bottom of the flower spike and continue opening upward, with buds nodding at the top. The flowers have 4 narrow, pink or magenta sepals; 4 obovate, clawed, pink or magenta petals; and 8 stamens that are often unequal. Like all plants in the evening primrose family, the flowers have an inferior ovary. The fruit is a linear capsule, up to 4" long, that splits open and releases tiny seeds tipped with a tuft of fine hairs that catch the wind.

Flowering time: July–September

Habitat/range: Open places, often in recently burned areas; mixed conifer, montane, subalpine, and alpine zones; 5,900–11,500'.

Similar plants: Dwarf Alpine Fireweed (*Chamerion latifolium*, previously *Epilobium latifolium*) has almost identical flowers, but it's less than 20" tall and has leaves that are opposite or nearly so. In Yosemite, the plant is known to grow in only one location, a gully in the cirque between Mount Hoffmann and Tuolumne Peak.

TWO-LOBED CLARKIA

Clarkia biloba ssp. *biloba*
Evening Primrose family (Onagraceae)

Description: This erect annual has a simple or branched stem, 7–31" tall. Its scant, narrowly lanceolate leaves are up to 1¼" long and are often minutely toothed. The drooping flower buds become erect when they bloom. The flowers have 8 unequal anthers and 4 sepals that are united at the tips. The 4 pale pink to magenta, wedge-shaped petals are up to 1" long. The petals are generally less than 1½ times longer than they are wide, and the lobes are often divided halfway to the base. The inferior ovary develops into a straight, 8-ribbed capsule, up to 1" long.

Flowering time: May–June

Habitat/range: Dry, grassy, open areas; chaparral/oak-woodland zone; up to 4,800'.

Comments: This is one of those clarkias that can grow in such profusion that they turn roadbanks and grassy flats almost solid pink.

Similar plants: Two-lobed Clarkia grows inside the park in the Hetch Hetchy area, and it grows around El Portal. Closely related Mariposa Clarkia (*Clarkia biloba* ssp. *australis*) grows close to the park boundary near El Portal. Its petals are generally more than 1½ times longer than they are wide, and the lobes are divided no more than a third of the way to the base. These are the only clarkias in the park that have 2-lobed petals.

DUDLEY'S CLARKIA

Clarkia dudleyana
Evening Primrose family (Onagraceae)

Description: Dudley's Clarkia is an annual with an erect, hairy stem that's 4–24" tall and is often branched above. Its alternate, lanceolate leaves are up to 3" long and are sometimes minutely toothed. Its flower buds droop at first and become erect when they bloom. The bowl-shaped flowers have an inferior ovary and 4 pink or purplish-red sepals that are twisted to the side and fused at the tips. The 4 wedge- or fan-shaped, pale pink to lavender petals are up to 1⅛" long, are distinctly narrowed at the base, sometimes have red dots, and usually have white streaks. The 4 outer stamens have lavender anthers, and the inner 4 stamens are smaller and paler. The style is longer than the anthers and has a 4-lobed stigma. The fruit is a cylindric, 8-grooved capsule.

Flowering time: May–July

Habitat/range: Dry, open, grassy and rocky areas; chaparral/oak-woodland and mixed conifer zones; up to 5,000'.

Comments: This common clarkia often grows in pink masses along Wawona Road, in the Hetch Hetchy area, and around El Portal.

Similar plants: This is the only clarkia in the park that has both nodding flower buds *and* fan-shaped, unlobed petals.

DIAMOND CLARKIA
Clarkia rhomboidea
Evening Primrose family (Onagraceae)

Description: Diamond Clarkia is an annual with an erect stem, 8"–3¼' long. Its lanceolate to ovate leaves, up to 3½" long, are sometimes minutely toothed. The plant has nodding flower buds, and its flowers have 4 free, reflexed sepals and a wheel-shaped corolla with 4 pinkish-lavender, diamond-shaped petals that sometimes have magenta dots. The petals are up to ½" long and narrow abruptly to a claw that has 2 lateral lobes. The flowers have an inferior ovary, 8 stamens, and a style with a 4-lobed stigma that does not extend beyond the anthers. The fruit is a cylindric, 4-grooved capsule.

Flowering time: April–August

Habitat/range: Dry, grassy, often rocky areas; chaparral/oak-woodland, mixed conifer, montane, and subalpine zones; up to 8,200'.

Similar plants: Diamond Clarkia is one of four clarkias in the park that have clawed petals. Southern Clarkia (*C. australis*) also has 2 lateral lobes on its petal claws, and it looks a lot like Diamond Clarkia, but its petals can be up to ⅝" long and its stigma extends beyond its anthers. Elegant Clarkia (*C. unguiculata*) has no lateral lobes on its petal claws, and its sepals are all fused at the tips. Mountain Clarkia (*C. heterandra*) has much smaller flowers with petals that narrow gradually to a claw. Unlike all the other clarkias in California, its fruit is spherical rather than cylindric.

FORT MILLER CLARKIA
Clarkia williamsonii
Evening Primrose family (Onagraceae)

Description: This showy annual has an erect stem, 7–30" long. Its alternate leaves, ¾–3" long, are linear to narrowly lanceolate. The flower buds are erect and have unfused sepal tips **[inset]**, which might require a close look to see. In bloom, the sepals are free or fused in 2 pairs. The bowl-shaped corolla has 4 fan-shaped, pale pink to lavender petals, up to 1³⁄₁₆" long, with a darker splotch in the middle or at the tip. The stigma extends slightly beyond the 8 equal stamens. The fruit is a cylindric, 8-grooved capsule.

Flowering time: April–August

Habitat/range: Dry, grassy areas; chaparral/oak-woodland and mixed conifer zones; up to 6,500'.

Similar plants: Dudley's Clarkia (*C. dudleyana*) also has fan-shaped petals, but its buds are nodding and its petals don't have a dark splotch. Four-spot Winecup Clarkia (*C. purpurea* ssp. *quadrivulnera*) and Slender Winecup Clarkia (*C. purpurea* ssp. *viminea*) are the only other clarkias in the park with fan-shaped petals and erect buds, but the tips of their sepals, in bud, are fused and their petals do not get over 1" long. The stigma of Four-spot Winecup Clarkia does not extend beyond its anthers, and its petals are less than ⅝" long. The stigma of Slender Winecup Clarkia does extend beyond its anthers, and its petals can be up to 1" long.

ALPINE WILLOWHERB
Epilobium anagallidifolium
Evening Primrose family (Onagraceae)

Description: This common perennial has leafy stolons that root at the nodes and enable the plant to spread vegetatively. Its curving, erect or trailing, densely clustered stems are 1–6" long and often have lines of stiff hairs. The leafy stems are usually purplish, and the leaves, which are ¼–1" long, often have purplish margins. The hairless basal leaves are spoon shaped to oblong, and the stem leaves are elliptic to lanceolate and often have sparse, stiff hairs. Only a few flowers grow in each drooping, spreading, or ascending, terminal flower cluster. The flowers have 4 pink to purple sepals and 4 light pink to magenta, notched petals that are about ¼" long. The inferior ovary becomes a smooth, linear capsule that's up to a little over 1½" long and has a stalk that's often longer than the capsule. The capsule splits open and releases tiny seeds with a tuft of fine, white hairs.

Flowering time: July–September

Habitat/range: Meadows, streambanks, seeps, and moist, rocky places; montane, subalpine, and alpine zones; 6,500–12,100'.

Similar plants: Clavate Willowherb (*Epilobium clavatum*) is the only other willowherb in the park with densely clustered stems. Its inflorescences are strictly erect, and its capsule stalk is much shorter than the capsule. The plant has been documented only once in the park, near Young Lakes.

AUTUMN WILLOWHERB
Epilobium brachycarpum
Evening Primrose family (Onagraceae)

Description: Autumn Willowherb is a wispy annual with an erect stem, 8"–6½' tall, that has peeling layers toward the base and is glandular-hairy toward the top. The linear to narrowly elliptic, mostly hairless leaves are up to 2" long, minutely toothed, and folded along the midrib. The flowers grow in open racemes from the axils of bract-like upper leaves. The flowers have an inferior ovary, 4 pointed sepals, and 4 pale pink to purple (or white), deeply notched petals that are up to ½" long. The 8 stamens are much shorter than the petals. The fruit is a 4-angled, linear, sometimes glandular capsule, up to 1¼" long, that produces seeds with a tuft of white hairs.

Flowering time: June–September

Habitat/range: Dry to moist, open or partially shaded areas; chaparral/oak-woodland and mixed conifer zones; up to 7,000'.

Similar plants: Two other willowherbs in the park have peeling layers on the lower part of the stem, have flowers that are not tucked in among leaves, and have seeds with a tuft of hairs, but neither of them are glandular and both of them are less than 1½' tall. The leaves of Leafy Willowherb (*E. foliosum*) are folded along the midrib, and its upper leaves are somewhat clustered. The leaves of Little Willowherb (*E. minutum*) are flat and, its upper leaves are not clustered.

GLANDULAR FRINGED WILLOWHERB

Epilobium ciliatum ssp. *glandulosum*
Evening Primrose family (Onagraceae)

Description: The stems of this common perennial are 8"–3' tall, are erect from the bottom to the top, and have no peeling layers at the base. The stems have lines of short, appressed hairs and are glandular toward the top. The ovate leaves, up to 4¾" long, have conspicuous veins, are not much reduced in size upward, and are minutely toothed. The inflorescence is a dense, leafy raceme. The flowers have 4 sepals and 4 pink to rose-purple petals, up to 5⁄16" long. The fruit is a cylindric, hairy capsule.

Flowering time: June–August

Habitat/range: Open to shaded streambanks, seeps, and meadows; mixed conifer, montane, subalpine, and alpine zones; 4,000–11,000'.

Similar plants: The park has three other perennial willowherbs with stems that are erect from bottom to top and that have no peeling layers at the base. The leaves of Fringed Willowherb (*E. ciliatum* ssp. *ciliatum*) also have conspicuous veins, but the leaves are noticeably reduced in size upward and its petals are pink or white and up to ¼" long. The leaves of Hall's Willowherb (*E. hallianum*) and Mountain Willowherb (*E. saximontanum*) have obscure veins. Hall's Willowherb has slightly nodding inflorescences, and its fruit stalk is ⅜–1" long. Mountain Willowherb's inflorescences are erect, and its fruit stalk is less than ¼" long.

DENSE-FLOWERED WILLOWHERB

Epilobium densiflorum
Evening Primrose family (Onagraceae)

Description: Dense-flowered Willowherb is an annual with a stiffly erect, sometimes branched, densely leafy stem that's 10–40" tall and has peeling layers toward the base. Its linear to lanceolate lower leaves are ¾–2" long and are opposite. The leaves become shorter, wider, and alternate toward the top of the stem, though the leaves are so crowded that it can be difficult to determine how they're positioned. The flowers are tucked in among the leaves toward the top of the stem. Each flower has 4 pink to rose-purple (sometimes white) petals, up to ⅜" long, that usually have conspicuously darker veins. The petals are often so deeply lobed that the flowers appear to have 8 petals. The fruit, which is usually concealed by the leaves, is cylindric and has no beak.

Flowering time: May–August

Habitat/range: Streambanks, drainages, marshy areas, and seasonally moist flats; chaparral/oak-woodland and mixed conifer zones; up to 6,500'.

Similar plants: Torrey's Willowherb (*Epilobium torreyi*) also has peeling layers toward the base of its stem, and it's the only other willowherb in the park with flowers that are somewhat tucked in among the leaves and whose leaves usually conceal the fruit. Its flowers grow in leaf axils all along the stem, not just toward the top, its petals are ¼" long or less, and its fruit has a beak.

SMOOTH WILLOWHERB
Epilobium glaberrimum ssp. *glaberrimum*
Evening Primrose family (Onagraceae)

Description: Smooth Willowherb is a perennial with clumped, often purplish, ascending stems, 8"–2¾' long, that are not perfectly erect. Its stems have no peeling layers near the base and are usually unbranched. The foliage is mostly smooth and waxy but can be minutely glandular-hairy in the inflorescence. The clasping leaves are ¾–2¾" long and are more or less narrowly lanceolate. The erect to drooping flowers, which grow from the upper leaf axils in crowded inflorescences, have 4 sepals and 4 notched, pink **[inset]**, rose-purple, or white petals, up to ⅜" long. The fruit is a cylindric, ascending to erect capsule.

Flowering time: June–September

Habitat/range: Well-drained, gravelly soils, roadsides and streambanks; mixed conifer, montane, and subalpine zones; 3,900–9,900'.

Similar plants: Two other willowherbs in the park have mostly hairless herbage and ascending stems that are not perfectly erect and have no peeling layers near the base. Small Smooth Willowherb (*E. glaberrimum* ssp. *fastigiatum*) also has clumped stems and crowded inflorescences, but the stems are less than 14" long and its leaves are less than 1½" long. Oregon Willowherb (*E. oregonense*) usually has a solitary stem that's less than 12" long, and it has open, uncrowded inflorescences.

ROCK FRINGE
Epilobium obcordatum
Evening Primrose family (Onagraceae)

Description: Rock Fringe is a lovely perennial with sprawling, woody stems, up to 6" long. The plant forms cushion-like mats around the edges of rocks and boulders. Its crowded, ovate leaves, up to ¾" long, are thick, toothed, and hairless and often have a bluish tinge. The large flowers are 1–1½" wide and grow solitary in the axils of the upper leaves. The flowers have 4 green or magenta-tinged sepals, 4 heart-shaped, rose to magenta petals, 8 stamens, and a long style with a purple, 4-lobed stigma. The elongated, velvety ovary often becomes reddish as the fruit develops.

Flowering time: July–September

Habitat/range: Rocky ridges, gravel slopes, and dry talus; subalpine and alpine zones; 9,000–11,600'.

Comments: It's such a delight to come upon these well-named rock-garden beauties tucked into cracks and encircling rocks and boulders high up in the mountains. It's also refreshing to encounter a plant in the *Epilobium* genus that's easy to identify. The plant's less showy willowherb relatives are often challenging to identify with confidence.

PURPLE OWL'S-CLOVER

Castilleja exserta ssp. *exserta*
Broomrape family (Orobanchaceae)

Description: Purple Owl's-clover is an annual with erect, usually reddish, simple or branched stems, 4–16" long, and glandular-soft-hairy herbage. Its alternate leaves are deeply divided into thread-like segments. Its broad inflorescence is a dense spike of flowers nestled among ascending to erect bracts. The bracts are 5–7 times palmately lobed and have lavender tips, which makes the inflorescence look like a paintbrush that's been dipped into lavender paint. The flowers resemble owls with a white or yellow head and a purple body. The protrusion at the top of the upper corolla lip is a densely shaggy-hairy beak with a curved tip.

Flowering time: March–May

Habitat/range: Dry, open, grassy slopes and flats; chaparral/oak-woodland and mixed conifer zones; up to 4,600'.

Similar plants: Dense-flowered Owl's-clover (*Castilleja densiflora* ssp. *densiflora*) looks a lot like Purple Owl's-clover, but the beak at the top of its upper corolla lip is short-soft-hairy (rather than shaggy-hairy) and the beak doesn't have a curved tip. Dense-flowered Owl's-clover grows near El Portal and in the Hetch Hetchy and Ackerson Meadow areas. Purple Owl's-clover also grows near El Portal and has been reported to grow in Yosemite Valley and near Ackerson Meadow.

LEMMON'S PAINTBRUSH

Castilleja lemmonii
Broomrape family (Orobanchaceae)

Description: This attractive perennial is the characteristic paintbrush of subalpine and alpine meadows. It's the most common paintbrush in the park and often grows in the company of Brewer's Lupine and Alpine Goldenrod. The plant has a single unbranched stem, 4–8" long, that's glandular hairy below and soft-hairy above. Its linear to narrowly lanceolate leaves, ¾–1½" long, have 2 lateral lobes. The bracts in the slender inflorescence have 3–5 narrow lobes that are all about the same size. The bracts and the calyxes are magenta toward the top and are much showier than the small, tubular, pale yellow corollas.

Flowering time: July–August

Habitat/range: Moist to dry meadows; subalpine and alpine zones; 7,800–11,000'.

Similar plants: Somewhat similar Short-flowered Owl's-clover (*Orthocarpus cuspidatus* ssp. *cryptanthus*) **[inset]** also has a slender, paintbrush-like, pink to magenta inflorescence. Its single stem is sometimes branched, and its inflorescence bracts have a broad central lobe and 2 much smaller lateral lobes toward the base of the bract. Although the plant is common north of Yosemite, it's been reported only a few times in the park, in the Pate Valley area east of Hetch Hetchy.

ALPINE PAINTBRUSH
Castilleja nana
Broomrape family (Orobanchaceae)

Description: Alpine Paintbrush is a common, tufted-looking perennial, 2–9" tall, that has soft-hairy herbage throughout and usually has clustered stems. Its foliage can vary considerably in color, and the entire plant can be pale green to cream to more or less pink or purple. Its leaves, up to 1½" long, are linear to narrowly lanceolate and often have 3–5 lobes. The inflorescence, 1–5" long, has 4-lobed calyxes and bracts that are yellow-green or more or less purple. The bracts have greenish or cream-colored margins and 3–5 lobes that gradually taper to a point. The narrow upper lip of the 2-lipped, tubular corolla is pale yellow with dark purple margins near the base, and the dark stigma extends beyond the corolla. The lower corolla lip is greenish and has shallow pouches.

Flowering time: July–August

Habitat/range: Rocky or gravelly slopes and flats; subalpine and alpine zones; 9,000–12,000'.

Similar plants: Hairy Paintbrush (*Castilleja pilosa*) also grows in the subalpine and alpine zones, but it's much less common in the park. It also has clustered stems and pale green to cream to pinkish herbage, but its inflorescence bracts have whitish margins and their lobes are rounded or truncate at the tip rather than pointed.

LITTLE ELEPHANT'S HEAD
Pedicularis attollens
Broomrape family (Orobanchaceae)

Description: This common perennial, 3–24" tall, has stout, ascending to erect stems that are densely soft-hairy above. Its basal and alternate stem leaves, 1–8" long, are pinnately cut into 17–41 linear, toothed segments. The basal leaves are on short petioles, and the stem leaves are sessile and reduced upward. The inflorescence, up to 12" long, is a densely hairy, spike-like raceme. The calyx has 5 lance-linear, unequal, hairy lobes, and the 2-lipped corolla is pale pink to purple with darker markings. The upper corolla lip has a narrow beak (the elephant's trunk), up to ¼" long, that curves upward and off to one side. The lower lip has 3 broad lobes that are rounded at the tips. The outer 2 lobes (the elephant's ears) are broader and longer than the middle lobe. At the base of the upper lip, the flowers often have 2 purple dots that look like the elephant's eyes.

Flowering time: June–September

Habitat/range: Moist meadows, bogs, and stream-sides; montane, subalpine, and alpine zones; 6,500–13,000'.

Similar plants: Bull Elephant's Head (*Pedicularis groenlandica*) has similar leaves and also grows in wet habitats. It also has pink to purple elephant-head flowers, but its inflorescence is hairless and its elephant trunk (the upper corolla lip beak) is up to ½" long.

BULL ELEPHANT'S HEAD
Pedicularis groenlandica
Broomrape family (Orobanchaceae)

Description: Bull Elephant's Head is a hairless perennial with 1 or more stout, ascending to erect stems that are 5–30" long. Its basal and alternate stem leaves are 1–10" long and are pinnately cut into 25–51 linear to oblong, sharply toothed segments. The inflorescence **[inset]** is a spike-like raceme, 1–12" long. The calyx has 5 pointed lobes, and the 2-lipped corolla is light pink to red-purple. The upper lip has a downward curved hood and a narrow, upward-curving beak (the elephant's trunk) that's up to ½" long, and the lower lip has 3 broad, mostly equal lobes that are rounded at the tips.

Flowering time: June–September

Habitat/range: Moist meadows and streamsides; subalpine and alpine zones; 8,000–11,200'.

Comments: Bumblebees pollinate the flowers of both Bull Elephant's Head and Little Elephant's Head, using a technique called buzz pollination. They hang from a flower and vibrate their flight muscles without moving their wings. The vibration shakes pollen loose.

Similar plants: Little Elephant's Head (*Pedicularis attollens*) has similar leaves and also grows in wet habitats. It too has pink to purple elephant-head flowers, but its inflorescence is densely hairy and its elephant trunk (the upper corolla lip beak) is only up to ¼" long.

PACIFIC BLEEDING HEART
Dicentra formosa
Poppy family (Papaveraceae)

Description: This hairless perennial is 8–18" tall, and it has masses of finely divided, fern-like, green to blue-green basal leaves, each on a petiole that's up to 20" long. The leafless stems extend well beyond the leaves and end with a collection of odd-looking, pink to rose-purple (occasionally white), nodding flowers that are flattened and shaped like a heart. The flowers have 4 petals in 2 sets of unlike pairs. The outer 2 petals are up to ¾" long, have spreading tips, and form the heart. The inner 2 petals run down the middle of the heart and are very narrow.

Flowering time: May–July

Habitat/range: Damp, shady areas; mixed conifer zone; 3,600–6,000'.

Comments: The heart-shaped flowers are pollinated by bumblebees and hummingbirds. Bumblebees have a long enough proboscis and hummingbirds have a long enough tongue to reach the nectar deep inside the flowers. The plants grow in patches that spread by rhizomes, underground stems that root at the nodes and produce new plants. Clodius Parnassian butterfly larvae feed on Pacific Bleeding Heart stems and leaves, which contain a toxin that's palatable to the larvae but not to other creatures. The toxin is passed on to the butterflies and makes them unpalatable to birds, who quickly learn to avoid the foul-tasting insects.

LONGHORN STEER'S-HEAD

Dicentra uniflora
Poppy family (Papaveraceae)

Description: Longhorn Steer's-head is an early blooming, low-growing, easily overlooked perennial, 1–3" tall, with 1–3 blue-green to grayish basal leaves that are irregularly divided into relatively broad lobes. Once you become familiar with the leaves, the plants are much easier to spot. Usually a single leafless flower stalk grows from the ground near each set of leaves, and each stalk has a solitary nodding or reclining flower that's shaped like the head of a steer. The flowers, about ⅝" long, have 2 sepals that are shed early. The 4 pink, lavender, or white petals are in 2 sets of unlike pairs. The outer 2 petals form the steer's horns, which become strongly curved when the flowers are mature. The outer curved portion of the horn is noticeably longer than the inner straight part. The inner 2 petals form the steer's head.

Flowering time: May–July

Habitat/range: Open, rocky or gravelly areas; mixed conifer, montane, subalpine, and alpine zones; 4,000–12,200'.

Similar plants: Shorthorn Steer's-head (*Dicentra pauciflora*) is similar, but it usually has 2 or 3 flowers per flower stalk. The outer curved portion of its horn is shorter than the broad inner portion, and the flowers look less like a steer's head. Shorthorn Steer's-head could be the rarest plant in the park, known to grow in only a few undisclosed sites.

BOLANDER'S MONKEYFLOWER

Diplacus bolanderi (*Mimulus bolanderi*)
Lopseed family (Phrymaceae)

Description: Bolander's Monkeyflower is a highly aromatic, distinctive annual with erect stems, 5–34" tall, and densely glandular-hairy herbage. Its opposite, sessile leaves, ¾–2½" long, are oblanceolate to ovate and are often toothed along the margins. The flowers have a stalk that's much shorter than the calyx, and they usually grow in pairs. The hairy, 5-lobed calyx is swollen, especially in fruit, and is strongly ridged, with pale tissue between the ridges. The magenta corolla has 5 broad, spreading lobes with a slightly narrower lower lobe. The white floor of the corolla throat is usually speckled with magenta dots.

Flowering time: April–July

Habitat/range: Damp, grassy, gravelly or rocky areas; chaparral/oak-woodland and mixed conifer zones; up to 5,500'.

Comments: Blue Monkeyflower (*Mimulus ringens*) is the only California monkeyflower that remains in the *Mimulus* genus, and it's known from only a single location in the lower Sierra Nevada foothills. One species is in the *Mimetanthe* genus, and all the rest have been assigned to one of two genera. Species with a flower stalk that's as long as or longer than the calyx are now in the *Erythranthe* genus. Species with sessile flowers or flowers with a stalk that's shorter than the calyx are now in the *Diplacus* genus.

241

PURPLE MOUSE EARS

Diplacus douglasii (*Mimulus douglasii*)
Lopseed family (Phrymaceae)

Description: This intriguing little annual, up to 1¾" tall, has more or less hairy, sometimes glandular herbage. Its shiny green, ovate to obovate leaves, up to 1⅛" long, are mostly crowded toward the base of the plant. The hairy calyx has 5 ridges, with pale surfaces in between, and 5 unequal lobes. The corolla has a yellowish tube that's much longer than the calyx. The tube widens gradually or more or less abruptly into a broadly funnel-shaped, magenta throat with bright gold stripes. The magenta upper lip of the 2-lipped corolla has 2 erect or arched mouse-ear lobes, and the lower lip is practically nonexistent (rudimentary).

Flowering time: March–May

Habitat/range: Open areas, usually in well-packed soil; chaparral/oak-woodland zone; up to 3,900'.

Comments: This little charmer appears to be singing the prolonged, final note of an operatic aria.

Similar plants: Congdon's Monkeyflower (*Diplacus congdonii*, previously *Mimulus congdonii*) **[inset]** is similar in several respects. It also looks as though it's in full-throated song, but its corolla has a well-developed lower lip. Neither plant has yet been reported in the park, but they are known to grow near the park's western boundary in the El Portal area.

GRANITE-CRACK MONKEYFLOWER

Diplacus graniticola
Lopseed family (Phrymaceae)

Description: Granite-crack Monkeyflower is an annual, up to 6" tall, with glandular-hairy herbage. Its opposite, mostly sessile leaves, ¾–1½" long, are lanceolate to ovate, and the spaces on the stem between the leaves are usually shorter than the leaves. The flowers grow on stalks that are much shorter than the calyx, and they usually grow in pairs. The pink to magenta corolla is not distinctly 2 lipped. It has 5 spreading, mostly equal lobes that are sometimes notched and usually have a dark line down the center. The floor of the lower lip has 2 bright yellow, elongated patches that are sometimes outlined in magenta.

Flowering time: May–August

Habitat/range: Granite cracks and crevices; chaparral/oak-woodland and mixed conifer zones; up to 4,600'.

Comments: In 2018, this species was segregated from Layne's Monkeyflower and became a newly described species. The plant is common on granite in the Hetch Hetchy area.

Similar plants: Layne's Monkeyflower (*Diplacus layneae*) sometimes has yellow patches on the floor of its lower lip, but the plant is much more open, and the spaces on the stem between the leaves are usually longer than the leaves.

KELLOGG'S MONKEYFLOWER
Diplacus kelloggii (*Mimulus kelloggii*)
Lopseed family (Phrymaceae)

Description: Kellogg's Monkeyflower is a distinctive annual with glandular-hairy herbage and an erect, sometimes branched stem, up to 12" tall. Its opposite, elliptic to obovate leaves, ¼–1¾" long, are mostly sessile. The somewhat inconspicuous flower stalk is much shorter than the glandular-hairy calyx, which has 5 prominent folded ridges, often with a dark line along each ridge top. The top calyx lobe is longer than the others. The magenta to red-purple, 2-lipped corolla has a long tube that gradually widens and becomes funnel-like. The 2 lobes of the upper lip are noticeably larger than the 3 mostly equal lobes of the lower lip. The corolla is darker toward the wide-open throat, and the floor of the lower lip is yellow with reddish spots.

Flowering time: March–June

Habitat/range: Sparsely vegetated, disturbed places, often on steep slopes; chaparral/oak-woodland zone; up to 4,300'.

Comments: This plant is widespread and somewhat common in the California Coast Ranges and in the Sierra Nevada foothills, but it's uncommon in the park, having been reported only along the Hetch Hetchy Trail and in the El Portal area. Unlike most plants, it seems to prefer to grow in precarious places, such as steep, rocky slopes with shifting substrates.

LAYNE'S MONKEYFLOWER
Diplacus layneae (*Mimulus layneae*)
Lopseed family (Phrymaceae)

Description: This common annual has short-hairy herbage and an erect stem that's 2–10" tall. Its opposite, mostly sessile leaves, up to 1" long, are elliptic to oblanceolate, and the spaces on the stem between the leaves are usually longer than the leaves themselves. The flowers, which usually grow in pairs, have a stalk that's much shorter than the calyx. The pale pink to magenta corolla is not distinctly 2 lipped and has 5 spreading, mostly equal, unnotched lobes, each usually with a dark line down the center. The floor of the lower lip has 2 white or pale yellow, elongated patches.

Flowering time: May–August

Habitat/range: Dry, open, sandy or gravelly flats and slopes; mixed conifer zone; 3,900–6,500'.

Similar plants: Granite-crack Monkeyflower (*D. graniticola*) has 2 bright yellow patches on its lower lip, and the spaces on its stem between the leaves are usually shorter than the leaves. Sticky Monkeyflower (*D. viscidus*, previously *Mimulus viscidus*) has been reported in the Wawona and Hetch Hetchy areas. It has a similar corolla, but its flowers don't grow in pairs and its herbage is extremely sticky. Layne's Monkeyflower and Granite-crack Monkeyflower have flowers that usually grow in pairs and they don't have extremely sticky herbage.

243

SLENDER MONKEYFLOWER

Diplacus leptaleus (*Mimulus leptaleus*)
Lopseed family (Phrymaceae)

Description: Slender Monkeyflower is a small annual with an erect, sometimes branched stem, up to 5½" tall, and herbage with short, soft, glandular hairs. Its opposite, untoothed leaves, up to 1" long, are linear to oblanceolate and sessile or short-petioled. The tiny flowers, which grow from leaf axils, have a stalk that's shorter than the calyx. The calyx has 5 ribs and 5 mostly equal lobes and is sometimes reddish. The tiny, dark pink to magenta corolla is not distinctly 2 lipped. The outer part of the throat is white with dark dots and the inner part is usually yellowish. The unnotched corolla lobes are often just barely spreading.

Flowering time: June–August

Habitat/range: Dry, open areas; mixed conifer, montane, and subalpine zones; 4,300–10,000'.

Similar plants: Two other monkeyflowers in the park have a tiny, pink to magenta corolla, Brewer's Monkeyflower (*Erythranthe breweri*), which is quite common, and Small-flowered Monkeyflower (*Erythranthe inconspicua*), which is uncommon. Both *Erythranthe* species have flower stalks that are much longer than the calyx, and their corolla lobes are more distinctly spreading. Small-flowered Monkeyflower's corolla lobes are notched. Brewer's Monkeyflower can have notched or unnotched corolla lobes.

TORREY'S MONKEYFLOWER

Diplacus torreyi (*Mimulus torreyi*)
Lopseed family (Phrymaceae)

Description: This erect annual has glandular-short-hairy herbage and a stem that's 2–14" long and sometimes branched. Its opposite, elliptic to oblanceolate leaves, up to 1½" long, have short petioles below and are sessile above. The tubular to narrowly funnel-shaped flowers, which grow from leaf axils, have a stalk that's much shorter than the calyx. The fused, pale green calyx has 5 ribs and 5 somewhat unequal lobes. The pale pink to magenta corolla is more or less distinctly 2 lipped, with lobes that are rounded to truncate at the tip and are often darker along the margins. The floor of the lower lip has 2 well-defined, elongated, yellow patches. The upper corolla lip curves backward, and the lower lip stretches forward. The stigma is hidden inside the corolla throat.

Flowering time: May–August

Habitat/range: Bare open, sometimes moist areas; mixed conifer zone; 3,000–6,800'.

Similar plants: Two other monkeyflowers in the park have a pink to magenta corolla with unnotched lobes and well-defined, elongated, yellow patches on the floor of the lower lip. The calyx of Granite-crack Monkeyflower (*D. graniticola*) has dark ribs and the lower lip of its corolla bends downward. Skunky Monkeyflower (*D. mephiticus*) has a stigma that is easily visible at the corolla throat and its foliage smells skunky.

KINGS RIVER MONKEYFLOWER
Erythranthe acutidens (*Mimulus acutidens*)
Lopseed family (Phrymaceae)

Description: This uncommon annual has hairless herbage and an erect, sometimes branched, often reddish stem, 1¼–12" tall. Its opposite, broadly ovate leaves, up to ¾" long, are mostly sessile, though the lower leaves are short-petioled and occasionally form somewhat of a rosette. The margins of the leaves are often reddish and have small, shallow teeth. The thread-like flower stalk is longer than the calyx. The mostly hairless calyx has 5 reddish-tinged ribs and 5 somewhat equal lobes. The rose to rose-purple, distinctly 2-lipped corolla is ½–⅝" long and becomes paler toward the throat. The corolla has 2 yellow ridges on the floor of the lower lip and often has thin pink lines leading into the throat. The upper corolla lip sometimes curves backward, the lower lip spreads outward, and all the lobes are notched.

Flowering time: April–June

Habitat/range: In partial shade near streams and seeps; chaparral/oak-woodland and mixed conifer zones; up to 4,000'.

Similar plants: Small-flowered Monkeyflower (*Erythranthe inconspicua*, previously *Mimulus inconspicuus*) **[inset]** is also uncommon and grows in similar habitats in the mixed conifer zone. It has similar leaves and it also has hairless herbage and notched corolla lobes, but its corolla is less than ½" long and is sometimes mostly white.

BREWER'S MONKEYFLOWER
Erythranthe breweri (*Mimulus breweri*)
Lopseed family (Phrymaceae)

Description: Brewer's Monkeyflower is a small annual with an erect, usually unbranched stem, 1–8" tall, and densely glandular-hairy herbage. Its opposite, sessile leaves, ⅛–1⅜" long, are more or less linear to narrowly oblong. The flowers grow on a stalk that's as long as or longer than the 5-lobed calyx. The tiny, pale pink to magenta corolla can be somewhat radially symmetrical or distinctly 2 lipped **[inset]**. The corolla has 5 spreading, equal lobes that are often shallowly notched. The 2 yellow ridges on the floor of the lower lip often have darker dots, and the lateral lobes of the lower lip are sometimes paler than the other lobes.

Flowering time: May–August

Habitat/range: Moist, open or shaded places; chaparral/oak-woodland, mixed conifer, montane, subalpine, and alpine zones; up to 11,200'.

Comments: This tiny plant is easily overlooked, but once you spot a single plant and start looking around, you'll often discover hundreds of them.

Similar plants: Two other monkeyflowers in the park have tiny, pink to magenta corollas. Less common Slender Monkeyflower (*Diplacus leptaleus*) also has hairy herbage, but its flower stalk is much shorter than its calyx. Small-flowered Monkeyflower (*Erythranthe inconspicua*) has hairless herbage and is rare in the park.

245

PINK MONKEYFLOWER, CALIFORNIA BLUSHING MONKEYFLOWER

Erythranthe erubescens (*Mimulus lewisii*)
Lopseed family (Phrymaceae)

Description: Pink Monkeyflower is a robust perennial, 1–3' tall, with glandular-hairy herbage. Its opposite leaves, up to 3" long, are oblong to elliptic and have wavy, minutely toothed margins. The flowers, which grow from the upper leaf axils, have a stalk that's considerably longer than the 5-ribbed calyx. The large, distinctly 2-lipped, pink corolla has 2 yellow, hairy ridges along the floor of the lower lip. The lobes of the 2-lobed upper lip and the 3-lobed lower lip are all about the same size and are often slightly notched at the tip.

Flowering time: June–September

Habitat/range: Wet places; mixed conifer, montane, and subalpine zones; 3,900–10,000'.

Comments: *Mimulus lewisii* was the scientific name for plants in the Sierra Nevada with pink corollas and plants in the Cascade and Klamath ranges with dark magenta corollas. Along with the genus change in 2018, each of the color variations was given species status. Our plants got the name *Erythranthe erubescens* and the northern plants kept the name *Erythranthe lewisii*. So, people who are familiar with this monkeyflower will have to give up the name Lewis' Monkeyflower and learn to call the plant Pink Monkeyflower or California Blushing Monkeyflower.

SLENDER-STEMMED MONKEYFLOWER, HETCH HETCHY MONKEYFLOWER

Erythranthe filicaulis (*Mimulus filicaulis*)
Lopseed family (Phrymaceae)

Description: This cheery little annual has an erect stem, 1½–12" tall, and sparsely glandular-hairy herbage. Its opposite, sessile or short-petioled leaves, up to 1" long, are narrowly elliptic to oblanceolate. The tubular flowers grow on a stalk that's as long as or longer than the calyx. The freckled calyx is covered with short, fine hairs and has 5 ribs and 5 equal lobes. The rose-purple to magenta corolla, which is not distinctly 2 lipped, has 5 equal, spreading lobes that are broad and conspicuously notched. The upper 2 corolla lobes have dark purple markings at the throat, and the middle lobe of the lower 3 lobes has a pair of hairy, bright yellow, elongated patches, usually with dark outlines and sometimes with small, dark spots.

Flowering time: May–July

Habitat/range: Moist, sandy and gravelly places; chaparral/oak-woodland and mixed conifer zones; up to 5,800'.

Similar plants: Small-flowered Monkeyflower (*E. inconspicua*) and Kings River Monkeyflower (*E. acutidens*) are the only other pinkish to purplish monkeyflowers in the park with elongated, yellow markings on the lower lip *and* with distinctly notched corolla lobes, but their herbage (including the calyx) is hairless.

PURPLE FOXGLOVE
(non-native)
Digitalis purpurea
Plantain family (Plantaginaceae)

Description: This showy biennial or perennial has unbranched, erect stems, 1½–6' tall, that are gray-hairy and glandular above. Its lanceolate to ovate leaves, 4–12" long, grow in a basal rosette and are alternate on the stem. The leaves are green and hairy above and grayish-woolly below. They taper to a short petiole and have shallow teeth along the margins. The nodding flowers, 1½–2½" long, grow in elongated, mostly 1-sided racemes. The 5 sepals are ovate to lanceolate. The broadly tubular, 5-lobed corolla is magenta, pink, pink-purple, or whitish and has decorative spots along the inner surface of the lower lip. The 4 stamens and the style are tucked away inside the corolla.

Flowering time: May–September

Habitat/range: Open to shady woodlands and disturbed areas; chaparral/oak-woodland and mixed conifer zones; up to 5,600'.

Comments: This European native has been extensively cultivated as a garden ornamental with a wide variety of corolla colors. All parts of the plant are poisonous, but an extract of the leaves, called digitalis, has been used (very carefully) since the late 18th century as a medication that can reverse heart failure. Several colonies of Purple Foxglove have become established in Yosemite Valley, in the Wawona area, and in the Mariposa Grove.

MOUNTAIN PRIDE, PRIDE OF THE MOUNTAINS
Penstemon newberryi var. *newberryi*
Plantain family (Plantaginaceae)

Description: Mountain Pride is a much admired, shrubby perennial with sprawling to ascending stems that are 6–12" long and often form extensive mats. Its herbage is glandular-hairy in the inflorescences but is mostly hairless below. The opposite, short-petioled, thick leaves, ⅜–1½" long, are elliptic, ovate, or obovate and have finely sharp-toothed margins. The flowers are ¾–1³⁄₁₆" long and grow in short, mostly 1-sided inflorescences. The calyx is often reddish and has 5 lanceolate lobes. The 2-lipped, broadly tubular corolla is dark pink to magenta and is somewhat pleated. The 2-lobed upper lip is more or less ascending, and the 3-lobed lower lip curves downward and is densely hairy inside. The woolly anthers extend beyond the corolla throat.

Flowering time: June–August

Habitat/range: Rock crevices and other dry, rocky places in the open; mixed conifer, montane, subalpine, and alpine zones; 4,000–12,000'.

Comments: Mountain Pride turns the granite areas along Tioga Road into beautiful rock gardens in mid to late summer. The species was named for John Strong Newberry (1822–1892), an American physician, geologist, paleontologist, and botanist. He was a member of many western expeditions, and he's believed to be the first geologist to visit the Grand Canyon.

NARROW-LEAVED COLLOMIA
Collomia linearis
Phlox family (Polemoniaceae)

Description: This attractive annual is somewhat hairy throughout. Its erect, leafy stems are 4–24" long and are usually unbranched. Its alternate, sessile, unlobed leaves are up to 2⅜" long, are lanceolate to linear, and are sometimes toothed. A head-like flower cluster, with 7–20 flowers, grows at the stem end, and smaller clusters sometimes grow from leaf axils. The flowers have pink to white (rarely yellow), trumpet-shaped, 5-lobed corollas that are ⅜–⅝" long. Plants that have flowers with mostly white corollas usually have some flowers with pink corollas mixed in.

Flowering time: June–August

Habitat/range: Open or partially shaded areas; mixed conifer, montane, and subalpine zones; 4,500–10,500'.

Similar plants: Much less common Staining Collomia (*C. tinctoria*) **[inset]** also has linear to lanceolate, unlobed leaves and clusters of trumpet-shaped flowers that can be pink, white, or pale yellow, but its stems are usually diffusely branched, with widely spreading branches. Variable-leaved Collomia (*C. heterophylla*) has been reported in El Portal and Hodgdon Meadow. It also has clusters of pink to white, trumpet-shaped flowers, but its lower leaves are pinnately lobed, and its middle leaves and at least some of its upper leaves are coarsely and irregularly toothed.

TRUE BABYSTARS
Leptosiphon bicolor (*Linanthus bicolor*)
Phlox family (Polemoniaceae)

Description: This petite annual has a slightly hairy stem that's 1–6" long. Its opposite leaves are deeply palmately divided into 3–7 linear segments that are less than ½" long. The dense flower heads have 1 or 2 flowers open at a time. The bristly calyx is deeply divided into 5 linear, pointed segments, and the membranes on the calyx margins are much narrower than the calyx lobes. The trumpet-shaped corolla, ½–1¼" long, has a reddish tube, a yellow throat, and 5 pink, magenta, or white **[upper inset]** lobes that are broadest toward the middle and have no spots at the base. The 5 yellow stamens extend beyond the throat.

Flowering time: March–June

Habitat/range: Dry, open areas; chaparral/oak-woodland and mixed conifer zones; up to 6,000'.

Similar plants: Mustang Clover (*Leptosiphon montanus*) and Whisker Brush (*Leptosiphon ciliatus*) have similar flower clusters, but the membranes on their calyx margins are at least as wide as the lobes, their corolla lobes are broadest at the tip, and the lobes usually have a spot at the base. Thread Linanthus (*Leptosiphon filipes*, previously *Linanthus filipes*) **[lower inset]** grows in the Ackerson Meadow and Hetch Hetchy areas. Its flowers are similar to the flowers of True Babystars, but they don't grow in dense clusters and they have a yellow center and distinct veins.

WHISKER BRUSH

Leptosiphon ciliatus (*Linanthus ciliatus*)
Phlox family (Polemoniaceae)

Description: Whisker Brush is a hairy annual with an erect stem, 1–12" tall, that's often branched from the base. Its pairs of opposite leaves are palmately divided into 5–9 linear, bristly-hairy segments, up to ¾" long. The dense flower clusters are nestled in deeply divided bracts that resemble the leaves. The membranes on the margins of the calyx lobes are at least as wide as the lobes. The trumpet-shaped corolla has a green to reddish tube. The 5 wedge-shaped, pink, magenta, or white corolla lobes are less than ³⁄₁₆" long and usually have a dark reddish or magenta spot at the base. The 5 yellow stamens extend slightly beyond the throat.

Flowering time: April–August

Habitat/range: Dry, open areas; chaparral/oak-woodland, mixed conifer, montane, and subalpine zones; up to 10,000'.

Similar plants: Mustang Clover (*Leptosiphon montanus*, previously *Linanthus montanus*), **[inset]** has very similar flower clusters and the membranes on the margins of its calyx lobes are also at least as wide as the lobes, but its corolla lobes are longer, ¼–⅜" long. Both species usually have a reddish or magenta spot near the base of each corolla lobe. True Babystars (*Leptosiphon bicolor*) has similar flower clusters, but the membranes on the margins of its calyx lobes are much narrower than the lobes and its corolla lobes have no spot at the base.

SLENDER PHLOX

Microsteris gracilis (*Phlox gracilis*)
Phlox family (Polemoniaceae)

Description: This common, widespread annual has glandular-hairy herbage and an erect to sprawling, branched or unbranched stem that's up to 7½" long. Its oblanceolate to lanceolate leaves are up to 1¼" long. The lower leaves are opposite and have a short petiole. The sessile upper leaves are opposite or alternate. The flowers grow in pairs from the upper leaf axils, though both flowers in a pair aren't necessarily open at the same time. The calyx is about the same length as the corolla tube, and it has 5 fused sepals with pointed tips. The trumpet-shaped corolla is up to ½" long, and it has a yellowish tube that is mostly hidden inside the calyx. The 5 pink, magenta, or white, spreading corolla lobes are broader toward the tip and usually have a shallow notch. The lobes of pink or magenta corollas are often white at the base.

Flowering time: March–August

Habitat/range: Dry to moist places; chaparral/oak-woodland, mixed conifer, montane, and subalpine zones; up to 9,000'.

Comments: This plant can be unbranched to much branched, and although its stature, leafiness, and hairiness are also variable, its flowers are fairly distinctive, even though their corollas can be pink or white **[inset]**.

BRIDGES' GILIA

Navarretia leptalea ssp. *leptalea*
(*Gilia leptalea* ssp. *leptalea*)
Phlox family (Polemoniaceae)

Description: This common annual often grows in large patches. It has a thread-like, branched stem, 3–13" tall, glandular herbage, and alternate, linear leaves. The flowers grow on long, slender stalks, usually in pairs, and have a calyx with 5 pointed lobes. The funnel-shaped corolla **[upper inset]** has a greenish-yellow tube and a purple throat, inside and out, though the throat is usually white at the top. The 5 broad corolla lobes are bright pink, magenta, or lavender, and the 5 anthers are blue.

Flowering time: June–August

Habitat/range: Dry to moist, open places; mixed conifer and montane zones; 3,000–7,000'.

Similar plants: Less common *N. leptalea* ssp. *bicolor* **[middle inset]** also has alternate, linear leaves. The tube and throat of its corolla are both greenish yellow, and the throat is usually white toward the top. The pale lavender to bright pink corolla lobes sometimes have purple marks at the base. The corollas of both *N. leptalea* subspecies are more than 5/16" long. Miniature Gilia (*N. capillaris*, previously *Gilia capillaris*) **[lower inset]** is uncommon in the park. It also has alternate, linear leaves, but its corolla is less than 5/16" long. Its corolla has a greenish-yellow tube, and the lobes are white, pale blue, or pink and often have purple or blue marks at the base.

SPREADING PHLOX

Phlox diffusa
Phlox family (Polemoniaceae)

Description: Spreading Phlox is common and widespread in the park. It's a low, sprawling perennial that's more or less matted but is not tightly cushion-like. The plant has a woody base and spreading stems that are 4–12" long and have crowded, linear or awl-shaped, pointed leaves. The leaves are usually hairless toward the tips but are typically white-woolly at the base. The sparsely hairy, 5-ribbed calyx has bristle-tipped lobes that are about as long as the tube. The pink, lavender, magenta **[inset]**, or white corolla is up to ¾" long and has a slender tube and 5 broad, spreading lobes.

Flowering time: May–August

Habitat/range: Dry, open places; mixed conifer, montane, and subalpine zones; 4,500–9,000'.

Similar plants: Although Spreading Phlox has a hairy calyx and leaves that are hairy at the base, the hairs have no sticky glands. The two similar matted *Phlox* species in the park, Condensed Phlox (*P. condensata*) and Cushion Phlox (*P. pulvinata*) have glandular-hairy calyxes. Granite Prickly-phlox (*Linanthus pungens*) is also somewhat similar, but its herbage is glandular-hairy throughout, and, unlike the *Phlox* species, it has needle-sharp leaf tips. The corollas of all these plants can be white or various shades of pink to pale blue.

SHOWY PHLOX

Phlox speciosa
Phlox family (Polemoniaceae)

Description: Showy Phlox is an eye-catching perennial with a woody base and an erect, sometimes branched stem that's 5–16" tall. Its opposite, linear-lanceolate leaves are up to 2" long and are widely separated, and the upper leaves are slightly glandular-hairy. The flowers grow at the stem and branch ends and have leaf-like bracts beneath them. The glandular-hairy calyx has 5 sharp-tipped lobes that are shorter than the tube. The trumpet-shaped, pale pink to magenta (rarely white) corolla is about 1" wide and has 5 narrowly heart-shaped lobes that are white at the base. The top of the throat sometimes has a magenta ring. The style and 5 stamens are hidden inside the tube.

Flowering time: May–June

Habitat/range: Rocky, wooded slopes; mixed conifer zone; 3,900–6,000'.

Comments: This plant is somewhat rare in the park, and though it reportedly grows in the vicinity of Crane Flat, you're more likely to see it along Highway 120 just west of the Big Oak Flat entrance.

PINK SPINEFLOWER

Chorizanthe membranacea
Buckwheat family (Polygonaceae)

Description: This slender annual has erect, woolly-hairy stems that are 4–40" tall, are usually branched above, and are often reddish. Its basal and alternate stem leaves are ½–2" long, are linear, and are mostly hairless on the upper surface and woolly underneath. Each flower grows solitary in a bowl-shaped involucre. The involucre is sometimes woolly-hairy and has 6 dark pink ribs, each with a hooked tip. The ribs are united by broad, paler pink membranes. The small flowers have 9 stamens and 6 pink or white tepals that are fused at the base. The upper flowers grow in dense clusters that have opposite or whorled, bristle-tipped bracts at the base. The bracts resemble the leaves but are smaller. Flowers also grow solitary or in smaller clusters at the branch and leaf nodes.

Flowering time: April–July

Habitat/range: Dry, grassy, gravelly or rocky places; chaparral/oak-woodland zone; up to 5,000'.

Comments: Pink Spineflower blends in so well in the sandy, gravelly areas where it typically grows that it's easy to walk through patches of the plant without noticing them. The plant got its common name from the narrow, spine-tipped bracts just below the flower clusters.

251

WAND BUCKWHEAT

Eriogonum roseum
Buckwheat family (Polygonaceae)

Description: Wand Buckwheat is a common annual with erect, hairy stems that are 4–32" tall and are usually branched above. Its basal and stem leaves are ¾–2¾" long, including the petiole. They have an oblanceolate to narrowly oblong, often wavy-margined blade and are white-woolly below and white-woolly to hairless above. Stem leaves often grow at the lower stem nodes. The tidy-looking flower clusters are somewhat evenly spaced along a branched inflorescence **[inset]**. The sessile, cylindric, 5-toothed involucres (the structures from which the flowers grow) are white-woolly and hold a single small flower. The pink or yellow perianth has 6 tepals, and the 3 outer tepals are broader than the 3 inner tepals. The 9 stamens in each flower tend to match the color of its tepals.

Flowering time: June–October

Habitat/range: Dry, sandy or gravelly places; chaparral/oak-woodland and mixed conifer zones; up to 6,000'.

Similar plants: Wright's Buckwheat (*Eriogonum wrightii*) is the only other *Eriogonum* species in the park with flowers that grow in clusters along inflorescence branches. Its flowers are always pink or white (never yellow), and they grow in more irregular, less rounded clusters. Also, its leaves are smaller, only up to ⅝" long, and most of the leaves are crowded toward the base of the plant.

WRIGHT'S BUCKWHEAT

Eriogonum wrightii var. *subscaposum*
Buckwheat family (Polygonaceae)

Description: This shrubby, somewhat mat-forming perennial has hairless to woolly-hairy stems that are 2–16" long. Its elliptic to oblanceolate leaves are ³⁄₁₆–⅝" long, are usually white-woolly-hairy, and are mostly at the base of the plant. The flowers **[inset]** grow in loose clusters along branched inflorescences. The hairless to woolly, narrowly bell-shaped involucres are sessile and solitary and have 5 erect teeth. The small flowers have 6 white tepals in 2 series, and each tepal has a reddish midrib. The 9 stamens have red pollen and extend beyond the tepals. The pink buds, reddish tepal midribs, and red pollen make the inflorescences look pink.

Flowering time: June–October

Habitat/range: Dry, rocky areas; mixed conifer, montane, and subalpine zones; 4,500–9,800'.

Comments: This plant often grows in crowded populations and can make an area look as though a misty pink haze has settled near the ground.

Similar plants: Wand Buckwheat (*Eriogonum roseum*) is the only other *Eriogonum* species in the park with flowers that grow in clusters along branched inflorescences. Its tidier-looking, ball-shaped flower clusters can be pink or yellow, its leaves are larger (¾–2¾" long), and it usually has leaves at the lower stem nodes.

LADY'S THUMB
(non-native)
Persicaria maculosa (*Polygonum persicaria*)
Buckwheat family (Polygonaceae)

Description: This Eurasian native is an annual
with a sprawling to erect, usually branched stem
that's 4"–2¾' long. The alternate, lanceolate
leaves, 1¼–6" long, often have a dark blotch on
the upper surface. Clusters of 4–13 flowers grow
in erect, dense, spike-like racemes at the branch
ends and from leaf axils. The racemes contain no
leaf-like bracts, and the flowers have a glandless
stalk and 4–8 stamens. The small, bell-shaped
flowers **[inset]** have 4 or 5 tepals that are pink or
rose in bud and usually become white when fully
open. The fruit is a flat or 3-angled, shiny brown or
black achene.

Flowering time: June–November

Habitat/range: Disturbed areas; chaparral/oak-
woodland and mixed conifer zones; up to 5,000'.

Similar plants: Lady's Thumb is one of three
smartweed (*Persicaria*) plants in the park that have
lanceolate leaves, dense, spike-like racemes with
no leafy bracts, and tepals that are pink in bud and
usually white when fully open. Water Smartweed
(*P. amphibia*, previously *Polygonum amphibium*)
also has erect racemes, but it's strictly an aquatic
plant. Willow Smartweed (*P. lapathifolia*, previously, *Polygonum lapathifolium*) has nodding rather
than erect racemes and its flower stalks are glandular. The upper surface of its leaves can also have
a dark blotch. Both plants are California natives.

KELLOGG'S KNOTWEED
Polygonum polygaloides ssp. *kelloggii*
Buckwheat family (Polygonaceae)

Description: Kellogg's Knotweed is a hairless
annual with an erect stem that's 1–6" long and
often has widely spreading branches. Its alternate,
linear, crowded leaves are up to 1½" long and are
sessile. The dense, spike-like inflorescences grow
at the stem and branch ends and from leaf axils.
The flowers are usually partially hidden within
crowded, spreading to ascending, leaf-like bracts.
The small flowers have 3 stamens and 5 pink or
white tepals with pointed tips.

Flowering time: June–September

Habitat/range: Damp, sandy soil; mixed conifer, montane, subalpine, and alpine zones;
4,500–11,500'.

Similar plants: This is one of three knotweed
plants in the park that have terminal inflorescences
with flowers that are at least partially concealed
within whorls of more or less crowded leaves or
leaf-like bracts. Less common Broad-leaved Dwarf
Knotweed (*P. minimum*) has sprawling to erect
stems. Its pink or white tepals have rounded rather
than pointed tips, its leaf blades are more or less
round, and it has 8 stamens. Prickly Knotweed
(*P. parryi*) has been reported twice in Yosemite
Valley and once in Poopenaut Valley. It's a tufted
plant with spiny-tipped leaves, and its flowers are
hidden within leafy bracts and the white, hair-like
remnants of its leaf sheaths.

WOODLAND THREADSTEM

Pterostegia drymarioides
Buckwheat family (Polygonaceae)

Description: Woodland Threadstem is a common foothill annual that has green or sometimes reddish, hairy herbage and can grow up to 3¼' in diameter. The plant has diffusely branched, sprawling and spreading stems and separate male and female flowers on the same plant. Its opposite, fan-shaped, petioled leaves, up to 1" wide, are usually wider than they are long, and most of them are broadly notched. The tiny, inconspicuous flowers grow in clusters of 2 or 3 and have 5 or 6 pink, rose, or white tepals. The male flowers **[inset]** have 6 stamens and a membranous, 2-winged bract at their base. The odd little fruit are obconic and often have red-edged wings.

Flowering time: March–July

Habitat/range: Damp, partially shaded areas; chaparral/oak-woodland and mixed conifer zones; up to 5,000'.

Comments: Woodland Threadstem is sometimes tucked away under overhanging rocks or beneath shrubs and often goes unnoticed, even by diligent plant hunters. However, after people become familiar with the unusual leaves, they spot the plant more easily. Fairy Mist and Fairy Bowties are two other common names for the plant. The *Pterostegia* genus is monotypic, which means that it contains only one species.

HENDERSON'S SHOOTING STAR

Primula hendersonii (*Dodecatheon hendersonii*)
Primrose family (Primulaceae)

Description: This attractive perennial is 5–19" tall, has only basal leaves, and is mostly hairless. Its leaves are up to 6" long, are sometimes slightly toothed, and have green petioles. The broadly elliptic to ovate leaf blade narrows abruptly to a petiole. The smooth, often reddish to maroon flower stalk ends with a loose umbel of 3–16 flowers with sepals that are hidden by the swept-back petal lobes. The nodding flowers have 4 or 5 magenta to deep lavender (rarely white) corolla lobes, up to ⅞" long, each with a strip of maroon at the base and a band of yellow or white (or both) next to the maroon strip. The dark anthers are fused around a longer style. The narrow, inconspicuous stigma is the same width as the style, as shown in the **inset**.

Flowering time: February–May

Habitat/range: Moist, shady places; chaparral/oak-woodland and mixed conifer zones; up to 5,600'.

Similar plants: The park has four shooting star species. Subalpine Shooting Star (*Primula subalpina*, previously *Dodecatheon subalpinum*) is the only other one with an inconspicuous stigma that is the same width as the style. Its leaves have pinkish petioles. It grows above 6,800', mostly south of Yosemite Valley. Its elevation range does not overlap the range of Henderson's Shooting Star, and it is *much* less common.

JEFFREY'S SHOOTING STAR
Primula jeffreyi (*Dodecatheon jeffreyi*)
Primrose family (Primulaceae)

Description: This common perennial is 6-24"
tall and has linear-oblanceolate to spatula-
shaped basal leaves that are 4–20" long and are
sometimes glandular-hairy. The flower stalk is
glandular-hairy (but not sticky), especially toward
the top. Magnification may be required to see the
tiny, glandular hairs. The leafless stalk ends with a
loose umbel of 3–18 nodding flowers with sepals
that are hidden by the corolla lobes. The flowers
have 4 or 5 magenta, lavender, or pink (rarely
white) corolla lobes, ⅜–1" long, each lobe with a
maroon strip at the base and a white or yellowish
band next to it. The 4 or 5 dark anthers are fused
around a longer style. The style has a stigma that
is noticeably, but not considerably, wider than the
style, as shown in the **inset**.

Flowering time: June–August

Habitat/range: Moist to dry meadows and streambanks; mixed conifer, montane, and subalpine
zones; 3,900–9,800'.

Similar plants: Four shooting star species grow in
the park. Alpine Shooting Star (*Primula tetrandra*,
previously *Dodecatheon alpinum*) grows in the
subalpine and alpine zones and is also common.
It's the only other shooting star in the park with a
stigma that is noticeably, though not considerably,
wider than the style. Its flower stalk has no hairs
or glands and its leaves are shorter, ¾–8" long.

SIERRA PRIMROSE
Primula suffrutescens
Primrose family (Primulaceae)

Description: Sierra Primrose is a sprawling,
woody subshrub with creeping, branched stems,
up to 8" long, and mostly hairless herbage. Its stiff,
crowded, evergreen leaves are ½–1½" long and
are arranged mostly in attractive basal rosettes.
The spoon- or spatula-shaped leaves are toothed
at the rounded tip. The flowers grow in loose,
minutely glandular-hairy umbels on a leafless
stalk, up to 4" long. The calyx has 5 triangular
lobes that are sometimes magenta tinged. The
beautiful trumpet-shaped corollas are ½–¾" wide,
and they have a bright yellow tube and throat and
5 bright magenta, spreading petal lobes that are
notched at the tip.

Flowering time: July–August

Habitat/range: Rock crevices, usually north facing;
subalpine and alpine zones; 9,000–11,300'.

Comments: In years with plenty of snow, Sierra
Primrose flowers can turn large swaths of rocky
slopes bright pink. A relatively easy place to find
the plants is at Polly Dome. They grow along the
north side of the dome's lower slopes and typically
bloom in mid to late July.

Similar plants: Somewhat similar Rock Fringe
(*Epilobium obcordatum*) is also a shrubby plant that
grows in rocky habitats. It has similar leaves and
also has magenta petal lobes that are flared and
notched, but its corolla has 4 lobes rather than 5.

WOOD ROSE

Rosa gymnocarpa
Rose family (Rosaceae)

Description: This shrub grows up to 6½' tall and has bristly stems with thin, mostly straight prickles. Its pinnately divided leaves have 5–9 leaflets, and the terminal leaflet has glandular teeth that often have teeth of their own. The flowers have 5 deciduous sepals, many stamens with yellow pollen, and 5–10 pistils. The 5 pink to reddish, ovate petals are about ⅜" long. The fruit is a red rose hip with no sepals attached.

Flowering time: May–July

Habitat/range: Dry, shady areas; mixed conifer zone; 3,600–5,000'.

Similar plants: Wood Rose is one of four rose species in the park. The other three species have flowers with 10 or more pistils. Sierra Dwarf Rose (*R. bridgesii*) is a low, delicate shrub, typically less than 2' tall, more like a shrub you'd trip over than one you'd stumble into. The other three species can grow up to 6½' tall and taller. California Rose (*R. californica*) is distinctive because it's the only rose species in the park with stout, rigid, backward-curved thorns, much like the thorns on typical garden rose bushes. That leaves Interior Rose (*R. woodsii* ssp. *ultramontana*). Like Wood Rose, it has thin, mostly straight prickles. Unlike Wood Rose, its sepals are persistent in fruit, its leaves are not glandular and have no double teeth, and its petals are more than ½" long.

MOUNTAIN SPIRAEA

Spiraea splendens (*S. densiflora*)
Rose family (Rosaceae)

Description: Mountain Spiraea is a deciduous shrub, up to 3' tall, with many stems and smooth to sparsely fine-hairy herbage. Its leaves are ½–2½" long, are mostly ovate, and usually have serrate teeth. The inflorescence is a compact, umbrella-shaped cluster of tiny, pink to rose flowers. The flowers have 5 sepals, 5 petals, and numerous stamens that extend beyond the petals and give the inflorescence a soft, fluffy appearance.

Flowering time: July–August

Habitat/range: Moist, rocky places; mixed conifer, montane, and subalpine zones; 3,900–10,800'.

Comments: In 1897, Felix Hoffmann was working as a chemist for the Bayer company. He was experimenting with material from willow bark and from a *Spiraea* plant in an attempt to create a compound to relieve his father's rheumatic pain. Using the plant material, Hoffmann synthesized a stable form of salicylic acid, which became the active ingredient in a breakthrough pharmaceutical medication called aspirin. The "spir" in the name is for *Spiraea*.

Similar plants: Western Snakeroot (*Ageratina occidentalis*), a shrub in the sunflower family, has similar pink to rose flower clusters, but the clusters are somewhat elongated rather than umbrella shaped.

MILK KELLOGGIA
Kelloggia galioides
Madder family (Rubiaceae)

Description: This common perennial has ascending to erect stems that are 4–16" long and are sometimes branched. Its opposite leaves, ¾–1½" long, are lanceolate to narrowly ovate, and smaller leaf pairs sometimes grow in the leaf axils. The flowers grow in small groups at the stem and branch ends. They have a tiny calyx with 4 or 5 claw-like lobes and a bright pink to white, funnel- to trumpet-shaped corolla with 4 or 5 lobes [inset]. The flowers have 4 stamens and 2 styles that are fused at the base. The developing fruit, at the base of the corolla, is covered with dense, hooked hairs.

Flowering time: May–August

Habitat/range: Open or partially shaded forested areas; mixed conifer, montane, and subalpine zones; 3,000–10,300'.

Similar plants: Botanists are often on the lookout for Sierra Starwort (*Pseudostellaria sierrae*), which is in the pink family (Caryophyllaceae) and is somewhat rare in the park. Sierra Starwort and Milk Kelloggia plants look almost identical when they have no flowers, and the plants grow in similar habitats and at similar elevations. When they have no flowers, the way to tell them apart is to look closely at the base of the leaves. Milk Kelloggia has tiny, fused, membranous bracts at the base of its leaves, and Sierra Starwort has no bracts at the base of its leaves.

SMALL-FLOWERED ALUMROOT, CREVICE ALUMROOT
Heuchera micrantha
Saxifrage family (Saxifragaceae)

Description: This frilly-looking perennial often grows in masses, making rocky slopes look as though a pink mist has settled over them. Its erect to ascending, pink to reddish stems are 4-40" long. The blades of the long-petioled basal leaves are up to 4¾" wide, are round or ovate in outline, and have 5–7 shallow, toothed lobes. The upper leaf surface is hairless, and the lower surface has long hairs on the veins. The alternate stem leaves, if any, are smaller. The wispy, pinkish, much-branched inflorescence sprays are glandular-hairy, and they have loose to dense clusters of numerous small flowers. Each flower has a bell-shaped, pink or white hypanthium, 5 tiny calyx lobes, 5 extended stamens, and 1 pistil. The 5 narrow, white or pink petals, less than ⅛" long, are usually reflexed.

Flowering time: May–July

Habitat/range: Rock crevices; chaparral/oak-woodland and mixed conifer zones; up to 7,000'.

Similar plants: Closely related Pink Alumroot (*Heuchera rubescens*) has similar flowers and leaves, but its sparsely branched inflorescence is much narrower and is often 1-sided, and its leaves are smaller, no more than 2¾" wide. The plant grows in similar habitats from the mixed conifer zone up into the alpine zone.

TWINING SNAKE-LILY

Dichelostemma volubile
Brodiaea family (Themidaceae)

Description: Twining Snake-lily is a hairless perennial with green or reddish, rough-surfaced flowering stalks, 1–5' long, that twine tightly around anything nearby. Its 3 or 4 linear, grass-like basal leaves are 11–28" long and are strongly keeled. Its dense, umbel-like inflorescence has 2–4 pinkish, papery bracts at the base. The 6–30 pink to rose, urn-shaped flowers are about ½" long, are narrowly constricted at the throat, and have 6 somewhat spreading lobes. The 6 white, narrowly lanceolate appendages inside each flower (the perianth crown) lean toward each other, mostly concealing the 3 staminodes (infertile stamens), the 3 fertile stamens, and the single style, which has a 3-lobed stigma.

Flowering time: May–July

Habitat/range: Dry, shrubby areas and woodland openings; chaparral/oak-woodland and mixed conifer zones; up to 5,000'.

Comments: This interesting plant has a unique way of getting its flowers up high where their pollinators are more likely to find them. The rough-surfaced flowering stalk is unable to support itself and twines around nearby objects and even around itself. Only the last few inches of the stalk are self-supporting. Even if the stalk breaks, the flowers often continue to bloom and set seed.

LONG-SPURRED SEABLUSH

Plectritis ciliosa
Valerian family (Valerianaceae)

Description: This slender annual has an erect, angled stem that's 2–16" tall. Its oblong leaves, up to ¾" long, grow along the stem in widely spaced, opposite pairs. The head-like flower clusters grow at the end of the stem. The small flowers have an extended style and 3 stamens with dark anthers, and the calyx is reduced to a narrow ring. The tubular, conspicuously 2-lipped, pink corolla has an erect upper lip with 2 lobes and a lower lip with 3 spreading lobes and 2 magenta dots where the lobes meet. The slender spur at the base of the corolla is much longer than the corolla tube.

Flowering time: March–May

Habitat/range: Open or partially shaded, grassy slopes; chaparral/oak-woodland zone; up to 3,500'.

Similar plants: White Seablush (*P. macrocera*) and Short-spurred Seablush (*P. congesta* ssp. *brachystemon*, previously *P. brachystemon*) have pink or white corollas that are radial rather than 2 lipped, and they have no dark dots. White Seablush's conspicuous, plump corolla spur is more than half the length of the corolla tube. Short-spurred Seablush's corolla has a short spur, less than half the length of the corolla tube, and the spur is often hard to see. White Seablush has been reported near El Portal. Short-spurred Seablush has been reported near Wawona. Long-spurred Seablush grows in the El Portal area and has been collected in Yosemite Valley.

BLUE, PURPLE, AND LAVENDER FLOWERS

Sky Pilot (*Polemonium eximium*)

The plants in this section cover a wide range of hues, from the palest lavenders and blues to the darkest blues and purples.

If you've looked through this section for a plant that has pale flowers and you couldn't find it, check the section for white to cream flowers. Many plants, especially plants in the sunflower family, have flowers that can range from white to blue or purple.

Since there's a fine line between pink and lavender, a plant that you haven't been able to find in this section could be in the section for pink, rose, and magenta flowers.

Note: The similar plants sections include plants that are not covered elsewhere in the book, as well as plants that have a separate photo unit of their own. The names of plants that have their own photo unit in the book are highlighted with green text.

LARGE CAMAS

Camassia leichtlinii ssp. *suksdorfii*
(*C. quamash* ssp. *quamash*)
Century Plant family (Agavaceae)

Description: Large Camas is an attractive perennial, 1–3' tall, that arises from a bulb and often grows in large populations in wet meadows. The long, narrow, grass-like basal leaves are keeled (V shaped). The showy flowers are 1–2" wide, range in color from sky blue to purple (occasionally white), and are clustered toward the top of a single leafless stem. Each flower has 6 tepals and 6 long, rather showy anthers. All parts of the plant are smooth and somewhat silky.

Flowering time: July–August

Habitat/range: Wet meadows; mostly in the montane zone; 5,000–8,000'.

Comments: After crossing the rugged Bitterroot Mountains in 1805, members of the Lewis and Clark Expedition were near starvation. They met a band of Nez Perce Indians who welcomed them and fed them. One of the foods they were given was bread made from *Camassia* bulbs, which are relatively large, quite nutritious, and sweet tasting. The bulbs were such an important staple food for many Native American groups that tribal wars and family disputes erupted over ownership of *Camassia* meadows. The people scrupulously managed the meadows, clearing them of rocks and brush and often burning them to encourage future growth.

GREATER PERIWINKLE

(non-native)
Vinca major
Dogbane family (Apocynaceae)

Description: This sprawling, evergreen perennial spreads along the ground, rooting at stem nodes. The glossy, dark green, opposite leaves are up to 2¾" long, are ovate and pointed at the tip, and have a leathery texture. The plant is hairless except for the hairy petiole and ciliate leaf and sepal margins. The showy, violet-purple, phlox-like flowers are up to 2" wide and grow solitary on upright stalks from the leaf axils.

Flowering time: May–July

Habitat/range: Damp, shady areas near structures; chaparral/oak-woodland and mixed conifer zones; up to 4,100'.

Comments: Greater Periwinkle is native to Europe and Africa and is often cultivated as ground cover. It grows around houses in El Portal and Yosemite Valley and occasionally escapes into meadows and other moist places. Once the plant becomes established, it's extremely difficult to eradicate. It spreads aggressively, forming dense masses that choke out native plants and change the ecology of an area. The genus name is from a Latin word that means to bind or wind around, possibly in reference to the long, flexible stems, which are used to make wreaths.

SIERRA DAISY
Erigeron algidus
Sunflower family (Asteraceae)

Description: This perennial has one or more unbranched, sparsely hairy, glandular stems that are 2–10" tall and are sometimes purplish. The narrow basal leaves, in a dense rosette, are up to 2¾" long, are broader toward the tip, taper abruptly to a distinct petiole, and are usually folded inward. The few alternate stem leaves are linear and much smaller. The flower heads, which grow solitary at the stem ends, have many yellow disk flowers and 30–125 ray flowers with lavender to pink or nearly white rays, up to ½" long. The bell-shaped involucre has purplish, hairy, minutely glandular phyllaries, about equal in size, with spreading or reflexed tips.

Flowering time: July–August

Habitat/range: Dry meadows and open, rocky areas; subalpine and alpine zones; 9,000–12,300'.

Similar plants: This is one of four composites in the park with similar flower heads and mostly basal leaves that are undivided and unlobed. Alpine Aster (*Oreostemma alpigenum*) has thinner, grass-like leaves and stems with no glands. The basal leaves of Dwarf Alpine Daisy (*E. pygmaeus*) taper very gradually to an indistinct petiole, and the plant is less than 2½" tall. Shining Daisy (*E. barbellulatus*), known from only a few remote locations in the park, has distinctive leaves; the enlarged base of each leaf is hard and white-shiny and encloses the base of the stem.

CALIFORNIA SAND-ASTER
Corethrogyne filaginifolia (*Lessingia filaginifolia*)
Sunflower family (Asteraceae)

Description: California Sand-aster is a white-woolly perennial to subshrub with reclining to erect, often much-branched stems that are up to 3½' tall. The alternate, hairy leaves, up to 2½" long, are variously shaped (linear to oblanceolate, spoon shaped, or ovate) and are sometimes toothed or lobed. The leaves are usually crowded toward the base of the stems and are smaller toward the top. The flower heads, which grow at the tips of the stem branches, are often glandular. Each head has up to 120 tightly packed, yellow disk flowers; up to 43 purple, lavender, pink, or white ray flowers; and a series of narrow, overlapping phyllaries that curl backward and become purple tipped with age.

Flowering time: August–October

Habitat/range: Open, rocky or gravelly areas; chaparral/oak-woodland, mixed conifer, and montane zones; up to 7,500'.

Comments: California Sand-aster, with its colorful flowers and silvery-hairy foliage, is a popular garden plant. Many attractive native plants can be purchased at native plant nurseries, and several chapters of the California Native Plant Society hold native plant sales once or twice a year. In a state where water is often at a premium, planting natives is a good idea. They evolved with dry summers and need to be watered only sparingly, if at all.

BREWER'S DAISY

Erigeron breweri var. *breweri*
Sunflower family (Asteraceae)

Description: Brewer's Daisy is a leafy perennial with prostrate to erect, often purplish stems, up to 2½' long, that are branched from the base and covered with dense, spreading hairs. Its herbage is generally not glandular but has dense, short, bristly hairs. The numerous, alternate stem leaves, up to 2½" long, are linear or somewhat wider toward the tip and are evenly sized and evenly spaced along the stem. Each stem usually has 1–5 flower heads, up to ¾" wide, with many yellow disk flowers and 12–45 lavender to pink (seldom white) ray flowers. The bell-shaped, densely glandular involucre has green-tipped phyllaries that overlap in 3–5 series.

Flowering time: July–August

Habitat/range: Open, rocky places; mixed conifer, montane, and subalpine zones; 4,900–9,500'.

Comments: William H. Brewer was a member of the famous Whitney geological survey party in the 1860s in California, and he was in charge of the team's botanical collections. Many plants have been named for him.

Similar plants: Much less common Tuolumne Daisy (*Erigeron elmeri*) is the only other similar composite in the park that has a leafy stem with leaves that are about the same size throughout. Instead of being dense and spreading, its stem hairs are sparse and lie flat against the stem.

WANDERING DAISY

Erigeron glacialis var. *glacialis*
(*E. peregrinus* var. *callianthemus*)
Sunflower family (Asteraceae)

Description: This common perennial, 3–19" tall, has stout stems that are often branched toward the top. The herbage is hairless or has short, stiff, appressed hairs. The basal and lower stem leaves are oblanceolate to spoon shaped; the alternate stem leaves are more or less clasping and get smaller toward the top. Each stem has 1–4 or more flower heads, 1–1¾" wide, with many yellow disk flowers and 30–100 pale pink, purple, or lavender ray flowers. The bell-shaped involucre has loosely spreading, sharp-tipped, more or less equal-sized phyllaries with dense stalked glands.

Flowering time: June–August

Habitat/range: Meadows and roadsides; montane, subalpine, and alpine zones; 6,000–10,800'.

Similar plants: This plant resembles several plants in the *Symphyotrichum* genus, but none of the plants in that genus, in the park, have glandular phyllaries. It also looks something like Thick-stemmed Aster (*Eurybia integrifolia*), which also has glandular phyllaries but only 8–27 ray flowers. Less common Hirsute Wandering Daisy (*Erigeron glacialis* var. *hirsutus*, previously *E. peregrinus* var. *hirsutus*) has flower stalks with spreading, bristly to soft-shaggy hairs; the flower stalks of variety *glacialis* have dense, tiny, stiff, appressed hairs, along with loosely appressed, slightly crinkled hairs.

DWARF ALPINE DAISY

Erigeron pygmaeus
Sunflower family (Asteraceae)

Description: This tiny, compact perennial, up to 2½" tall, has unbranched, sticky-glandular, often reddish stems. The densely clustered basal leaves, up to 1½" long, are linear or slightly broader at the tip, are partially folded at the midrib, and taper very gradually to an indistinct petiole. The alternate stem leaves, if any, are smaller. The flower heads, which grow solitary at the stem ends, have many yellow disk flowers and 20–37 ray flowers with blue or purple (rarely white) rays that are often angled downward and are up to ¼" long or slightly longer. The hairy, bell-shaped involucre has purplish-black phyllaries that are densely minutely glandular.

Flowering time: July–August

Habitat/range: Rocky, gravelly, or sandy places; subalpine and alpine zones; 10,000–13,000'.

Similar plants: This is one of four composites in the park with similar flower heads and mostly basal leaves that are undivided and unlobed. Alpine Aster (*Oreostemma alpigenum*) has thin, grass-like leaves and a stem with no glandular hairs. The basal leaves of Sierra Daisy (*E. algidus*) are more noticeably broader toward the tip and taper abruptly to a distinct petiole, and the plant can get up to 8" tall. Shining Daisy (*E. barbellulatus*), known from only a few remote locations in the park, has distinctive leaves; the enlarged base of each leaf is white-shiny and encloses the base of the stem.

THICK-STEMMED ASTER

Eurybia integrifolia (*Aster integrifolius*)
Sunflower family (Asteraceae)

Description: Thick-stemmed Aster is a perennial with several erect stems, up to 2½' tall, that are glandular-hairy toward the top and often purplish. Its basal and stem leaves are thick, are mostly hairless to sparsely soft-hairy, and have no teeth along the margins. The basal leaves are 1½–9" long, are oblanceolate to elliptic, and taper to a petiole. The smaller, alternate stem leaves have an expanded base that more or less clasps the stem. The raggedy-looking flower heads, which are alternate along the upper portion of the stem, have 20–50 bright yellow disk flowers and 10–21 unevenly distributed ray flowers with violet or purple rays that are up to ⅝" long. The bell-shaped involucre has 3 or 4 series of thick, densely glandular, recurved phyllaries with pointed tips and a disorganized look.

Flowering time: July–September

Habitat/range: Meadow borders and open, moist woodlands; mixed conifer, montane, and subalpine zones; 5,200–10,500'.

Similar plants: Hoary Tansyaster (*Dieteria canescens* var. *canescens*, previously *Machaeranthera canescens*) has almost identical flower heads with raggedy-looking ray flowers and recurved phyllaries, but its leaves are conspicuously toothed. The plant grows mostly east of the park but is occasionally reported along Tioga Road.

BLUE LETTUCE
Lactuca tatarica ssp. *pulchella*
Sunflower family (Asteraceae)

Description: This hairless, somewhat waxy perennial has a stout, leafy stem that's 12–40" tall. Its basal leaves are mostly gone by flowering time. The numerous, alternate stem leaves, which are mostly toward the base of the plant, are linear, elliptic, or lanceolate and are often lobed. Few to many flower heads, about ¾" wide, grow in more or less sparsely branched clusters on the upper part of the stem. Each head has 15–50 pale to deep blue, 5-lobed ray flowers. The cylindric involucre has phyllaries in 3 or 4 series, and the outer phyllaries are often purplish.

Flowering time: June–September

Habitat/range: Moist to wet areas near seeps and springs; mixed conifer zone; 3,400–5,000'.

Similar plants: Non-native Chicory (*Cichorium intybus*) has similar flower heads, but Chicory's flower heads grow stalkless along the stem and Blue Lettuce's flower heads all have an obvious stalk. Non-native Bachelor Buttons (*Centaurea cyanus*) **[inset]** has only disk flowers (no ray flowers), but the enlarged margins of the outer disk flowers make them look like ray flowers. The last herbarium specimen of Blue Lettuce collected in the park was in the 1940s, but the plant may persist. Chicory has been found near Wawona, El Portal, and Yosemite West. Bachelor Buttons is common around El Portal and has been collected in Foresta.

SIERRA LESSINGIA
Lessingia leptoclada
Sunflower family (Asteraceae)

Description: Sierra Lessingia is a hairless to densely woolly annual that's up to 3' tall and has long, stiff, reddish, ascending branches. The plant has a basal leaf rosette with spatula-shaped leaves that wither by blooming time. The alternate stem leaves are much smaller, are dotted with glands, and are sometimes toothed. The flower heads are about ¾" long and grow solitary or in small clusters at the branch tips. Each head has 6–25 pale to deep lavender disk flowers with 5 long lobes that make them look more like ray flowers. The tubular to cup-shaped involucre has 5–8 series of overlapping, silvery-woolly, usually glandless phyllaries with erect, green or purple tips.

Flowering time: July–October

Habitat/range: Dry, open areas, often along roads; chaparral/oak-woodland and mixed conifer zones; up to 6,000'.

Comments: Like many non-native plants, this decorative native plant often grows abundantly in disturbed soils such as road margins, where they look like a lavender haze floating above the ground. They bloom in late summer, often reaching their peak around Labor Day. The flowers are a distinctive lavender color, and they're sometimes called Summer Lavender.

ALPINE ASTER

Oreostemma alpigenum var. *andersonii*
(*Aster alpigenus* var. *andersonii*)
Sunflower family (Asteraceae)

Description: The unbranched, reddish stems of this perennial are up to 16" long and often bend toward one side and become erect toward the top. The herbage is glandless and more or less hairless, except that the upper stem and phyllaries are always somewhat hairy and sometimes woolly-hairy. The grass-like basal leaves are 1½–10" long and are linear to linear-elliptic, and the alternate stem leaves are fewer and smaller. The solitary flower head is up to 1" wide and has many yellow disk flowers and 10–40 pale to deep lavender or white ray flowers. The hemispheric involucre has more or less equal phyllaries that are sometimes reddish to purple along the margins or at the tip.

Flowering time: June–September

Habitat/range: Moist or wet meadows; montane, subalpine, and alpine zones; 6,800–11,000'.

Similar plants: This is one of four composites in the park with similar flower heads and mostly basal leaves that are undivided and unlobed. Sierra Daisy (*Erigeron algidus*) and Dwarf Alpine Daisy (*Erigeron pygmaeus*) have glandular-hairy stems. Shining Daisy (*Erigeron barbellulatus*), known from only a few remote locations in the park, has distinctive leaves; the enlarged leaf base is hard and white-shiny and encloses the base of the stem.

WESTERN MOUNTAIN ASTER

Symphyotrichum spathulatum var. *spathulatum*
(*Aster occidentalis* var. *occidentalis*)
Sunflower family (Asteraceae)

Description: This common perennial has stems that are up to 2' long. Its lanceolate to elliptic leaves are 2–6" long and less than ⅜" wide, and the stem leaves become smaller upward. The 3–10 flower heads have many yellow disk flowers and 15–40 lavender to violet ray flowers. The linear to oblong phyllaries have narrow tips. The outer phyllaries are not significantly shorter than the inner phyllaries, and the phyllaries are not strongly graduated.

Flowering time: July–September

Habitat/range: Mostly meadows; mixed conifer, montane, and subalpine zones; 4,000–10,200'.

Similar plants: Long-leaved Aster (*S. ascendens, Aster ascendens*) and Leafy Aster (*S. foliaceum* var. *parryi, A. foliaceus*) are less common. Long-leaved Aster's phyllaries are strongly graduated, and its outer phyllaries are much shorter than the inner. Both Western Mountain Aster and Leafy Aster have phyllaries that are not strongly gradu-ated. However, Western Mountain Aster's leaves are more than 7 times longer than wide and the largest are less than ⅜" wide; Leafy Aster's leaves are less than 7 times longer than wide and the largest are more than ⅜" wide. Yosemite Mountain Aster (*S. spathulatum* var. *yosemitanum*, previ-ously *A. occidentalis* var. *yosemitanus*) has linear leaves and 3–25 flower heads.

265

VIOLET DRAPERIA
Draperia systyla
Borage or Waterleaf family (Boraginaceae)

Description: This charming little plant is a low, spreading perennial with soft-hairy herbage and stems that are up to 16" long. The oval to ovate leaves are in opposite pairs, and the leaf blades are up to 2¾" long. The flowers, which grow in somewhat loose, terminal clusters, have a calyx with 5 long, tapering lobes and a funnel-shaped, pale lavender to white corolla that's up to ½" long and has 5 rounded lobes. The petals sometimes have a noticeable purplish line down the center.

Flowering time: May–September

Habitat/range: Dry, shady, often rocky areas; chaparral/oak-woodland and mixed conifer zones; up to 6,200'.

Comments: Violet Draperia is a delicate little plant that's often overlooked. It grows in masses in shady places and is quite common under coniferous trees in Yosemite Valley. The plant is found only in California, and the genus is monotypic, meaning that it has only one species. Golden-mantled Ground Squirrels consider the flowers to be tasty treats. The genus was named for John William Draper (1811–1882), an American historian and scientist. He produced the first detailed photograph of the moon and was well known for his somewhat controversial book *History of the Conflict between Religion and Science.*

CALIFORNIA YERBA SANTA
Eriodictyon californicum
Borage or Waterleaf family (Boraginaceae)

Description: California Yerba Santa is a leggy evergreen shrub, 3–8' tall, that often grows in clonal colonies. The leaves and the smaller branches are coated with a shiny resin and often have black fungus spots. The alternate, leathery leaves, up to 6" long, are lanceolate to oblong, are sessile or short-petioled, and are coarsely toothed. The upper leaf surface is shiny and sometimes sticky, and the lower surface is veiny and slightly hairy. The inflorescence is a cluster of funnel-shaped flowers with a calyx that's deeply divided into 5 narrow lobes and a lavender to whitish, sparsely hairy corolla, up to ½" long, with 5 rounded, spreading lobes.

Flowering time: April–July

Habitat/range: Open slopes and roadsides; chaparral/oak-woodland and mixed conifer zones; up to 6,000'.

Comments: Early Spaniards in California called the plant Yerba Santa, which means holy herb. They chose that name after they learned about the plant's medicinal value from Native Americans, who made a tea from the leaves to treat colds, coughs, sore throats, and asthma. The leaves have an odor that some people consider unpleasant, and they're unpalatable to most animals, although they are eaten by insects.

MEADOW STICKSEED
Hackelia micrantha
Borage or Waterleaf family (Boraginaceae)

Description: This common perennial has erect to ascending, branched, soft-hairy stems that are 11–40" long. The narrow basal leaves can be over 1' long and have long, winged petioles. The alternate, sessile stem leaves are sometimes rough-hairy and become smaller toward the top of the plant. The flowers **[upper left inset]** grow in open clusters, are less than ½" wide, and have a corolla with 5 blue lobes and a ring of white to pale yellow, tooth-like appendages at the throat. The calyx lobes and the corolla tube are about the same length. The ridges on the nutlets **[upper right inset]** have prickles that are conspicuously broader at the base and taper to a small, barbed tip.

Flowering time: July–August

Habitat/range: Meadow borders and damp, rocky places; montane, subalpine, and alpine zones; 7,000–11,000'.

Similar plants: Sierra Stickseed (*H. nervosa*) has almost identical flowers that are also less than ½" wide, but its corolla tube is longer than the calyx lobes and the prickles on its nutlets **[lower right inset]** are only a little bit broader at the base. Velvety Stickseed (*H. velutina*) has similar flowers with blue corollas, but its flowers are well over ½" wide.

VELVETY STICKSEED
Hackelia velutina
Borage or Waterleaf family (Boraginaceae)

Description: Velvety Stickseed is a perennial with several erect, hairy stems, 12–31" long, and velvety hairy herbage. Its narrow-elliptic to oblanceolate basal leaves are up to 7" long. The stem leaves get smaller upward and are clasping toward the top of the stem. The branched inflorescences have somewhat crowded flower clusters. The flowers are well over ½" wide and have a blue, 5-lobed corolla with a ring of 5 white, lobed appendages at the throat. The fruit is a nutlet with slender, barbed prickles.

Flowering time: June–August

Habitat/range: Dry forest openings and meadow borders; montane zone; 5,500–8,500'.

Comments: Bees pollinate Velvety Stickseeds. Fully developed flowers are blue and have a center that looks white to us but is ultraviolet to bees, which are attracted to both blue and ultraviolet. The stickseed buds are pink and the flowers turn pink after they're pollinated, presumably as a signal to bees that they have nothing to offer. The color differentiation may keep bees from wasting time on anything but mature, unpollinated flowers.

Similar plants: Velvety Stickseed is one of three blue-flowered stickseed species in Yosemite. The flowers of the other two species, Meadow Stickseed (*H. micrantha*) and Sierra Stickseed (*H. nervosa*), are smaller, less than ½" wide.

WESTERN WATERLEAF

Hydrophyllum occidentale
Borage or Waterleaf family (Boraginaceae)

Description: This leafy, sometimes hairy perennial has erect, fleshy stems, up to 2' tall, and mostly basal leaves. The basal and alternate stem leaves are 2–16" long and are pinnately lobed to pinnately compound with 7–15 divisions that are irregularly lobed or toothed. The upper leaf surface usually has paler, contrasting blotches. The lower leaflets are usually in distinct pairs, and the terminal leaflets are usually merged. The bell-shaped flowers are up to ⅜" long and grow in spherical clusters. They have a hairy, 5-lobed calyx; a 5-lobed, pale lavender to white corolla; and 5 long stamens.

Flowering time: April–July

Habitat/range: Shady places; chaparral/oak-woodland and mixed conifer zones; up to 7,000'.

Comments: *Hydrophyllum* is Latin for waterleaf, possibly referring to the irregular blotches on the leaves of some plants in the genus. The blotches look something like water stains on green paper.

Similar plants: This plant is similar to plants in the *Phacelia* genus. However, its leaves have much more surface area than the leaves of the park's *Phacelia* species. Its leaves usually have conspicuous pale blotches, which sets it apart from all the phacelias in the park except for Waterleaf Phacelia (*Phacelia hydrophylloides*), which can also have splotches on its much smaller leaves.

STREAMSIDE BLUEBELLS

Mertensia ciliata var. *stomatechoides*
Borage or Waterleaf family (Boraginaceae)

Description: This hairless perennial is common in the park's mid- to high-elevation meadows. It has several erect, leafy, branching stems that are up to 5' tall. Its lanceolate to ovate leaves have pointed tips and ciliate margins and are slightly rough to the touch. The petioled basal leaves are somewhat heart shaped at the base. The alternate stem leaves are sessile and have conspicuous lateral veins. The cylindric to bell-shaped flowers grow in open, drooping clusters at the branch tips. The flowers have a calyx with 5 pointed lobes and a tubular, 5-lobed corolla that's sky blue at maturity and up to ⅝" long. The corolla is pink in bud and becomes pink again as it begins to wither.

Flowering time: June–August

Habitat/range: Open or shady meadows, streambanks, and moist forest; mixed conifer, montane, and subalpine zones; 4,500–8,500'.

Comments: Streamside Bluebell's flowers are pink until they're ready to be pollinated, typically by bees, which perceive the color blue but can't distinguish shades of red, including pink. The color coding keeps pollinators from wasting time on flowers that aren't ready to be pollinated. The dangling flowers resemble billowing skirts, which accounts for another common name, Languid Ladies.

CHANGING FORGET-ME-NOT
(non-native)
Myosotis discolor
Borage or Waterleaf family (Boraginaceae)

Description: This charming annual or biennial has a slender, sometimes branched stem that's 4–20" long. Its leaves are up to 1½" long and are covered with straight, unhooked hairs. The basal leaves are oblanceolate, and the alternate stem leaves are linear to oblong. The flowers are arranged in coiled or curved clusters on the upper half of the stem. The tiny, funnel-shaped corolla, which is less than ¼" wide, is yellow or cream colored at first, then turns pink, and finally becomes blue at maturity. The fruit is a smooth, shiny, dark nutlet.

Flowering time: April–June

Habitat/range: Moist ground, wet meadows, and roadsides; chaparral/oak-woodland and mixed conifer zones; up to 5,400'.

Comments: Most plants in the forget-me-not genus (*Myosotis*) are native to western Eurasia and New Zealand. Alpine Forget-me-not, *Myosotis alpestris*, is a high-elevation, circumpolar native of the Northern Hemisphere. It is the state flower of Alaska and grows up to 14,000' in the Himalayas.

Similar plants: Small-flowered Forget-me-not (*Myosotis micrantha*), another non-native annual, has flower clusters all along the stem (not just the upper half), and the hairs on the lower surface of its leaves are hooked, especially along the midrib.

BABY BLUE-EYES
Nemophila menziesii var. *menziesii*
Borage or Waterleaf family (Boraginaceae)

Description: Baby Blue-eyes is an early blooming annual with stems that are 4–12" long. Its leaves are opposite and are pinnately divided into 1–13 lobes that can be further lobed or toothed. Its 5-lobed calyx has small, reflexed appendages between the lobes. The broadly bowl-shaped corolla is up to 1½" wide and has 5 petals that are bright blue toward the tip and white at the base. The petals often have dark blue veins and dots.

Flowering time: February–June

Habitat/range: Meadows and grasslands, often in partially shady areas; chaparral/oak-woodland zone; up to 4,000'.

Comments: This appealing annual often grows in profusion on open, grassy slopes around the park's western boundary and in the Wawona area. Since the plant is in much demand, most nurseries carry its seeds. However, even though the plants grow easily from seed, they don't reliably reseed themselves outside their native habitat.

Inset: Fivespot (*Nemophila maculata*) was collected in Yosemite Valley in 1938. It's also known to grow near Mather, in Ackerson Meadow, and in Hodgdon Meadow, but the plant is much more common at lower elevations in the foothills, where it grows in moist places, often in close association with Baby Blue-eyes.

EISEN'S PHACELIA
Phacelia eisenii
Borage or Waterleaf family (Boraginaceae)

Description: This small, easily overlooked annual has a slender, usually unbranched stem, 1–6" long, and sparsely short-hairy, sometimes glandular herbage. Its lanceolate to oval leaves are up to 1" long, taper to a petiole, and have no lobes or teeth. A few flowers grow on thread-like stalks in short, open inflorescences that are uncoiled or only loosely coiled. The deeply divided calyx has 5 linear to oblanceolate lobes. The deciduous, 5-lobed corolla is less than ¼" long, broadly bell shaped, and lavender to nearly white.

Flowering time: May–August

Habitat/range: Dry to damp, open, sandy or gravelly areas; mixed conifer, montane, and subalpine zones; 5,000–10,500'.

Comments: Some *Phacelia* species can cause contact dermatitis, giving people with sensitive skin a rash similar to the rashes caused by poison oak and poison ivy.

Similar plants: Less common Racemose Phacelia (*Phacelia racemosa*), also an annual, is the only other phacelia in the park with few-flowered inflorescences that are uncoiled or only loosely coiled. Its deciduous corolla is narrowly bell shaped rather than broadly bell shaped, and its leaves grow up to 1½" long. The plants grow in similar habitats and in the same vegetation zones.

WATERLEAF PHACELIA
Phacelia hydrophylloides
Borage or Waterleaf family (Boraginaceae)

Description: Waterleaf Phacelia is a woody-based perennial with reclining to ascending, hairy stems that are 4–12" long. Its alternate, silky-hairy leaves are up to 2½" long, are evenly distributed along the stem, and sometimes have pale blotches on the upper surface. The leaf blades are oblong to ovate, are coarsely toothed or lobed, and usually have 1 or 2 pinnate pairs of leaflets below a larger terminal leaflet. The flowers are numerous in dense, head-like clusters. The narrowly oblong calyx lobes are densely hairy on the margins. The broadly bell-shaped, wide-open corolla is about ¼" long and has 5 fused petals that are greenish yellow or sometimes red tinged at the throat and base. The widely spreading corolla lobes are purplish blue (rarely white) and are conspicuously curled under along the margins. The stamens have purple pollen and extend well beyond the corolla.

Flowering time: June–September

Habitat/range: Open, dry slopes and flats; montane and subalpine zones; 6,000–9,500'.

Comments: The word *hydrophylloides* is derived from Latin and means like waterleaf, referring to the plant's resemblance to plants in the *Hydrophyllum* genus. Like Waterleaf Phacelia, the leaves of *Hydrophyllum* species sometimes have pale spots on the upper surface.

CHANGEABLE PHACELIA
Phacelia mutabilis
Borage or Waterleaf family (Boraginaceae)

Description: Changeable Phacelia is a biennial or short-lived perennial with a few unbranched, reclining to erect stems that are up to 24" long. Its herbage is sparsely stiff-hairy, but not glandular. The lanceolate to ovate, green leaves are up to 14" long and sometimes have 1 or 2 pairs of lateral leaflets at the base of a much larger terminal leaflet. The smaller, alternate stem leaves sometimes have 3 lobes or a pair of lateral leaflets. By the time the plant is flowering, many of its basal leaves are withering or withered, leaving mostly stem leaves. Numerous flowers grow in 1-sided, coiling inflorescences toward the stem tops. The densely bristly calyx lobes are linear to oblanceolate. The tubular to bell-shaped corolla is about ¼" long and has 5 fused, lavender to white petals, and the hairy stamens extend well beyond the corolla lobes.

Flowering time: June–September

Habitat/range: Open to shady, dry or moist, sometimes rocky areas; mixed conifer and montane zones; 3,800–8,000'.

Similar plants: Timberline Phacelia (*Phacelia hastata*) is a higher-elevation perennial with stems that are up to 10" long. Its leaves are unlobed or have 1 or 2 lobes or 2 leaflets at the base of the blade. Most of its silvery or grayish-green leaves are clustered at the base of the plant, and the leaves are not withered when the plant is in bloom.

GRANITE PHACELIA
Phacelia quickii
Borage or Waterleaf family (Boraginaceae)

Description: Granite Phacelia is an annual with a reclining to erect stem that's 1½–7" long and is sometimes branched. Its herbage, which is covered with short, sometimes glandular hairs, is usually reddish and often has a skunk-like odor throughout. The alternate, linear to linear-oblong leaves are ½–2" long, taper to a petiole, and are unlobed. The flowers grow in loose to dense, coiled clusters at the top of the stem (and at the branch tips when there are branches). The 5 unequal, short-hairy calyx lobes are narrowly oblanceolate to linear. The broadly bell-shaped corolla is less than ¼" long, is pale blue or lavender to violet, and remains in place when the fruit starts to develop. The stamens extend beyond the corolla and have white to purple filaments and cream to pale yellow pollen.

Flowering time: May–July

Habitat/range: Open areas in granitic gravel; mixed conifer and montane zones; 3,900–8,000'.

Similar plants: Mariposa Phacelia (*Phacelia vallicola*) is also an annual. It looks a lot like Granite Phacelia, but its herbage isn't skunky smelling, its tubular-bell-shaped corolla falls off as soon as the fruit begins to develop, and its stamens do not extend beyond the corolla.

ELEGANT ROCKCRESS

Boechera arcuata (*Arabis sparsiflora* var. *arcuata*)
Mustard family (Brassicaceae)

Description: This showy perennial is 12–32" tall and has several stems that are sometimes branched and are often reddish at the top. Its herbage is coarsely hairy and grayish throughout. The petioled lower leaves are 1–4" long, are narrowly lanceolate, and are sometimes toothed. The sessile stem leaves are smaller, are narrowly triangular, and have 2 narrow, triangular, sometimes toothed lobes at the base. The showy inflorescence **[inset]** has 12–70 tube-shaped flowers with 4 purple petals that are ⅜–½" long. The slender, curved siliques (fruit) are 2–5" long and are ascending and then spreading.

Flowering time: March–July

Habitat/range: Dry, rocky places; chaparral/oak-woodland and mixed conifer zones; up to 6,000'.

Similar plants: Elegant Rockcress is one of six purplish-flowered rockcress species in the park that can have mostly spreading siliques.

Two of the six species, Spreading Rockcress (*B. divaricarpa*, previously *Arabis* x *divaricarpa*) and Davidson's Rockcress (*B. davidsonii*, previously *A. davidsonii*) are the only species in the group with hairless upper stem leaves that look green rather than grayish. Spreading Rockcress is less than 6" tall; Davidson's Rockcress is 11"–2' tall and sometimes has whitish flowers.

The other four species have grayish looking leaves. Within that group, Inyo Rockcress (*B. inyoensis*, previously *A. inyoensis*) is the only one, besides Elegant Rockcress, with petals that are more than ¼" long, but it grows only above 8,500'.

Two other species in the grayish-leaved group have petals that are less than ¼" long. Those two are Soldier Rockcress (*B. depauperata*, previously *A. lemmonii* var. *depauperata*) and Lemmon's Rockcress (*B. lemmonii*, previously *A. lemmonii* var. *lemmonii*). Soldier Rockcress's siliques are distributed somewhat evenly around the stem. Lemmon's Rockcress differs from the other rockcresses in this group of six in that its siliques grow mostly on one side of the stem.

WILD RADISH
(non-native)
Raphanus sativus
Mustard family (Brassicaceae)

Description: The stems of this invasive annual or biennial are 1¼–4¼' tall and are often branched toward the top. The lower leaves are up to 2' long, are pinnately cleft into 1–12 pairs of lateral lobes, and have a large, rounded terminal lobe. The flowers, which grow in an elongated inflorescence, have 4 sepals and 4 long-clawed petals, ½–1" long, that are usually lavender to purple but can be white or shades of yellow. The inflated-looking mature fruit (siliques), 1–6" long, are not constricted or are only slightly constricted between the seeds.

Flowering time: May–July

Habitat/range: Disturbed areas; chaparral/oak-woodland and mixed conifer zones; up to 5,000'.

Comments: This plant became domesticated in Europe in pre-Roman times and is now cultivated in temperate areas worldwide as a salad vegetable.

Similar plants: Jointed Charlock (*Raphanus raphanistrum*) has mature fruit that are strongly constricted between the seeds. Its petals are yellow or creamy white. Both of these plants are native to Mediterranean Europe and have become naturalized throughout North America, often becoming invasive weeds. They hybridize with each other and produce plants that are highly variable in flower color and fruit constriction.

CALIFORNIA HAREBELL
Asyneuma prenanthoides
(*Campanula prenanthoides*)
Bellflower family (Campanulaceae)

Description: California Harebell is a mostly hairless perennial with erect or reclining, branched stems that are 5"–4' long and are square-sided, at least toward the base. Its alternate stem leaves are ½–2½' long and are lanceolate to ovate with a pointed tip. The leaves are sessile or short-petioled, are thin to leathery, and have teeth along the margin. The long, narrow inflorescence has clusters of 2–5 flowers. The fused, urn-shaped calyx has 5 narrow, spreading to recurved lobes. The pale blue to deep blue, widely funnel-shaped corolla is up to ½" long and has 5 petals with narrow lobes that are often curled backward. The flowers have 5 short stamens and a long style that extends far beyond the corolla.

Flowering time: June–September

Habitat/range: Dry, shady forest; mixed conifer and montane zones; 4,500–7,000'.

Comments: Even though California Harebells are fairly common and the flowers are an eye-catching color, the plants often go unnoticed because they blend in so well with other vegetation in the shady places where they grow.

SIERRA CALICOFLOWER
Downingia montana
Bellflower family (Campanulaceae)

Description: This interesting, hairless annual has reclining to erect, sometimes branched stems, 1–6" long. The alternate stem leaves are up to a little over ¼" long and are linear and sessile. The small flowers are also sessile and are solitary in the upper leaf axils. The calyx has 5 linear lobes, the upper 3 much longer than the lower 2. The upper lip of the 2-lipped, tubular corolla has 2 narrow, pointed lobes that are blue, lavender, or purple. The 3-lobed lower lip is usually the same color as the upper lip, but with a large, white or cream-colored central area and 2 purple and yellow folds near the throat. The flower has an elongated, linear, inferior ovary that looks like a flower stalk.

Flowering time: May–August

Habitat/range: Damp to dry meadows and roadside ditches; mixed conifer zone; 3,000–5,500'.

Comments: This plant grows in the Hetch Hetchy area and at Ackerson Meadow. The genus was named for Andrew Jackson Downing (1815–1852), an American landscape designer, architect, and writer. He had great influence on the landscape architect Frederick Law Olmsted and collaborated with him in the design that was adopted for Central Park in New York City. Olmsted played a role in the preservation of Yosemite Valley and the Mariposa Grove of Giant Sequoias, and Olmsted Point was named in his honor.

COMMON BLUECUP
Githopsis specularioides
Bellflower family (Campanulaceae)

Description: Common Bluecup is an annual with an erect stem, 1–6" tall, that's square below and sometimes branched. Its herbage is hairless or has spreading hairs. The alternate, sessile stem leaves are up to ¾" long, are ovate to oblong, and are irregularly toothed along the margin. The small flowers grow solitary at the end of the stem and branches. The funnel-shaped corolla is up to about ½" long. Its lobes are purple, lavender, or deep blue, and the throat and tube are white. The calyx has linear, spreading, sometimes toothed lobes that extend well beyond the corolla lobes, and the calyx lobes are as long as or longer than the inferior ovary at their base. The narrowly cone-shaped ovary has a long-tapered base, is somewhat narrowed at the top, and has 10 prominent ribs.

Flowering time: May–June

Habitat/range: Open areas; chaparral/oak-woodland and mixed conifer zones; up to 5,000'.

Comments: Common Bluecup grows in the El Portal area and has been reported to grow on the north side of Hetch Hetchy and near Wawona.

Similar plants: San Gabriel Bluecup (*Githopsis diffusa* ssp. *robusta*), which has been reported to grow near the park's western boundary, has a cylindric to cone-shaped ovary that's narrowed near the middle and somewhat swollen at the base.

WESTERN PEARLFLOWER

Heterocodon rariflorum
Bellflower family (Campanulaceae)

Description: This charming little annual has a slender, square stem, 2–12" long, that's sprawling to erect, sparsely hairy, and sometimes branched from the base. Its alternate, sessile stem leaves are less than ½" long, roundish to ovate, prominently triangular toothed, and usually the most noticeable part of the plant. The flowers are solitary in the leaf axils. The lower flowers are self-fertilizing, and their little pearly-white buds never open. The 5 leaf-like, spreading sepals, above the cup-shaped inferior ovary, are widely triangular and are often bristle tipped. The blue or bluish-purple, cylindric corolla is less than ¼" long and has dark veins and 5 spreading to erect, triangular lobes.

Flowering time: April–July

Habitat/range: Vernally moist, open to shady places; chaparral/oak-woodland and mixed conifer zones; up to 5,500'.

Comments: Once you become familiar with the plant's distinctive little leaves, you'll begin to realize how common it is. The trick is to find it in bloom.

Similar plants: Small Venus Looking-glass (*Triodanis biflora*) **[inset]**, which is reported to grow in the Hetch Hetchy area, also has tiny, blue to purple flowers that grow in the leaf axils, but its corolla is wide open, with little or no tube, and its sepals are narrowly triangular and are not leaf-like.

PURPLE SAND-SPURRY

(non-native)
Spergularia rubra
Pink family (Caryophyllaceae)

Description: Purple Sand-spurry is an erect to sprawling annual or perennial that forms dense, low mats. Its stems are much branched toward the base and are glandular toward the ends. The tiny, linear leaves are up to ½" long, grow in whorls of 2–5, and have a membranous, silvery-shiny bract that tapers to a sharp point. The 5 distinctive canoe-shaped sepals are partially fused at the base, are often glandular-hairy on the outside, and have membranous margins. The 5 lavender to purple petals are less than ¼" long and are about the same length as the sepals.

Flowering time: March–September

Habitat/range: Roadsides and other disturbed areas; chaparral/oak-woodland, mixed conifer, montane, and subalpine zones; up to 8,700'.

Comments: The genus name was derived from *Spergula*, the genus of a plant called Corn Spurry (*Spergula arvensis*). Corn Spurry is a European native that was cultivated historically for cattle feed because it was believed to increase milk production. The plant has become a worldwide noxious weed and has recently been reported in the Hetch Hetchy area. Although Purple Sand-spurry grows from low elevations up into the subalpine zone in the park, it's not considered noxious or invasive and often grows where little else will grow.

FRECKLED MILKVETCH

Astragalus lentiginosus var. *ineptus*
Pea family (Fabaceae)

Description: Freckled Milkvetch is a perennial with sprawling stems, 4–12" long, and gray-hairy herbage. Its pinnate leaves are ½–2" long and have 9–27 obovate, crowded leaflets, up to ⅜" long, that are opposite or offset. The inflorescence is a crowded cluster of pea flowers, up to ½" long, at the branch ends. The cylindric calyx has 5 triangular lobes, and the corolla has cream-colored petals with lavender tips. The strongly inflated, greenish to cream-colored pods are red mottled and are sometimes slightly hairy. The pods have a curved beak and are sessile in the calyx (with no stalk between the base of the pod and the calyx).

Flowering time: June–August

Habitat/range: Open, gravelly areas; montane, subalpine, and alpine zones; 7,900–12,000'.

Comments: This milkvetch is one of just a few plants in the *Astragalus* genus that have detachable pods that can be blown by the wind or can float on water to other locations, aiding in seed dispersal.

Similar plants: Whitney's Milkvetch (*Astragalus whitneyi* var. *whitneyi*) also has strongly inflated, slightly hairy, red-mottled pods, but the pods grow out of the calyx on a short stalk. The 2 papery bracts at the base of its lower leaves are fused into a sheath. Freckled Milkvetch's lower leaf bracts are not papery and are not fused into a sheath.

WOOLLY-POD MILKVETCH

Astragalus purshii var. *lectulus*
Pea family (Fabaceae)

Description: This high-elevation, sparsely to densely matted perennial has reclining stems, up to 5½" long, and its herbage has dense, cottony, tangled hairs that are gray or silvery. Its pinnate leaves, up to 6" long, have 3–17 narrowly elliptic to somewhat round leaflets with blunt or notched tips. The inflorescences, which are usually nestled among the leaves, have 1–5 pale purple to pink pea flowers with a banner up to ½" long. The pods **[left inset]** are egg shaped in outline, and they're densely covered with long, white-woolly hairs.

Flowering time: July–September

Habitat/range: Dry, rocky areas; subalpine and alpine zones; 10,500–12,000'.

Comments: Milkvetches are often called locoweed, and some species contain various toxins that can make livestock ill, causing such symptoms as erratic behavior, aggression, lethargy, depression, loss of balance, and nervousness.

Similar plants: Spiny Milkvetch (*Astragalus kentrophyta* var. *danaus*) **[right inset]** grows in dry, rocky areas in the alpine zone. Its similar flowers are pale blue, pink-purple, or mostly white, and the banner is up to ⅜" long. Its small pods are finely hairy. The plant's linear, spine-tipped leaves distinguish it from the other *Astragalus* species that grow in the park.

LANSZWERT'S PEA

Lathyrus lanszwertii var. *lanszwertii*
Pea family (Fabaceae)

Description: Lanszwert's Pea is a perennial with fine, short-hairy herbage and climbing or ascending stems, up to 2½' long. Its pinnate leaves end with a coiled tendril that can attach to other vegetation. The leaves have 4–10 opposite or offset, linear to narrowly lanceolate leaflets, ¾–4" long, with pointed tips. The small pea flowers are up to ⅝" long and grow in loose clusters on long stalks from the leaf axils. The calyx has 5 triangular lobes, and the corolla is pale blue, lavender, or sometimes white and turns yellow with age. The flat, hairless pea pods resemble culinary snow peas.

Flowering time: May–July

Habitat/range: Dry, moist, open or shaded slopes and flats; mixed conifer zone; 3,900–6,000'.

Similar plants: The leaflets of Lanszwert's Pea are considerably longer than they are wide. Somewhat similar non-native Spring Vetch (*Vicia sativa* ssp. *nigra*) also has some leaflets that are longer than they are wide, but the leaflets have notched rather than pointed tips. American Vetch (*Vicia americana*), a native plant, often has some leaflets that are noticeably longer than they are wide, but most of its leaflets are widely elliptic; if in doubt, check the style (see page 198). Another variety of Lanszwert's Pea has been reported in the park, *Lathyrus lanszwertii* var. *aridus*; its leaves end with a bristle rather than a coiled tendril.

SIERRA NEVADA PEA

Lathyrus nevadensis var. *nevadensis*
Pea family (Fabaceae)

Description: This hairless or sparsely hairy perennial has erect to ascending, angled stems that are 4–15" long. Its pinnate leaves, which occasionally end with a tendril, but more often a bristle, have 4–8 elliptic to widely ovate leaflets that are ½–1½" long and are opposite or slightly offset. Showy pea flowers, up to 1" long, grow in open clusters of 2–4 from the leaf axils. The green or purplish-tinged calyx has 5 triangular lobes, and the corolla has a lavender to purplish banner petal and white or purplish wing petals. The smooth pea pods resemble culinary snow peas.

Flowering time: April–July

Habitat/range: Forest and woodland openings; chaparral/oak-woodland and mixed conifer zones; up to 6,000'.

Comments: Plants in the pea genus (*Lathyrus*) and the vetch genus (*Vicia*) have an even number of pinnate leaflets and no terminal leaflet, but they often have a terminal tendril or bristle.

Similar plants: Sierra Nevada Pea is similar to non-native Spring Vetch (*Vicia sativa* ssp. *nigra*) and native American Vetch (*Vicia americana*), but Spring Vetch and American Vetch both have leaves with at least 8 leaflets and invariably have some leaves with more than 8 leaflets, and Sierra Nevada Pea has leaves with only 4–8 leaflets.

NARROW-WINGED LUPINE

Lupinus albicaulis
Pea family (Fabaceae)

Description: Narrow-winged Lupine is a leafy perennial with ascending to erect, branched stems, 1–3½' long. Its leaves are palmately divided into 5–10 oblanceolate leaflets that are up to 2¾" long and are covered with appressed, silky hairs on both surfaces. The uncrowded inflorescences are 4–17" long and have whorled pea flowers, up to ⅝" long, with purple, pale yellow, or white petals. The slender banner petal, which often has a pointed tip, has a narrow, white center on purple-petaled flowers. The tip of the strongly upcurved, hairless keel protrudes beyond the narrow wing petals. The silky pods are up to 2" long.

Flowering time: May–August

Habitat/range: Dry, open or somewhat shaded places; chaparral/oak-woodland, mixed conifer, montane, and subalpine zones; up to 8,900'.

Similar plants: Narrow-winged Lupine, in the photo on the left, is one of five erect lupines in the park with a mostly hairless keel (magnification required) and leaves that are hairy, at least on the upper surface. It's the only one in the group with narrow wing petals that usually fail to conceal the keel tip.

Green-stipuled Lupine (*L. fulcratus*) **[upper left photo in the photos to the right]** is the only one

in the group with a pair of green, leaf-like bracts at the base of the leaves. Its keel is usually completely hairless, though it can have a few scattered hairs on the upper keel margins near the middle.

That leaves three other lupines, Anderson's Lupine (*L. andersonii*), Summer Lupine (*L. formosus* var. *formosus*), and Forest Lupine (*L. adsurgens*). Of the three, Anderson's Lupine **[lower left]** is the only one with bright green leaves, though they are hairy. Summer Lupine **[upper right]** has gray to silvery leaves, and Forest Lupine **[lower right]** has silver to dull green leaves.

Summer Lupine differs from Forest Lupine in that its inflorescences and leaflets can be longer, and it has rhizomes (horizontal underground stems), which Forest Lupine lacks. Summer Lupine's inflorescences are 4–12" long, and its leaflets can be up to 2¾" long. Forest Lupine's inflorescences are ¾–9" long, and its leaflets can be up to 2" long.

The lupines in this group don't always conform reliably to their descriptions, and they can be difficult to identify with any certainty.

The *Jepson eFlora* (2020) indicates that three species in the group need more study. Under *L. albicaulis* it says, "doubtfully distinct from *L. andersonii*." Under *L. andersonii* it says, more or less "indistinct morphologically from *L. albicaulis*." And, under *L. fulcratus* it says, "may be part of *L. andersonii*." Forewarned is forearmed.

BUSH LUPINE

Lupinus albifrons var. *albifrons*
Pea family (Fabaceae)

Description: This leafy shrub has branched stems, 2–6' long, and usually has a distinctly woody trunk. Its palmate leaves have 6–10 oblanceolate leaflets, ½–1¾" long, with silvery-silky hairs above and below. The loosely whorled inflorescence, 3–12" long, has uncrowded flowers, about ½" long, with violet to lavender petals. The banner petal has a yellow or white center that turns magenta with age. The upper margins of the keel are ciliate from the middle to the tip (under magnification).

Flowering time: March–June

Habitat/range: Open areas; chaparral/oak-woodland and mixed conifer zones; up to 5,000'.

Comments: Since Bush Lupine is the only lupine in the park that's distinctly a shrub, it's easy to identify. There are about 20 other lupine species in the park, and the similarity of several species can make identification difficult at best. Magnification of the hairs (or lack thereof) on the keel petal is required to identify several species. Petal color can also confuse matters. Several lupines that usually have blue to purple petals can have pink, lavender, pale yellow, cream-colored, or white petals. Whitewhorl Lupine (*Lupinus microcarpus* var. *densiflorus*) is the only lupine that always has white (or yellow) petals, and it isn't known to grow within the park boundaries. So, if you find a lupine in the park that has pale petals, look for it in this color section.

SPURRED LUPINE

Lupinus arbustus
Pea family (Fabaceae)

Description: This leafy perennial has many erect stems, 8–26" tall. Its green leaves are palmately divided into 7–13 oblanceolate leaflets, ⅜–2¾" long, with appressed hairs. The somewhat whorled inflorescence, 2–7" long, has mostly uncrowded pea flowers that usually have blue petals (sometimes pink, lavender, violet, or white). The wing petals have short, dense hairs toward the tip, and the keel is ciliate along the upper margins (both requiring magnification). The upper calyx lip **[inset]** has a small, but noticeable bulge (spur) at its base. The silky pods are up to 1" long.

Flowering time: May–July

Habitat/range: Dry, open to shady area; mixed conifer and montane zones; 4,000–7,500'.

Similar plants: If you find a lupine over 8" tall in the park's middle elevations, take a close look at several of its flowers. If some of them have a small, but distinct bulge at the base of the upper calyx lip, it's probably Spurred Lupine. The spur can be up to ⅛" long and doesn't require magnification to see. Spurred Lupine grows along the trail to McGurk Meadow and in other places along Glacier Point Road. Silvery Lupine (*Lupinus argenteus* var. *heteranthus*) is the only other lupine in the park with a spur on its upper calyx lip. Its leaves have silvery-silky hairs and its wing petals have no hairs. The plant is known from only a few locations in the park.

MINIATURE LUPINE
Lupinus bicolor
Pea family (Fabaceae)

Description: Miniature Lupine is a slender annual, 4–15" tall, with branched stems and soft-hairy herbage. Its leaves are palmately divided into 5–7 linear to oblanceolate leaflets, ⅜–1⅝" long. The inflorescence is up to 3" long and has more or less whorled, blue (or rarely pink) pea flowers that are up to ⅜" long. The flower stalks are less than ⅛" long. The banner petal is longer than it is wide, and it has a white, often blue-speckled center that turns magenta to purple with age. The wing petals usually completely conceal the keel, which is ciliate on the upper margins near the pointed tip. The hairy pods are ½–1" long.

Flowering time: March–June

Habitat/range: Dry, open, grassy areas; chaparral/oak-woodland and mixed conifer zones; up to 5,200'.

Similar plants: Very similar Sky Lupine (*Lupinus nanus*) is also a low-elevation annual with blue petals and a white, usually speckled patch on the banner petal. The plant is generally more robust than Miniature Lupine, and its flower stalks can be more than ⅛" long. Its banner petal is as wide as or wider than it is long. The two plants can sometimes be difficult to tell apart with certainty. In its description of Miniature Lupine, the *Jepson eFlora* (2020) says that vigorous plants with larger flowers may be confused with *Lupinus nanus*.

BREWER'S LUPINE
Lupinus breweri var. *breweri*
Pea family (Fabaceae)

Description: This hairy, mat-forming, somewhat woody-based perennial has 1–6" long, sprawling stems that end in upward-turning inflorescences. The palmate, silvery-silky leaves are crowded and mostly basal but are also scattered along the stem. The leaves have 7–10 leaflets that are wider toward the tip and are ¼–¾" long or a tad longer. The flowers are up to ⅜" long and are in dense, head-like racemes that are up to 1¼" long. The petals are violet or blue, and the banner petal has a yellow or white center. The keel has no hairs on its upper or lower margins (which can require magnification to determine). The bract below each flower detaches early. The silky fruit pods are about ½" long.

Flowering time: June–August

Habitat/range: Dry, open or partially shaded areas, meadow borders; mixed conifer, montane, subalpine, and alpine zones; 5,500–11,000'.

Similar plants: Lobb's Tidy Lupine (*Lupinus lepidus* var. *lobbii*) is also a low-growing, hairy lupine with a head-like inflorescence, and it looks a lot like Brewer's Lupine. Most of its leaves, which can also be silvery-silky, are at the base of the plant and form somewhat of a tufted rosette rather than a mat. Its leaflets are ½" long or less, the bract below each flower is persistent, and its keel petal has ciliate hairs on the upper margin. Both plants are common in the park.

SHAGGY LUPINE
Lupinus covillei
Pea family (Fabaceae)

Description: This large perennial, up to 3' tall, has several erect, unbranched stems. Its herbage has long, soft, shaggy hairs or short, appressed hairs. The leaves, which are more numerous toward the top of the plant, are palmately divided into 5–9 linear to narrowly elliptic leaflets that are 1–4⅜" long and less than ½" wide. The inflorescences are 4–9" long and have scattered to loosely whorled pea flowers with pale blue, deep blue, or purple (rarely white) petals. The bracts in the inflorescences are linear, conspicuous, and remain in place when the flowers are mature. The upper keep margins are ciliate toward the tip. The woolly pea pods are up to 1½" long.

Flowering time: July–September

Habitat/range: Moist to wet areas; montane, subalpine, and alpine zones; 8,000–10,500'.

Similar plants: Shaggy Lupine is one of three relatively tall, high-elevation lupines that have hairy leaves with narrow leaflets that can be more than 3" long. Slender Lupine (*L. gracilentus*) is less common, and its inflorescences have thread-like, inconspicuous, deciduous bracts. Inyo Meadow Lupine (*L. pratensis* var. *pratensis*) is known from only two sites in the park in the vicinity of the Lyell Fork of the Tuolumne River. Its inflorescence bracts are conspicuous and persistent, but its flowers are so dense that they mostly hide the flower stalk.

GRAY'S LUPINE
Lupinus grayi
Pea family (Fabaceae)

Description: This attractive perennial has several reclining to erect stems, 7–14" long. Its leaves are mostly basal and are palmately divided into 5–11 oblanceolate leaflets, up to 1⅜" long. The leaves are so densely silver-hairy that they appear to be gray-green rather than green. The somewhat whorled inflorescence, 4–6½" long, has a tidy arrangement of pea flowers **[inset]**, ⅜–⅝" long, with pale bluish to lavender petals (sometimes white in recently burned places). The banner petal has a pale yellow center that turns reddish with age. The keel upper margins are densely hairy, and the lower margin is usually ciliate near the base (requiring magnification to see). The pods, up to 1⅜" long, are covered with stiff, appressed hairs.

Flowering time: May–July

Habitat/range: Dry forest openings; mixed conifer and montane zones; 3,400–7,000'.

Similar plants: Several other similar lupine species that grow in the mixed conifer and montane zones also have hairy leaves and a keel with hairs on the upper margin. Spurred Lupine (*Lupinus arbustus*) has mostly stem leaves, which are green rather than gray-green, and its upper calyx lip has a distinctive spur. All other similar lupine species that have both hairy leaves and a keel with hairs on the upper margin, also have flowers that are smaller, less than ⅜" long.

281

BROAD-LEAVED LUPINE

Lupinus latifolius var. *columbianus*
Pea family (Fabaceae)

Description: Broad-leaved Lupine is a robust perennial with erect stems, 1–4' tall, and herbage that's mostly hairless or sometimes has tiny, stiff, appressed hairs. Its leaves are palmately divided into 5–11 broadly oblanceolate, sparsely hairy or hairless leaflets that are 1½–4" long. The somewhat whorled Inflorescence is 6–18" long and has mostly uncrowded pea flowers that are up to ½" long and have blue to purple or pinkish petals. The keel has ciliate upper margins from the base to the middle (under magnification).

Flowering time: May–September

Habitat/range: Moist places along roads, streams, and meadows; mixed conifer, montane, subalpine, and alpine zones; 3,000–10,700'.

Similar plants: Broad-leaved Lupine and Large-leaved Lupine (*Lupinus polyphyllus* var. *burkei*) are the only tall lupines that grow at higher elevations *and* have mostly hairless leaves. Broad-leaved Lupine grows in moist places, and it typically has no leaflets that are more than 4" long. Large-leaved Lupine grows in wet places, often near streams, springs, or seeps; it has at least some leaflets that are more than 4" long, and they can get up to 6" long. To be certain, use magnification to check the upper keel margins. Broad-leaved Lupine has hairs on its upper keel margins. Large-leaved Lupine's keel has no hairs on the upper margins.

MEADOW TIDY LUPINE

Lupinus lepidus var. *confertus*
Pea family (Fabaceae)

Description: This perennial has reclining to erect stems that are up to 2' long. Its leaves are well distributed along the stem and are palmately divided into 5–8 leaflets that are sparsely silky-hairy and are up to 1⅝" long. The densely packed inflorescence is 2–12" long and has many flowers that are less than ⅜" long and have lavender to purple petals. The keel is ciliate on the upper margins (under magnification).

Flowering time: June–August

Habitat/range: Moist to wet areas; mixed conifer and montane zones; 3,800–7,600'.

Similar plants: This is one of five perennial lupines in the park that have reclining to erect stems, that have keel petals that are ciliate on the upper margins, and that have distinctly hairy leaves with leaflets that are less than 2½" long. Donner Lake Tidy Lupine (*L. lepidus* var. *sellulus*) also has an elongated, densely packed inflorescence, but its leaves are mostly basal and it grows in dry places. Branched Tidy Lupine (*L. lepidus* var. *ramosus*) has an open inflorescence and its leaves are long-shaggy-hairy. Small-flowered Lupine (*L. argenteus* var. *meionanthus*) also has an open inflorescence, but its leaves have appressed, silvery hairs. Gray's Lupine (*L. grayi*) has flowers that are ⅜–⅝" long. The other lupines in this group have flowers that are less than ⅜" long.

PARASOL CLOVER
Trifolium bolanderi
Pea family (Fabaceae)

Description: Parasol Clover is a hairless perennial with several ascending stems, 3–8" long, that are branched from the base. Its mostly basal, palmate leaves have 3 elliptic to obovate, finely toothed leaflets, up to ⅝" long, that are often notched at the tip. The flower head grows at the end of an unusually long stalk, 2⅜–6" long, and has no whorl of bracts (involucre) beneath it. The 10–20 narrow, drooping pea flowers are up to ½" long and have a dark purple or black calyx with 5 lanceolate, unequal lobes and a lavender to pale pink corolla.

Flowering time: June–July

Habitat/range: Moist or wet meadows; montane zone; 6,800–7,500'.

Comments: This rare clover is known only from montane meadows in Mariposa, Madera, and Fresno counties. In Yosemite, it grows mostly in meadows along Glacier Point Road.

Similar plants: Tree Clover (*Trifolium ciliolatum*) also has an unusually long flower stalk, about the same length as Parasol Clover's. It also has no whorl of bracts under its flower head, but its flowers are erect at maturity and begin to droop only with age. Tree Clover grows in dry, grassy places below 5,600' and has been reported near the Mather area and within the park's western boundary in the El Portal area.

CLAMMY CLOVER
Trifolium obtusiflorum
Pea family (Fabaceae)

Description: Clammy Clover is a robust annual with an ascending to erect stem, 11–20" long, that's branched below. Its glandular-hairy herbage feels wet and sometimes sticky. The palmate leaves have 3 narrowly elliptic, sharply toothed leaflets. The somewhat rounded flower head is ¾–1¼" wide and has a wheel-shaped involucre with irregular, sharp teeth. The flowers have a glandular-hairy calyx with a yellowish-green tube and 5 green, needle-like teeth. The corolla is up to ¾" long, is pale lavender or white, and has a dark magenta to purple spot in the central part of the banner petal.

Flowering time: April–July

Habitat/range: Moist, grassy or marshy areas and gravel bars; chaparral/oak-woodland and mixed conifer zones; up to 5,900'.

Comments: Clammy Clover exudes a dew-like, acidic liquid that makes the plant feel wet to the touch. Native Americans ate the plants raw but usually rinsed off the acidic substance first. This plant has a wheel-shaped whorl of united bracts, called an involucre, just below the flowers. Many clovers have such bracts but others don't, and the presence or lack of the bracts is often used to distinguish species. The involucre can be made up of separate bracts or it can have bracts united into a bowl or bell shape or a flat, wheel shape. The bracts have various sorts of irregular teeth.

283

WHITE-TIPPED CLOVER, VARIEGATED CLOVER

Trifolium variegatum var. *geminiflorum*
Pea family (Fabaceae)

Description: This mostly hairless annual has sprawling to erect stems, ½–12" long. Its palmate leaves have 3 wedge-shaped leaflets, less than ⅜" long, with elongated, bristly teeth. The inflorescence has 1–5 tubular flowers and an irregularly toothed, wheel-shaped involucre (whorl of bracts) at the base. The calyx has 5 lobes with sharp tips that are often dark purple-black. The distinctive corollas are up to ⅜" long, are lavender, magenta, or purple, and have white tips.

Flowering time: April–July

Habitat/range: Dry, open, grassy slopes and disturbed areas; chaparral/oak-woodland, mixed conifer, and montane zones; up to 8,000'.

Comments: The name *variegatum* refers to the variability of plants in the species. This plant's variety, *geminiflorum*, is Latin for twin flowers, probably because the inflorescences often have only a pair of flowers. The *Jepson eFlora* (2020) reports that the clover has about 30 named entities and suggests that molecular research is needed.

Similar plants: With its mostly hairless herbage and tidy, white-tipped flowers, this plant is fairly easy to recognize. Another variety of the clover has been reported at Ackerson Meadow and at Hetch Hetchy, var. *variegatum*. It's quite similar in most respects, but its inflorescences have 5–10 flowers.

TOMCAT CLOVER

Trifolium willdenovii
Pea family (Fabaceae)

Description: Tomcat Clover is a small to robust, hairless annual with a sprawling to erect stem that's 8–20" long and is sometimes branched at the base. Its palmate leaves have 3 linear to narrowly oblong leaflets, up to 2" long, with short, bristly teeth and a pointed tip. Its flower head is broader than it is tall, and the wheel-shaped whorl of bracts (involucre) beneath the flower head is irregularly, sharply toothed or lobed. The flowers have a shiny, 5-lobed calyx, which is often cream colored with brilliant reddish stripes. The corolla is up to ⅝" long and has a lavender banner petal. The lavender to magenta wing petals have a white tip and a dark spot in the center.

Flowering time: March–June

Habitat/range: Open, grassy areas with spring moisture; chaparral/oak-woodland and mixed conifer zones; up to 4,500'.

Comments: Clovers typically have leaves with 3 leaflets, but if you're lucky, you might find a 4-leaf clover, or more accurately a 4-leaflet clover. For some reason, luck has become associated with clovers. The shamrock of Irish lore isn't a particular species, and the name shamrock simply means little clover. When the Irish haggle over what plant is the true shamrock, it comes down to a contest between three species of clover and one species of medick (*Medicago* genus).

AMERICAN VETCH

Vicia americana ssp. *americana*
Pea family (Fabaceae)

Description: American Vetch is a sparsely hairy or hairless perennial with a stem, up to 3¼' long, that can be short and erect or sprawling or climbing. Its pinnate leaves have 8–16 leaflets and are usually tipped with a branched tendril. The widely elliptic, oval, or oblong leaflets are up to 1⅜" long, are rounded or truncate at the tip, and often have small teeth. The inflorescences have 3–9 flowers, up to 1" long. The upper 2 teeth of the calyx are shorter than the lower 3. The lavender, magenta, or purple corolla turns blue with age. The pods are up to 1½" long and look like culinary snow peas.

Flowering time: March–June

Habitat/range: Open areas; chaparral/oak-woodland and mixed conifer zones; up to 6,000'.

Similar plants: American Vetch has flower stalks with 3–9 flowers. Non-native Spring Vetch (*V. sativa* ssp. *nigra*) **[upper inset]** has 1–3 flowers per flower stalk. Non-native Purple Vetch (*V. benghalensis*) **[lower inset]** has 3–12 crowded flowers and differs from the other two vetches in that its flowers are pendant and their banner petal is less erect. Lanszwert's Pea (*Lathyrus lanszwertii*) and Sierra Nevada Pea (*Lathyrus nevadensis*) are similar, but they have no more than 10 leaflets. American Vetch almost always has some leaves with more than 10 leaflets, but, if in doubt, check the style (page 198).

EXPLORER'S GENTIAN

Gentiana calycosa
Gentian family (Gentianaceae)

Description: This attractive, hairless perennial usually has several ascending stems that are 4–18" long. Its opposite, glossy green stem leaves are up to 2" long and are ovate to more or less round. At the end of the stem, 1–3 flowers grow above a pair of leafy green bracts. Flowers can also grow from the upper leaf axils. The narrowly bell-shaped calyx has 5 unequal, narrow to widely ovate lobes. The deep blue or violet, bell-shaped corolla is 1–2" long and has 5 broad lobes with whitish dots inside. The appendages between the petal lobes are divided into 2 or 3 triangular segments that are thread-like at the tip.

Flowering time: July–September

Habitat/range: Wet meadows and streambanks; montane zone; 7,000–8,000'.

Comments: This plant is rare in the park and has been reported in only two locations, along Sentinel Creek near Sentinel Dome and along Tenaya Creek below Tenaya Lake.

Similar plants: Explorer's Gentian looks something like Sierra Gentian (*Gentianopsis holopetala*) and Hiker's Gentian (*Gentianopsis simplex*), but those two gentians have corollas with 4 lobes and Explorer's Gentian has 5-lobed corollas.

NORTHERN GENTIAN

Gentianella amarella ssp. *acuta*
Gentian family (Gentianaceae)

Description: Northern Gentian is a slender, delicate annual with ascending, usually branched stems that are up to 16" long. The lanceolate to ovate leaves, ½–1" long, grow at the base of the plant and in opposite pairs along the stem. The small flowers, which grow in crowded clusters from the leaf axils and at the branch ends, have 4 or 5 long, narrow, pointed-tipped sepals. The tubular, pale lavender to purple corolla is ¼–⅝" long and has 4 or 5 spreading, lanceolate lobes and a ring of fringe in its throat **[left inset]**.

Flowering time: July–September

Habitat/range: Wet meadows, seeps, and bogs; subalpine and alpine zones; 8,200–11,000'.

Comments: The few small annuals that live in the Sierra Nevada alpine zone may be descendants of plants that survived the last ice age because the peaks where they grew stood like islands above the surrounding glacial ice sheets.

Similar plants: Dane's Dwarf Gentian (*Comastoma tenellum*, previously *Gentianella tenella* ssp. *tenella*) **[right inset]** is another delicate, high-elevation annual with opposite leaves. Its small flowers, which look much like Northern Gentian's flowers, are pale violet-blue to white, but they grow solitary on slender stalks rather than in clusters and they always have only 4 petals.

SIERRA GENTIAN

Gentianopsis holopetala
Gentian family (Gentianaceae)

Description: This hairless annual has an ascending to erect stem, 1½–10" tall. The stem is usually branched at the base, but the branches look more like individual stems. The crowded lower leaves are obovate or spoon shaped, and 1 or 2 opposite pairs of slightly smaller, linear-oblong leaves grow on the stem. The flowers are solitary at the stem or branch ends. The partially fused calyx has 4 lanceolate, pointed lobes and often has a dark midvein along the length of each sepal. The trumpet-shaped corolla is ¾–1¼" long and has 4 deep blue or violet lobes with rounded tips that sometimes have tiny, wavy teeth. The outside of the corolla tube usually has longitudinal stripes that match the color of the petal lobes.

Flowering time: July–September

Habitat/range: Wet meadows; montane, subalpine, and alpine zones; 7,000–11,000'.

Similar plants: Hiker's Gentian (*Gentianopsis simplex*) has a solitary, unbranched stem and has only one flower per plant; its blue to violet corolla also has 4 lobes, but the lobes are distinctly sharp toothed. Explorer's Gentian (*Gentiana calycosa*) has similar flowers, but their corollas have 5 lobes.

HIKER'S GENTIAN
Gentianopsis simplex
Gentian family (Gentianaceae)

Description: Hiker's Gentian is a slender, hairless annual with a single erect, unbranched stem that's 2–16" tall. The spoon-shaped, clasping basal and lower stem leaves wither early. The opposite upper stem leaves, up to 1" long, are broadly to narrowly lanceolate with a rounded or pointed tip. Each plant has a solitary flower at the end of the stem. The calyx has 4 long, lanceolate lobes that are pointed at the tip. The blue or violet, tubular corolla, ¾–1¾" long, has 4 long, spreading, sometimes overlapping lobes that are usually somewhat twisted and have irregular, sharp teeth on the margins.

Flowering time: July–September

Habitat/range: Wet meadows; montane and subalpine zones; 6,500–8,500'.

Comments: Alpine gentian species grow in the Alps, in the Andes, in the higher elevations of Australia and New Zealand, and in the Himalayas, where one gentian species grows on the slopes of Mount Everest at 18,000'. Antarctica is the only continent where gentians don't grow.

Similar plants: Sierra Gentian (*Gentianopsis holopetala*) has more than 1 flower stalk per plant, and its petal lobes typically have smooth margins, though they sometimes have tiny, wavy teeth. Explorer's Gentian (*Gentiana calycosa*) has flowers with 5 petals.

STAR GENTIAN
Swertia perennis
Gentian family (Gentianaceae)

Description: This hairless perennial usually has a single slender, unbranched stem, 4–20" tall. Its basal leaves, 1–6" long, are spoon shaped to obovate. The smaller, opposite or alternate, sessile stem leaves are widely lanceolate to somewhat oval. The flowers grow in elongated panicles at the top of the stem. The calyx is fused at the base and has 5 narrow lobes with pointed tips. The corolla is ¼–½" long and is also fused at the base. It has 5 (rarely 4) lanceolate to oblong, blue to violet lobes with conspicuous veins. Each corolla lobe has a pair of round nectar pits near the base.

Flowering time: July–September

Habitat/range: Wet meadows and bogs; subalpine and alpine zones; 8,200–10,500'.

Comments: Star Gentian is a circumboreal plant, growing around the world in the Northern Hemisphere. It often goes unnoticed because it's usually camouflaged by other tall plants. The plant has been reported to grow along the Lyell Fork of the Merced River, along Echo Creek, and near Isberg Pass. However, the plant has not been documented in the park. If you find Star Gentian in Yosemite, please report it to yose_web_manager@nps.gov and provide precise location information.

LONG-BEAKED STORKSBILL
(non-native)
Erodium botrys
Geranium family (Geraniaceae)

Description: This European native is a short-hairy annual with reclining to ascending stems, up to 3' long, and opposite leaves. Its shallowly to deeply lobed lower leaves are 1½–6" long. The flowers have 5 hairy, lanceolate sepals and 5 stamens. The 5 pink to purple, obovate, dark-veined petals are up to ⅝" long, and they overlap at the bases. The fruit, which is 3¾–5" long, is a 5-parted fruit body with 5 elongated styles (the stork's bill).

Flowering time: March–June

Habitat/range: Disturbed areas; chaparral/oak-woodland and mixed conifer zones; up to 4,000'.

Similar plants: Four *Erodium* species have been reported in the park, all of them non-native. Long-beaked Storksbill and Short-beaked Storksbill (*E. brachycarpum*) have petals that overlap at the bases. Short-beaked Storksbill's fruit is less than 3¼" long. The other two species, Red-stemmed Storksbill (*E. cicutarium*) **[inset]** and Green-stemmed Storksbill (*E. moschatum*) have petals that do not overlap at the bases. Red-stemmed Storksbill's sepal tips have 1 or more bristles, and its stems and flower stalks are usually reddish. Green-stemmed Storksbill's sepal tips can have hairs but not bristles, and its stems and flower stalks are usually green. *Geranium* species are similar, but they have 10 stamens rather than 5.

CUT-LEAVED GERANIUM
(non-native)
Geranium dissectum
Geranium family (Geraniaceae)

Description: This weedy annual has branched stems, 8–24" long, and glandular-hairy herbage. The blades of its long-petioled leaves are deeply palmately divided into 5–7 parts, which are again divided into smaller, usually linear segments. The flower stalks have 1 or 2 flowers with 10 stamens and 5 lanceolate sepals tipped with a prong-like appendage. The 5 lavender to purple petals are less than ¼" long and are sometimes notched. The 5-parted fruit, a little less than ½" long, has 5 united styles. The spreading hairs on the fruit are usually gland tipped and are less than ¹⁄₁₆ long.

Flowering time: March–July

Habitat/range: Disturbed areas; chaparral/oak-woodland and mixed conifer zones; up to 4,200'.

Similar plants: Cut-leaved Geranium is one of four annual *Geranium* species that have been reported in the park. Non-native Robert's Geranium (*G. robertianum*) is the only one with compound leaves that are twice pinnately divided. The leaves of non-native Dove's-foot Geranium (*G. molle*) are distinctly round in outline and are not deeply lobed, and it's the only one of the four with sepals that have no appendages at the tip. The fruit of native Carolina Geranium (*G. carolinianum*) has ascending hairs with no glands, and at least some of the hairs are more than ¹⁄₁₆" long.

RICHARDSON'S GERANIUM
Geranium richardsonii
Geranium family (Geraniaceae)

Description: Richardson's Geranium is a perennial
with erect, more or less soft-hairy stems, 6–35"
long, and opposite leaves that are 1¾–5" wide.
The larger leaf blades are deeply palmately divided
into 5–7 parts that are diamond shaped in outline
and that are again divided into smaller segments.
The flower stalks have hairs tipped with red or
purple glands. The flowers, which are 1⅛–1⅝"
wide, have 5 lanceolate, bristle-tipped sepals and
5 rounded, lavender-tinged to white petals with
purplish veins. The flowers are densely soft-hairy
in the center, and they have 10 stamens when
fully mature. The fruit is a 5-parted fruit body with
5 united styles, together less than 1" long. The
stigma on each style is less than ³⁄₁₆" long.

Flowering time: June–August

Habitat/range: Moist areas; mixed conifer, montane, and subalpine zones; 3,900–9,000'.

Similar plants: The flower stalks of perennial
California Geranium (*Geranium californicum*)
have hairs tipped with white or yellow glands.
Its leaf segments are wedge shaped in outline,
its flowers are less than 1¼" wide, and its stigmas
are more than ³⁄₁₆" long. Magnification might be
required to see the color of the glands. These
two perennial geraniums have a wheel-shaped or
shallow saucer-shaped corolla. The park's annual
geraniums have a cup-shaped to broadly funnel-
shaped corolla.

WESTERN BLUE FLAG
Iris missouriensis
Iris family (Iridaceae)

Description: Western Blue Flag is a hairless
perennial, 8–20" tall, with a single rarely branched
stem that ends with 1 or 2 showy flowers. Its
linear basal leaves are about ⅓" wide, are pointed
at the tip, and sometimes have a waxy coating
that rubs off. The flowers are various shades of
blue, bluish purple, purple, lavender, or white. The
spreading, spatula-shaped sepals, which are the
outer 3 petal-like parts, are 1½–2¾" long, are paler
than the petals, and have prominent, contrasting
veins. The 3 shorter, narrower, ascending to erect
petals grow alternate the sepals. The 3 petal-like
style branches are upturned and notched at the tip
and have a stigma on the lower surface, just below
the notch. Each style branch arches over a sepal,
and a stamen is hidden between them.

Flowering time: May–July

Habitat/range: Wet meadows, streambanks, and
drainages; chaparral/oak-woodland, mixed conifer,
montane, and subalpine zones; up to 11,000'.

Similar plants: Western Blue Flag grows in moist
to wet places, often in colonies. Hartweg's Iris
(*Iris hartwegii*) usually has yellow, cream-colored,
or white flowers, but the flowers can be blue or
purple. It grows alone or in small groups in dry forest openings. So, if you find an iris in the park with
pine needles nearby, it's likely to be Hartweg's Iris,
no matter what color its flowers are.

IDAHO BLUE-EYED GRASS

Sisyrinchium idahoense var. *occidentale*
Iris family (Iridaceae)

Description: This hairless perennial is 4–17" tall and has a flattened, winged, unbranched stem. Its linear, grass-like leaves are sheathed and overlapping at the base, are shorter than the stem, and are mostly basal, though the stem does have a pair of leaf-like bracts below the inflorescence. Each plant has 1 few-flowered inflorescence, which often has only a single flower in full bloom at a time. The flowers are yellow in the center and have 6 blue to bluish-violet (occasionally white) tepals that are about ½" long. The 3 outer tepals are broader than the 3 inner tepals, and the tepals usually have a notched tip with a short needle-like projection. The flowers have 6 stamens with yellow anthers.

Flowering time: May–August

Habitat/range: Open, moist, grassy areas; mixed conifer, montane, and subalpine zones; 3,000–9,500'.

Similar plants: The flowers of Western Blue-eyed Grass (*Sisyrinchium bellum*) look almost identical to those of Idaho Blue-eyed Grass, and both plants grow in moist, grassy habitats. However, Western Blue-eyed Grass, which grows only in the mixed conifer zone in the park, has a branched, leafy stem and has 2 or more inflorescences per plant. Idaho Blue-eyed Grass has only 1 inflorescence per plant.

CANADA MINT

Mentha canadensis (*M. arvensis* var. *canadensis*)
Mint family (Lamiaceae)

Description: Canada Mint is a peppermint-scented perennial that's 4–23" tall and has ascending to erect, square stems that are branched and leafy. Its herbage is smooth to densely hairy. The opposite, short-petioled leaves are ½–2" long, are linear to lanceolate, and have a pointed tip and toothed margins. The flowers are up to ¼" long and grow in dense, well-separated whorls in the leaf axils. The calyx has 5 triangular lobes. The corolla is up to ¼" long and is pale lavender, pale violet, or white. Although the corolla is 2 lipped, it looks as though it has 4 lobes, with a notched upper lobe. The 4 stamens extend well beyond the corolla.

Flowering time: July–October

Habitat/range: Damp to wet areas; chaparral/oak-woodland and mixed conifer zones; up to 5,000'.

Similar plants: Spearmint (*Mentha spicata*), a European native that has become naturalized in California, also grows in wet habitats. It's also aromatic and has similar pale lavender to white flowers, but its flowers grow in dense, elongated spikes at the stem or branch ends. Northern Bugle-weed (*Lycopus uniflorus*) is a native that grows in wet places. Like Canada Mint, its flowers grow in dense, well-separated whorls in the leaf axils, but its flowers are always white and have only 2 visible stamens. All three plants have been reported from Yosemite Valley meadows.

PURPLE MOUNTAIN PENNYROYAL

Monardella odoratissima ssp. *glauca* (*M. glauca*)
Mint family (Lamiaceae)

Description: This aromatic, leafy subshrub, 6–14"
tall, is slightly woody at the base and has stems
and branches that often look somewhat powdery.
Its lanceolate to oblong leaves, ½–1½" long, are
usually distinctly short-hairy, but they can also be
hairless. The stem is leafy throughout, even when
the plant is in full bloom. The purplish, overlapping
bracts under each flower head are ovate to round,
and they taper abruptly to a small, narrow pointed
tip. The flowers, up to ¾" long, have purple-tipped
sepals, a 2-lipped, lavender to purple corolla, and 4
stamens that extend beyond the corolla lobes and
match the color of the corollas.

Flowering time: June–August

Habitat/range: Dry, sandy areas; mixed conifer,
montane, and subalpine zones; 4,000–10,500'.

Similar plants: The park has two other *Monardella*
species with purplish flowers. Mustang Mint (*M.
breweri* ssp. *lanceolata*, previously *M. lanceolata*)
is an annual with a single stem, and its lower
leaves are mostly withered by the time the plant
is in bloom. The mostly green bracts beneath its
flower heads are broadly lanceolate and taper
gradually rather than abruptly to a pointed tip.
Coyote Mint (*M. sheltonii*) has green rather than
purplish bracts beneath its flower heads, and
several of the middle bracts bend conspicuously
downward.

LANCE-LEAVED SELF-HEAL

Prunella vulgaris var. *lanceolata*
Mint family (Lamiaceae)

Description: This common perennial has short-
hairy herbage and 1 or more reclining to erect,
square stems that are 4–20" long. Its opposite,
ovate, elliptic, or lanceolate leaves are 1–4" long
and are sometimes irregularly toothed along
the margins. The flowers grow in a club-like,
somewhat square head at the end of the stem.
The 2-lipped calyx is green or purple-maroon. The
2-lipped corolla, up to ⅝" long, is finely hairy inside
and is lavender to blue-violet (sometimes pink or
white). Its upper lip forms a hood above 4 stamens,
and the reflexed lower lip has 3 lobes, 2 rounded
lateral lobes and a finely toothed middle lobe.

Flowering time: March–September

Habitat/range: Moist, shady or open areas; mixed
conifer and montane zones; 3,400–7,500'.

Similar plants: Two non-native mint family plants
have similar flowers. Unlike Lance-leaved Self-
heal, they have round to kidney-shaped leaves
with scalloped margins. Common Henbit or Giraffe
Head (*Lamium amplexicaule*) **[left inset]** has flowers that grow at the stem end *and* from leaf axils.
The flowers of Ground Ivy (*Glechoma hederacea*)
[right inset] grow only in the leaf axils, and it has
creeping stems. Clasping Henbit grows near the
park's western boundary and may grow in the park.
Ground Ivy grows in meadows around Yosemite
Village and possibly elsewhere.

DANNY'S SKULLCAP

Scutellaria tuberosa
Mint family (Lamiaceae)

Description: This attractive little perennial has a reclining or weakly erect stem, 2–9" long, that's usually branched from the base and is covered with spreading hairs. The opposite, thin, ovate leaves, up to ¾" long, are coarsely scalloped or toothed and are either mostly hairless or have soft, spreading hairs on both surfaces. The upper leaves are mostly sessile. The flowers grow solitary from the leaf axils, often in pairs from the axils of opposite leaves. The 2-lipped calyx has a ridge-like appendage on the upper lip. The blue to purple, 2-lipped, tubular corolla is ½–¾" long. It has a smaller, hood-like upper lip and a larger, 3-lobed lower lip with a white patch or mottling in the center.

Flowering time: March–July

Habitat/range: Dry, grassy areas; chaparral/oak-woodland zone; up to 5,400'.

Similar plants: Somewhat similar Grayleaf Skullcap (*S. siphocampyloides*) **[left inset]** has a blue or purple corolla that's longer, 1–1⅜" long, and its leaves are linear-oblong and densely glandular-hairy. Danny's Skullcap and Grayleaf Skullcap grow around the western park boundary, and Danny's Skullcap was collected near Wawona. Sierra Skullcap (*S. bolanderi* ssp. *bolanderi*) **[right inset]** resembles the other two skullcaps, but its flowers are mostly white and it's known to grow in the park only in Wawona Meadow.

VINEGAR WEED

Trichostema lanceolatum
Mint family (Lamiaceae)

Description: Vinegar Weed is a strong-scented, erect annual, 3–22" tall, with a stem that branches from the base. Its herbage is covered with long, soft, spreading hairs, mixed with short, glandular hairs. The opposite, lanceolate leaves are ¾–3" long, are mostly sessile, and are narrow (acute) at the tip. The intricate flowers, which grow from leaf axils, have a bell-shaped calyx with 5 triangular lobes. The upper lip of the blue to blue-violet corolla has 2 spreading, deeply divided lobes. The lower lip has 3 deeply divided, oblong lobes. The strongly arched style and stamens are at least ½" long and ascend between the upper corolla lobes.

Flowering time: June–October

Habitat/range: Dry, open, usually sparsely veg-etated, disturbed areas; chaparral/oak-woodland and mixed conifer zones; up to 5,000'.

Comments: These plants smell more like turpen-tine than vinegar, and you don't have to crush a leaf to smell it. Just barely touch a leaf with a finger and take a careful whiff.

Similar plants: The leaves of Mountain Blue-curls (*Trichostema oblongum*), which are also glandular-hairy and highly aromatic, are more rounded and have a broad (obtuse) tip. Their flowers **[inset]** are like miniature versions of Vinegar Weed's flowers, with stamens that are ¼" long or less.

WESTERN BLUE FLAX
Linum lewisii var. *lewisii*
Flax family (Linaceae)

Description: This hairless perennial has several erect, leafy stems that are 2–30" long and are often branched at the base. Its sessile, mostly alternate leaves are ½–¾" long, are linear to lanceolate or narrowly oblanceolate, and taper to a narrow, pointed tip. The wheel-shaped flowers grow in open, sometimes 1-sided clusters. The 5 ovate sepals have smooth, translucent edges, and the outer 3 sepals overlap the inner 2. The 5 obovate, blue to purplish-blue (rarely white) petals, up to ⅝" long, are greenish or greenish yellow in the center and are often shed in the warmer temperatures of the afternoon. The fruit is a small, round capsule.

Flowering time: May–September

Habitat/range: Dry, open, rocky slopes and flats; chaparral/oak-woodland, mixed conifer, montane, subalpine, and alpine zones; up to 11,000'.

Comments: This plant is common throughout the western states. Native Americans used the stems of the plant to make cordage, mats, snowshoes, fishing nets, and baskets. Linen fibers and linseed oil come from Common Flax (*Linum usitatissimum*), a plant that's native to Eurasia and doesn't grow in the park. Common Flax seeds contain nutrients that have many recognized health benefits, and they're sold whole or ground in markets, large and small, throughout the United States.

NAKED BROOMRAPE
Aphyllon purpureum (*Orobanche uniflora*)
Broomrape family (Orobanchaceae)

Description: Naked Broomrape is a glandular-hairy plant that has no chlorophyll and is completely parasitic on other plants. Its stem, up to 2" long, is mostly underground. The tubular flowers are usually solitary (or 1–3) on a delicate stalk, 1–5" long. The calyx is deeply divided into 5 narrow, pointed lobes. The 2-lipped, arching corolla is pale to dark purple (sometimes yellowish or white) with darker veins, and the throat is yellow at the base. The corolla has rounded, more or less spreading lobes that are shorter than the tube. The upper lip usually has 2 lobes (sometimes 3), and the lower lip has 3 lobes.

Flowering time: April–August

Habitat/range: Moist, shaded or open places; chaparral/oak-woodland and mixed conifer zones; up to 7,000'.

Comments: Naked Broomrape often grows on wet, rocky, north-facing slopes, where it parasitizes mostly plants in the stonecrop (*Sedum*) genus. The plant also grows in open areas or on forest floors, where its hosts are usually members of the saxifrage family or the sunflower family. The leaf rosettes in the photo belong to Broad-leaved Stonecrop plants (*Sedum spathulifolium*), which are being robbed of nutrients.

SMALL-FLOWERED BLUE-EYED MARY
Collinsia parviflora
Plantain family (Plantaginaceae)

Description: This dainty annual has an ascending to erect stem that's 1–16" long. Its opposite, hairless leaves, up to 1½" long, are oblong-lanceolate. The open, leafy inflorescences are not hairy but are sometimes sparsely glandular. The tiny flowers grow 1 or 2 in the upper leaf axils. The calyx has 5 narrow, sharply pointed lobes. The 2-lipped corolla has a white tube and throat and an angular pouch that's somewhat hidden by the calyx. The upper lip has 2 oblong, ascending to erect lobes that are blue tipped or whitish. The lower lip has 2 blue, oblong, spreading outer lobes and a smaller, keel-shaped central lobe that encloses the stamens and the style.

Flowering time: April–August

Habitat/range: Moist, shady places; mixed conifer, montane, subalpine, and alpine zones; 3,000–11,500'.

Similar plants: Several similar *Collinsia* species grow in the park, but they all have glandular-hairy inflorescences and somewhat blunt-tipped calyx lobes, and the pouch on the top of their corollas is not mostly hidden by the calyx. False Pimpernel (*Lindernia dubia*) **[insets]** is similar, but the central lobe on its lower corolla lip is essentially identical to the 2 lateral lobes rather than being keel shaped. The plant is much less common and has been reported in Yosemite Valley and around Mather.

TORREY'S BLUE-EYED MARY
Collinsia torreyi var. *torreyi*
Plantain family (Plantaginaceae)

Description: This small annual has a spreading, branched, glandular-hairy stem that's 2–8" long. Its opposite, broadly linear to oblong leaves are ½–1½" long, are sessile or short-petioled, and sometimes have tiny teeth along the margins. The flowers are in loose, glandular-hairy whorls toward the stem and branch ends. The 5-lobed calyx has somewhat blunt tips. The 2-lobed, erect upper lip of the corolla is mostly white, and the blue or purplish-blue lower lip has 2 lateral lobes that hide the lower, keel-shaped lobe. At least some of the corollas are more than ¼" long.

Flowering time: April–August

Habitat/range: Dry, sandy areas; mixed conifer, montane, and subalpine zones; 3,400–9,000'.

Similar plants: Very similar Wright's Blue-eyed Mary (*C. torreyi* var. *wrightii*) has no corollas that are more than ¼" long. The upper and lower corolla lips of much less common Child's Blue-eyed Mary (*C. childii*) are essentially the same color, either white, pale lavender, or pale blue. Narrow-leaved Blue-eyed Mary (*C. linearis*) also has a corolla with a blue to purple lower lip and a white upper lip, but its corolla is up to ½" long. The inflorescences of Small-flowered Blue-eyed Mary (*C. parviflora*) can be slightly glandular, but they have no hairs, and it's the only species in this group with calyx lobes that are sharply pointed.

DAVIDSON'S PENSTEMON

Penstemon davidsonii var. *davidsonii*
Plantain family (Plantaginaceae)

Description: Davidson's Penstemon is an attractive, somewhat shrubby, mat-forming perennial, up to 4" tall, with woody, short-hairy stems and crowded leaves. Its thick, opposite, mostly basal leaves, up to 1³⁄₁₆" long, are elliptic to round, short-petioled, and often gland-dotted. The glandular-hairy inflorescence is a few-flowered raceme. The red-purplish calyx has 5 narrow lobes. The 2-lipped corolla, ¾–1³⁄₈" long, has an inflated tube and can be pale blue, lavender, blue-violet, blue-purple, or magenta. The 2-lobed upper lip is spreading to erect, and the 3-lobed lower lip is mostly spreading and is densely long-hairy along the ridges in the throat **[inset]**. The stamens and style are mostly concealed inside the corolla.

Flowering time: July–August

Habitat/range: Rocky slopes and flats; subalpine and alpine zones; 9,000–12,500'.

Similar plants: Showy Penstemon (*Penstemon speciosus*) is a similar showy penstemon that grows at subalpine and alpine elevations, and it has been reported to grow in the park. Its corollas can exhibit the same impressive color variation as Davidson's Penstemon, but they can also be royal blue or sky blue. Its inflorescences are sometimes slightly hairy, but they're not glandular and its corollas are hairless inside and out.

SIERRA PENSTEMON

Penstemon heterodoxus var. *heterodoxus*
Plantain family (Plantaginaceae)

Description: Sierra Penstemon is a common perennial with ascending to erect stems, 2–10" long. Its thin, hairless leaves, ½–2" long, form a basal rosette and are opposite on the stem. The short-petioled basal leaves are linear-oblanceolate to spatula shaped, and the sessile or clasping stem leaves are oblanceolate or lanceolate. The glandular inflorescence has 1–4 somewhat dense whorls of flowers that are ³⁄₈–⁵⁄₈" long. The calyx has 5 pointed lobes. The 2-lipped, tubular corolla is blue-purple, but the buds and tubes are often magenta to deep purple. The 2-lobed upper lip is spreading to ascending, and the 3-lobed, slightly longer lower lip arches downward.

Flowering time: July–August

Habitat/range: Dry, open meadows and rocky areas; montane, subalpine, and alpine zones; 7,500–12,500'.

Similar plants: Only two other penstemons in the park have distinctly whorled inflorescences, but their inflorescences are hairless and have no glands. Meadow Penstemon (*P. rydbergii* var. *oreocharis*) grows in Yosemite Valley and ranges up into the subalpine zone. Its corollas extend straight outward and are ³⁄₈–⁹⁄₁₆" long. Pincushion Penstemon (*P. procerus* var. *formosus*) grows in the subalpine and alpine zones. Its corollas bend at least slightly downward and are ¼–³⁄₈" long.

295

MOUNTAIN BLUE PENSTEMON

Penstemon laetus var. *laetus*
Plantain family (Plantaginaceae)

Description: This common perennial has ascending to erect stems that are 7–31" long and are branched below. Its opposite leaves are ½–10" long. The lower leaves are linear to oblanceolate and taper to a petiole. The lanceolate upper leaves are sessile. The inflorescences are conspicuously glandular-hairy. The calyx has 5 widely lanceolate, spreading lobes. The 2-lipped, tubular corolla **[inset]** is ⅞–1⅜" long. The narrow base of the corolla is usually magenta, the expanded portion is usually blue or blue-lavender, and the spreading lobes are deep blue or purple-blue. The lower lip has 2 narrow, oblong, white nectar guides.

Flowering time: May–July

Habitat/range: Dry places, gravelly slopes and flats and roadsides; chaparral/oak-woodland, mixed conifer, and montane zones; up to 7,000'.

Similar plants: Three similar penstemons have been reported in the park. Roezli's Penstemon (*P. roezlii*) also has a glandular-hairy inflorescence, but its corollas are smaller, ½–⅞" long. The other two penstemons, which have rarely been reported in the park, have inflorescences that have no hairs or glands. Azure Penstemon (*P. azureus* var. *angustissimus*) has leaves that are broadest at the base and often clasp the stem. Foothill Penstemon (*P. heterophyllus* var. *purdyi*) has leaves that taper to a narrow base.

AMERICAN SPEEDWELL

Veronica americana
Plantain family (Plantaginaceae)

Description: American Speedwell is a fairly robust, hairless perennial with shallow rhizomes and creeping stems, up to 40" long. Its opposite, lanceolate to ovate leaves, up to 3½" long, have fine teeth along the margins, and the lower leaves have a short, but distinct petiole. The flowers, ¼–⅜" wide, are in elongated racemes that grow opposite each other from the upper leaf axils. The flowers have 4 sepals, 2 stamens, and 1 style. The violet-blue to lilac corollas have a lower lobe that is noticeably narrower than the other 3 lobes.

Flowering time: May–August

Habitat/range: Moist to wet soil, slow streams and meadows; mixed conifer, montane, and subalpine zones; 3,200–8,200'.

Similar plants: American Speedwell is one of three *Veronica* species in the park with a stem that does not end in a raceme of flowers. Instead they have open, elongated racemes that grow from leaf axils. Water Speedwell (*V. anagallis-aquatica*) and Marsh Speedwell (*V. scutellata*) are the other two species. Water Speedwell, a European native that has become naturalized in North America, also has inflorescences that grow *opposite* each other from leaf axils, but none of its leaves have a petiole. Marsh Speedwell is a native and has inflorescences that grow *alternate* in the leaf axils, with only a single inflorescence per leaf pair.

CORN SPEEDWELL

(non-native)
Veronica arvensis
Plantain family (Plantaginaceae)

Description: This small, noninvasive European annual has soft-hairy herbage and a reclining to erect, sometimes branched stem that's 1½–14" long. Its opposite, mostly sessile stem leaves, up to ⁵⁄₁₆" long, are ovate to triangular and have rounded teeth. The flowers grow in compact, leafy-bracted terminal racemes on stalks that are less than ⅛" long. Each flower has 2 stamens, 1 style, and 4 narrow, unequal sepals. The tiny corolla is less than ⅛" wide and has 4 deep blue lobes. The fruit is a tiny, flattened, heart-shaped capsule.

Flowering time: April–July

Habitat/range: Moist meadows; chaparral/oak-woodland and mixed conifer zones; up to 5,000'.

Similar plants: Corn Speedwell is common in the Ackerson Meadow area, and it also grows around Wawona and in Yosemite Valley. Two other small annual speedwells grow in the park. Hairy Purslane Speedwell (*V. peregrina*), a native plant, also has a tiny corolla, less than ⅛" wide, but its corolla is white. Bird's-eye Speedwell (*V. persica*), also called Persian Speedwell, is a noninvasive Eurasian native that's been reported only a few times in the park but is probably often overlooked. Its corolla **[inset]** is more than ¼" wide and has a white center, and its flower stalks are more than ½" long.

THYME-LEAVED SPEEDWELL

Veronica serpyllifolia ssp. *humifusa*
Plantain family (Plantaginaceae)

Description: Thyme-leaved Speedwell is a somewhat hairy perennial with sprawling stems that are 4–15" long. The stems root at the nodes and become erect only toward the tips. The opposite, ovate to oblong leaves are ½–1" long and are often minutely toothed on the margins. The lower leaves are short-petioled, and the smaller upper leaves are sessile and often clasping. The flowers, which grow in a glandular-hairy raceme at the end of the main stems, have 4 equal, elliptic or oblong sepals, 2 stamens, and 1 style. The blue, 4-lobed corolla is ¼–⁵⁄₁₆" wide and has dark blue stripes. The lower lobe is smaller and sometimes paler than the other lobes. The fruit is a heart-shaped, somewhat flattened capsule that's wider than it is long.

Flowering time: April–August

Habitat/range: Moist meadows and streambanks; mixed conifer, montane, and subalpine zones; 3,900–8,700'.

Similar plants: This plant is the only speedwell in the park that has *all* of the following characteristics. Its flowers grow in racemes at the stem ends rather than from leaf nodes; the lower part of its stems sprawls along the ground; and its corolla is at least ¼" wide. A similar European native, *Veronica serpyllifolia* ssp. *serpyllifolia*, which has a white corolla, has been reported to grow in lawns in Yosemite Valley.

297

AMERICAN ALPINE SPEEDWELL
Veronica wormskjoldii
Plantain family (Plantaginaceae)

Description: American Alpine Speedwell is a somewhat common perennial with an erect, rarely branched stem that's 4–12" long. Its herbage has long, soft, wavy hairs. The opposite, sessile leaves are up to 1½" long, are lanceolate to elliptic, and sometimes have obscure teeth along the margins. The flowers grow in a crowded, glandular-hairy raceme and seem to be squeezed tightly together at the tip of the stem. Each flower has 4 sepals, 2 stamens, and a very short style, less than ⅛" long. The violet-blue, 4-lobed corolla is ¼–⅜" long, and its lower lobe is slightly smaller than the other lobes. The fruit is a notched, slightly flattened capsule that's noticeably longer than it is wide.

Flowering time: June–August

Habitat/range: Moist meadows, streambanks, and lakeshores; montane, subalpine, and alpine zones; 6,000–12,000'.

Similar plants: Cusick's Speedwell (*Veronica cusickii*) is the only other *Veronica* species in the park that has an erect stem, corollas that are at least ¼" wide, and flowers that grow in terminal racemes. Its flowers can also be crowded at the top of the stem, but its long style extends well beyond the corolla lobes and the corolla lobes have a conspicuous white patch at the base. The plant is rare in the park and has been reported only near May Lake and on the east side of Tuolumne Peak.

DENSE FALSE GILIA
Allophyllum gilioides ssp. *gilioides*
Phlox family (Polemoniaceae)

Description: This slender annual has an erect to ascending, sometimes branched stem, up to 16" long, and glandular-hairy herbage that's not skunky smelling. The basal and alternate stem leaves are 1–3" long and are pinnately lobed, with a terminal lobe that's longer than the lateral lobes. The lower leaves have 5–11 lobes, and the stem leaves have 3–5 lobes. The flowers grow in somewhat dense clusters of 4–8 at or near the branch and stem tips. The dark blue or blue-violet, trumpet-shaped corolla is ¼–⅜" long. It has a narrow tube that's twice as long as the calyx and 5 spreading lobes that are sometimes paler than the tube.

Flowering time: April–July

Habitat/range: Open, dry to damp, sandy or grassy areas; chaparral/oak-woodland and mixed conifer zones; up to 6,600'.

Similar plants: *A. gilioides* ssp. *violaceum* has an open inflorescence with only 1–3 flowers, its stem is usually less than 6½" long, and its lower leaves have only 3–7 lobes. It grows from the chaparral/oak-woodland zone up into the subalpine zone. Another similar, lower-elevation plant, Purple False Gilia (*A. divaricatum*) **[inset]** has glandular-hairy, skunky-smelling foliage. Its corolla is ⅜–⅞" long and is distinctly 2-toned, with a reddish-purple tube and pink to lavender lobes, and its corolla tube is usually about 3 times as long as the calyx.

BIRD'S-EYE GILIA
Gilia tricolor ssp. *diffusa*
Phlox family (Polemoniaceae)

Description: Bird's-eye Gilia is an intricate annual with an erect to ascending, sometimes branched stem that's 4–16" long, is often hairy, and is usually densely glandular toward the top. The lower leaves, which sometimes form a rosette, are ¾–4" long and are pinnately divided once or twice into linear segments. The upper leaves are smaller and become bract-like. The flowers grow in open, loose clusters from the leaf axils, and at least some of the flower stalks are distinctly longer than the corolla, which is about ¼–½" long. The fused calyx has 5 pointed lobes. The corolla tube and the lower part of the throat is yellow. The upper part of the throat has 5 pairs of dark purple lines that can appear to form a ring. The spreading corolla lobes are usually pale in the center and blue-violet along the margins.

Flowering time: March–June

Habitat/range: Open, grassy slopes and flats; chaparral/oak-woodland zone; up to 5,000'.

Similar plants: The flowers of closely related *Gilia tricolor* ssp. *tricolor* grow in tighter clusters, and the flower stalks, which are mostly less than ¼" long, are much shorter than the corolla. Both subspecies grow near the park boundary in the El Portal area and might grow within the park. If you happen to be driving in the Sierra Nevada foothills or the Coast Range foothills in the spring, you're likely to see pale purple patches of the plants.

CALIFORNIA JACOB'S LADDER
Polemonium californicum
Phlox family (Polemoniaceae)

Description: This attractive perennial has clustered, glandular-hairy stems, 4½–9½" long. Its alternate, pinnately compound leaves, up to 6" long, are sparsely hairy to densely glandular-hairy. The leaves have 9–25 leaflets, up to 1" long, and the terminal 3 leaflets of at least some of its leaves are partially fused at the base. The flowers **[inset]** are in loose clusters of 5–25 at the stem ends, and they have 5 stamens with white pollen and a style with a 3-lobed stigma. The glandular-hairy calyx has 5 pointed lobes. The light blue to blue-purple, bell-shaped corolla, ¼–½" wide, has 5 spreading lobes and a tube that's mostly hidden by the calyx.

Flowering time: June–August

Habitat/range: Dry, open to shaded forest areas; montane and subalpine zones; 7,000–10,000'.

Similar plants: Less common Western Jacob's Ladder (*P. occidentale*) also has pinnately compound leaves that often have 3 fused terminal leaflets, but its leaves are hairless. It usually has a single stem that's 1¼–3¼' long, its stamens have yellow pollen, and it's the only *Polemonium* species in the park that grows in wet places. Like California Jacob's-Ladder, Showy Jacob's Ladder (*P. pulcherrimum*) has clustered stems and pinnately compound leaves, but its terminal leaflets are unfused. The plant grows only in dry, rocky places in the alpine zone and is rare in the park.

299

SKY PILOT
Polemonium eximium
Phlox family (Polemoniaceae)

Description: Sky Pilot is a notoriously beautiful alpine perennial. It has an erect, hairy to glandular-hairy stem that's 4-16" tall. Its densely clustered leaves are mostly at the base of the plant and are 1½–5" long. The leaves are sticky-glandular and strong scented, and they have 10–35 crowded leaflets that are deeply divided into 3–5 blunt-tipped lobes. The stem leaves are much smaller than the basal leaves. The flowers grow in distinctive, dense, head-like clusters. The glandular-hairy, sometimes purplish calyx has 5 lobes. The funnel-shaped corolla is up to 1¼" long. It has a magenta throat and 5 blue to purple, rounded, spreading lobes. The 5 stamens have cream-colored pollen.

Flowering time: July–August

Habitat/range: Among rocks and boulders near the summits of the highest peaks; alpine zone; 11,400–13,100'.

Comments: Sky Pilot grows only in the Sierra Nevada. It's strictly an alpine plant, and in Yosemite it grows only in the upper reaches of the alpine zone. Unlike most alpine species, it's a robust plant that can be spotted from a considerable distance. Sky Pilot is so popular that many people who aren't partial to mountain climbing will make the trek if they think they might find the plant in bloom.

SHOWY JACOB'S LADDER
Polemonium pulcherrimum var. *pulcherrimum*
Phlox family (Polemoniaceae)

Description: This showy perennial has sparsely glandular-hairy herbage and erect, clustered stems that are 4–8" long. Its densely clustered basal leaves are pinnately divided into 9–23 ovate to round, smooth-margined leaflets, and the 3 terminal leaflets are all separate rather than fused to each other at the base. The alternate, pinnately lobed stem leaves are smaller than the basal leaves. The flowers grow in somewhat dense clusters of 4 or 5 at the stem ends. The calyx has 5 pointed lobes and is sometimes reddish. The shallowly bell-shaped corolla is about ⅜" wide. It has 5 widely spreading, blue to purplish, ovate lobes and a greenish-yellow throat. The 6 stamens have white pollen, and the style is 3 lobed at maturity.

Flowering time: July–August

Habitat/range: Dry talus slopes; alpine zone; 10,300–12,200'.

Comments: All *Polemonium* species have elongated, pinnately compound leaves that could be said to resemble ladders.

Similar plants: Sky Pilot (*Polemonium eximium*) is the only other Yosemite *Polemonium* species that grows in rocky alpine places. It has a distinctive densely clustered, head-like inflorescence.

MONKSHOOD

Aconitum columbianum ssp. *columbianum*
Buttercup family (Ranunculaceae)

Description: Monkshood is a common perennial with erect stems that are 1–6½' tall and are
soft-hairy to glandular-hairy in the inflorescence.
Its alternate leaves are 2–6" wide and are deeply
palmately cleft into 3–5 wedge- to diamond-
shaped segments that are toothed or irregularly
lobed and have pointed tips. The leaves become
gradually smaller toward the top of the stem. The
inflorescence is an open, sometimes branched
raceme. The flowers have 5 petal-like, lavender to
deep blue-purple or white sepals. The upper sepal
forms a hood, the 2 lateral sepals are roundish and
opposite each other, and the 2 lower sepals are
smaller and bend downward. The flowers have 2
small, blue or whitish petals that are concealed by
the hood. Each flower has 25–50 stamens.

Flowering time: July–August

Habitat/range: Streambanks and wet meadows;
mixed conifer, montane, subalpine, and alpine
zones; 5,000–10,800'.

Comments: Alaskan natives hunted whales from
kayaks, and they used Monkshood to poison their
spear tips. The tips were so lethal that a single
one could paralyze a whale, causing it to drown.

Similar plants: Monkshood resembles larkspur
species, in the *Delphinium* genus, but all larkspurs
have a conspicuous spur and Monkshood doesn't.

DWARF LARKSPUR

Delphinium depauperatum
Buttercup family (Ranunculaceae)

Description: This perennial has a slender, nearly
hairless stem that's 3–16" tall. Its minutely hairy or
hairless, long-petioled leaves grow mostly on the
lower third of the stem. The leaves are roundish in
outline and are palmately cleft into 5–10 segments
that are often lobed. The few-flowered inflorescence is short-hairy to glandular-hairy and is more
or less 1-sided. The flowers have 5 dark blue to
purplish-blue, petal-like, spreading sepals that are
hairless or slightly hairy, and the upper sepal forms
a straight, horizontal spur. The 4 small, white petals are somewhat inconspicuous. The upper 2 are
notched and sometimes have blue-purple tips.

Flowering time: May–July

Habitat/range: Moist meadows or drier, sometimes rocky areas; mixed conifer, montane, and
subalpine zones; 3,900–9,500'.

Similar plants: The park has two other blue-
flowered larkspurs that are less than 20" tall.
Slender Larkspur (*D. gracilentum*) has leaves with
5 or fewer segments. Nuttall's Larkspur (*D. nuttal-
lianum*) has leaves with 7–25 segments. The three
plants hybridize with each other and with other
Delphinium species and are often impossible to
tell apart. So, if you're having trouble identifying a
blue-flowered larkspur in the park that's less than
20" tall, you might want to settle for "identifying"
it as one of the troublesome trio.

MOUNTAIN MARSH LARKSPUR

Delphinium polycladon
Buttercup family (Ranunculaceae)

Description: This lofty, hairless perennial has erect stems that are up to 4' tall and have no waxy coating. Its petioled leaves are palmately cleft into 3–5 wedge-shaped, irregularly lobed segments. The leaf blades are round to pentagonal in outline and are up to 5" wide. The open, sometimes branched inflorescences have 3–35 flowers with 5 showy, dark blue to blue-purple, petal-like sepals. The flowers have 4 small petals. The upper 2 petals are mostly white, and the lower 2 are blue-purple. The upper sepal forms a downward-curving spur that contains the nectar spurs of the 2 upper petals.

Flowering time: July–September

Habitat/range: Meadows, wet streambanks, and wet talus; montane, subalpine, and alpine zones; 7,500–11,500'.

Similar plants: Mountain Marsh Larkspur is one of two blue-flowered larkspurs in the park that can grow over 2' tall. The other one, Giant Mountain Larkspur (*Delphinium glaucum*) can get up to 6½' tall and grows in similar habitats at similar elevations. Its inflorescences usually have more than 50 flowers, and, unlike Mountain Marsh Larkspur, the lower part of its stem has a waxy coating. The park also has three smaller, blue-flowered larkspurs that are less than 20" tall. Those three species are often difficult to impossible to distinguish from each other.

FRESNO MAT

Ceanothus fresnensis
Buckthorn family (Rhamnaceae)

Description: Fresno Mat is a ground-hugging evergreen shrub, 2–12" tall, with spreading stems that root at the nodes and form extensive, rigid mats. Its opposite, elliptic to oblanceolate, short-petioled leaves, up to ½" long, are stiff and leathery. The leaves sometimes have short, flat hairs and are sometimes minutely toothed. The upper leaf surface is shiny green, and the lower surface is paler. The small, blue to lavender or white flowers grow in umbel-like clusters at the branch ends. The 5 triangular sepals often bend toward each other, concealing the 3-lobed ovary. The sepals are fused at the base and are united with an urn-shaped hypanthium. The 5 spoon-shaped petals and 5 or 6 stamens are attached to the hypanthium. The fruit is a 3-segmented capsule with 3 spreading horns.

Flowering time: May–June

Habitat/range: Dry forest and chaparral openings; mixed conifer and montane zones; 5,400–6,500'.

Similar plants: Fresno Mat is common on road cuts in Yosemite Valley, near Crane Flat, and along Wawona Road. Pinemat (*Ceanothus diversifolius*) is the only other low, mat-forming *Ceanothus* species in the park. It also has blue, lavender, or white flowers, but its leaves are alternate and are thin and flexible rather than leathery and stiff. It grows in the Wawona and Foresta areas.

CHAPARRAL WHITETHORN
Ceanothus leucodermis
Buckthorn family (Rhamnaceae)

Description: Chaparral Whitethorn is a robust evergreen shrub, 5–13' tall, with erect, stiff, spreading branches and rigid, thorn-like twigs. Its smooth bark is pale gray to gray-green and has a waxy or powdery coating. Its alternate, 3-veined leaves are ⅝–1½" long, are ovate to elliptic, and have a powdery or waxy coating. The leaves are somewhat thick and leathery and are sometimes minutely toothed. The leaf blades are light green above and grayish green below. The small, pale blue or white flowers are in rounded or elongated clusters, up to 6" long, at the branch ends. The 5 triangular sepals, which often bend toward each other, are fused at the base and are united with an urn-shaped hypanthium. The 5 spoon-shaped petals and 5 or 6 stamens are attached to the hypanthium. The green ovary is surrounded by a fleshy, gray or bluish nectary, and the fruit is a 3-segmented capsule.

Flowering time: April–June

Habitat/range: Dry, rocky slopes; chaparral/oak-woodland and mixed conifer zones; up to 5,000'.

Similar plants: Mountain Whitethorn (*Ceanothus cordulatus*) is the only other *Ceanothus* species in the park with rigid branches and thorny twigs. It grows only up to 5' tall, it has shorter flower clusters (⅜–2" long), and its flowers are always white and have a yellow nectary.

LITTLE-LEAVED CEANOTHUS
Ceanothus parvifolius
Buckthorn family (Rhamnaceae)

Description: This erect, deciduous shrub is up to 4' tall and has slender, spreading, flexible branches and twigs. Its thin, alternate, short-petioled leaves are ⅜–1" long, are oblong-elliptic to elliptic, and have 1 to 3 veins from the base. The upper leaf surface is shiny green and hairless, and the lower surface is paler and usually hairless. The small, vivid blue flowers are in somewhat dense clusters. The 5 triangular sepals, which often bend toward each other, are fused at the base and are united with an urn-shaped hypanthium. The 5 spoon-shaped petals and 5 or 6 stamens are attached to the hypanthium. The green ovary is surrounded by a fleshy, yellowish to greenish nectary, and the fruit is a 3-segmented capsule.

Flowering time: May–July

Habitat/range: Partially shaded forest openings; mixed conifer and montane zones; 4,000–7,000'.

Similar plants: Two other *Ceanothus* species in the park have alternate leaves, are not mat-forming, and have twigs that are not thorny. Deer Brush (*C. integerrimus*) has larger leaves (¾–2½" long). Its flowers are usually white, but they can be pale blue. Snowbrush Ceanothus (*C. velutinus*) is known in the park only from Virginia Canyon. It has white flowers, and its shiny, broad, roundish leaves have tiny, gland-tipped teeth along their margins.

303

CHAPARRAL NIGHTSHADE

Solanum xanti
Nightshade family (Solanaceae)

Description: Chaparral Nightshade is a much-branched perennial to subshrub, up to 3' tall, with erect to reclining stems and grayish-hairy herbage. Its alternate, lanceolate to ovate leaves are ¾–2¾" long, sometimes have 1 or 2 lobes at the base, and often have wavy margins. The slightly nodding flowers grow in open, sometimes branched, umbel-like clusters. The calyx has 5 broadly triangular lobes. The wheel-shaped to shallowly bowl-shaped corolla is ⅝–1¼" wide and has 5 fused, pale lavender to deep purple petals with 2 green spots at the base. The spots are outlined in white or pale green. The 5 stamens have bright yellow anthers at maturity, and the fruit is a greenish, round berry.

Flowering time: May–August

Habitat/range: Dry openings in wooded or shrubby areas; chaparral/oak-woodland, mixed conifer, and montane zones; up to 7,000'.

Comments: Chaparral Nightshade's berries look like tiny green tomatoes, but the plant's berries and its foliage are extremely toxic. The nightshade family includes several widely cultivated agricultural crops, such as tomatoes, potatoes, bell peppers, chili peppers, tomatillos, and eggplant. Tobacco and petunias are also members of the family.

HARVEST BRODIAEA, ELEGANT BRODIAEA

Brodiaea elegans ssp. *elegans*
Brodiaea family (Themidaceae)

Description: This common, hairless perennial has a stout, rigid flowering stem, 4–18" tall, and 1–6 linear, grass-like basal leaves, 4–18" long, that are crescent shaped in cross section and are usually withered by flowering time. The inflorescence is an umbel with stalks that are 2–3" long. The funnel-shaped flowers, up to 1¾" long, have a pale green tube and 6 bluish-purple to magenta, outward-arching lobes, 3 of which are narrower than the other 3. The 3 flat, white staminodes (infertile stamens) are positioned away from the center of the flower. The 3 fertile stamens have linear anthers and are more or less pressed together around the single style in the center of the flower.

Flowering time: April–July

Habitat/range: Moist, grassy areas and meadows; chaparral/oak-woodland, mixed conifer, and montane zones; up to 7,500'.

Comments: Harvest Brodiaea is common in the park's lower elevations, such as in Yosemite Valley, in the Mather area, and around Hetch Hetchy. It got the common name Harvest Brodiaea because it blooms around the time of the hay harvest.

Similar plants: Ithuriel's Spear (*Triteleia laxa*) closely resembles Harvest Brodiaea in overall appearance, but it has 6 fertile stamens that look alike but are somewhat unequal in length.

BLUE DICKS

Dichelostemma capitatum ssp. *capitatum*
Brodiaea family (Themidaceae)

Description: This perennial has an erect, stout, leafless flowering stem, 4–25" tall, and 2 or 3 linear, grass-like, slightly keeled basal leaves, 4–26" long. Its dense, terminal inflorescence has 5–15 horizontal to erect flowers that are ⅜–1" long. The 2–4 papery bracts below the inflorescence are purple or greenish with purple stripes. The flowers **[left inset]**, which are not noticeably narrowed above the ovary, have 6 erect to ascending, bluish-purple, pinkish-purple, or white lobes. The 3 white, lanceolate appendages inside each flower (the perianth crown) are deeply notched and lean toward the anthers, nearly concealing them. The 6 unequal stamens are all fertile, and the single style has 3 stigmas.

Flowering time: March–May

Habitat/range: Meadows and grassy slopes and flats; chaparral/oak-woodland and mixed conifer zones; up to 4,200'.

Similar plants: Round-toothed Ookow (*Dichelostemma multiflorum*) **[right inset]** looks a lot like Blue Dicks, but its flowers have 3 stamens and 3 unnotched, purplish or white, erect appendages between the corolla lobes and the stamens, and the flower tube is conspicuously narrowed above the ovary. It blooms later, from May through July. Both plants grow in the park's lower elevations, mostly in the El Portal and Foresta areas but also around Wawona.

ITHURIEL'S SPEAR

Triteleia laxa
Brodiaea family (Themidaceae)

Description: Ithuriel's Spear is a hairless perennial with an erect, leafless flowering stem that's 4–28" tall. Its 1–3 linear, grass-like basal leaves are 7¾–16" long, are slightly keeled, and are often withered by flowering time. The open, umbel-like inflorescence has ascending to erect stalks that are ½–4" long. The bluish-purple, funnel-shaped flowers are ¾–1¾" long, are tapered at the base, and have 6 gradually spreading lobes. The 6 fertile stamens are more or less equal, and the single style has a 3-lobed stigma.

Flowering time: April–June

Habitat/range: Open to partially shaded, grassy areas; chaparral/oak-woodland and mixed conifer zones; up to 4,000'.

Comments: This plant grows in the El Portal area and has been reported several times in Yosemite Valley. It was named for the angel Ithuriel's multipronged spear in John Milton's *Paradise Lost*. Ithuriel could touch the Devil with the spear to reveal his true form when he was in disguise.

Similar plants: Harvest Brodiaea (*Brodiaea elegans*) looks a lot like Ithuriel's Spear, in general, but its flowers have 3 conspicuous flat, white, infertile stamens that are positioned away from the flower center and 3 completely different fertile stamens in the center of the flower.

305

WESTERN VERVAIN

Verbena lasiostachys var. *lasiostachys*
Vervain family (Verbenaceae)

Description: Western Vervain is a much-branched
perennial with several erect to ascending,
4-angled stems, 10–28" long, and herbage that's
covered with soft, spreading hairs. Its opposite,
oblong-ovate, somewhat lumpy-looking leaves
are up to 4" long, have saw-toothed margins,
and often have 3 or 5 lobes. Each stem has 1–3
cylindric, dense, hairy flower spikes that are 3–10"
long, are less than ½" wide, and typically have
only a few flowers in bloom at the same time.
The small flowers have 1 pistil, 4 stamens, and
a tubular calyx with 5 long, tapered lobes. The
purple to pale lavender, 2-lipped corolla, about
¼" long, has a narrow tube and 5 spreading lobes
with rounded tips. Concealed within the calyx are
4 oblong nutlets.

Flowering time: May–September

Habitat/range: Open, dry to wet places;
chaparral/oak-woodland, mixed conifer, and
montane zones; up to 8,100'.

Comments: This weedy-looking native grows at
Happy Isles and has been reported at other locations in Yosemite Valley and in the Pate Valley
area. This plant and other plants in the *Verbena*
genus have been used medicinally for many years.
Tea made from the flowers and leaves is used
to alleviate cold symptoms and to calm upset
stomachs.

WESTERN DOG VIOLET

Viola adunca ssp. *adunca*
Violet family (Violaceae)

Description: This common perennial has erect to
reclining stems that are 2–8" long. Its somewhat
thick basal leaf blades are 1½–2" wide, are round
or ovate, are sometimes heart shaped at the base,
and are smooth to slightly hairy. The petioles are
sometimes longer than the blade. Its alternate
stem leaves are similar to the basal leaves. The
flowers, which grow from the leaf axils, have
5 lanceolate sepals and 5 stamens. The showy
corolla has 5 bluish-purple to violet petals that
are ¼–⅝" long. The 2 upper petals are erect or
reflexed, and the 3 lower petals are more or less
spreading and are white at the base. The middle,
spurred petal has purple nectar guides, and the 2
side petals have dense, white hairs that scrape
pollen off of insects as they follow the guidelines
to reach the nectar in the spur.

Flowering time: May–July

Habitat/range: Streambanks, bogs, and moist
meadows; mixed conifer, montane, and subalpine
zones; 3,900–9,200'.

Comments: Western Dog Violet's flowers and
leaves are edible, but its roots and fruit are poisonous to humans. Some Native American groups
use an infusion of the leaves and roots to treat
sore and swollen joints. This is the only violet in
the park that has bluish-purple petals. The other
violets have yellow or white petals.

GREEN AND BROWN FLOWERS

Monument Plant (*Frasera speciosa*)

This section contains plants with flowers that are various shades of green, brown, and maroon. Some plants in the section have green flowers with white hairs that can be thick enough to make the flowers appear to be white.

Many plants in the buckwheat family (Polygonaceae) have flowers that start out green but that quickly become various shades of red. Those plants are included in the section for red and orange flowers.

The last three pages of the section (pages 319–321) have photographs of 12 plants with such small, inconspicuous flowers that they are often overlooked. Those wee-flowered plants can be some of the most fun plants to learn, and once you become accustomed to paying attention to tiny plants, it's easy to acquire a penchant for them.

Note: The similar plants sections include plants that are not covered elsewhere in the book, as well as plants that have a separate photo unit of their own. The names of plants that have their own photo unit in the book are highlighted with green text.

HARTWEG'S WILD-GINGER

Asarum hartwegii
Pipevine family (Aristolochiaceae)

Description: This evergreen perennial grows from a shallow, ginger-scented rootstock, or rhizome. The heart-shaped, deep green leaves have white marbling along the major veins, soft-woolly hairs along the margins, and longer, shaggy hairs on the petioles, and they have a lemon/ginger fragrance. The solitary flower has shaggy, white hairs on the outside and grows near the ground at the base of the petioles; if a plant appears to have more than one flower, multiple plants are growing close together. The flower has no petals. The 3 brownish-purple parts are sepals that are fused near the base and have spreading, gradually tapered lobes that are 1–2½" long. The sepals have dark lines and bands of hair on the inside. The fruit is a fleshy capsule with numerous seeds.

Flowering time: May–June

Habitat/range: Dry, shaded forest floor; chaparral/oak-woodland and mixed conifer zones; up to 6,900'.

Comments: This is one of two *Asarum* species that grow in Yosemite. They aren't closely related to the plant that produces the ginger root sold in grocery stores, and they look nothing like it. They were named wild-ginger because their roots smell and taste like culinary ginger root, and their roots *are* sometimes used to flavor food. To attract pollinators, many plants have flowers that are brightly colored, sweet smelling, and grow near the top of the plant. The flowers of wild-ginger are drab colored and grow close to the ground, tucked away under the leaves and out of sight of most pollinating insects. The flowers have a stinky, fetid odor, which attracts small flies that appear in early spring. The color of the flowers may also play a part in attracting the flies. As soon as the flies emerge from the ground, they begin to use their sense of smell to search for the thawing carcass of an animal that failed to survive the winter; the rotting flesh will provide food for the fly larvae when the eggs hatch. Some of the meat-seeking flies mistake a wild-ginger flower for rotting flesh, and they crawl inside the flower to lay their eggs, sometimes pollinating the flower and always dooming their offspring to starvation. Wild-ginger seeds have a fleshy, protein-rich appendage that seems to have evolved solely to attract ants. The ants eat the appendage, leaving the seed behind. When they're full, they grab another seed and haul it off to their nest, where the fleshy material will soon be eaten. If they leave the seed in the nest, it will be safe from seed-eating rodents and may be in a perfect habitat for germination next spring.

Similar plants: Lemmon's Wild-ginger (*Asarum lemmonii*) is quite similar at first glance, but its leaves have green rather than white veins, its sepal lobes **[inset]** are usually red or reddish and are only about ½" long, and it grows in damp habitats.

LAMB'S QUARTERS
(non-native)
Chenopodium album
Goosefoot family (Chenopodiaceae)

Description: This common annual has erect to sprawling stems that are 7"–6½' long and are usually much branched. The alternate leaves are irregularly toothed along the margin, and they become less toothed to untoothed toward the top of the stem. The arrowhead- or diamond-shaped leaf blades are ⅝–2¾" long, are about twice as long as the petioles, and are dull green above and powdery gray-green beneath. The small flowers, which have no petals, grow solitary or in thick spikes at the branch ends or from leaf axils. The ovate, powdery sepals are usually keeled.

Flowering time: June–October

Habitat/range: Disturbed areas; chaparral/oak-woodland and mixed conifer zones; up to 6,000'.

Comments: This nutritious plant is cultivated as a grain and a vegetable crop in Asia and Africa. Its close relative Quinoa (*Chenopodium quinoa*) is cultivated specifically for its nutritious seeds.

Similar plants: Much less common Pinyon Goosefoot (*Chenopodium atrovirens*) is a native plant. It has similar flowers and also has powdery gray leaves, but its leaves are untoothed and are oblong or elliptic rather than arrowhead or diamond shaped.

JERUSALEM OAK GOOSEFOOT
(non-native)
Dysphania botrys (*Chenopodium botrys*)
Goosefoot family (Chenopodiaceae)

Description: This Eurasian native is an erect to ascending annual with glandular stems that are 5½"–2' long and are sometimes branched at the base. Its aromatic, short-petioled leaves are ovate to elliptic, have prominent deep veins, and are densely glandular underneath. The leaf blade **[inset]** is up to 2½" long, is wavy to pinnately lobed, and looks like an oak leaf. The lower leaves have lobes that are often squared off and toothed at the tips, and the lobes themselves are often lobed. The small, short-stalked flowers grow in arching, often elongated clusters at the branch ends and from leaf axils. The flowers have no corolla. The calyx has 5 distinct, glandular, somewhat flat lobes.

Flowering time: June–October

Habitat/range: Roadsides and disturbed, sandy areas; chaparral/oak-woodland and mixed conifer zones; up to 6,000'.

Similar plants: Less common Clammy Goosefoot (*Dysphania pumilio*, previously *Chenopodium pumilio*), native to Australia, has leaves with a simpler margin of evenly rounded lobes, and its flower clusters, in the leaf axils, are spherical rather than elongated. According to *Flora of North America*, Jerusalem Oak Goosefoot has "aromatic" leaves, and Clammy Goosefoot has "malodorous" leaves.

TURKEY MULLEIN

Croton setiger (*Eremocarpus setigerus, E. setiger*)
Spurge family (Euphorbiaceae)

Description: Turkey Mullein is a densely soft-hairy, often mound-like annual, up to 1¾' tall, with spreading to ascending, branched stems and separate, tiny male and female flowers on the same plant. Its alternate, gray-green leaves are 1–4½" long, are ovate with a rounded tip, and have dense, clustered hairs. The male flowers grow in terminal clusters and have 5 or 6 sepals, no petals, and 6–10 stamens. The female flowers grow 1–3 in the lower leaf axils and have no sepals or petals.

Flowering time: May–October

Habitat/range: Dry, open roadsides and other disturbed areas; chaparral/oak-woodland and mixed conifer zones; up to 6,000'.

Comments: Although Turkey Mullein is a native plant, it often grows in disturbed areas. It blooms throughout the summer, after most other annual plants have died back. To catch fish, Native Americans mashed the plants and put the mashed material in pools. Turkey Mullein's narcotic properties stupefied the fish, which then floated to the surface. Early Spaniards who settled in California also used the plants to catch fish, and they called it Yerba del Pescado, the fishing herb. The plant is also called Dove Weed because Mourning Doves commonly eat the seeds. Indians hunted Mourning Doves in areas where Turkey Mullein grew in profusion.

CHINESE CAPS

Euphorbia crenulata
Spurge family (Euphorbiaceae)

Description: Chinese Caps is an erect, hairless annual, 5"–2' tall. Its leaves are up to 1½" long and are elliptic to oblanceolate or somewhat spoon shaped. The leaves are alternate from the base upward until they get to the point where the stem bears a whorled set of usually 3 leaves. Above that is an umbel-like, loose cluster of inflorescence branches. Fused, leaf-like bracts form a platform under each set of flowers, and 2 more inflorescence branches develop from the center of the bracts. Separate male and female flowers are cupped by a calyx-like, bell-shaped involucre. Along its edge are 4 crescent-shaped, yellowish or greenish nectar glands with 2 distinctive, tapered horns. Each involucre has several male flowers and a single female flower, none of which have sepals or petals. The male flowers have a single stamen with a short filament and an anther with yellow pollen. The female flowers have a forked style. The ovary enlarges as the fruit develops and becomes a dangling orb, which is often the most noticeable feature of the inflorescence.

Flowering time: March–August

Habitat/range: Dry, open places; chaparral/oak-woodland and mixed conifer zones; up to 5,600'.

Comments: The plant got its common name from the resemblance of its upper leaf bracts to conical Asian hats.

BUSH CHINQUAPIN
Chrysolepis sempervirens
Oak family (Fagaceae)

Description: This common, much branched, evergreen shrub, 1–7½' tall, has smooth, brown bark. Its leathery, oblong leaves are 1–3¾" long, including the petiole, and are green to yellow-green on top and golden or rusty colored below. Densely packed, tiny, flat scales give the lower leaf surface its color. The shrub has separate, small male and female flowers that grow on stiff, erect catkins from the axils of bracts. The male and female flowers can grow on separate catkins, or the female flowers can grow below the male flowers on the same catkin. The fruit is a round, green to brownish-gold, densely spiny bur, up to 1⅜" wide, that encloses 1–3 chestnut-like nuts.

Flowering time: July–August

Habitat/range: Dry, rocky slopes; mixed conifer, montane, and subalpine zones; 4,000–8,600'.

Similar plants: It might seem a bit of a stretch to compare Bush Chinquapin with Huckleberry Oak (*Quercus vacciniifolia*), but they're similar in size and shape, their leaves are similar, and they're both common throughout the park's montane zone. When the plants have fruit, they're unmistakable, one having a spiny bur and the other, an acorn. When they have no fruit, people who are familiar with both shrubs often turn a leaf over to make sure which one it is. Huckleberry Oak's leaves are green on both surfaces, though they are paler below.

FREMONT'S SILK TASSEL
Garrya fremontii
Silk Tassel family (Garryaceae)

Description: Fremont's Silk Tassel is an uncommon, wind-pollinated shrub, up to 10' tall, with male and female flowers growing on separate plants. Its twigs are silky-hairy, and its opposite, leathery, evergreen leaves are ¾–2" long and are elliptic to ovate. The inflorescences are narrow, pendulous, catkin-like clusters. The small flowers have no petals and grow from sets of fused bracts. The longer male inflorescences (shown in the photo) usually have 3 flowers in each set of bracts, and the female inflorescences have 1–3 flowers. The male flowers have 4 stamens, and the female flowers have 2 styles. The fruit is a black to purplish berry.

Flowering time: February–April

Habitat/range: Dry, rocky, open areas; mixed conifer and montane zones; 4,000–6,000'.

Comments: The genus was named for Nicholas Garry (c. 1782–1856) who accompanied renowned botanist David Douglas in his explorations of the Pacific Northwest. Douglas named the genus in Garry's honor. The species was named for John Charles Fremont (1813–1890), an intrepid explorer, geographer, and naturalist who was nicknamed Pathfinder. He became a millionaire in the 1848 California Gold Rush. In 1850 he became one of the first two U.S. senators from California, and he ran for president in 1856 but lost to James Buchanan.

MONUMENT PLANT, GREEN GENTIAN

Frasera speciosa (*Swertia radiata*)
Gentian family (Gentianaceae)

Description: This striking perennial has a single erect stem, 3–7' tall, and mostly hairless herbage. Its basal leaves are 2½–20" long, grow in an attractive rosette, and are broader toward the tip. The stem leaves, which grow in whorls of 3–7, become progressively smaller upward. All the leaves have parallel veins. The flowers are 1–2" wide, and they grow in narrow panicles that are more crowded toward the top of the stem. The calyx is fused at the base and has 4 narrow lobes that are visible between the petals. The 4 oval petals are light green and white, and they have a dark midvein, dark flecks, and a pair of hairy glands toward the middle. Each flower has 4 stamens and 1 pistil.

Flowering time: July–August

Habitat/range: Meadows, meadow borders, and open woodland; mixed conifer, montane, and subalpine zones; 6,000–9,500'.

Comments: A Monument Plant makes its first appearance as a rosette of large leaves that wither and die at the end of the growing season. For the next 20 to 80 years, the plant will grow only a leaf rosette each year. Finally, when the plant has stored enough energy, it sends up a tall, robust stem with numerous, intricate flowers. After it blooms, the plant sets seed and dies.

PURPLE FRITILLARIA

Fritillaria atropurpurea
Lily family (Liliaceae)

Description: Purple Fritillaria is a hairless perennial with an erect stem that's 4"–2' long. Its linear to narrowly lanceolate leaves are 1½–5" long, grow in sets of 2 or 3 per node on the lower stem, and are alternate upward. The 1–6 nodding flowers are wide open and are shaped like a saucer or a shallow bowl. The 6 oblong to diamond-shaped tepals are up to 1" long and have conspicuous cream-to-green and purple-to-maroon splotches on both the outer and inner surfaces. The flowers have a 3-branched style and 6 stamens. The fruit is a 6-angled capsule.

Flowering time: April–July

Habitat/range: Meadow borders and forest openings; mixed conifer, montane, subalpine, and alpine zones; 3,200–10,500'.

Similar plants: Pine Fritillaria (*F. pinetorum*) looks a lot like Purple Fritillaria. Its flowers [left inset] are also wide open, but, instead of nodding, they face outward or upward. Checker Lily (*F. affinis*) has been reported to grow in the El Portal area and along the old dirt road bordering Wawona Meadow. Its lower leaves are in whorls of 2–8, and it has nodding flowers [right inset] that are bell shaped rather than wide open. Brown Bells (*F. micrantha*) has nodding, bell- or cup-shaped flowers, but its tepals lack conspicuous mottling on their outer surface, though they often look smudged.

BROWN BELLS

Fritillaria micrantha
Lily family (Liliaceae)

Description: This hairless, bulbed perennial has an erect stem, 7"–2½' tall, and linear to narrowly lanceolate leaves, 2–6" long. The lower stem leaves are in 1–3 whorls of 4–6 leaves, and the upper leaves are alternate. The 4–12 broadly bell- or cup-shaped, nodding flowers have 6 pale green or purplish, oblanceolate tepals, up to ¾" long. The tepals can be conspicuously mottled on the inner surface, but they are either unmottled or only obscurely mottled on the outer surface, though the outer surface often looks smudged. The flowers have 6 stamens and a style with 3 strongly curved branches. The fruit is a capsule with 6 wide wings.

Flowering time: April–June

Habitat/range: Dry, sometimes rocky forest openings; mixed conifer zone; 2,900–5,000'.

Comments: Fritillarias don't bloom every year. When a bulb does not have enough nutrients to grow a flowering stalk, it grows a large nurse leaf instead **[inset]**. The leaf spends the growing season producing nutrients for the bulb. Once the bulb has absorbed enough nutrients, it's ready to grow a flowering stalk during the next growing season.

Similar plants: This is the only *Fritillaria* species in the park with tepals that are unmottled or only obscurely mottled on their outer surface, though their inner surface can be conspicuously mottled.

STREAM ORCHID

Epipactis gigantea
Orchid family (Orchidaceae)

Description: Stream Orchid is a hairless, leafy perennial, 12–30" tall, that usually has several unbranched stems in clumps. Its alternate, sessile leaves, 2–6" long, are lanceolate to widely elliptic and are distinctly veined. Up to 20 flowers grow in a 1-sided raceme. The 3 spreading, lanceolate sepals have in-rolled margins and are greenish to slightly reddish, with darker veins. The lateral sepals are ⅝–1" long. The 2 lateral petals are spreading or folded forward and are greenish with red or purple tinges and conspicuous veins. The variously colored lip petal has dark veins and is constricted in the middle into 2 parts, a concave base and a yellow or greenish, tongue-like lobe with a groove along the middle. The stamens and style are fused into a curved, yellowish-green column.

Flowering time: April–August

Habitat/range: Seeps, streambanks, and wet meadows; mixed conifer zone; 3,900–6,000'.

Similar plants: Broad-leaved Helleborine (*Epipactis helleborine*) is a European native that has been reported to grow along Big Oak Flat Road. Its lip is more pouch-like at the base and the tongue is ungrooved or only slightly grooved. Its lateral sepals are shorter, ⅜–½", and it grows in dry places. Stream Orchid is rare in the park and has been reported from only four locations in Yosemite Valley.

313

BROAD-LEAVED TWAYBLADE

Listera convallarioides
Orchid family (Orchidaceae)

Description: Broad-leaved Twayblade is an intricate perennial, 2–14" tall, that's densely glandular-hairy above. The distinctive pair of opposite, sessile, spreading stem leaves, ¾–2¾" long, are broadly ovate to round. The inflorescence is a somewhat open terminal raceme of 5–16 yellowish-green flowers that have 3 sepals and 3 petals (2 lateral petals and 1 lip petal). The sepals and the lateral petals are bent strongly backward and look somewhat alike, though the 2 linear petals are slightly shorter than the 3 lanceolate sepals. The long, flat, wedge-shaped lip is notched at the tip and often has a small tooth in the notch. The lip tapers to a pair of triangular teeth and narrows again to a slender claw. The stamens and style are fused into an arched column that's slightly expanded at the tip. The fruit is an elliptic capsule.

Flowering time: May–August

Habitat/range: Moist areas along small streams; mixed conifer and montane zones; 4,000–8,000'.

Comments: Charles Darwin studied the mechanisms of twayblade pollination. One species has a foul odor that attracts flies and fungus gnats. An insect that lands on a flower comes into contact with a trigger mechanism that shoots a squirt of sticky glue and a pollen packet onto the insect's head. The insect might then transport the pollen packet to a nearby twayblade flower.

ALASKA REIN ORCHID

Piperia unalascensis
Orchid family (Orchidaceae)

Description: This slender, hairless perennial, 6–28" tall, has 2–4 narrowly lanceolate to broadly oblanceolate basal leaves that are 2–7" long, are up to 1⅝" wide, and are *not* particularly grass-like. The flowers **[inset]** grow in a sparse to slightly dense spike, 1½–16" long. The greenish, somewhat translucent flowers have 3 sepals and 3 petals (2 lateral petals and 1 lip petal). The upper sepal is ascending or pointed forward, and the 2 lateral petals, on each side of the upper sepal, are more or less erect to pointed forward. The 2 lateral sepals are spreading to curled backward. The spur, less than ¼" long, is horizontal or curved downward and is at least as long as the lip.

Flowering time: June–August

Habitat/range: Dry, open or shady places; mixed conifer, montane, and subalpine zones; 5,200–10,000'.

Comments: This orchid has a strong nocturnal fragrance that lingers into the day. The fragrance is described as musky, soapy, or honey-like.

Similar plants: Coleman's Rein Orchid (*Piperia colemanii*) is the only similar plant in the park that grows in dry habitats and has green flowers. It has grass-like leaves that are less than ⅜" wide, the spur of its flowers is shorter than the lip, and its flowers have no fragrance.

SPARSE-FLOWERED BOG ORCHID

Platanthera sparsiflora
Orchid family (Orchidaceae)

Description: Sparse-flowered Bog Orchid is an erect, hairless perennial, 10"–3' tall. Its alternate stem leaves are 1½–6" long, are linear to elliptic or lanceolate, and are reduced upward. The inflorescence is an uncrowded spike, 6–16" long, and the green to yellowish-green flowers have 3 sepals and 3 petals (2 lateral petals and 1 lip petal). The upper, broad, hood-like sepal and the 2 lateral petals are about the same length, and the petals usually curve toward each other, forming an unfused hood with the upper sepal. The lateral sepals bend downward or spread outward. The narrow, linear to lance-linear lip hangs downward and gradually narrows to a tip. The cylindric spur curves downward, narrows to a tip, and is about the same length as the lip.

Flowering time: May–August

Habitat/range: Wet meadows, seeps, and stream-banks; mixed conifer, montane, and subalpine zones; 5,900–10,500'.

Similar plants: The rare Yosemite Bog Orchid (*Platanthera yosemitensis*) also grows in wet meadows and has green to yellowish-green flowers. Its flowers have a somewhat oblong lip that doesn't narrow toward the tip and doesn't hang down, and its spur is sac-like rather than cylindric. In Yosemite, the plant grows mostly in meadows along Glacier Point Road.

ENGLISH PLANTAIN

(non-native)
Plantago lanceolata
Plantain family (Plantaginaceae)

Description: This invasive perennial has erect, short-hairy stems that are 4–24" long and have longitudinal grooves. Its lanceolate to lance-oblong leaves, 2–10" long, all grow at the base of the stem. The leaves taper to a petiole, have 3–5 parallel veins, and are often finely toothed. The inflorescence **[left inset]** is a dense spike that becomes longer with age. The tiny flowers have a deeply 4-lobed calyx and 4 conspicuous white stamens. The brownish, wheel-shaped corolla has 4 tiny, spreading lobes.

Flowering time: April–August

Habitat/range: Disturbed areas; chaparral/oak-woodland and mixed conifer zones; up to 5,500'.

Comments: This wind-pollinated plant grows in highly disturbed areas and doesn't tend to displace native plants in natural settings. The plant is used in herbal remedies, and a tea made from the leaves is used as a cough remedy. The mucilaginous seeds have been used to stiffen fabrics.

Similar plants: Common Plantain (*Plantago major*) **[right inset]** is somewhat similar and is less common. It also has only basal leaves, but the leaves are broadly elliptic rather than lanceolate, and its flowers have shorter, less conspicuous stamens. Both plants are European natives.

FENDLER'S MEADOWRUE

Thalictrum fendleri var. *fendleri*
Buttercup family (Ranunculaceae)

Description: This somewhat leggy perennial has erect, branched stems that are 2–6' tall. The plant is dioecious, with female and male flowers on separate plants. The leaves are 3–18" long and are divided into 3 or 4 sets of 3-lobed leaflets. The upper leaves are finely glandular-hairy on the lower surface. The wind-pollinated flowers grow in elongated panicles, are greenish white to purplish, and have 4 or 5 thin, elliptic sepals and no petals. The male flowers have drooping clusters of stamens with thread-like filaments and elongated anthers, and the spiky-looking female flowers have numerous pistils. The fruit **[inset]** are clusters of somewhat flattened achenes.

Flowering time: May–August

Habitat/range: Moist meadows and riparian areas; chaparral/oak-woodland, mixed conifer, montane, subalpine, and alpine zones; up to 11,000'.

Similar plants: Another, almost identical variety, var. *polycarpum*, grows in the Hetch Hetchy area. Unlike var. *fendleri*, its upper leaves are glandless and hairless on the lower surface. Few-flowered Meadowrue (*Thalictrum sparsiflorum*), the only other meadowrue that grows in the park, is less common. Its leaves look just like the leaves of Fendler's Meadowrue, but its showier, insect-pollinated, bisexual flowers have both male and female parts and have white, petal-like sepals.

BIRCH-LEAF MOUNTAIN MAHOGANY

Cercocarpus betuloides var. *betuloides*
Rose family (Rosaceae)

Description: Birch-leaf Mountain Mahogany is an evergreen shrub or small tree, up to 10' tall. Its stiff branches have grayish bark, and its twigs are reddish. The petioled, alternate or clustered leaves are up to 1¾" long, are obovate to more or less roundish, and are wedge shaped below the middle and coarsely toothed above the middle. The upper leaf surface is dark green with conspicuous veins, and the lower surface is paler and sometimes sparsely hairy. The inflorescences are clusters of mostly 2 or 3, or occasionally as many as 6 flowers. The small, pendulous flowers have a silky-hairy stalk and a broadly bell- or cone-shaped, sometimes silky-hairy, greenish-yellow hypanthium. The 5 broadly triangular sepals are fused to the rim of the hypanthium. The flowers **[inset]** have 15 or more stamens in 2 or 3 rows, 1 pistil, and no petals. The fruit is an achene with an elongated, feathery style that spirals as the fruit matures.

Flowering time: March–May

Habitat/range: Dry, often rocky slopes and flats; chaparral/oak-woodland zone; up to 5,000'.

Comments: This plant has inconspicuous flowers, but its showy, feathery fruit *are* conspicuous and definitely attract attention. When most of the fruit are mature, an entire shrub is adorned with feathery swirls that glow in the sunlight.

SEQUOIA BEDSTRAW

Galium sparsiflorum ssp. *sparsiflorum*
Madder family (Rubiaceae)

Description: Sequoia Bedstraw is a perennial with erect, 4-angled stems that are woody at the base and are 8–20" long. Its oval to round leaves grow in whorls of 4, are ¼–1" long, and are sometimes sparsely hairy. The plants are dioecious, with female and male flowers growing on separate plants. The tiny flowers grow from leaf axils, the female flowers usually solitary and the male flowers in loose clusters **[inset]**. The flowers have a green or yellowish, 4-lobed corolla and no calyx. The fruit is a hairless or sparsely hairy berry.

Flowering time: June–August

Habitat/range: Forested, partially shady to open areas; mixed conifer zone; 3,000–6,200'.

Comments: This attractive plant is common in the park's Giant Sequoia groves and is easily identified by its erect stems and whorls of 4 oval to round leaves.

Similar plants: Climbing Bedstraw (*G. porrigens*) and Bolander's Bedstraw (*G. bolanderi*) also have 4-lobed corollas, leaves in whorls of 4, stems that are woody at the base, and male and female flowers on separate plants, but their leaves are linear to narrowly elliptic.

SIERRA BOLANDRA

Bolandra californica
Saxifrage family (Saxifragaceae)

Description: This inconspicuous perennial has slender, ascending to erect stems that are 6–20" long and are glandular-hairy toward the top. Its basal leaves have a petiole that's longer than the blade. The thin, pale green, roundish leaf blade is ¾–2" wide, is palmately veined, and has 3–7 round to ovate lobes with rounded to pointed teeth. The alternate stem leaves are smaller and sessile. The glandular, panicle-like inflorescences have a few nodding or spreading flowers with a turban- or barrel-shaped hypanthium. The 5 green, triangular sepals are curled backward, and a purple stamen filament is attached near the base of each sepal. The 5 narrowly triangular, long-tapered, white petals are about ¼" long, are also curled backward, and have red to purple margins.

Flowering time: June–July

Habitat/range: Wet rock crevices; mixed conifer, montane, and subalpine zones; 3,200–8,600'.

Comments: Sierra Bolandra blends in well with other vegetation in the shady, wet places where it grows, and people typically notice the leaves before they spot the flowers. The genus was named for renowned botanist Henry Nicholson Bolander (1831–1897), who worked for the California Geological Survey in the late 1800s and collected many plants in the Yosemite region.

BREWER'S MITERWORT

Pectiantia breweri (*Mitella breweri*)
Saxifrage family (Saxifragaceae)

Description: Brewer's Miterwort is a common perennial that's 4–12" tall and has basal leaves only. The petiole of the sparsely hairy leaves is 1¼–3" long, and the roundish to kidney-shaped blade is 1–3" wide and is heart shaped at the base. The leaf blades have 7–11 shallow lobes with irregular, rounded teeth. The mostly hairless flowering stems have an uncrowded to somewhat crowded raceme **[upper inset]**. The tiny, green to yellow-green flowers have a broadly saucer-shaped hypanthium, 5 broad sepals, 5 spreading petals, 5 short stamens, and 1 pistil. The unusual petals have 5–11 mostly opposite, linear lobes and look something like double-sided combs that have lost some of their teeth. Each of the 5 stamens grows near the base of one of the rounded sepals. The fruit is a cone-shaped capsule.

Flowering time: June–August

Habitat/range: Moist, shady places; mixed conifer, montane, subalpine, and alpine zones; 6,000–10,000'.

Similar plants: Much less common Five-pointed Miterwort (*Pectiantia pentandra*, previously *Mitella pentandra*) **[lower inset]** looks a lot like Brewer's Miterwort at first glance, but each of its 5 stamens grows near the base of one of the comb-like petals rather than near the base of a sepal.

DWARF NETTLE

(non-native)
Urtica urens
Nettle family (Urticaceae)

Description: This wind-pollinated annual has an erect, sometimes branched stem that's 4–24" tall. Its opposite, elliptic to broadly elliptic leaves, ¾–3" long, have 3 or 5 veins from the base. The blades have painful stinging hairs and are coarsely toothed along the margins. The head- or spike-like flower clusters grow from the leaf axils. Each cluster has tiny, unisexual male and female flowers with no petals. The male flowers have 4 bristly, mostly equal sepals and 4 stamens. The female flowers have 4 sepals, the outer 2 smaller than the inner 2.

Flowering time: January–June

Habitat/range: Disturbed places and streambanks; chaparral/oak-woodland, mixed conifer, montane, and subalpine zones; up to 8,600'.

Comments: This European native has been collected around the horse stables in Yosemite Valley and Tuolumne Meadows.

Similar plants: Hoary Stinging Nettle (*Urtica dioica* ssp. *holosericea*) is a native plant that has been reported on the west side of Mount Gibbs and at Happy Isles. It looks a lot like Dwarf Nettle and also has stinging hairs that can cause intense pain, but it's much taller, 3¼–9¾' tall, and its female and male flowers grow on separate, elongated flower clusters.

PLANTS WITH SMALL, GREENISH, INCONSPICUOUS FLOWERS

The plants on this page and the next two pages have flowers that are easily overlooked, and most of the plants grow at lower elevations. Some species have been reported only near the park's western border, but chances are good that they grow within the park. Plants with an asterisk to the right of their common name are not native to the Yosemite area.

TUMBLEWEED*
Amaranthus albus
Amaranth family (Amaranthaceae)

PROSTRATE PIGWEED
Amaranthus blitoides
Amaranth family (Amaranthaceae)

STEMLESS DWARF-CUDWEED
Hesperevax acaulis
Sunflower family (Asteraceae)

CALIFORNIA COTTONROSE
Logfia filaginoides (*Filago californica*)
Sunflower family (Asteraceae)

DAGGERLEAF COTTONROSE*
Logfia gallica (*Filago gallica*)
Sunflower family (Asteraceae)

SLENDER COTTONWEED, Q-TIPS
Micropus californicus
Sunflower family (Asteraceae)

SLENDER WOOLLY-MARBLES
Psilocarphus tenellus
Sunflower family (Asteraceae)

FIELD BURRWEED*
Soliva sessilis
Sunflower family (Asteraceae)

ROUGH COCKLEBUR*
Xanthium strumarium
Sunflower family (Asteraceae)

HAIRY RUPTUREWORT*
Herniaria hirsuta var. *hirsuta*
Chickweed family (Caryophyllaceae)

GERMAN KNOTGRASS*
Scleranthus annuus ssp. *annuus*
Chickweed family (Caryophyllaceae)

NUTTALL'S POVERTYWEED
Monolepis nuttalliana
Goosefoot family (Chenopodiaceae)

LOWLAND TOOTHCUP
Rotala ramosior
Loosestrife family (Lythraceae)

MARSH SEEDBOX
Ludwigia palustris
Evening Primrose family (Onagraceae)

PHOTOGRAPHER CREDITS

The photographers, listed in alphabetical order, hold the copyright to the photos they've let us use in this book. The page numbers of their photographs are shown in parentheses.

Michael Charters: *Veronica peregrina* ssp. *xalapensis* (76).

Debra L. Cook: *Dichelostemma multiflorum*, right inset in *Dichelostemma capitatum* photo (305); *Draba verna*, inset in *Arabidopsis thaliana* photo (25); *Galium sparsiflorum*, inset (317); *Lupinus fulcratus*, upper middle photo with *Lupinus albicaulis* photo (278); *Sorbus californicus* (100); *Tropidocarpum gracile* (152).

John Doyen: *Aphyllon fasciculatum*, inset (165); *Chaenactis alpigena* (13); *Drymocallis glandulosa* var. *reflexa*, lower right inset in *Drymocallis lactea* photo (93); *Epilobium glaberrimum*, inset (237); *Erigeron algidus* (261); *Erigeron canadensis*, left inset (14); *Euphorbia serpillifolia* ssp. *serpillifolia*, inset (49); *Euthamia occidentalis* (128); *Geum macrophyllum*, inset (181); *Horkelia tridentata*, lower inset in *Horkelia fusca* photo (95); *Lactuca tatarica*, primary photo (264); *Lepidium virginicum*, inset (29); *Lupinus formosus*, upper right photo with *Lupinus albicaulis* photo (278); *Micranthes aprica*, inset (107); *Micranthes bryophora*, primary photo (107); *Polygonum aviculare* ssp. *depressum*, inset (83); *Polygonum shastense* (84); *Primula jeffreyi*, inset (255); *Rumex crispus*, inset (207); *Sanicula tuberosa*, lower inset in *Lomatium uticulatum* photo (117); *Silene gallica*, lower right photo with *Silene antirrhina* photo (36).

John Game: *Downingia montana*, inset (274).

George W. Hartwell: *Drosera rotundifolia*, inset (43).

Dave Jigour: *Sphaeromeria cana* (19).

Doug Krajnovich: *Apocynum cannabinum* (10); *Astragalus congdonii*, inset in *Astragalus bolanderi* photo (50); *Draba albertina* (150); *Croton setiger* (310); *Toxicoscordion venenosum* (60); *Epilobium obcordatum*, inset (237); *Penstemon davidsonii*, primary photo and inset (295).

Neal Kramer: *Artemisia rothrockii*, inset (122); *Calochortus invenustus*, inset in *Calochortus leichtlinii* photo (56); *Cerastium arvense*, inset (32); *Dysphania botrys*, inset (309); *Leptosiphon bicolor*, upper inset (248); *Lithophragma heterophyllum*, lower right inset in *Lithophragma affine* photo (105); *Lupinus adsurgens*, lower right photo with *Lupinus albicaulis* photo (278); *Micranthes californica*, lower inset in *Micranthes nidifica* photo (108); *Mollugo verticillata*, inset in *Galium aparine* photo (101); *Monolepis nuttalliana* (321); *Symphoricarpos mollis*, primary photo (218); *Triantha occidentalis* (113); *Vicia benghalensis*, lower inset in *Vicia americana* photo (285).

Steve Matson: *Amaranthus albus* (319); *Astragalus kentrophyta*, right inset in *Astragalus purshii* photo (276); *Cardamine oligosperma*, inset (28); *Chrysolepis sempervirens*, lower inset (311); *Circaea alpina*, inset (67); *Claytonia nevadensis* (62); *Comastoma tenellum*, right inset in *Gentianella amarella* ssp. *acuta* photo (286); *Cynoglossum occidentale*, upper inset (193); *Draba breweri*, upper inset (28); *Eriogonum lobbii*, inset (81); *Galium bifolium*, inset (101); *Gentianella amarella*, left inset (286); *Hulsea heterochroma*, inset in *Hulsea brevifolia* photo (132); *Lupinus andersonii*, lower middle photo with *Lupinus albicaulis* photo (278); *Lupinus breweri* var. *breweri* (280); *Maianthemum stellatum*, inset in *Maianthemum racemosum* photo (103); *Mentzelia dispersa* (162); *Menyanthes trifoliata* (61); *Micranthes odontoloma*, inset (108); *Mimetanthe pilosa*, inset in *Erythranthe suksdorfii* photo (173); *Phacelia ramosissima* (24); *Pyrola picta*, inset (47); *Ranunculus cymbalaria*, inset (177); *Ribes inerme* (53); *Rumex triangulivalvis*, inset (208); *Scleranthus annuus* (321); *Solanum americanum*, inset (111); *Spiranthes romanzoffiana* (72); *Thalictrum sparsiflorum*, inset (89); *Trifolium breweri* (51); *Trifolium variegatum* var. *geminiflorum* (284); *Utricularia macrorhiza* (161).

Peggy Moore: *Astragalus purshii* var. *lectulus, primary photo* (276).

Keir Morse: *Acmispon brachycarpus*, upper inset in *Acmispon strigosus* photo (157); *Asyneuma prenanthoides*, inset (273); *Chorizanthe membranacea*, inset (251); *Chrysolepis sempervirens*, upper inset (311); *Eriogonum spergulinum* var. *reddingianum*, inset (82); *Glechoma hederacea*, right inset in *Prunella vulgaris* photo (291); *Hackelia micrantha*, upper left inset (267); *Kalmia polifolia* (221); *Kelloggia galioides*, inset (257); *Lindernia dubia*, insets in *Collinsia parviflora* photo (294); *Lithophragma glabrum*, inset (106); *Ludwigia palustris* (321); *Lupinus microcarpus* var. *densiflorus*, inset (50); *Marah fabacea*, inset (42); *Minuartia pusilla*, inset in *Sagina saginoides* photo (35); *Montia fontana*, inset in *Montia chamissoi* photo (65); *Navarretia leptalea* ssp. *bicolor*, middle inset in *Navarretia leptalea* ssp. *leptalea* photo (250); *Navarretia leptalea* ssp. *leptalea*, upper inset (250); *Oxyria digyna*, inset (206); *Parnassia palustris*, inset (73); *Pectiantia pentandra*, lower inset in *Pectiantia breweri* photo (318); *Pectocarya pusilla*, primary photo (22); *Persicaria maculosa*, primary photo and inset (253); *Platanthera dilatata*, inset (71); *Pterostegia drymarioides*, inset (254); *Ranunculus aquatilis* var. *diffusus*, inset (88); *Ranunculus flammula*, inset (178); *Scutellaria bolanderi*, right inset in *Scutellaria tuberosa* photo (292); *Silene bridgesii*, upper right photo with *Silene antirrhina* photo (36); *Silene menziesii*, middle right photo with *Silene antirrhina* photo (36); *Stellaria nitens*, inset (39); *Tribulus terrestris*, inset (189).

Anuja Parikh and Nathan Gale: *Eriogonum hirtiflorum* (206).

Jean Pawek: *Boechera retrofracta*, inset (26).

Steven Perry: *Antirrhinum leptaleum* (74); *Bolandra californica*, inset (317)

Lynn Robertson: *Anemone occidentalis*, inset (86); *Ceanothus leucodermis* (303); *Cryptantha nubigena* (20); *Erythranthe erubescens* (246); *Scrophularia californica*, primary photo and inset (210); *Swertia perennis* (287); *Torilis arvensis* (9).

Wojtek Rychlik: *Saxifraga hyperborea* (110).

Steve Schoenig: *Erythranthe inconspicua*, inset in *Erythranthe acutidens* photo (245).

Aaron Schusteff: *Fritillaria pinetorum*, left inset in *Fritillaria atropurpurea* photo (312); *Micranthes nidifica*, upper inset (108); *Parnassia palustris*, primary photo (73); *Pectiantia breweri*, upper inset (318); *Pectocarya pusilla*, inset (22); *Piperia unalascensis*, inset (314); *Triodanis biflora*, inset in *Heterocodon rariflorum* photo (275).

Mike Spellenberg: *Hesperevax acaulis* var. *acaulis* (319).

Dean Wm. Taylor: *Potentilla pseudosericea* (184).

GLOSSARY

This section defines the botanical terms that are used in this book, plus a few other common terms. For definitions of botanical terms that are not included in this glossary, we recommend the book *Plant Identification Terminology, An Illustrated Glossary* by James and Melinda Harris.

achene: A small, single-chambered fruit that contains a single seed and that doesn't split open when ripe (a sunflower hull and seed, for example).

acute: Having a short-tapered, pointed tip or base, the sides rounded outward (convex) or straight and coming together at less than a 90-degree angle.

alternate: Growing singly at each node, such as leaves on a stem, or positioned between rather than over other organs, such as stamens between petals.

annual: A plant that grows from a seed, flowers, sets seed, and dies in the same year.

anther: Expanded, pollen-bearing part of the stamen at the tip of the filament.

appressed: Pressed close to or flat against another plant part, such as hairs that lie flat against the surface of a stem or leaf.

ascending: Slanting or curving upward during growth.

axil: The attachment point in the upper angle formed between the stem and any part growing from the stem (typically a leaf).

banner: The upper and usually the largest petal of a plant in the pea family.

basal: Positioned at or arising from the base, such as leaves arising from the base of the stem.

beak: A narrow or elongated tip.

biennial: A plant that lives for two years, often forming a basal rosette of leaves the first year and flowers and fruit the second year.

bilaterally symmetrical: Having only one plane of symmetry, which divides two mirror images, such as a human being or a pea flower.

blade: The broad portion of a leaf or petal.

bract: A reduced leaf or leaf-like structure at the base of a flower or inflorescence.

bractlet: A small, often secondary, bract.

bristle: A short, stiff hair or hair-like structure.

bulb: An underground storage structure with thickened fleshy scales like the layers of an onion.

bulblet: A small bulb or a bulb-like structure borne above ground, usually in a leaf axil.

calyx: Collective term for all the sepals of a flower (the outer perianth whorl).

capsule: A dry fruit that splits open when ripe and has one or more seed-containing compartments.

catkin: A thin, cylindrical flower cluster with unisexual flowers that have no petals.

ciliate: Having a fringe of hairs along the margin.

circumboreal: Occurring throughout the northern (boreal) areas of North America and Eurasia.

clasping: Completely or partially surrounding the stem.

claw: The narrow base of some petals and sepals.

cleft: Cut or split about halfway to the middle or base.

clones: Multiple plants originating from a single parent plant by vegetative reproduction.

composite: A member of the sunflower family, which has multiple flowers in a flower head.

compound: Having two or more similar parts, such as a leaf that's separated into two or more distinct leaflets. The leaflets themselves can be further separated into smaller leaflets. To determine if a structure is a leaf or a leaflet, look for a bud at the point of attachment. If there is a bud, the structure is a leaf. If there is no bud, the structure is a leaflet.

compound umbel: An umbel inflorescence in which each primary ray ends with a smaller, secondary umbel called an umbellet (like many plants in the carrot family).

corolla: Collective term for all the petals of a flower.

corymb: A flat- or round-topped raceme-like inflorescence in which the lower, outermost flower stalks are longer than the upper, innermost flower stalks, bringing the flowers up to a common level.

cyme: A flat- or round-topped, branched inflorescence in which the central or uppermost flower opens before the peripheral or lowermost flowers on any branch.

deciduous: Falling off at more or less the same time, such as leaves from a deciduous tree or petals from a flower.

dioecious: Having male flowers on one plant and female flowers on another.

disk flower: Tubular flowers in the sunflower family. A flower head can have only disk flowers or it can have disk flowers in the central area of a flower head and an outer set of ray flowers.

dissected: Deeply divided into segments.

divided: Cut or lobed all the way or most of the way to the base or to the central rib or vein.

elliptic: In the shape of a flattened circle, with both ends evenly curved or pointed.

endemic: Confined to a specific geographic area.

entire: Not toothed, notched, lobed, or divided, such as the continuous margin of some leaves. Margins can be hairy or glandular hairy and still be entire.

erect: Upright, vertical to the ground, not leaning in any direction.

evergreen: Having green leaves throughout the year, not deciduous.

filament: The stalk portion of a stamen.

flower head: A more or less dense cluster of stalkless flowers, such as some clovers in the pea family and all plants in the sunflower family.

foliage: All the leaves of a plant.

genome: The complete set of genetic material in a set or organism.

gland: A structure that secretes a sticky or oily, sometimes scented, substance.

glandular: Having glands.

graduated: In the sunflower family, describes an involucre that has phyllaries of unequal length, with the outer phyllaries the shortest, the inner phyllaries the longest, and a gradual transition through several series in between.

haustoria: Specialized roots of a parasitic plant. The roots drill into the roots of other plants to steal water and essential minerals.

hemispheric: Shaped like half of a sphere.

herbaceous: Not woody, often referring to a somewhat shrubby plant without a woody base.

herbage: All parts of a plant that are not woody and are not involved in reproduction.

hypanthium: A tube-, cup-, or bowl-shaped structure, formed from the fused lower parts of a flower's sepals, petals, and stamens and from which those parts appear to be growing.

inferior: Attached below, such as an ovary that is attached below the point of attachment of sepals and petals, making those parts look as though they arise from the top of the ovary.

inflorescence: A flower cluster or the arrangement of flowers on a flower stalk.

involucre: A whorl of free or fused bracts immediately beneath a flower or flower cluster.

keel: A central ridge on the long axis of a structure, usually on the underside. Also, the two lowermost, fused petals on the flowers of many members of the pea family.

lanceolate: Lance-shaped, much longer than wide, with the widest point near the point of attachment.

leaflet: A distinct leaf-like segment of a compound leaf.

limb: The expanded part at the tip of a calyx or corolla, whether or not the sepals or petals are united, free, or nearly free.

linear: Long and narrow with more or less parallel sides.

lobe: A usually rounded division or segment of a plant part, such as lobes on a leaf blade and the unfused tips of a fused corolla.

midrib: The main or central rib of a leaf or other structure.

midvein: The main or central vein of a leaf.

monoecious: Having separate male and female flowers on the same plant.

mycelia: The root-like strands of soil fungi.

mycoheterotroph: A plant that is a parasite of fungi, getting some or all of its food from the fungi's root-like mycelium and providing nothing in return.

naturalized: Indicating that a species has spread outside its native range through deliberate or accidental human activity (also referred to as introduced, non-native, alien, and exotic).

nectar guides: Lines or dots that direct pollinators toward a nectary. The guides are often invisible to the human eye except under ultraviolet light.

nectary: A nectar-secreting structure in a flower or on a stem or leaf.

node: A place on a stem where a leaf or branch originates.

ob-: In a reverse or opposite direction (inverted). For example, a lanceolate leaf is broader toward the base and an oblanceolate leaf is broader toward the tip.

oblanceolate: Lance-shaped, much longer than wide, with the widest point toward the tip, rather than toward the point of attachment (inversely lanceolate).

oblong: Two to four times longer than wide with nearly parallel sides.

obovate: Egg-shaped in outline and attached at the narrow end (inversely ovate).

obtuse: Having a blunt tip or base, the sides rounded outward (convex) or straight and coming together at more than a 90-degree angle.

opposite: Growing across from each other at the same node, such as a stem with two leaves per node, or positioned over rather than between other organs, such as stamens over petals.

oval: Broadly elliptic, the width more than half the length.

ovary: The enlarged, basal part of a pistil, the part that contains one or more immature seeds.

ovate: Egg-shaped in outline and attached at the wider end.

palmate: Having three or more parts (leaflets, lobes, or veins) that radiate from a single point, somewhat like the fingers of a hand.

panicle: A branched, raceme-like inflorescence with flowers that mature from the bottom upward.

parasite: An organism that gets all or some of its food or water from another organism.

pappus: In the sunflower family, the modified calyx that forms a crown of awns, bristles, or scales at the top of the fruit (achene). The fluff on the top a dandelion "seed" is its pappus.

pedicel: The stalk of a single flower in a flower cluster.

pendant: Hanging or drooping downward.

perennial: A plant that lives for three or more years.

perianth: Collective term for both the calyx (set of sepals) and corolla (set of petals), whether or not they are distinguishable. Also a term that refers to the calyx of a flower that has no corolla.

persistent: Remaining attached rather than falling off.

petal: A segment of the corolla (collection of petals).

petiole: Stalk at the base of leaf blade.

phyllary: A bract in the whorl of bracts (involucre) directly beneath the flower head of plants in the sunflower family.

pinnate: Having leaflets, lobes, veins, or other structures arranged along each side of an axis, in two dimensions (one plane).

pistil: The female reproductive organ of a flower, usually having a stigma, a style, and an ovary.

prostrate: Lying flat on the ground.

protandrous: Describing a stigma that remains undeveloped until the anthers no longer have pollen, preventing self-pollination.

raceme: An elongated, unbranched inflorescence with stalked flowers that open from the bottom to the top.

radial: With structures radiating from a central point.

radially symmetrical: Having symmetry in multiple planes around a central axis, such as a starfish or a lily.

ray: A branch of an umbel, or the strap-like part of ray flower in the sunflower family.

ray flower: In the sunflower family, flowers that have a strap-like structure called a ligule; ray flowers can occur with or without accompanying inner disk flowers.

receptacle: The expanded part of a flower stalk that the flower parts are attached to. In the sunflower family, multiple flowers of a flower head are attached to a single receptacle.

reclining: Lying on something and being supported by it, or bending or curving downward.

recurved: Curved backward.

reflexed: Bent backward or downward.

rhizome: A horizontal stem that grows partly or completely underground. Also called a rootstalk.

rosette: A radiating cluster of leaves (or other structures) usually at or near the ground.

saprophyte: An organism that gets its energy from dead and decaying organic matter.

scale: A thin, flat, dry, membranous structure.

sepal: A segment of the calyx (collection of sepals).

serrate: Having a margin with sharp saw-like teeth that point forward.

sessile: Stalkless, attached directly at the base, such as a leaf without a petiole.

sheath: A part of an organ that surrounds another organ, at least partially, such as the base of a leaf that surrounds a stem.

sheathing: Forming a sheath, such as a leaf base that forms a sheath as it surrounds a stem.

shrub: A woody perennial plant that's shorter than a typical tree and has multiple stems.

silicle: In the mustard family, a short, dry fruit that's usually not more than twice as long as wide.

silique: In the mustard family, an elongated, dry fruit that's at least three times as long as wide.

simple: Undivided, such as an unbranched stem and a leaf that isn't separated into leaflets, though the blade may be deeply lobed or toothed.

spike: An elongated, unbranched inflorescence with sessile flowers that open from the bottom to the top.

sprawling: Lying on and being supported by something.

spur: Slender, hollow projection or expansion of a flower part, usually containing nectar.

stamen: The male reproductive organ of a flower consisting of a filament and an anther.

staminode: A modified stamen that's sterile and produces no pollen.

stellate: Star-shaped, such as hairs with a few to many branches that radiate at or near the base (often requiring magnification to be Use a 10x hand lens to see them.)

stem: Central support of a plant with nodes, leaves, and buds, usually above the ground.

stigma: The part of the pistil that is receptive to pollen, usually at or near the apex of the pistil.

stipule: One of a pair of leaf-like structures at the base of a leaf petiole.

stolon: An elongated, horizontal stem that creeps along the ground, roots at the nodes or at the tip, and gives rise to new plants (strawberry plants, for example).

stomata: Tiny pores on the surface of a leaf or herbaceous stem that serve as the sites for gas exchange. Each pore is surrounded by a pair of guard cells that regulate its opening and closing.

style: The part of a flower's female organ (the pistil) that connects the ovary to the stigma.

subshrub: A plant with a woody base and with stems and twigs that are less woody or not woody and die back seasonally.

superior: Attached above, such as an ovary that's attached above the point of attachment of the sepals and petals.

tendril: A slender twining or coiling growth that provides support by grasping objects.

tepal: A segment of the perianth of a flower in which the calyx and corolla segments (which together make up the perianth) are nearly indistinguishable, as they often are in onions and lilies.

terminal: At the tip or apex.

throat: In a corolla with united petals, the expanded area between the tube and the limb (corolla lobes).

toothed: Having small lobes or points along a margin.

truncate: Having a tip or a base that's squared off, as if it's been cut off.

tube: A hollow, cylindrical structure, such as the constricted (tubular) lower part of a corolla with united petals.

tuber: An enlarged part of a rhizome or stolon that's used for nutrient storage and usually has nodes and buds (such as a potato).

tubercle: A small, tuber-like, rounded structure.

tuft: A dense cluster.

tufted: Arranged in a dense cluster.

umbel: A convex or flat-topped flower head with flower stalks that originate more or less from a single point, like the struts of an umbrella.

umbellet: A secondary umbel in a compound umbel.

urn-shaped: Having a narrowed opening near the mouth end of a rounded body.

vein: A small bundle of thread-like tubes in a leaf or other structure that are often visible and that transport water, minerals, and nutrients.

vine: A plant with a stem that is not self-supporting, one that climbs or trails on other plants or structures.

whorled: Having three or more parts in a ring-like arrangement, such as multiple leaves growing at one node on a stem.

wing: One of the two lateral petals of an irregular corolla, often in the pea family. Also, a flat, thin margin bordering or extending from a structure.

FAMILY INDEX

Bold page numbers are used for plants that have their own photo unit.

GENERAL INDEX

Bold page numbers are used for plants that have their own photo unit.

ABOUT THE AUTHORS

Judy and Barry grew up several states apart from each other. Both of them developed an interest in nature in their early years. Judy spent her childhood years in Fort Worth, Texas, and Barry spent his in the San Francisco Bay Area. In their formative years, they both spent much of their time outdoors, learning about their native flora and fauna. Barry became a California State Park ranger and eventually found his perfect niche at Henry W. Coe State Park, which is the second largest state park in California and is located in the rugged ridges of the Inner South Coast Ranges. Judy moved to California in 1981 and began backpacking and hiking in the beautiful parks and open spaces that have been preserved in the Bay Area. In 1987, when she got back to park headquarters after a glorious three-day backpacking trip at Coe Park, she went straight to the visitor center, without thinking to remove her backpack, and asked a volunteer how she could become involved with the park. She became a uniformed Coe Park volunteer in 1988, spent much time in the park learning the plants, and started leading wildflower walks in 1990. In 1995, Judy and Barry got married, and in 2007 they retired and moved to Greeley Hill, in the central Sierra Nevada foothills, about 35 minutes from Yosemite's Big Oak Flat entrance. Since that time they've spent many hours in the park, becoming familiar with its plants and animals. They used the resources available to learn the plants, but longed for a comprehensive Yosemite wildflower guide that would be small enough to fit in a book bag. Eventually, they decided they'd have to write one.